STREETWISE®

SMALL
BUSINESS
SUCCESS KIT

STREETWISE®

SMALL BUSINESS SUCCESS KIT

The Ultimate Source
for Forms and Tools for
Starting and Growing a
Small Business

by **Suzanne Caplan**

with contributions by
Alan E. Cech, Esq.

Adams Media Corporation
Holbrook, Massachusetts

Dedication

To Larry Kemp
For your contributions to my thoughts, my work, and my life.
S.C.
To my wife, Francie, who believed in me before I believed in myself.
A.E.C.

A Streetwise® Publication.
Streetwise® is a registered trademark of Adams Media Corporation.

Published by Adams Media Corporation
260 Center Street, Holbrook, MA 02343 U.S.A.
www.adamsmedia.com

ISBN: 1-58062-367-0

Printed in the United States of America.

J I H G F E D C B A

Library of Congress Cataloging-in-Publication Data
Caplan, Suzanne.
Streetwise small business success kits / Suzanne Caplan,
with material contributed by Alan E. Cech.
p.   cm.
ISBN 1-58062-367-0
1. New business enterprises. 2. Small business. I. Title.
HD62.5 .C367   2001
658.02'2–dc21   00-069966

This publication is designed to provide accurate and authoritative information with regard to the subject matter covered. It is sold with the understanding that the publisher is not engaged in rendering legal, accounting, or other professional advice. If legal advice or other expert assistance is required, the services of a competent professional person should be sought.

— From a *Declaration of Principles* jointly adopted by a Committee of the American Bar Association and a Committee of Publishers and Associations

Cover illustration by Eric Mueller.

This book is available at quantity discounts for bulk purchases.
For information, call 1-800-872-5627.

Visit our exciting small business Web site: www.businesstown.com

CONTENTS

SECTION I: EARLY STAGE VENTURE

SECTION II: THE GROWING BUSINESS

SECTION III: TAKING YOUR VENTURE TO THE NEXT LEVEL

ACKNOWLEDGMENTS

The authors are grateful to Laurie Harper, who is a friend, a contributor, and a supporter in all regards as well as an agent. To Sherry Truesdell, who once again worked her organizational magic, the words are the same but the meaning ever more sincere—Thank You!

To Jere Calmes, the vision and the reality seem to meet where you work. And to Dawn Thompson, it's good to have you on our team.

To Linda Kress, you have been a stalwart, organizing Alan, humoring us both, and making sure the material was where it should be, when it should be.

And finally, Suzanne Caplan is grateful to Alan Cech for what he added to this work that will provide readers with a primer on success. His sense of humor didn't hurt either.

INTRODUCTION

The decision has been made—you have joined or are about to join millions of other men and women in the exciting life of an entrepreneur. You have made a plan (or are in the midst of one) and now you are taking the steps to put it into action. There are times when you wonder if the whole process is too complex for one individual to accomplish successfully. In a way, this is a fair question. The information you need to launch a new venture comes from a variety of disciplines and expertise, and a person attempting to tackle this project alone faces a daunting task. This book is meant to give you a good part of the outside information that you are seeking, including strategies that work and inside tips from the pros.

We will begin from the best starting point—your business plan. (One chapter may not be sufficient for you, however, and if you need more detail, excellent books have been written on the topic.) No venture can get to where it wants to be without a plan. It acts as a roadmap that you should revisit from time to time to measure your progress and perhaps plan a detour if needed. Periodically updating a business plan is a smart move.

The entire first section of this book is devoted to the Early Stage Venture. Beginning with elements of the plan, you will learn how to make the right choice for the legal entity for your company. You will also learn how to find the right attorney for the job, along with tips on hiring accountants and consultants when and if the time comes that you need them.

Money is the fuel that moves a venture forward, and this section covers how to budget your start-up costs and where to look for capital or credit. It also discusses finding the right location and understanding what you need to know about your lease or the purchase of property. Financial record keeping, a critical element in your business, is also described at length.

The art of business comes next—determining your best market and finding your customers. You will need to hire, motivate, and train employees to serve your customers in a way that will bring them back again and again.

This section also teaches you how to measure your success by reading your financials and setting benchmarks and goals. And you

> The information you need to launch a new venture comes from a variety of disciplines and expertise.

will explore the complicated and challenging role of the leader in a start-up venture.

Section Two concentrates on business in the growth mode. This starts, as you probably expect, with money. Finding sufficient capital from lenders, partners, or even venture capitalists is covered. Your financial records will become more sophisticated and your knowledge in this area will have to be kept current.

At this point in your business, there are sophisticated legal considerations as well, and we will review some of the contract language and nuances you need to understand. Even when your attorney is handling the details, you must be an informed client.

The bottom line is always a major concern, and this section covers the two key elements in profit controlling costs and adequate pricing. Finding new markets that offer growth as well as higher margins is also a feature of this section. We'll also discuss strategies on successfully dealing with customers—you need to keep them happy, but you also need to be paid promptly and in full, as cash flow is critical to the growth of a company. You will also find tips on finding the best vendors and getting adequate credit. And we will look at strategies to minimize taxes.

The larger your business becomes, the more complicated it is to manage employment issues. We will look at these issues in depth, beginning with job descriptions and covering performance reviews, documentation, and dismissals.

Once an organization has started to grow, the founder must learn to redefine his or her role. In the early days, you may have done all or most of the jobs and closely supervised the work of others. This section explains how to delegate tasks and spend your days in working on new relationships and strategic planning.

Section Three is about taking your business from start-up through early growth to the next level. This usually happens from years two through ten, and what you establish during this time will assure a long and healthy life for your company.

You will find that almost as soon as you complete the task of creating a company of sufficient size to be strong and profitable, you will have to go back and reinvent it. Products, services, and markets change rapidly, and learning how to stay on the cutting edge is one

> The larger your business becomes, the more complicated it is to manage employment issues.

of the most critical issues for a young company. Should you have missed some opportunities, this section will show you how to trouble-shoot and make the corrections that are needed.

This section also discusses how to invest your excess cash once your profitability has reached steady levels. You will also learn how to find partners that are a good fit, and how to leverage your bottom line by strategic alliances and joint ventures.

Long-term banking relationships are covered, as they are important to long-range planning—you want your bank to be there whenever you need them.

Eventually, you may want to move on, so this section discusses the sale or merger of your business—you may as well enjoy the fruits of your labor. While you are active in your business, however, you assume the role of a mature leader—perhaps preparing a successor and taking a place in your community. Balancing that with the needs of the business is covered in this final section.

The life of an entrepreneur is a creative one—the learning never quite ends. There are always ways of making your company run smoother, your profits greater, and your own work more productive. This book is dedicated to teaching you those ways. It is written from the perspective of those who have been there and done it—from my own 25 years of business experience to the important contributions of working professionals such as Alan Cech who has been in the practice of business law for over 20 years. Read the sections you need and keep the book handy to refer to as your company grows and changes.

Some chapters contain what I call the "Streetwise® Reality Tour." Here you will get some good street-smart insights to consider—some issues to consider that you may not have thought of on your own. Here is where the pros—those who have been there and done it—can really be of help.

This book is dedicated to your success.

> Long-term banking relationships are covered, as they are important to long-range planning.

Early Stage Venture

In this section, you'll learn:

- **the importance of a comprehensive business plan**
- **how to choose which business entity is best for your situation**
- **what to look for in the outside professionals your business hires**
- **where to find start-up financing**
- **strategies for selecting the best location for your business**
- **how to set realistic goals for your business**
- **how to hire loyal employees and manage them effectively**

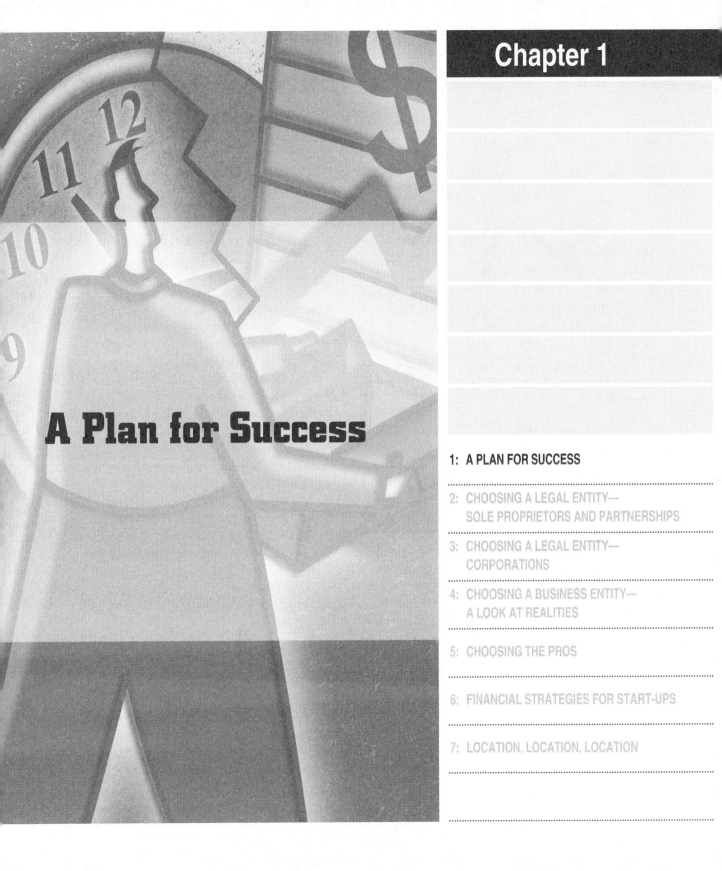

A Plan for Success

Chapter 1

J ust as you would not head out on a trip to new territory without a map, you should not begin a new business venture without a plan. You need to do the thinking, research, and background work required for a plan before you begin spending money or obligating yourself to the financial and time commitments of a new business. Since you are the person who will be working from the plan, you must understand its elements and identify the challenges, as well as develop the solutions. This is why you should write your own plan, not pay someone else to do it.

This chapter provides an overview of all of the elements of a plan. One chapter in a book, however, is not sufficient to tell you everything you need to know about a business plan. There are excellent books, including the one by Bob Adams, called *Streetwise® Complete Business Plan* that you can use for greater details.

> The basic elements of the plan will be the same, but the order in which they are placed may vary.

There may be some variations in recommendations from one book to another. The basic elements of the plan will be the same, but the order in which they are placed may vary. There is a wide variety of acceptable formats, and you will want to customize your plan to the type of business you are starting.

Your type of business (manufacturing, retail, wholesale, service, etc.) will differ from someone else's and will therefore require a change in emphasis. For example, a wholesale company dealing in a few commodities will require a simpler explanation than a high-tech manufacturing business. The former may need to emphasize its sales strategy while the latter will need to explain products and operations in greater detail. It will be helpful to read as many plans as you can in the business category while planning.

See "Business Plan—Imago Press" (Form 01-01) in the Appendix for an example.

Management Summary

Begin your plan by describing your business in a few sentences. For example, "ABC Corporation will manufacture oak furniture for sale to high-end decorating firms." Or, "XYZ Associates will design and install computer networks for small service companies." You should identify exactly what you are doing and for whom. This will allow your reader to look through the plan with advance knowledge of the core of your business and determine whether your plan is comprehensive enough to accomplish your goal.

Following are additional elements of the management summary:

- The current status of the business venture. This is where you will describe whether you are starting from scratch or purchasing all or part of another existing business. If the business was previously operated on a part-time basis, you should include that fact in this summary.
- Your personal reasons for starting this business. Are you experienced in the industry? Have you seen a need that isn't being filled? Is a large contract coming up that you think you can win?
- Your vision for the future of the company. If you don't know where you are going, you are not likely to get there. You must be able to describe where you hope the company will be in three years and in five years. Be realistic when you describe how you expect to grow and expand. Will you handle more products or sell over a wider geographical area? The people who see your plan (bankers, investors, advisors) may be able to make suggestions that will help you get where you want to go. Let them know where that is.

> You must be able to describe where you hope the company will be in three years and in five years.

Description of Your Product/Service

This section of the plan is where you describe in detail exactly what you hope to create, manufacture, distribute, and sell to your customer. Cover in detail what makes your product/service different from what is already available. For example, perhaps you have made a design improvement in what is currently available. Or, your company is opening a retail business in an area where no one else is handling the particular product line. This is your competitive edge.

Included in this section is information about what products/ services you expect to be able to provide in the future. What expansion plans do you have regarding additional product lines or services?

Market Analysis

This section begins with your research. What is the size of the entire market for your product/service? How many total dollars are spent in the area you expect to cover? This figure is used to substantiate your estimation of the revenue you expect, because you will only get a percentage of the total volume and it will be small in the beginning. For example, if the total number of pizzas sold in your area is 500,000, you cannot expect sales beyond a percentage of that amount.

Next, you need to address the current trends in the market you expect to serve. Are existing companies expanding into more products? Is the use of the service growing (i.e., computer networking)? Are larger companies leaving the business, providing opportunities for smaller businesses to grow?

You must then establish what segment of the market you expect to target. Are you looking to attract senior citizens to your restaurant? Will you be concentrating on sales to school districts? Services to nonprofit agencies? Be specific and show that you know exactly who your best potential customer will be.

Have you discovered any special niches where there is little or no competition? For example, perhaps no one is providing computer learning classes specifically for small business owners. They require early classes, in-office learning, and specific business software. If you can provide this service, you may be able to virtually corner the market and charge at a price point that is profitable. Remember, the more competition, the lower the margins.

> Address the current trends in the market you expect to serve.

The Competitive Analysis

This section should begin with a description of the general competition in the industry. Are there many other companies currently in the same field? Over the past few years, has the overall competition been growing or shrinking? This information will give you (and your reader) an idea about what the competition will look like in the future–less or more.

Next you should describe the immediate competition—that is, those who are doing the same work in the area in which you expect to operate. List each company by name and include as much general data about them as you can find. This information may include the name of the president (owner, etc.), how much volume they do, how long they have been in operation, a credit rating, and some notes on their strengths and weaknesses. You will be surprised how much you will learn about the industry from looking at this overview. For example, if you believe that most of the existing companies share a similar weakness (e.g., they are not meeting the needs of their customers), you can put your emphasis on solving this problem. The more you can distinguish yourself from the competition, the better off you will be.

The next section of the competitive analysis should feature a full discussion of the opportunities that exist in the industry. Is the competition extremely busy and profitable, leaving room for a new kid on the block? Is there one or a few products or services that are needed but not readily available? Is there a price point that isn't being served? Do potential customers have to travel a long distance to get a service that your business provides locally? For example, maybe there is no day-care center within five miles, yet there are families that have the need. Or perhaps there is an upscale shopping area without a comparable restaurant for lunch and dinner. Each business exploits its own set of opportunities. You must identify yours.

Finally, you must take a candid look at the challenges. Is the current level of competition high, but you believe you bring something extra that will make the difference? Have others in the business been there such a long time that you will have to work to get noticed? Is your market spread over a large geographical area so it will take both time and money to get your message out? Do you have enough of both? Is what you are planning so innovative that you will have to educate your customers?

Be very honest about this section—the work will be valuable to you in getting ready to steer your venture towards success, and anyone who reads your plan will know you have thought through all the aspects of your business. It builds confidence.

> The more you can distinguish yourself from the competition, the better off you will be.

What Is Your Sales Strategy?

You have identified your customers, and now you must explain how you will reach them. Will you have a sales force? Will you advertise and where? Will you use direct mail? Do you have special access to potential customers that gives you an edge? For example, you may be well known because you are active in local sports leagues. If you are selling a service or product that is sports related, you have a ready clientele. Describe your strategy in detail.

Another issue of your overall sales strategy is your pricing. This establishes which segment of the market you are going after—the bargain shoppers or the high-end buyer. Your advertising and marketing effort must be directed at the type of buyer you have targeted.

You will also need to discuss customer-development issues, or how you will create client loyalty. This can be achieved in many ways, such as partnering with customers or offering frequent buyer programs. Each first-time sale comes at a higher cost of marketing and advertising than a repeat sale. An ongoing client/customer base is where your profits lie. Discuss special promotions you will utilize from the opening or as an ongoing program.

> An ongoing client/customer base is where your profits lie. Discuss special promotions you will utilize from the opening or as an ongoing program.

Operations

If you are planning to manufacture, you should begin this section with descriptions of your tangible assets (those you have or intend to acquire) such as machinery and equipment. You should also discuss the facility you will utilize and the material you will need, particularly if it is specialized.

If your company is in sales or service, the key part of your operation will probably be personnel. If they are management or technical and they are already a part of the team, include their resumes. Again, these are key elements to your success, and you should emphasize them.

If your business is labor intensive and a shortage of labor may be a concern, discuss your strategy for meeting that challenge. Will you recruit in a special way? Do you have a training program to develop the necessary skills in your workers?

Is the distribution of your product a concern, or do you have a way to take advantage of opportunities in this area? Will you need service professionals who can respond quickly and you have solved that problem? Include it. This is the place to promote all the ways you will be profitable and competitive by running a smooth and effective operation.

Financial Information

Although it is last, this section is of great importance. Begin with information about the start-up operations. What will be your start-up budget (include a complete list of needs) and where will this capital come from? We will cover this in depth later in this book.

Include a current balance sheet—that is, a list of all of your assets and liabilities. If you have acquired any equipment or inventory along the way, list it here, along with any cash set aside for use by the business. Likewise with any debts you may have incurred thus far in the process.

The most difficult part of business plan financials is establishing the pro formas. You want to project the first few years' revenue and expenses in order to determine how long it will take you to become profitable and how much money you will need to sustain you until you get to that point. This also will be covered later in this chapter.

This chapter has been meant as an overview of what is included in your business plan. If you are just beginning to write one, I again suggest that you read one or more books that cover this topic in greater detail.

> The most difficult part of business plan financials is establishing the pro formas.

Streetwise Reality Tour

Here are some good reminders:

1. Use your plan as a marketing tool—show it to others who might have ideas and advice. Then give serious consideration to their advice. Of course you are an authority on the

business you are planning, but remember that sometimes you are too close to the project to be objective. Keep an open mind.

2. Be conservative about your financials. The revenue seldom meets expectations in the early days of any business. It takes a while (likely longer than you think) for customers to realize you are there and for them to change their buying habits.

3. A business plan is not the same thing as a loan proposal. While you are likely to show your plan to your potential banker, there is another document that may be more effective. It asks for a specific amount of money and establishes exactly how it will be paid back. We will discuss this later in this book.

The next step is to put a team together and take the first steps towards success.

> A business plan is not the same thing as a loan proposal.

For more information on this topic, visit our Web site at www.businesstown.com

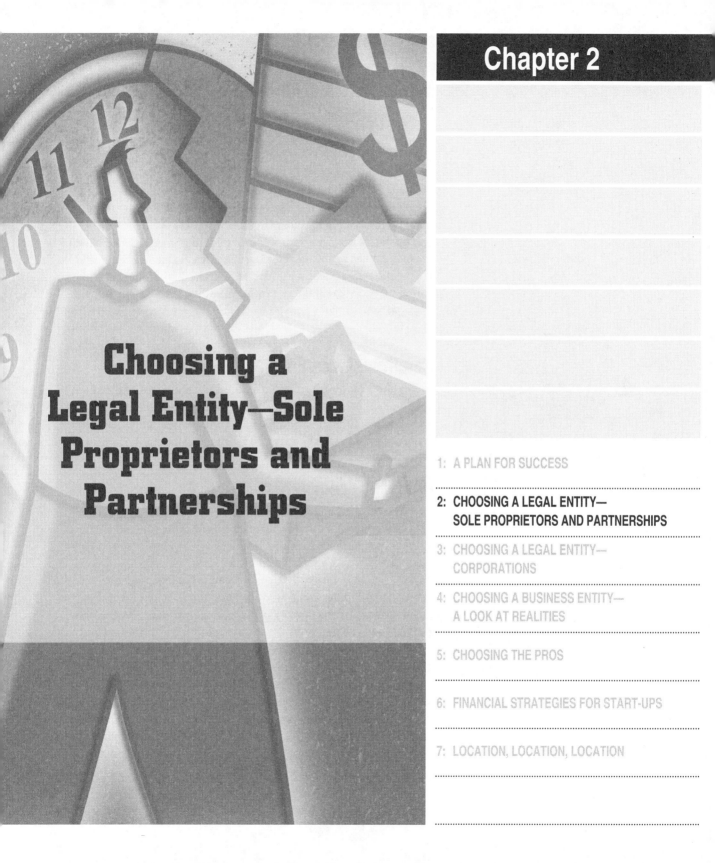

Chapter 2

Choosing a Legal Entity—Sole Proprietors and Partnerships

First, you must learn about the various types of entities that may be used to set up your business, and understand the advantages and disadvantages of each. We begin with a summary of how businesses are supposed to operate in the "perfect world."

If you think that businesses really operate the way the textbooks say they should, you are mistaken. You are also mistaken if you think that your business will operate in the same fashion that a *Fortune* 500 company does. Recognizing this distinction between the "perfect world" and the "real world" is the goal of the second section of this chapter. In part three, you will be given some common sense ideas to put into practice when forming your business.

Small Business Entities

In forming a business, you will have a variety of options available to you. While some of you may already be familiar with these forms, we are including a complete discussion of the available options and the major features of each.

Proprietorship

Description

Sole proprietorship is what many people think of when they think of going into business for themselves. It is a business in its simplest form. The proprietorship consists of a single individual owning the business, which includes all of its assets. While a proprietorship may conduct business under a trade name (for example, "John Doe, doing business as 'Doefingers'"), there are no partners, shareholders, or Board of Directors.

A sole proprietor or owner may have any number of employees and may even delegate business decisions to those employees. Ultimately, however, the owner is responsible for all business decisions; he takes all of the risks and reaps all of the profits.

A proprietorship is often thought of as being small in terms of employees, income, and assets. In fact, there is no legal limit to the size of a proprietorship. It can be as big or as small as the founder desires.

> The proprietorship consists of a single individual owning the business, which includes all of its assets.

While most owners are associated with smaller businesses, the reasons for the choice are related to factors other than size, such as tax considerations, the need for additional capital, and transferability of interests. These types of concerns are more easily addressed through other business forms, such as the corporation and the limited liability company.

Management

Management decisions are most likely made by the proprietor or any designated supervisory managers.

Personal Liability

The proprietor is personally liable for all debts incurred by the business, including money owed to trade creditors, wage claims of employees, taxes collected and those owed on profits, operating expenses, etc.

Advantages

The proprietorship is simple to set up and operate. You may be able to avoid various taxes, such as a corporate stock tax, as well as the costs associated with corporate record keeping and multiple tax returns. There are no partners to deal with and, perhaps most importantly, the owner will not find himself responsible for the consequences of financial decisions made by someone else.

Disadvantages

The biggest disadvantage is the fact that the owner is liable for most or even all debts of the business, which may be significant.

A second disadvantage is the possibility that the owner may have difficulty raising capital. If, after forming the business, the owner needs additional operating capital, he will not be able to sell partial interest to an investor and will have few options other than to borrow from a bank, which may be impractical or outright impossible.

Another disadvantage is the difficulty of transferring ownership of the business. When the owner wishes to retire, or dies, transferring the business is made more difficult because there is no "entity" to transfer. Remember, more often than not, the value of the proprietorship is in its cash flow. Selling the assets will net

> The biggest disadvantage is the fact that the owner is liable for most or even all debts of the business, which may be significant.

almost nothing for the owner's family. In order to maximize the return there has to be a sale or transfer of an operating entity. Unless there is a contingency plan for someone to keep the business running during the transition, a valuable asset may be lost.

Partnership

Description

A partnership is a business that consists of two or more owners/ managers. This business form is considered a legal entity, separate and apart from its partners. The partners do not own any of the assets of the partnership but, instead, own an interest in the partnership, which, in turn, owns the assets. (In a proprietorship, the proprietor and the business are considered as one and the same, and the assets are owned by the proprietor.)

> This business form is considered a legal entity, separate and apart from its partners.

Management

The management of a partnership can take many different forms. The structure will depend, to a great extent, upon the type of business, the amount of individual investment, the desired involvement of the partners, their level of business expertise, and the trust that each has in the others.

Owners in smaller partnerships, in which they have daily interaction and mutual trust, often opt for an informal management structure where routine decisions are made by the partner in charge at the time. More important decisions are made by consensus when the partners meet during the business day or week.

Whether small or large, every partnership should have a written "Partnership Agreement" (Form 02-01 in the Appendix), which spells out such things as:

1. The duties and authority of the partners;
2. How to resolve disputes between the partners (if there are only two partners, disagreement often means "deadlock," and deadlock leads to liquidation;
3. Buy-outs of a partner's share upon dissolution or deadlock;
4. Tax treatment.

The most dangerous aspect of partnership management is the concept of "apparent authority."

Assume that Jason, Bob, and Carl have agreed, and even have a partnership agreement, which states that no partner can obligate the partnership for any expenditure exceeding $1,000, without the consent of the other partners. Sounds great!

One day, Bob meets with a particularly effective salesman and is convinced that he would be a fool not to purchase a new $100,000 piece of equipment for the company. He can't reach either of his partners and the deal must be locked down now or it will be lost forever. Bob signs the contract and orders the equipment.

When Jason and Carl find out about the purchase they tell the seller about their partnership agreement and that Bob did not have authority to bind the partnership for the purchase. The seller says, "That's nice, the equipment will be delivered Tuesday."

Even though Bob did not have actual authority to bind the partnership, he had apparent authority; and that's enough!

Personal Liability

As you might expect, the partnership entity is always responsible for the debts of the partnership. What is more important is that, as in a proprietorship, each of the partners is also responsible for the debts of the partnership.

What might be troubling to most partners is that a creditor can collect all of the debt from any one of the partners and is under no obligation to collect equally from each.

For example, imagine that Jason, his friend Bob, and Carl (Bob's well-to-do uncle who just wanted to help Bob get started in business) are partners in a restaurant. Uncle Carl is a partner but he lives out of state, has no role in business management, never visits the business, and has

> The partnership entity is always responsible for the debts of the partnership.

chosen to limit his involvement to his initial capital investment of $100,000. He leaves the management of the business to Jason and Bob, who share management responsibilities but have not contributed a penny to the business.

For various reasons, Jason and Bob have neglected to pay federal withholding taxes, and the partnership now owes Uncle Sam over $200,000. When the IRS comes knocking, the restaurant goes out of business and Jason and Bob, whose assets can't fill the trunk of a small car, are judgment-proof (legalese for "broke").

Conclusion: Carl is forced to write the IRS a check for $200,000. This, plus his initial investment of $100,000, makes his total loss $300,000.

Advantages

This is easy: there are very few, if any at all.

Then why do people form partnerships? As an attorney in a partnership once said, "Lawyers in partnerships are a lot like puppies, they like to huddle together for warmth."

Think! If you have a good idea for a business or profession and you are reasonably capable and energetic, why do you need a partner, anyway? If it is for money, why not attract an investor instead?

Disadvantages

The partners have personal liability for partnership debts, even if another partner made the decision that resulted in the liability. Even worse, the partners may not be aware that the debt has been created because, even though the partnership agreement says that all decisions must be voted on, the partner who made the decision to buy the expensive new machinery for the business had "apparent authority" to bind the partnership.

> The partners have personal liability for partnership debts, even if another partner made the decision that resulted in the liability.

Limited Partnership

A limited partnership is one in which the business is managed by one or more entities, referred to as "general partners." Like the partners in a general partnership, the general partners are personally liable for all partnership debts.

However, in this form of partnership, people can become "limited partners." This means that they can invest money and share in the profits but they cannot be held liable for business debts. In this regard, they are very similar to shareholders in a corporation.

Limited partnerships are used primarily in businesses such as real estate development and management or oil and gas ventures. As a vehicle for operating a small business, there are other, better, options.

In some situations, family businesses are converted into "family limited partnerships" for the estate-tax planning benefits that exist at present.

> Limited partnerships are used primarily in businesses such as real estate development and management or oil and gas ventures.

For more information on this topic, visit our Web site at www.businesstown.com

Chapter 3

Choosing a
Legal Entity—
Corporations

Corporations

Description

This entity is meant for any business consisting of one or more participants (called "shareholders"). Like a partnership, a corporation is considered as a legal entity, separate and apart from its shareholders. The shareholders do not own any of the assets of the corporation but, instead, they own an interest in the corporation, which in turn owns the assets.

Management

The management of a corporation is traditionally two tiered. First, the shareholders elect a board of directors, who are responsible for establishing the general policies of the corporation. Second, the board of directors appoints officers (president, vice president, etc.) who carry out the wishes and directions of the board of directors.

Every corporation is required to maintain a set of bylaws (Form 03-01 in the Appendix), which provides the rules of conduct and the respective rights of the board of directors, the officers, and the shareholders.

> Unlike the proprietorship and the partnership, a shareholder is not liable for the debts of the corporation.

Personal Liability

Unlike the proprietorship and the partnership, a shareholder is not liable for the debts of the corporation. In most circumstances, all a shareholder stands to lose is his investment. This is probably the single biggest reason that attorneys and accountants advise their clients to form corporations for the operation of their business. (In view of the problems associated with maintaining the integrity of the corporate entity, which will be discussed, it is appropriate to wonder why the corporation is so frequently recommended).

Advantages

Problems aside, this lack of shareholder liability for the debts of the corporation makes the corporation the form of choice for most attorneys and accountants.

In addition, the corporate entity makes it easier to raise new capital. The corporation can issue and sell new shares of stock; thereby raising needed funds for such things as corporate expansion or research and development. The issuance of stock can also allow investors to take various percentages of interests in the corporation, becoming as active or inactive as they desire.

The corporate form also allows a shareholder to sell or otherwise transfer his shares to family members, or others, when the shareholder retires or dies.

Disadvantages

The biggest disadvantage of a corporate form for the small business is the formality required. For example, a corporation requires bylaws, shareholder meetings at least annually, and board of director meetings. What's more, minutes of those meetings must be prepared and filed in the corporate minute book.

Failure to observe these formalities can subject the shareholders to personal liability. Remember, the avoidance of personal liability is the biggest reason most entrepreneurs choose the corporate form in the first place.

Close Corporations

Most states allow a corporation to elect to be treated as a "close corporation." (This is not the same thing as a Sub-Chapter "S" corporation, which is discussed later in this chapter.)

In a close corporation, the shareholders are allowed to treat the corporation much like a partnership, at least for management purposes, while still maintaining the shareholders' immunity from corporate debt.

A close corporation also allows the shareholders to vote against having a board of directors, and to have the shareholders manage the corporation. The shareholders may also limit the ability of any shareholder to purchase additional shares of stock if, in doing so, it allows that shareholder to take increased control over the corporation. The shareholders can also limit the transferability of shares in the corporation. Because most close corporations rely heavily on the compatibility of the individual shareholders who make it up, there is a great

> A corporation requires bylaws, shareholder meetings at least annually, and board of director meetings.

interest in making certain that one shareholder does not sell his shares to someone outside of the initial core group. The shareholders can insist that the seller give the corporation a right of first refusal, which means they may buy the stock at the same or a higher price.

Sub-Chapter "C" and "S" Corporations

Even many attorneys fail to understand the relationship between a corporation and Sub-Chapter "C" or "S" corporate election.

Corporations are created by state law. In terms of creation, management, and shareholder issues, "a corporation is a corporation is a corporation."

Under the Internal Revenue Code and most state statutes, a corporation may elect to be treated, *solely for tax purposes*, as a Sub-Chapter "S" corporation (Forms 03-33, 03-34, and 03-35 in the Appendix). In effect, a Sub-Chapter "S" election allows the income and expenses of the corporation to be "passed through" directly to the shareholders. Profit is taxed only once to the individual shareholder based on his/her percentage of ownership. In a "C" corporation, profit is taxed only to the corporation, which pays taxes on that profit. If a dividend or payout is given to the shareholder, that amount is taxed again to the individual. Both corporation types operate the same otherwise.

Limited Liability Company (LLC)

Description

Similar to a corporation, this is a business consisting of one or more participants, called "members" (not "shareholders").

Like the corporation, the limited liability company (LLC) is considered a legal entity, separate and apart from its members. The members do not own any of the assets of the LLC but, instead, own an interest in the LLC, which owns the assets.

Management

The management of a corporation is governed by an operating agreement, which is a cross between a partnership agreement and

> The members do not own any of the assets of the LLC but, instead, own an interest in the LLC, which owns the assets.

corporate bylaws (Form 03-36 in the Appendix) The management can be handled by a committee or by a manager, as dictated by the operating agreement.

Personal Liability

Similar to a shareholder in a corporation, a member is not liable for the debts of the LLC. All a shareholder stands to lose is his investment.

Advantages

Flexibility is the key word. With a limited liability company, the shareholders can allocate job responsibilities among themselves and may even alter the voting requirements for crucial corporate action. This can be very useful when, for example, a minority shareholder wishes to exercise some control over expenditures of funds. In a routine corporate setting, the board of directors will make the decision regarding expenditures. In a less formal close corporation, the majority of shareholders will make that decision. In either case, the minority shareholder has no control over the situation. This can be modified with a limited liability company.

Assume the following situation:

Jim has been the sole shareholder of a corporation for the past ten years. He likes to live large, and money pours through corporate coffers like water. Jim is now at a point where he needs additional capital (new investors) but he isn't willing to give up controlling interest in the corporation. Mike would like to invest but is smart enough to know that, without controlling interest, his money will disappear at a high rate of speed.

With a limited liability company Mike can invest his money, hold a minority interest, and still impose controls over corporate expenditures.

Disadvantages

Surprisingly few disadvantages exist with respect to a limited liability company. While a limited liability company requires some of

> With a limited liability company, the shareholders can allocate job responsibilities among themselves and may even alter the voting requirements for crucial corporate action.

the same tax and accounting work required by a corporation, there is, at present, no requirement for the formality that is essential to preserving the corporate veil.

Limited Liability Partnership (LLP)

Description
This type of partnership carries limited liability of the partners for partnership debt.

Management
As with the general partnership, management is by the partners and may be as formal or informal as they desire. An operating agreement is essential.

Personal Liability
The benefit of the limited liability partnership (LLP) is the fact that the partners are insulated from partnership debt.

Advantages
The partners have limited liability.

Disadvantages
Even though the disadvantages of the partnership are reduced with the limited liability partnership, it can still be unwieldy. It is also limited in many states to professional partnerships such as law and accounting firms.

> The benefit of the limited liability partnership (LLP) is the fact that the partners are insulated from partnership debt.

For more information on this topic, visit our Web site at www.businesstown.com

Chapter 4

Choosing a Business Entity— A Look at Realities

N ow that we have briefly examined the range of options available to the prospective entrepreneur, let's examine the "reality" of business entities and how these realities can affect the small business. Following are some thoughts and concerns that every prospective business owner should consider:

A corporate entity does not always protect the shareholders from personal liability for corporate obligations. As we mentioned in the discussion of corporations, the protection of shareholders from corporate obligations is the primary reason many attorneys and accountants recommend that their clients incorporate their businesses.

The reality is that, when the business does not have enough money to pay its debts, creditors will look for any way to pierce the "corporate veil" in order to get to the assets of the shareholders. In fact, depending upon the state in which you operate, there are as many as seventeen different theories that creditors can use in trying to pierce the corporate veil. Success under any one of these theories will allow the creditor to reach the assets of the shareholders; exactly what the entrepreneur was trying to avoid when he decided to use a corporate form.

Some of the more successful attacks on shareholder protection follow.

Tort Liability

Tort liability is something that should be considered by every shareholder who is also an employee because it allows a creditor to reach the shareholder's personal assets.

The concept of the corporate shell protects the shareholder only from corporate (that is, business) debt. It does not provide immunity to the shareholder when he commits a tortious act as an employee.

For example, Sarah, Bob, and Jill are the only three shareholders of a corporation that owns and operates a restaurant. In addition to their roles as shareholders, the three are also officers and employees of the corporation.

> A corporate entity does not always protect the shareholders from personal liability for corporate obligations.

One evening, Sarah and Bob are tending bar. A patron becomes intoxicated and, as a result, becomes involved in an auto accident. A lawsuit is filed against the corporation, as well as Sarah and Bob for their negligence as employees in serving alcohol to the patron when he was visible intoxicated. Just because they are owners, they cannot shield themselves from personal responsibility for any act.

Failure to Observe Corporate Formality

One of the most common problems encountered by the small corporation is the failure to observe corporate formality. The concept is simple enough: if the shareholders do not respect the corporate entity, don't expect a creditor to. For example:

Sarah, Bob, and Jill hire an attorney to form a corporation for their new business. The corporate registration is filed and advertised and a federal identification number is obtained. An organizational meeting is held, officers are elected, and the first minutes are approved, which adopt the bylaws and the corporate seal.

The shareholders take their corporate minute book, seal, and share certificate book, and go happily on their way.

Five years later a creditor, seeking to pierce the corporate veil, demands to see the corporation's books and records (something they are entitled to see when they are trying to collect money). In the creditor's examination of those records he discovers that, in the intervening five years, not one shareholder meeting has been held, no corporate resolutions have been voted upon, no salaries have been approved and personal expenses of the shareholders have often been paid out of corporate bank accounts.

Conclusion: Sarah, Bob, and Jill are personally liable for the debts of the corporation.

> The concept is simple enough: if the shareholders do not respect the corporate entity, don't expect a creditor to.

Remember, a creditor does not have to win the case. More often than not, cases are settled prior to trial. By ignoring corporate formality the shareholders have allowed the creditor to "get his foot in the door." The shareholders will pay something to the creditor rather than risk a total defeat at trial. The shareholders will also pay to avoid the loss because it will be an invitation to every other corporate creditor to come after their personal assets as well.

Statutory Liability

The government knows that corporations are often utilized to avoid shareholder liability and to limit access to the real parties in control of the corporation.

Consequently, federal, state and even local governmental bodies pass laws which, while obligations of the corporation, are also imposed against the responsible officers of the corporation. Some of these are as follows:

Trust Fund Taxes (Withholding, Sales Tax)

An employer is required to withhold monies from the paychecks of the employee and to pay those to the federal and state governments on a regular and timely basis. If the employer fails to do so, the IRS will make a penalty assessment against the corporate officers.

Wage Claims

Virtually all politicians can benefit from being the protector of the "working man." For this, and for other very good reasons, many state laws allow an unpaid wage earner to sue the corporate officers for failing to pay wages (including severance, vacation, or health benefits).

Unless you are very large and successful or publicly traded, don't expect a bank to lend the business money without a personal guarantee signed by the owners, and perhaps with a mortgage on their homes.

Many entrepreneurs form corporations with the idea that they will be protected from corporate debt. As you just read in the

> Unless you are very large and successful or publicly traded, don't expect a bank to lend the business money without a personal guarantee signed by the owners, and perhaps with a mortgage on their homes.

preceding section, however, there are a number of situations where this simply is not true.

Having read this, you may think that the exceptions to the rule arise in circumstances that are entirely beyond the control of the entrepreneur (that is, tort liability, lack of corporate formality, and statutory liability) and that you would never voluntarily agree to be liable for the debts of the corporation. What you may find amazing, however, is just how fast you will be putting yourself "on the hook" for the corporation's debt, and willingly so.

Sooner or later your business will need capital (for expansion, to meet payroll, to carry the business over the "off" months). If you are like most small businesses, this means a trip to the bank.

Assuming that everything looks good (and this will be discussed later in this book) the bank will agree to make the loan. The terms are acceptable and all you have to do is sign on the dotted line—not as president of the corporation, but personally. If you are married, you had better prepare your spouse for the fact that the bank is going to want to see their signature as well. Over the past several years, however, more and more spouses are refusing to sign and due to a change in credit laws, the banks are relenting.

Later in the book we will discuss why the bank wants these "personal guarantees," but the reality is that the bank wants them and it will get them, or you won't get the loan.

There you have it. After selecting the corporate form to avoid corporate liability, you have just agreed to be personally liable for what will probably be the biggest debt the business will ever face. From this point on, your car, your home, your savings, and everything else that has the word "your" in front of it, will be at risk. However, with only one signature, assets that you own jointly will be spared.

If you don't maintain controlling interest in the business, you're working for somebody else. Most businesses in America are not *Fortune* 500 companies—they are small organizations consisting of fewer than five members. In many cases, the principals of the business are family members. What does this mean to you? Let's look at some examples.

> Sooner or later your business will need capital.

Nancy, Beth, and Carl are longtime friends. They formed a corporation, with each one owning one-third of the stock. Each of them has contributed $50,000 of their savings and have, over the last ten years, made the company their life. In addition to being shareholders in the company, they are the only officers and the only employees.

As Nancy, Beth, and Carl get older, they develop differing goals and each has different demands made upon his time. For example, Carl has a wife and three small children who require a great deal of his time. He wants to make a nice living but does not care if he ever lives in a mansion. Nancy and Beth, however, are high-energy, achievement-oriented individuals who are becoming increasingly frustrated with Carl.

One day, Carl shows up for work only to be advised that he has been fired. In addition, by special action of the board of directors (which Nancy and Beth control), he has been removed as an officer of the corporation.

What does Carl have to show for his years of effort and his sizeable capital contribution? Almost nothing. Carl is still a shareholder and still holds one-third of the stock in the company. But because the company (as do most small companies), pays out its income to the shareholders by way of salary, and because Carl is no longer an employee of the company, he does not share in any of the income.

Carl is now without a job, without income, and he cannot even compel the company to liquidate because that would require a vote of the majority of shareholders. In short, Carl's share certificate for 33% of the company is not worth the paper it's printed on.

The scenario does not change unless Carl owns at least 51% of the company. Until that time, Carl is at the mercy of any one, two, or three shareholders who decide that they want something different.

Any small business with two or more owners is a "marriage." Don't take it for granted. If you have a partner in your small business,

> Any small business with two or more owners is a "marriage." Don't take it for granted.

whether he be called a "shareholder," a "member," or anything else, you are going to have to deal with that person on a personal level. Forget stock transfer restrictions, covenants not to compete, pre-emptive rights, and almost everything else you may have learned about shareholders' or partners' rights.

The fact that you have detailed bylaws may help, but ultimately, your best protection is to select partners who share your goals, interests, and work ethic. More importantly, keep the lines of communication open so that disputes over personality matters and personal values do not become impediments to the continued operation of the business. For example:

> Adam is a financial whiz. He can balance numbers, perform cost estimates, and actually finds bankers to be great conversationalists (hey, we said this was hypothetical).
>
> John is the creative end of the team. He couldn't care less about the numbers and thinks that Adam places profitability ahead of quality and inventiveness.
>
> In anticipation of possible creative differences, Adam (always a planner) has retained a majority interest in the company and can outvote John on any issue that arises.
>
> Unfortunately, when the break occurs, John and his entire creative team walk out. Adam's majority interest hasn't protected him at all. He is still a master at numbers but, without John's involvement, the only numbers he is crunching are in his Chapter 11 bankruptcy petition.
>
> John isn't much better off. He is out of a job, his 49% interest in the company is valueless, and the "covenants not to compete" that he signed years earlier frighten away potential employers.

If you think that this is fun, consider the "family business." Where a family business is concerned, you will be dealing with much more than simple business decisions and the personalities of your partners. Many business disputes, in the family-owned business, are not business disputes at all. Conflicts between parents and children

> Keep the lines of communication open so that disputes over personality matters and personal values do not become impediments to the continued operation of the business.

or among siblings can take the form of a business dispute but the cause is often much deeper. (Forget about being sued by your partners. What are you going to do when your father gets home?)

Your Decision-Making Process

Assuming that you haven't skipped any pages (or at least very many pages) you are now at least familiar with the options available to you for the formation of your business.

More importantly, you have seen examples of how what you may have understood about the various types of business entities does not always hold up in the real world.

So, what is the best form of business?

That depends on you. There is no single "best form" that applies to everyone. You have to analyze and understand your current capabilities, your goals, and your needs.

Following are several scenarios to show how you might analyze your own business needs.

> You have to analyze and understand your current capabilities, your goals, and your needs.

Scenario I

You want to start or acquire a business. You have always preferred to work alone and you don't plan on having any partners or shareholders. You can keep a low-overhead shop and, with some intelligent budgeting, keep the lights burning and food on the table. Under these circumstances, a proprietorship may be right for you.

If you choose to operate as a proprietorship, you avoid the start-up costs of the corporation as well as the capital stock tax that some states assess simply for the privilege of existing.

You can avoid the extra accounting fees at tax time and skip altogether the aggravation of maintaining corporate minute books and records simply to show that you have observed corporate formality.

But what about protection from liability for business debts?

1. Is your business one in which you anticipate paying for materials and supplies as they are ordered? or

2. Do you anticipate that your receivables will be paid promptly and, therefore, that you will not be carrying any payables? or
3. Is your business largely a service business where the debts of the business will never be significant?

If your answer to any of these is yes, do you need to be overly concerned about your personal liability for business debts? If not, then the corporation may provide little or no additional protection—certainly not enough to justify the trouble of incorporation.

But what about tort liability? Remember that even a corporate shell will not insulate the employees and responsible officers (and in a small corporation almost everyone is a responsible officer) from actions for negligence (auto accidents while on company business, slip and falls in the customer area, over-serving the intoxicated bar patron, improper food handling) What will protect you from tort liability? Insurance will!

Because people may become injured in almost any setting, you should talk to your insurance agent about comprehensive coverage for your business. Try to structure your financial affairs so that you are always judgment proof, although it can be an awful way to live. Also, if you are in business for the long haul (and if you aren't, you should get out now) you can't grow when you are always looking over your shoulder.

If, on the other hand, you anticipate that the business may generate significant trade debt, then a corporation or limited liability company may be the way to go. (We limit the concern to "trade debt" because as we said, any bank loans will be personally guaranteed by you anyway, so a corporation will not protect you from the bank.)

> If you anticipate that the business may generate significant trade debt, then a corporation or limited liability company may be the way to go.

Scenario II

You and two of your friends have an idea for a business. You each have a unique skill to offer the business and, for a variety of reasons, you would feel better if someone else was around to help with the work, shoulder the responsibility, and worry right along with you.

Because of the nature of the business, you are going to have trade debt almost immediately. In addition, you anticipate that collections may trail payables by several weeks. Under these circumstances, a corporation or limited liability may be right for you. (Remember what we said about partnerships. We are not going to consider them here.)

If you acquire more debt than you can pay, the ability to walk away (after making certain that withholding taxes and wage claims are paid) with only your investment lost can be a big comfort.

If you go with the corporation, you can draft the bylaws to clearly define everyone's responsibilities (so long as you are disciplined enough to follow them).

Here's a neat idea! If the business has valuable assets (for example, real estate, building, fixtures, and the like) have the shareholders purchase them personally (or through another corporation) and then lease them to a corporation that they form. Then, if the business takes a turn for the worse, the debt stays with the corporation while the shareholders take the more valuable assets of the business with them.

Just make sure that the corporation was adequately funded (that is, "capitalized") to begin with and that the shareholders keep scrupulous records to document purchase of the assets and observance of corporate formality. If not, be prepared to find yourself on the receiving end of a lawsuit seeking to pierce the "corporate shell" and establish personal liability. This works only for property acquired prior to formation of the corporation, or else you will encounter yet another theory for piercing the corporate shell, "usurpation of a corporate opportunity."

Take some time, consider your needs, and think hard about the "reality" of your situation.

> If you go with the corporation, you can draft the bylaws to clearly define everyone's responsibilities.

For more information on this topic, visit our Web site at www.businesstown.com

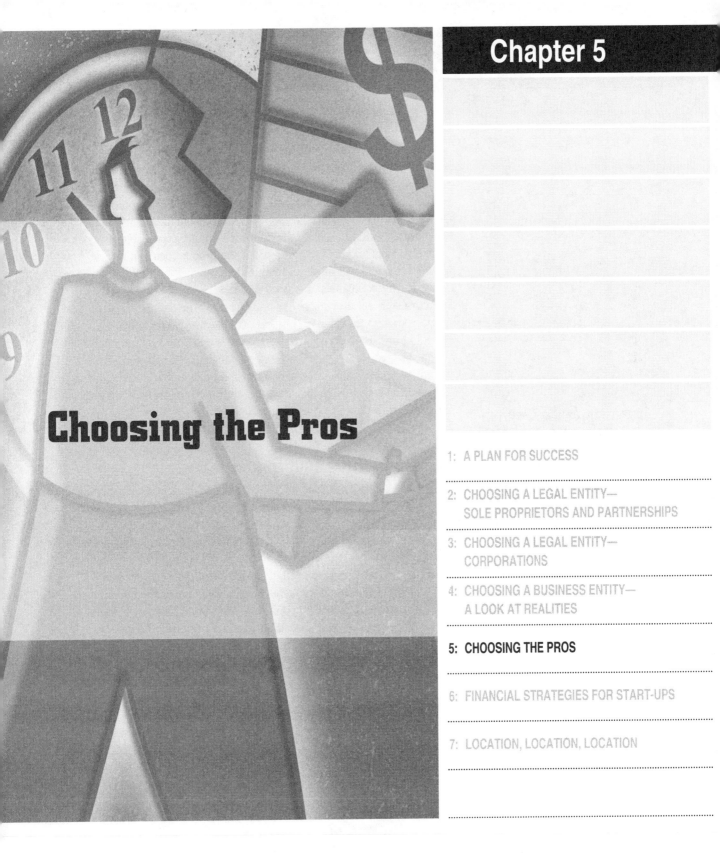

Chapter 5

Choosing the Pros

By now you should realize that one of the first decisions you will make is about the legal formation of your company—whether it will be a proprietorship, partnership, corporation, or limited liability company. This decision will be based on a number of considerations—some purely legal and some financial. You must understand the concepts, but you will need the advice of an attorney and an accountant to make the best decision. In many instances, you will also need an attorney to file all of the proper documents with state, local, and federal governments.

If your company's operation will be fairly straightforward, you can probably set up your books on your own. The details of this aspect are covered later in this section. However, if you anticipate needing investors, expect large early losses that will have tax implications; or if you will need complicated financing, you will want to bring on an outside accountant early in the game. You would be wise to take some time to choose carefully and find professionals that can do your work now and grow with you as well.

Where to Start Your Search

Do not pick a name at random from the phone book and entrust your company's future to that individual. In the first place, all of the potential lawyers may not be listed, even fewer advertise because until a few years ago, only a minority had the marketing sense to do so and the bar frowned on the practice. The accountants usually only list their names, so you get absolutely no additional information. And, more importantly, an ad will give you very little information about how any professional will respond to you and your company's needs.

What you should do is ask for referrals from people you trust. Start with other members of the business community. Do they have a good lawyer or accountant they would recommend? You may be able to find someone who has a track record with a client very similar to you.

You might also ask your banker for a recommendation. Bankers may be particularly knowledgeable about accountants. They see financial records on a regular basis and they know who produces

> If you anticipate needing investors, expect large early losses that will have tax implications; or if you will need complicated financing, you will want to bring on an outside accountant early in the game.

timely and comprehensive reports—and timeliness is critical. Some accountants (and lawyers as well) overbook their clientele and they routinely do not produce work product when it is required. It may be necessary to file for extensions on tax returns and legal papers from time to time, but a professional who makes a habit of this may put you in jeopardy.

Your end-of-the-year financials will be required by your lenders on a certain date, and not having them by the deadline may affect your loan approval or loan renewal. Most bankers will hold you responsible for the behavior of your professional advisors, so choose carefully and find someone who doesn't operate in this manner.

Another referral source may be your insurance agent. He/she may have done business and estate planning with attorneys and accountants, and may have recommendations for several who operate efficiently and provide well-thought-out advice.

Other sources might come from professional organizations, community groups such as Rotary or Lions, and your local Chamber of Commerce. But remember, this is only a starting point.

The Large Firms vs. the Smaller Ones

Perhaps one of the most difficult questions to answer is whether you should work with a large firm of lawyers/accountants, with the smaller firms, with only a few professionals, or with a sole practitioner. The cost is understandably higher at the larger firms; they have more overhead to cover and their areas of expertise may be greater because many subspecialities will be covered by partners and associates.

Specific skills of taxation, international business, and intellectual property, to name a few, will be more likely be covered in a large firm and less likely in a smaller one. Your question is, do you need all of these specialties at this point in your business, and can you afford to pay for access you don't need? Unless you have unlimited capital, a prestigious firm may be too expensive for most start-ups.

In addition, a big firm will often assign their smaller clients to inexperienced associates, so you won't get the benefit of the

> The cost is understandably higher at the larger firms; they have more overhead to cover and their areas of expertise may be greater because many subspecialities will be covered by partners and associates.

high-powered advice you may believe you are getting. You will be more likely to interact directly with the professional handling your work in a small or mid-size firm.

The downside with a smaller firm is that with fewer professionals on staff (perhaps only one), your work may get pushed back to meet a current emergency. The tradeoff of cost vs. benefit is a judgment call only you can make.

The Initial Meeting

Before hiring any professional, you should sit down with him or her and discuss your company, the goals you've set, and the challenges you expect. In the past, many attorneys would offer a free initial consultation, but that happens very infrequently in the current business climate. A small firm or sole practitioner may still do this, however, as will a number of accounting firms. Don't let a fee stop you from sitting face to face with the individual who will become an important advisor to your company—you need to find out how you will interact and whether you can trust the advice you will be given in the future. There are times when the most knowledgeable advisor will have to make a judgment call and you must have confidence in their ability to listen to all of the facts—and their instincts as well.

Questions to Ask

Don't make the fees the deciding criteria; be prepared to ask specific questions about money, such as the following:

1. What is your hourly rate? The range can be staggering—from less than $100/hour to over $300/hour.
2. Do you have less-experienced associates that can handle some of the work at a lower rate?
3. Do you require a retainer against your billings?
4. Are your bills detailed as to the nature of the work and time spent?

> There are times when the most knowledgeable advisor will have to make a judgment call and you must have confidence in their ability to listen to all of the facts—and their instincts as well.

It is important that you are comfortable with the financial arrangements before hiring any attorney or accountant, but there are other, and perhaps more important, issues to consider.

- Do they have experience with start-up or early stage companies?
- Do they already work for or represent any of your important vendors, anticipated customers, or your bank? This is an important legal question, because if you have a dispute with those individuals or companies, your lawyer will have a conflict of interest and not be able to represent you.
- Do they have any special experience in your industry? For example, you may require an accounting system that is very specialized, and this could be critical.
- Do they have any special relationships with lending institutions that may be helpful to you?
- If considering a smaller firm, do they have a relationship with other professionals with a specialization that you might eventually need, and are they comfortable about making a referral?

Trust Your Instincts

You will be working closely with these professionals over many years—sometimes during great stress—when, for example, you are involved in any legal action. You must have a compatible relationship that includes mutual respect and trust. You will want this trust to be present from day one, so take time to assess the attitude of your professional before hiring them. Don't ever let yourself get intimidated by their education and status. Always remember—they work for you, not the other way around. Better yet, you should be working together to reach your goals.

> The more prepared you are before you meet with your advisor, the better the information you will get and the lower the cost will be.

Saving Money on Fees

The more prepared you are before you meet with your advisor, the better the information you will get and the lower the cost will be.

Taking a shoebox full of receipts into your accountant's office and asking for a profit-and-loss statement will cost you a fortune. However, taking balanced and checked records in for a quarterly review will be cost effective. End-of-the-year tax planning should be done at the end of the third quarter once your records to date have been compiled.

If you are in the middle of any negotiations over a contract, talk to your attorney first with a list of issues, not along the way as you are working out details. Any questions you have can be answered at one time, and you should always make a deal subject to your attorney's review.

Most professionals round off any time billed to a 10- or 15-minute increment. A two-minute phone call could cost you a good bit of money, so ask your questions in one call, instead of ten.

> End-of-the-year tax planning should be done at the end of the third quarter once your records to date have been compiled.

Professional Courtesy

Your calls should be answered in a timely fashion, and work should be completed when it is due. You have the right to expect this kind of treatment and if you are not getting it, don't hesitate to say so and leave if the situation doesn't change. It is your money that is being spent and it may be your success that is at risk.

Using (and Choosing) Consultants

This is a fairly gray area of professional advice, because there is no official licensing of consultants. Virtually anyone can print a card and call themselves a consultant. So be careful when choosing one—referrals are a necessity in finding the best consultants.

You can have a good bit of expertise in marketing, human resources, computer technology, and finance available to you on a cost-effective basis by hiring a consultant. You don't have to bring anyone on to your staff; you pay only for the work you need. The individual who has set up a sole practice may give you a great value, as they specialize in a single aspect of business and have become very experienced in their field.

The general business consultant (or management consultant) may be a bit more problematic. If they can't tell you exactly what areas they will cover and what they will accomplish for you, it may be best to stay away from them. Few new businesses need or can afford the work of a generalist.

Check References on any Consultant

You will want to begin on a referral but then go further and check with other previous clients. Ask for a list and call them. You will want to ask about the following:

- Was the work satisfactory?
- Was it completed on time and within budget?
- Did the original scope give an accurate description of what needed to be done?
- Were there many add-ons (work needed but not included in the original scope)?

You may want to hire a software consultant to design or customize a program for your use. In which case, you should find out if previous clients got all they expected, when they expected it. When you are in the middle of a systems change, your whole business could be put at risk if data is lost.

If you can't get a list of satisfied customers, be cautious.

> It is possible to get excellent advice and assistance at no cost to you.

A Source of Free Advice

It is possible to get excellent advice and assistance at no cost to you. Sponsored in part by the Small Business Administration (SBA) and state government is a group of Small Business Development Centers housed primarily in universities throughout the United States. They provide classes as well as trained consultants who give you one-on-one, specific business advice. Their interest is the growth of new (and existing) companies, and they can assist with loan proposals as well as marketing plans and expert advice. The only downside here is the time factor. With many businesses needing their help, most of the consultants have limited time to spend with any client. You must really do your part of the work and use the help wisely. For a company on a budget, this could be a critical factor in success. Call your local university or college or the closest SBA office.

Letters of Engagement

Any lawyer, accountant, or consultant should send you a letter that spells out your arrangement in detail. All fees and retainers should be covered, as well as, in many instances, the specific work to be done. This is not as likely with an attorney, who will be giving ongoing advice, but your accountant may spell out what he will be doing in addition to tax returns. Also, any consultant should describe fully the project they are undertaking and when and how it will be completed. This letter of engagement is a form of contract between you and your advisor and it may be referred to if any dispute arises at a later date. Read it carefully and ask questions about what you don't understand.

Streetwise Reality Tour

There are some important issues regarding your professional advisors for you to keep in mind.

1. The risk is yours, and the decisions should be yours as well. Your job is leadership, collecting information and advice, and proceeding in a way that you believe is best.
2. It is always easier to give advice than to take it. Your confidence and optimism may need some tempering from time to time. Be a bit humble.
3. The amount of money you spend is not directly proportional to the quality of advice. It may be the surroundings, the charm, or the connections of a professional that allows them to charge high fees. Don't be swayed by the superficial.

> This letter of engagement is a form of contract between you and your advisor and it may be referred to if any dispute arises at a later date.

For more information on this topic, visit our Web site at www.businesstown.com

Chapter 6

Financial Strategies for Start-Ups

The key questions for the new business owner to consider are how much is it going to cost, and where can I find an adequate amount? Understanding both of these issues and developing a plan is the most important element in the successful future of your venture. Your strategy begins with a comprehensive assessment of what it's going to cost to get into the game.

There are two different categories of start-up costs, and you should analyze these as separate issues. The first are nonrecurring expenses, those you spend only once and which have long-term payback. It may very well be disastrous to borrow short-term money to pay these costs—the capital should come from investment or at the very least, long-term and liberal debt. The second category is operating and working capital—the cash you need to finance the early stages of the venture when you may be losing money and to fund growth if cash flow won't meet the needs. We will review these separately.

> Your strategy begins with a comprehensive assessment of what it's going to cost to get into the game.

One Time Start-Up Expense

There are basically five kinds of nonrecurring expense, which are as follows.

Organizational Costs

The bulk of this money will go for professional fees, primarily paid to your attorney to create your business entity. You may also have a filing fee to register your name and/or your corporation with your state (Forms 06-02, 06-03, and 06-04 in the Appendix). You may also be paying an accountant to help you decide what form you are going to use (sole proprietor, LLC, or corporation, etc.) and to set up original books and records to attract investors or lenders.

Preparing Your Location

If you are not operating out of your home, you will need to lease a space and prepare it for your use. You are likely to need a security deposit for your landlord and, because you are a new company, he may also require a few months' rent.

Unless you are renting office space only, there may be work needed to prepare the site for your occupancy. Some landlords are willing to contribute a portion of the cost of the work as an incentive for a new tenant, or you may be able to pay for it over the term of the lease. Determine as closely as you can the total cost of this renovation and see if there are ways to keep the costs down.

Remember also to include the cost of putting in phone and other telecommunication lines such as fax and data lines. The phone company will charge to run the wire to the building, and all of the interior wiring will be done at your expense as well. Also, don't forget the cost of the phone instruments themselves—you may either purchase or lease them. A phone system may cost thousands of dollars.

Deposits, Fees, and Licenses

There are other deposits beyond those that are required by the landlord. Your phone company and the other utilities will also need some money to turn on your new service. The amount will depend on the size of the space and the number of lines you need. Gas and electric companies will want an average of two months' charges.

You will require insurance to cover your tangible assets (loss from fire, theft, etc.); to protect from any liability such as product failure; and to protect you and your workers from the cost of injuries (workers' compensation). Most insurance agents require a substantial portion of the annual premium (in the 25% range) to activate your coverage.

In addition, there may be fees to pay to local government for occupancy permit or professional licenses. These may have annual renewal costs as well. If your business is any type of professional service, you may need licensing for that as well.

> There may be fees to pay to local government for occupancy permit or professional licenses.

Fixtures, Furniture, Machinery, Etc.

The needs here may cover a wide range—from a few desks and some PCs to a full-fledged factory full of state-of-the-art equipment. For many new businesses, this is where the bulk of the money is spent. Remember that you may be able to use lease financing here instead of outright purchases. Equipment companies often do their own leasing.

A company car may be nice, but not necessary. Be careful, because anything in the company name will have to be insured by the company, and the level of coverage may be higher than you require individually. You may need a small truck for deliveries, so don't forget the costs of coverage for that as well. Again, a lease may be the answer.

Marketing Material and Promotions

You will want to get off the ground with a good image and as much fanfare as is reasonable. Potential customers will make judgments about your business based in part on the creativity and quality of your printed material and advertising. You need to have sufficient funds to design and print material to distribute and do some advertising and/or direct mail marketing. The payback for this expense is long term because it takes some time for these programs to show results.

> Potential customers will make judgments about your business based in part on the creativity and quality of your printed material and advertising.

Working Capital

This item is the most complex one you will have to estimate. You must have sufficient cash to fund your business in the early stages until you reach the break-even point and have a positive cash flow. If you sell on credit, you will have to have capital to fund your receivables.

You will need a pro forma cash flow statement. Each month, you will estimate the total amount of your revenues and your total expense. It is very likely that your revenues will not cover those expenses for a period of up to a year or more. Larger businesses routinely expect this as a cost of doing business, small start-ups often neglect this concern. *USA Today* was in business for years before it made its first dollar, and Amazon.com has poured hundreds of millions into its early years of losses. You won't be covering these enormous amounts of money, but regardless of what your losses are, if you don't have enough cash on hand to sustain yourself, you won't be around to celebrate your own success. If you aren't sure how to figure what you need, get the help of an accountant, because the more accurate your numbers, the higher your potential for success.

Once you have these target numbers, you must line up the money or the credit to meet your needs.

Sources of Start-Up Capital

Many new business owners think it is possible to come up with a good idea and then fund it with a bank loan. This seldom works, for several reasons. First, most banks won't lend money to a new business without a track record, and second, few new companies have the cash flow to pay back loans early in the life of the venture. In recent years, banks have been marketing loans that they describe as business loans, although they are actually home equity loans. They are more concerned with the value of your collateral than the cash flow of your business. If you get into any struggle at all over money, you could lose your home.

The second most problematic source of start-up capital is unsecured personal lines on your credit cards. These carry a high interest rate and add to your cost of doing business. Perhaps they can be useful as a last resort, but they are not good as a primary source to get cash.

> Most banks won't lend money to a new business without a track record, and few new companies have the cash flow to pay back loans early in the life of the venture.

You Need Equity and/or Investment

The best way to fund a new business venture is with your own savings that you have put aside specifically for this reason. You can then use this as a long-term investment and build your equity as you build your company. Someday you can sell off the business and use the money to retire—a good long-range plan.

Perhaps you don't have quite enough. How about going to family and friends? You're the best judge of their ability to help. Should you make it a loan or an investment?

Unless you are absolutely sure you will have the cash to pay back a loan, don't risk a relationship by borrowing money. If things get tough, you will need the friendship even more. However, if there is someone who is in a position to lend without an immediate payback for the first year, that may be a solution. You can pay interest only at the end of the year and then begin paying back the principal when your cash flow can sustain it.

Here is where you may want to consider simply finding an investor. Previously we discussed corporate structures that will allow you to approach individuals about making an investment in your venture. You must be sure that you have the proper documentation in place and that you make it perfectly clear that money is at risk and may be lost if the venture does not succeed. If the level of investment is small enough and the potential is great enough, this could be a very good deal for a few family members, friends, or business associates.

The major question is, how much interest in the company should they get for their cash? You must decide how to value the various elements required to start the company. For example:

> Eric has a new concept for a home improvement company, which he has spent two years working on. It will take another year to perfect it. He needs $100,000 capital. After deciding that his idea was 50 percent of the value of the company and his time over three years had a value of $150,000, he concluded that 50 percent of the business was worth $250,000 (his time and the cash). Therefore, each $25,000 investment is worth 5 percent of the ownership. He put in an extra $25,000 and sold off 15 percent of the business for $75,000.
>
> There is no scientific formula for this, so you must create your own. Put a fair value on your own idea and the work you have put in and then you can determine what the financial support is really worth.

Noncash Resources

Whether you want to or expect to, it is likely that in the early stages of your business, you will be working for free or for lower wages than you might have earned elsewhere. This is known as sweat equity, and the value of this free work enhances the value of your business. It also decreases your need for cash—the lower your

> You must be sure that you have the proper documentation in place and that you make it perfectly clear that money is at risk and may be lost if the venture does not succeed.

personal overhead, the more comfortable you will be about putting your efforts into the business.

> Joan started a small gift shop with some items that were homemade crafts, some items on consignment, and a line of products she purchased from the manufacturer. Her largest expense was preparing the shop to open and paying wages once the shop was doing business.
>
> With the help of her family and friends, the decorating was completed for the price of the paint. Labor was donated, and shelves were installed for free. Cabinets and tables to use for display were given or lent for her use. She fully expected to work for free for the first six months. The only start-up costs she anticipated were the cost of beginning inventory, utilities, rental deposit, and advertising. A bootstrap way to get into business.

Vendor Credit

Most new companies are required to pay in advance or by COD for their raw materials and finished products—and the money won't come in until the products are sold. Depending on how quickly you move your inventory and how often you must fill in by purchasing more, this is a major use of your working capital.

Needless to say, if you can get terms such as net 30 days to pay your bills, the pressure for cash will be less. This is something you want to work up to from the beginning.

Try to negotiate with new vendors to pay part up front and the balance in 15 days. Any starting terms may be the beginning of a good credit relationship. Be very sure that you adhere to the terms given so that you can get to the next level of more liberal terms.

> Try to negotiate with new vendors to pay part up front and the balance in 15 days.

Barter

Whether done informally or through an organized barter group, you can contribute the goods or services that you sell and get equivalent goods/services in return. For example, if you are starting a restaurant and need to install a computerized order/cash register system, perhaps you can issue gift certificates for food in lieu of all or part of the cash payments. The credit decisions are looser and you will have the margin of your profitability to cushion you as well.

This is a major caution: just because you are not spending cash, don't be tempted to spend more than you need or more than is budgeted. Remember, a bootstrap operation with the safety of extra capital can always upgrade.

> Just because you are not spending cash, don't be tempted to spend more than you need or more than is budgeted.

Streetwise Reality Tour

1. Everything you spend and borrow as a start-up will have an effect on your profitability and your competitiveness for years to come. The more you spend, the higher your costs, and the more you have to charge for your goods/services. If your prices are higher than your competitors, you will not attract the customers you need.

2. The revenue stream seldom flows as quickly as you want and expect. Once you have projected your sales revenue for the first year, cut it down by one-third. Be conservative. Customers do not change their buying patterns as quickly as you may hope and expect, and first-year sales are frequently less than anticipated. Prepare for less revenue, cash flow, and profit, and you will be able to last until you've reached the break-even point.

3. Always keep cash in reserve—you may need it for a variety of reasons. When times are good, you will need to increase inventory. Opportunities may arise to purchase goods at a discount, and having the cash to do so will directly improve your bottom line. Also, should business become a bit slow, you will require capital to fill in when operating cash flow gets low.

For more information on this topic, visit our Web site at www.businesstown.com

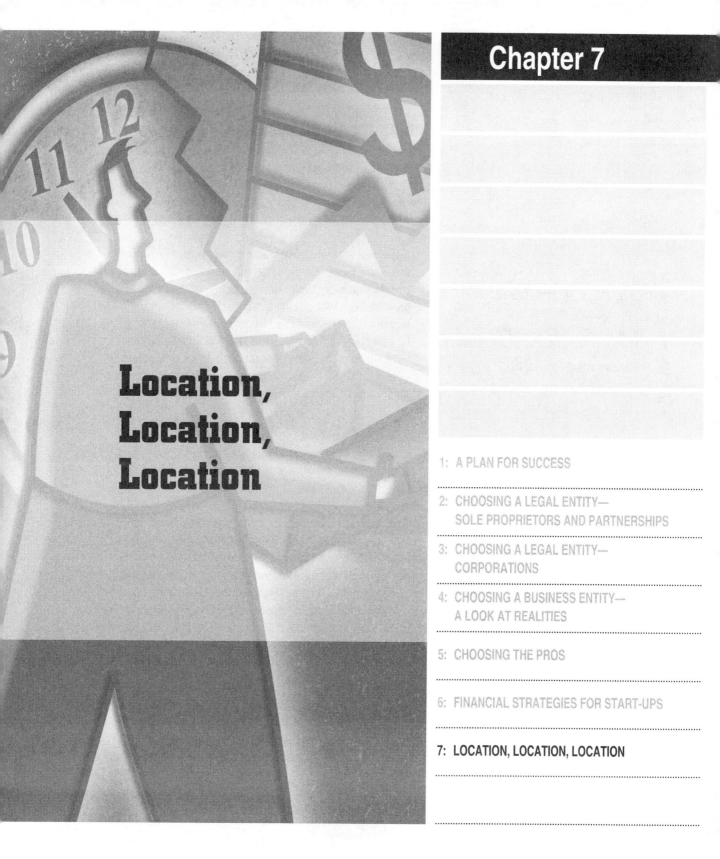

Chapter 7

Location,
Location,
Location

Finding the Right Location

As the story goes, a wealthy businessman was asked to list the three most important factors in the success of his business. His response was, "LOCATION, LOCATION, and LOCATION!" Regardless of whether the story is true, for many of you, location may be a major factor in the success of your business.

Adam had a great idea for an upscale restaurant with an expensive menu. He prepared his business plan and worked out every detail of purchasing, preparation, and presentation. What he hadn't considered, however, was the fact that there were too many expensive restaurants where he had chosen to locate. Even these other restaurants were suffering because of a diminishing local population. Without that sufficient customer base, Adam's restaurant, great idea or not, failed within the year.

How Much Can You Spend?

One of the first issues you have to resolve is how much you can afford to spend for your business location. The answer to this will vary greatly, depending upon the type of business and your space requirements.

In a restaurant, occupancy costs should be five to seven percent of gross sales, more in a fine dining establishment or a fast food restaurant that requires heavy traffic for volume.

Most manufacturing operations can locate anywhere, and cost becomes the most important consideration, except perhaps convenience of labor. Retail operations need to be near their most likely customers. Service firms do much of their work at customer locations, so that is not a concern. You must decide on your own priorities.

Lease or Buy?

Once you have determined how much you can (or more importantly, should), spend on a business location, you will have to decide whether you want to lease or purchase that location.

Some of the things you will need to consider are as follows.

> One of the first issues you have to resolve is how much you can afford to spend for your business location.

Tax Ramifications

When you buy commercial real estate, the purchase is usually financed by a lender (usually a bank), which takes a mortgage on the property as collateral for the loan. The interest on the loan, as well as the points (fee charged) and closing costs, are deductible for income tax purposes.

But remember, as with any loan, interest is amortized over the life of the loan. What this means is that most of the interest is paid during the first half of the loan term. During each year of the loan you will be making the same payment amount, but less and less of it will be deductible as interest. When the loan is finally paid off, there will be no interest deduction at all, but you will have collateral that is free and clear. On the other hand, when you lease real estate, all of the lease payments are deductible for as long as you rent the property. One last thing that benefits a business owner who buys his property is the concept of "depreciation."

While a complete discussion of depreciation is beyond the scope of this chapter, generally, under the current tax code, an owner of business property is allowed to take depreciation (an artificial deduction) over a specific period of years. This allows the property owner to shelter a portion of his income from taxation. It accounts for the likely wear and tear on the property and necessary repairs. A simple example of this complex tax concept is as follows:

> Michelle purchases a warehouse for $200,000. Assuming that she is allowed to depreciate that purchase over 20 years, she will be allowed to take depreciation of $10,000 per year. If Michelle receives $100,000 per year in gross income, she can reduce that gross income amount by $10,000 in depreciation. Her income tax is then calculated on $90,000 rather than $100,000.

There is no absolute rule for whether, from a tax standpoint, it is better to buy or lease a business property. Assuming that all other factors are equal, you will want to sit down with your accountant and "crunch the numbers" to determine whether purchasing or leasing is in your best interest.

> The interest on the loan, as well as the points (fee charged) and closing costs, are deductible for income tax purposes.

Build Equity

One of the primary benefits of ownership over leasing is that you can build equity and ultimately end up owning the property.

If you purchase the property, you don't have to worry about losing your lease or putting up with a troublesome landlord. You can renovate and modernize without having to obtain permission. You can also spend as much or as little on maintenance and upkeep as fits your budget, as opposed to your landlord's.

If the property is likely to appreciate, you get the benefit of the appreciation. Even if the property does not appreciate, you will have more than rent receipts to show for your years of payments; you will have the deed.

Don't forget, however, that property can also depreciate in value. The area may change, or the structure may deteriorate. At some point, you may realize that the neighborhood is not as good for business as you had hoped or that a new highway did not generate the business you had expected. If you lease the property, you can always move at the end of the lease.

Distraction of Operating Real Estate

One of the biggest drawbacks of owning real estate is that you will have to divide your time, efforts, attention, and energy between running your business and taking care of the property.

Most business owners are kept busy enough with the details of running their business. It is just fine with them if someone else takes care of the leaks in the roof, the potholes in the parking lot, the peeling paint, the property taxes, and general maintenance of the property.

It is not that you *cannot* do these things, but if you wanted to manage commercial real estate, you would probably be working for a real estate management company. And, with the time you save from managing the property, maybe you can even see your family from time to time.

Seller Financing

If you decide to purchase a business location, you can always try to get a bank loan. But, unless you can afford to make a down

> One of the primary benefits of ownership over leasing is that you can build equity and ultimately end up owning the property.

payment of at least 30% of the purchase price or have enough other assets to put up for collateral, you may find this difficult, if not impossible.

What you can do is ask if the seller will finance the purchase. You can do this to finance the purchase of real estate or even of an entire existing business. The seller will hold the mortgage with the same rights of foreclosure of any lender.

> Ask if the seller will finance the purchase.

After years of looking for just the right opportunity, Greg found a small auto repair business whose owner wanted to retire.

Greg does not have enough money to make a sizeable down payment and has no other property to put up for collateral. A bank loan is out of the question.

The owner has not been flooded with offers. He has known Greg for years and believes that Greg can successfully run an auto body business. He also knows that Greg may be his last chance to sell the business.

Greg and the owner agree that Greg will purchase the business and real estate for $200,000. At the closing, Greg will get a deed to the property and a bill of sale for the equipment and other assets of the business. The owner will get a mortgage on the property that he is selling to Greg.

Greg will make his monthly mortgage payments to the owner, not a bank. And, if the owner finds that Greg cannot afford the mortgage payments, he will be able to foreclose on the property to protect his investment.

The benefit of seller financing is that Greg is able to finance the purchase, even though he would never qualify for a bank loan. The owner is able to sell the property to someone on whom he is willing to take a risk. The sale also provides a cash flow to the owner during his retirement years. Finally, if Greg does not succeed, the owner can take back the property.

Sale Leaseback

This is similar to the previous example but, in this situation, the seller leases the property to Greg with the agreement that once Greg has paid a certain amount of the lease, the transaction will turn into a purchase. You can also lease with an option to buy at a certain date.

Assess Your Needs

Before you sign on the dotted line and obligate yourself, and your untested business, to a multiyear lease, step back and consider what your business needs are in terms of location.

Some of the things to consider are as follows:

- *Type of business.* Depending upon your type of business, you will need to decide whether you need industrial space, commercial space, office space, storefront, or a combination.
- *Square footage.* The rent you pay may be the single biggest expense facing your business. You need to decide how much space your business really needs (usually calculated as square footage). For example, you may see office space advertised as 1,000 square feet available at $20 per square foot. One thousand square feet multiplied by $20 totals $20,000. Dividing this number by 12 (the number of months in the year) results in a monthly rent of $1,666. In some areas, the prices are quoted per month to make them more attractive. In this case, it would be $1.66 per square foot. Taking too much space (and too much rent) as a fixed monthly expense can mean the difference between making money for yourself and making money for your landlord.
- *Access to the Business.* Can customers find your business and can they get to it without difficulty? This is particularly important with respect to a retail business that sells to the public.
- *Access for Employees.* Can the labor force you want and need easily reach your business? Is it on a transportation line?
- *Storage and display area.* If your business requires a large inventory, you will need to have enough space to store and display your merchandise.

Before you sign on the dotted line and obligate yourself, and your untested business, to a multiyear lease, step back and consider what your business needs are in terms of location.

- *Room to expand.* While you don't want to take on too much square footage, you have to consider whether you will have enough room to expand if your business goes as well as you hope. If you find yourself with no room to grow, you may have to incur significant costs in moving the business. You may also find that your new location, while roomy, is not as good as the one you just outgrew.
- *Option to Renew.* A great location with room to expand is good only for as long as the lease lasts.

Matt finally raised the money necessary to open a child care center. After five years of struggling, he was able to see "light at the end of the tunnel."

Unfortunately, the lease Matt signed five years before did not give him the right to renew. In the meantime, the landlord has made other plans for the space occupied by Matt's day care.

Matt is going to have to relocate, but the new space is too far from his old location for his day care clientele to get to. For all practical purposes Matt has to start over, but because he only had enough savings to fund one start-up day care business, he has to close down entirely.

- *Zoning.* If your business involves manufacturing, assembly, or fabricating, you are going to have to be aware of local zoning ordinances. You may hope that the landlord warns you about them, but it is your responsibility to know. Once the lease is signed, it's too late. You're on the hook for rent for the entire five-year term of the lease.
- *Relationship with Nearby Businesses.* You will also want to see what other businesses are in the immediate area and whether those businesses will be a draw for your business.

Laurie opened a used car lot on a busy stretch of highway. There were no other auto dealerships for fifteen miles in any direction. Laurie thought that she was guaranteed success because she had no immediate competition.

> If your business involves manufacturing, assembly, or fabricating, you are going to have to be aware of local zoning ordinances.

What Laurie realized later was that her potential customers did not want to travel to her area just to see the selection of cars offered by her one lot. Instead, they were traveling to the "Miracle Mile" on the far side of town because there were ten auto dealerships within a three-mile section of highway. There was selection, there was activity, and there was a perception on the part of the customers that the dealerships would be competitive with one another in terms of price. In short, there was something for everyone.

For more information on this topic, visit our Web site at www.businesstown.com

Chapter 8

Negotiating a Lease

I f you decide not to purchase your business location, then, sooner or later, your are going to have to negotiate a lease.

A Lease Is a Contract

A lease is a contract that details the rights and responsibilities of both the landlord and the tenant (Form 08-01 in the Appendix). The terms of the lease are enforceable in a court of law by either the landlord or the tenant.

The lease is usually written by the landlord or his attorney, and it usually contains provisions that heavily favor the landlord.

Most leases are a virtual "wish-list" of things the landlord's attorney wants you to agree to, and no one would be more surprised than the landlord's lawyer if you signed the lease without some attempt to negotiate changes. (And if you do, get a new lawyer for yourself.)

In fact, many commercial leases contain particularly onerous lease provisions ("throw-away clauses") just so the landlord can give them up as part of the negotiation process. You feel that you got something in the negotiations and the landlord gives away the clauses he never expected to enforce anyway, while keeping the provisions he really wanted.

Weigh Your Negotiating Power

Depending on the type of business you own and your specific needs, you may have anywhere from tremendous bargaining power to no bargaining power at all.

David wants to open a bookstore in the brand new supermall. The mall is operated by a professional management company that manages malls throughout the country. The management company has already been approached by five other national booksellers about taking space in the new mall.

David is presented with a proposed lease that calls for a high rent, charges high common-area fees, dictates hours of operation, requires that the mall be paid a

> A lease is a contract that details the rights and responsibilities of both the landlord and the tenant.

percentage of your yearly sales, and guarantees you practically nothing in return.

David reads the clause that requires that he pledge one of his vital organs as collateral. Because David has read this chapter carefully, he figures that it is one of the throw-away clauses that the landlord expects to give up in negotiations. WRONG! For this landlord, and this lease, in this mall, you will sign the lease as presented or go somewhere else.

Paul, on the other hand, has located a spot for his bookstore in an older building in an area of town that is attempting a comeback. The building has been vacant for several years and the landlord will let Paul practically write the lease just to get him into the building and generate the first positive cash flow the landlord has seen in years.

Don't think, however, that Paul necessarily got the better deal. The mall charges more and puts more restrictions on its tenants because the number of customers drawn to the mall may dwarf anything that Paul will ever see.

Triple Net Lease

This is a lease that includes payment for rent plus real estate taxes, plus insurance (for the structure) plus maintenance. If you sign such a lease, make sure the total cost is spelled out.

Hours of Operation

In certain retail locations such as shopping centers and malls, the landlord directs that your business will be open for specific hours of the day.

This type of lease terms ensures that, during the busy hours of the day, all of the stores are open and drawing customers. A customer drawn to the card store at the end of the plaza may also realize that she needs a birthday cake from the bakery four stores away.

> If you sign a triple net lease, make sure the total cost is spelled out.

Common Area Maintenance ("CAM")

When there are several tenants in a building, the landlord may attempt to allocate the cost of maintenance and upkeep among the tenants.

For example, roof repair, resurfacing the parking lot, snow removal, and general maintenance will be charged to the tenants on a monthly basis, in addition to their rent. The lease may also state that the landlord has absolute discretion in deciding what repairs and maintenance are to be performed on the property.

> The lease may also state that the landlord has absolute discretion in deciding what repairs and maintenance are to be performed on the property.

Christina leases a storefront in a small five-store shopping plaza. The stores are equal in size so that each tenant pays the same common area maintenance charge. Christina pays a monthly rent of $1,000 and a monthly common-area maintenance charge of $250. It's more rent than Christina wanted to pay but she can afford it.

The following year the landlord decides to resurface the parking lot and notifies the tenants that their common area maintenance fee will be increased to $500 per month.

Read the common area maintenance clause carefully. Disputes often arise as to whether an expense is a maintenance expense (which may be passed along to the tenant as CAM), or an improvement to the property, which is usually solely the landlord's responsibility. Whether or not it is usually the landlord's responsibility, it will become yours if the lease says that it is.

Also, make sure you understand how the CAM is allocated among the tenants. It can be allocated among the available stores or among the tenants. For example:

Ian is one of five tenants in the shopping plaza. He is content to pay his 20 percent of the common area maintenance charge.

In the second year of his lease, two of the tenants move out of the shopping center. Ian is now being requested to pay for 33% of the common area maintenance.

Closely related to the CAM is the fact that leases often allow the landlord to pass along to the tenants any increases in property taxes, assessments, and insurance.

Lease Renewal

As mentioned earlier, you will want to make sure that the lease can be renewed beyond its original term.

It is not uncommon for a tenant to insist upon one, two, or even three, five-year extensions of the lease. In this way, the tenant obtains the benefit of permanency, customer recognition, and established clientele. The lease can also include terms for increases in rent should you exercise the renewal options. You may be able to limit the increase to a certain percentage.

Noncompete

If you are in a small shopping center you may want the landlord to agree not to lease one of the other storefronts to a business substantially similar to yours.

> Adam operates a card store. Three years into his lease the landlord decides to rent one of the storefronts to a gift shop. What Adam did not realize is that 40 percent of the gift shop's income is from the sale of cards. Adam has lost a substantial part of his business but, without an agreement from the landlord, can do nothing about it.

Escalation Clause

Should you default on your regular monthly rental payment, many leases have a provision that the total value of the lease becomes payable immediately.

For example, Bill leases a building for three years at $1,000 per month. The total lease value is $36,000. At the end of the sixth month, his business gets into trouble and he stops paying rent. There is $30,000 remaining on the lease, and the landlord may sue for that amount as a result of the escalation clause.

> It is not uncommon for a tenant to insist upon one, two, or even three, five-year extensions of the lease.

Deferral

It may be possible to negotiate a deferral (or delay) of rent during the initial months of the lease, when you are first getting established at the new location and before your cash starts flowing.

Percentage Lease

In a percentage lease, you have to pay your monthly rent plus a percentage of your gross sales. This type of lease is seen most often in retail storefront leases, or those in shopping centers and malls. It is in recognition of the fact that the amount of your sales is a factor of the management of the mall and the number of customers who are drawn to the stores in the mall.

Insurance

Once you decide whether to purchase or lease a business space, and before you take possession (in the case of a purchase, at the time of the sales agreement) you should talk to your insurance agent about the types of insurance you will need. In fact, most sophisticated landlords will have a clause in the lease requiring you to acquire insurance for damage to the property that is attributable to your business.

- Renter's Insurance. If you are leasing a business space, you will want insurance to protect the contents of your business. Computers, furniture, inventory—all should be insured from loss by theft or fire.
- Liability Insurance. If a customer slips on water that you allowed to collect on the floor, expect a lawsuit.

Streetwise Reality Tour

1. More often than not, the landlord will want personal guarantees to secure your promise to pay rent. You can take all the steps you want to minimize your personal exposure for

> Most sophisticated landlords will have a clause in the lease requiring you to acquire insurance for damage to the property that is attributable to your business.

business debts. You can form a corporation and you can keep your spouse out of business affairs. Nevertheless, if you want to lease a particular space for your business, the landlord may insist that you and your spouse execute personal guarantees to assure payment of the rent.

Landlords know that if a corporate tenant defaults on the lease his chances of collecting the rent are slim to none. The landlord also knows that probably the biggest reason that you decided to operate in a corporate form is so that you can do just that, should circumstances warrant.

Consequently, the landlord will, more likely than not, insist upon personal guarantees. He cannot make you sign them, but he does not have to lease the space to you if he does not want to.

Because leases often extend for years and can be the most significant part of your operating budget, you may lose the benefit of the corporate form by agreeing to personally guarantee your corporation's debt on the lease.

Suggest instead that you post an additional security deposit or limit the personal guarantee to a six- to twelve-month period or a specific dollar amount.

2. If you default on the lease and move out of the premises, the landlord does not necessarily have the obligation to release the property. He may be able to let the property sit vacant and sue you for the balance on the lease. If you have signed personal guarantees, be prepared to pay or file bankruptcy.

If you are at all familiar with contract law, you have learned that when one party breaches a contract the other party has a duty to take steps to reduce his damages. This is the concept of mitigation of damages.

For example, if Carol agrees to purchase seafood from a seller and then defaults on the agreement, the seller cannot simply let the inventory go to waste on a loading dock. He must make efforts to locate a new purchaser.

With regard to a lease, however, that is not always the case. If the tenant defaults after the first year of a five-year lease, the landlord may be able to let the property sit vacant

> Because leases often extend for years and can be the most significant part of your operating budget, you may lose the benefit of the corporate form by agreeing to personally guarantee your corporation's debt on the lease.

for the remaining four years and simply send bills to Adam for the rent payments and common area maintenance charges.

3. Once you are in the leased premises, you have lost a great deal of negotiating power in the event that disputes arise during the course of the lease.

Your greatest negotiating power lies in the period of time before you sign the lease. Once you are in the location, with furniture in place, inventory on display, and after you have incurred additional expenses for signage and advertising, it is not at all likely that you are going to move out over a minor dispute with your landlord.

Your landlord knows this, and he also knows that if you try holding back rent he will exercise one of the variety of default clauses in the lease to declare you in default, to accelerate the balance on your lease, and to commence legal collection activity against you.

> Your only recourse, once you have taken possession of the property, is to file suit against your landlord for his breach of the lease.

Your only recourse, once you have taken possession of the property, is to file suit against your landlord for his breach of the lease. Because your landlord can make your life miserable in so many ways, this is also not an appealing option. Nevertheless, it may be all you have.

4. Just because you signed a lease on your apartment does not make you an expert on commercial leases. Hire an attorney to help you review the lease and to understand each and every one of the provisions in it, before you sign.

A commercial lease can be anywhere from two to sixty pages long. Many landlords hire attorneys who, over the years, justify their bills by adding new and different clauses to pre-existing lease forms. The result is a sixty-page lease form with clauses for every possible contingency, which always favor the landlord, and which are, in most cases, practically unintelligible to the new business owner.

No one likes to hire attorneys, and no one likes to pay those attorneys. The consequences are too great, however, to go into a commercial lease without adequate review and preparation.

Chapter 9

Setting Up the Books

From day one of your venture planning, you will want to begin to set up the financial books of your company. All of the costs associated with starting a business are deductible from any income you derive from its operations for tax purposes.

Bob was planning to open an antique store and he spent over six months renovating a small storeroom at night and over the weekend while still working at his soon-to-be-former job. He spent several thousand dollars in material for the shop and then prior to the mid-September opening, he spent $1,500 on advertising and a mailing. Once the store was opened, he devoted all of his time to its operation and the first three months were pretty good. In addition to his operating expense (rent, utilities, and salaries), Bob was able to deduct his start-up expense from the income, and because of that, his first year showed a loss. This was used as a credit against his income earned while still on his job.

You will want to sit down with an accountant and determine together the criteria for the accounting system you will use. Following are some issues to consider:

> Even if you are a very small business, you should consider using a software accounting system.

- *What type of record keeping: manual or computerized?* Even if you are a very small business, you should consider using a software accounting system. The most popular one is Quickbooks, and it comes in several versions, which can be enhanced and customized for your use. Another frequently used program is Peachtree Accounting, which can work well for more complicated businesses such as manufacturing companies, and when there is the need for multiple users.

  Both systems are menu driven, fairly easy to understand, and will provide you with good ongoing records and reports that will tell you how the business is progressing. You will also be able to find out other information such as how much is owed to you and how much you owe at any point in time.

This is management information you must have access to on a regular basis.

- *Will you set up on a cash or accrual basis?*
There are two basic types of accounting systems. A cash method shows income (or revenue) at the time it is received, not necessarily when the transaction is made. It will record an expense at the time it is paid, not necessarily when it is incurred. This works best for small service businesses and cash-heavy businesses such as restaurants.

Linda has a successful Italian restaurant doing over $70,000 of business per month. Her money comes in the form of cash or credit card payments that go into her bank within 48 hours. Her expenses are wages paid every two weeks and food paid often upon delivery. Each month she pays her rent, utilities, insurance, and loan payments. At the end of each month, her accountant computes her total revenue, deducts her expenses, and gives her a profit and loss statement that shows the results of the period. A cash basis system works here because most transactions are done in cash.

The accrual-based system recognizes income whenever it is earned, whether the money comes in or not (when an expense is incurred, even if it is not paid). This type of system works for a business that sells on credit (as opposed to credit cards, which turn into cash quickly) and also buys on credit. This is the best way to match the timing of income and expense for the purpose of determining profitability.

- *How much detail will you require?* When you are in the process of setting up your books, you should be deciding what type of information will be helpful to you in the sales, pricing, and future planning aspects of your business. You will then set up your books to give you the detail you require.

> The accrual-based system recognizes income whenever it is earned, whether the money comes in or not (when an expense is incurred, even if it is not paid).

For example, if you have a retail business selling a large number of items, you will want to track which ones are the best sellers and which move more slowly. This is accomplished by creating detail in your chart of accounts on the revenue side.

On the other side of the ledger, if you are manufacturing a product and there are a number of different raw materials and processes that are involved, you will want great detail in order to track your costs.

You can categorize all income and expense of your company in as much detail as you desire. Work with your accountant to determine what will give you the information you need to make solid financial decisions.

Understanding the Financial Reports

> There are two types of profit: gross and net.

There are a number of reports that will be generated by your accounting system, and you must know what they are and how to read them. The primary one is the income or profit-and-loss statement. It tells you just what the name implies: how much profit or loss you've generated from the operation of your company. There are two types of profit: gross and net. Gross profit is what remains after subtracting the actual cost of the goods. These costs are called direct expense or variable expense. The actual material and labor that is directly involved in the product is what makes up the expense. It is variable because the more you sell, the more you will spend. The bottom line profit is the net (before tax) profit, which deducts all of your overhead (indirect or fixed) cost from the gross profit.

Following is a sample income or profit-and-loss statement for a distribution company. They purchase in large quantity and then resell to industrial users.

XYZ Distribution Corporation	

INCOME STATEMENT
YEAR ENDING 12/31/00

Total Revenue	**500,000**
Less returns and allowances	18,000[1]
Less discounts earned	5,000[2]
Net sales	477,000
Cost of Goods Sold (Variable)[3]	
Material purchased	286,200[4]
Freight in	3,800[5]
Total direct costs of sales	290,000
Gross Profit	187,000
Administrative Expense (Fixed)[6]	
Advertising	2,500
Accounting fees	1,500
Truck expense	5,000
Commission	10,000[7]
Insurance	12,000
Interest	9,600[8]
Legal fees	1,500
Officer's salary	45,000
Office salary	25,000
Office expense (incl. phone)	5,000
Postage	1,500
Rent	6,000
Sales salaries	42,000[9]
Utilities (heat and light)	3,600
Total expense	**170,200**[10]
Net (before tax) profit	**16,800**

[1] Refunds and allowances are all credits you give for returns and discounts to move merchandise. Monitor this number to make sure you are not losing money by having to grant too many concessions to customers.

[2] If you allow discount for fast payment, list it separately. You must decide on the value of these discounts. A new company may need to generate the cash flow, but a more established one can borrow more cheaply.

[3] The costs of goods vary on the volume of sale because each item or service has a direct cost associated with it.

[4] The major cost for most companies is the raw material (for manufacturers) or the cost of the finished product offered for sale.

[5] You should include the freight inbound as it is part of the cost of the material.

[6] The administrative and selling expense is for the most part fixed (or constant) and not dependent on sales.

[7] Commission is a cost which is semi-fixed (or semi-variable) as it is pegged to the volume sold.

[8] Only the interest paid on a loan is deducted from the Income Statement. Principal is, however, deducted from a Cash Flow Statement, which will be discussed later.

[9] Sales salaries may be tied to sales volume and therefore also be semi-variable.

[10] The total expenses are deducted from the gross profit to produce the net (before tax) profit.

The Balance Sheet

The second-most important financial report that will be generated is the balance sheet, which is a document describing the economic health and stability of your company. In short, it is a list of assets and liabilities of the business. When the latter is deducted from the former, you will be able to determine the net worth of the business or the value of your equity. As important as that number is, perhaps the determination of solvency is more critical to the ongoing operation. Solvency is a measure of how adequate your current assets are to meet your current obligations.

The typical balance sheet is arranged as follows:

Assets
    Current assets
        Cash and cash items[11]
        Accounts receivable
        Inventory[12]
        Notes payable–short term[13]
        Total current assets

    Fixed assets
        Land and buildings
        Machinery and equipment
            Less depreciation[14]
        Long-term notes[15]
        Total fixed assets

    Total assets

Liabilities
    Current liabilities
        Accounts payable
        Payroll taxes due[16]
        Accrued vacations due[17]
        Loans–current portion[18]
        Long-term liabilities[19]
            Stockholder equity

    Total liabilities

[11] Cash may be bank deposits or credit card charges in transit. This item may also include any short-term money investments such as CDs that you may use to house excess cash.

[12] Inventory can be a deceptive time because a certain percentage may be obsolete or unsaleable. Make these adjustments to get an accurate picture.

[13] Short-term notes may include loans to stockholders or employees that are due to be paid back over the next few months.

[14] Depreciation reduces the value of machinery and equipment sometimes below its market value. It may also not reflect the low value of some equipment, particularly computer systems, which often have almost no resale value.

[15] The portion of a loan or note that is due beyond one year.

[16] Taxes that have been withheld and not remitted.

[17] Vacation time due to employees this year from time worked previously.

[18] Loan payments (principal and interest) due over the next 12 months.

[19] Any portions of loans due beyond the next 12 months.

Current Assets vs. Current Liabilities

It is possible for a company to have a positive net worth yet have cash flow problems that threaten its survival. By the same token, a company may have a good current cash flow yet have a negative net worth. The key here is investing money and resources in productive assets like inventory or machinery in constant use. If capital is tied up in a building or seldom-used equipment, it is not productive.

Our hypothetical distribution company may have the following balance sheet.

> It is possible for a company to have a positive net worth yet have cash flow problems that threaten its survival.

XYZ Distribution Company	

BALANCE SHEET
12-31-00

Assets

Cash in Bank	30,000
Accounts Receivable	75,000
Notes Payable	3,000
Inventory	40,000
	148,000

Long-term assets

Utility deposits	2,500
Total assets	150,500

Liabilities—current

Accounts payable	39,000
Payroll taxes due	6,000
Current portion loans	30,000
	75,000
Long-term note due	102,000
	177,000
Owner's equity	(26,500)
Total Liabilities and Equity	150,500

On first examination, this business looks to be in trouble. But the fact that the current assets ($148,000) are twice as much as the current liabilities, the operations should be easy to manage. If the profits continue and long-term debt is reduced, in a few years, the net worth will grow to be positive.

Break-Even Analysis

This is where your understanding of the financial side of your business becomes very important. Unlike a profit-and-loss statement or balance sheet, a break-even analysis is not automatically generated. It is, however, a valuable document to determine where your volume must be in order to begin to make a profit. You will not start your business at this level, so you must find out what this goal should be.

The break-even volume is where all overhead expenses are covered by the gross profits from operations. You begin by establishing what the ongoing fixed overhead amount will be. You will want to divide it into a monthly number, so if there are expenses that are billed on an annual basis, you will need to divide them by 12 to get the monthly numbers.

For example, our distribution company may have fixed expenses as follows:

Salaries (all)	10,000
Commissions	1,000
Insurance	1,000
Rent	500
Utilities	300
Truck	500
Postage	125
Marketing (including advertising)	300
Office expense	500
Miscellaneous	1,000
Interest	300
	$15,525

> The break-even volume is where all overhead expenses are covered by the gross profits from operations.

With a gross profit margin of 40 percent, the break-even number of this company is $40,000 per month so that they generate a $16,000 gross profit amount. Until this company reaches this number, they will not be profitable.

You can change your break-even number by doing one of the following:

- Lower direct expense, which raises the gross profit margin.
- Control overhead, which lowers the volume required.
- Raise prices, which will also raise profit margins.

Look at this number on a quarterly basis to see how you are meeting volume/cost goals.

Cash Flow Statement

This is not the same as an income statement, as here you are dealing *only* with the inflow and outflow of cash. If sales are made on credit, this statement will only reflect that cash that has been received. Following are some other items to consider when you construct a cash flow.

- Depreciation is expensed on your profit-and-loss statement, but since it is a noncash item, it is not reported on a cash flow statement.
- Only interest is deducted on the income statement, but the full loan statement (principal and interest) is shown on the cash flow.

> Only interest is deducted on the income statement, but the full loan statement (principal and interest) is shown on the cash flow.

A cash flow statement is formatted as follows:

Income
 Less direct expense
  = gross profit
 Less operating expense
  = net (before tax) profit

Starting cash
 Plus cash sales and receivable collections
 Plus loan proceeds (if available and needed)
  = total available cash
 Less direct expense
 Less operation (administrative) expense without depreciation
 Less debt service (principal payment)
  = ending cash

The ending cash from any period becomes the beginning cash for the next period.

When your company begins to grow, it will put a strain on cash flow. You will need accurate pro formas to determine what sort of outside capital you will require.

> The goal is not just to acquire assets, but to acquire productive assets.

Streetwise Reality Tour

1. You must learn about your accounting system and review the reports on a regular basis. Look beyond the bottom line to see the trends that are occurring.
2. The goal is not just to acquire assets, but to acquire productive assets. You must be making a profit on the use of the space, equipment, or inventory you own, or it will be a drag on your operation.
3. Cash flow is critical, so volume must be adequate to fund overhead and finance any receivables.

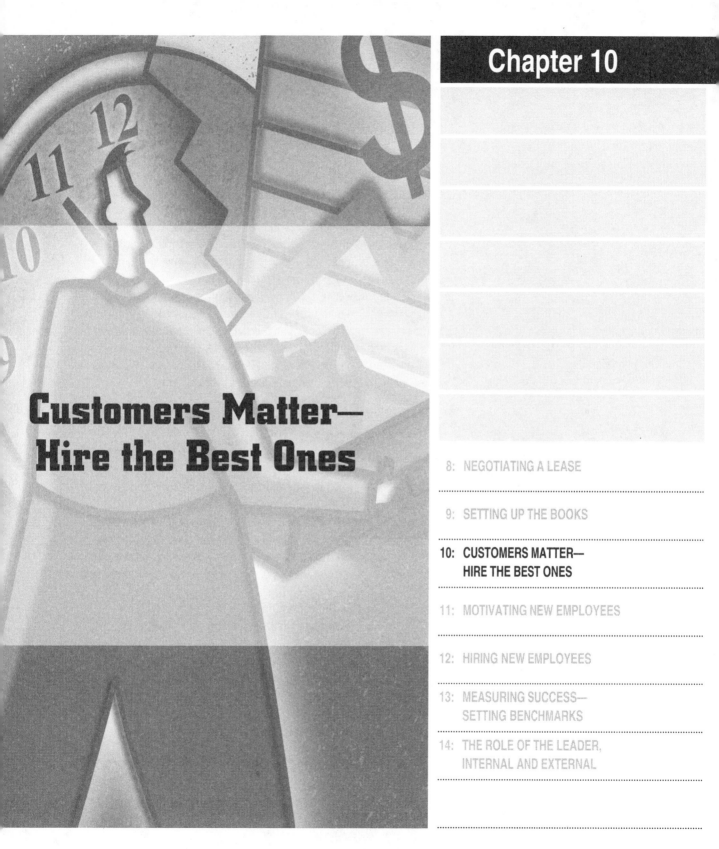

Chapter 10

Customers Matter—
Hire the Best Ones

There is a large variety of reasons business owners start their companies. Some may have learned a skill and realize that there is profit and freedom available in their own venture. Some may have a special talent such as photography or design, or a special educational degree such as a law degree. Or it may be special product knowledge or access to products that inspires them to create a venture to profit from this ability. The chance to be creative and independent is appealing, but it is important to give substantial thought to who your customers are likely to be.

If your answer to this question is "Anyone who uses (your product/service)," then you haven't done your homework. In your business plan phase, you looked at the size of the market for your business; and the closer you get to opening, the more you must narrow your target so you deliver the goods to the people or businesses most likely to become frequent customers.

> You must narrow your target so you deliver the goods to the people or businesses most likely to become frequent customers.

Market Research Includes Competitive Analysis

You must be very detailed about your review of existing and potential competition. Don't just list their names and make a casual consideration of what they produce, sell, or service. If possible, experience the competition yourself. Visit their stores or eat in their restaurant or make inquiry about their services. Begin grading them by their physical location and go on from there. Consider some of the following issues.

- Is the location convenient?
- Is the building well maintained and well designed?
- Is there parking?
- Do you feel welcome on your initial visit?
- Is merchandise displayed attractively?
- Is there a variety of merchandise?
- Do prices seem reasonable for what you are getting?
- Are the hours convenient?
- Is there sufficient staff?
- Do they follow up after the sale to determine your satisfaction?

Alice decided to open a beauty parlor day spa in a small, suburban strip mall. She determined that her clientele was primarily women between the ages of 29 and 44, mostly working full or part time. Her shop would be located in a good demographic area. In the months prior to opening, Alice personally visited 8 of the 12 salons in the area. What she found was very helpful to her own plans.

Few were open late every night and only one had hours on Sunday. Only two salons gave pedicures and neither had foot massage available. No salon she patronized called to remind her of her appointment and only one called a few weeks later to solicit additional business. Alice saw the value and the necessity for all of these accommodations and incorporated them in her salon. She also offered e-mail reminders to those who wanted them.

Alice also used her research to help in pricing. She felt the value of her services would sustain higher pricing, so she began at that level. The busiest times were likely to be late afternoon through evening, so she offered discounts for off-peak appointments. This combination of high service and perceived value made the salon successful from the beginning.

What Is Perceived Value?

Any new business owner who starts out with the simplistic idea that he will give high quality and low prices is deluding himself. It simply isn't possible. You must learn to strike a balance between the two. High quality and high service has a cost, and you must pass it on to customers.

> High quality and high service has a cost, and you must pass it on to customers.

What really attracts customers to a business once they have tried it is a feeling that they are getting good value for their money. There is always a customer base that will pay high prices for very exclusive service. The top-of-the-line-restaurants, hotels, and retail shops are a testament to that. But this is a small segment of the market and you may not be set up to attract them. Perhaps the largest segment are those who will pay a good price when they feel they are getting their money's worth. For most new businesses, these are the customers you want.

Alice found that her potential client put a premium on convenience in her hours of operation and a higher level of personal services offered. How does your company meet the extra needs of your customers? Some of the things you can do at a reasonable cost that will give that look of value are as follows:

- Be open longer hours.
- Make it easy to reach you via phone, fax, or the Internet.
- Offer delivery service.
- Offer special orders.
- Provide special discounts for frequent or off-peak users.
- Offer free parking/day care.
- Provide inhome or office consultation or demonstration.
- Provide follow-up service.

The explanation is simple: make your customer feel as if his business is welcome, listen to his needs and wants, and you will make it easy for him to do business. The customer wants to spend money where it is noticed and where there is a return.

Your Costs Must Be Covered

You have a specific amount of capital available to you early in your business life. It should be spent where there is a return. The items that directly affect your ability to serve your customers and keep them happy should be the top priority.

Office furniture that no one sees, a luxury car lease for you, selective entertainment for favored customers—all of these perks are nice, but they won't show a return for their expenditure.

You have a finite amount of money to spend for your overhead, and its costs will be reflected in your pricing. So, if you want to be competitive and yet give that perceived good value, keep the

> You have a finite amount of money to spend for your overhead, and its costs will be reflected in your pricing.

overhead low and keep it focused on improving the quality of your product or your service.

Communicate with a Target Audience

One of the most confusing items in a start-up budget is the marketing and advertising expense. Many novice entrepreneurs think that if you throw a great deal of money at the project then you will be successful—and there is no shortage of marketing consultants who will do expensive projects for you.

Many new business owners do need this type of help. A comprehensive strategy is very valuable, but few can afford the full-blown assistance. What you can do to cut the costs is to identify exactly who your customer is by their various characteristics, such as:

- Age
- Location
- Gender
- Income level
- Family status
- Other hobbies or interests

> There is no shortage of marketing consultants who will do expensive projects for you.

There are other items you can use to sort out this targeted person (or in some cases, business). Take the time to do so. Then, learn as much as you can about how they would receive information. Do they:

- Watch TV?
- Read local papers?
- Read specific magazines?
- Use the Internet frequently?
- Purchase from catalogs or by mail?

Once you have decided which one or two methods are best to announce and promote your new business, then you can focus your time and energy on creating the format of your message.

You want your potential customer to know you are here and to be enticed to try your product or service. You should, by now, have decided which items of service or convenience are most important to them. That is what you want to stress—be specific, inform a potential customer why they should be a customer!

You may try incentives such as grand opening specials and discounts to get people in your door, perhaps you even want to schedule a special guest or event. But once they are there, the spotlight is on you and your employees. How well you deliver the goods will determine how strong a business you can grow.

Streetwise Reality Tour

1. You can't be all things to all people. Some customers will be attracted and others will not. Focus your time and attention on the most likely candidates.
2. The highest quality and the lowest price are theories in conflict. Choose some combination of the two to provide good perceived value to customers.
3. Spend your time and money on what will make you money. Put resources in areas that benefit customers, not you.
4. Market and advertise in limited ways, targeting the customers most likely to patronize your venture. Don't use a shotgun approach.

> How well you deliver the goods will determine how strong a business you can grow.

For more information on this topic, visit our Web site at www.businesstown.com

Chapter 11

Motivating New Employees

If you are asked to identify one of the single most important aspects of your business, there are a number of issues you could identify.

You might say that your business plan is the most important aspect of your business. In fact, you can identify any number of different things: the availability of capital, the location of your business, its organizational structure, and its marketing efforts. The one thing you probably wouldn't say is that the most important aspect of your business's success is what your employees think and feel about their jobs.

But the fact is, if your business operates with any employees, what they think and feel about their work determines whether they are motivated to do their jobs. And employees without motivation can sap the life from any business, including yours.

If you are like most small business owners, the idea that you should be concerned about what your employees think and feel about their jobs may surprise you. It may even frustrate you. Don't you have enough to deal with already?

> Employees without motivation can sap the life from any business, including yours.

One day, Joe was reading a magazine on business management and came across an article that suggested that he place his employees' thoughts and feelings about their jobs ahead of all else.

As he read the article, Joe started to mutter to himself.

After all, he was the one who had the idea for the business, he had taken the time to investigate the product, hire the professionals, and develop the marketing plan. He was the one who borrowed the money to start the business and he was the one who gave the bank a mortgage on his home. He is the one who goes without a paycheck when money gets tight and he is the one who loses everything if the business fails.

Joe's employees, on the other hand, work a 40-hour week, get a guaranteed lunch break, receive their paychecks on time, and don't wake up in the middle of the night worrying about whether the customer wire-transferred the funds that will allow them to make the mortgage payment the next morning.

When Joe couldn't stand it any more he slammed down the magazine and yelled, "Worry about what my employees think and feel about their jobs? They're lucky to even have jobs. If they don't want them, there are others who do."

If this reaction doesn't sound familiar, don't worry; it will soon enough!

The Value of Job Satisfaction

The fact is that your employees' satisfaction with their jobs may account for a major fluctuation in the profit margins you achieve. The rest of your profitability is explained by such things as the current market, the general economy, and a range of other things like local competition and location.

Like it or not, your employees' satisfaction with their jobs may make the difference between the success or failure of your business.

Don't Fight It, Use It!

Recognize that people have a strong desire to do well. As a child you sought the approval of your parents. As you got older you strived to impress your teachers. You may say that you were trying to get good grades to get into college but, if you are at all honest with yourself, you have to admit that you liked the feeling of accomplishment, the sense that your teacher was pleased or impressed with your efforts, and that you were something special and apart from your classmates. You may also have enjoyed working on a challenging project with a teacher who provided guidance and support, but not direction.

For those same reasons, most of your employees do not come to work with the intention of doing a bad job. They like doing a good job and they like feeling good about themselves afterward. With this little bit of human nature firmly in mind, you are halfway to a satisfied, and motivated, employee.

> The fact is that your employees' satisfaction with their jobs may account for a major fluctuation in the profit margins you achieve.

Don't be misled, however. You are not doomed to failure if you are not a motivational wizard. In fact, some of the successful business owners you know don't have a clue when it comes to motivating employees. But, just think of how much more successful they would be if they could motivate their employees to their fullest potential. And, think about what it could mean to a new business like yours, which operates on "razor-thin" margins.

Don't Punish, Motivate

There is a world of difference between the quality of work performed by an employee who simply does not want to do a bad job and the quality of work performed by an employee who is truly motivated. Unfortunately, many business owners have neither the time nor the patience to design and implement a motivation plan for their employees.

> Steve's business is growing faster than he can keep up with it. After six months of 80-hour work weeks, Steve decides that he needs to hire an administrative assistant. Because he is so busy, however, Steve doesn't have the time to think about exactly what the assistant will be doing for him.
>
> Because Steve is three weeks behind in filling customer orders, it takes him an additional two months to get around to interviewing and another month before he actually hires someone.
>
> Having finally completed the hiring of his new assistant Steve believes he has done all that is necessary and promptly runs off to "put out the next fire" affecting his business.
>
> Because the new administrative assistant hasn't had the job fully explained to him, however, much less gone through a training period, there is still no real help in sight for Steve. He is just as busy as he was before, only now his overhead is higher.

> Some of the successful business owners you know don't have a clue when it comes to motivating employees. But, just think of how much more successful they would be if they could motivate their employees to their fullest potential.

Training and motivating employees is both time consuming and requires a great deal of thought. All too often busy business owners focus their attention, instead, on catching employees making mistakes, and then taking punitive steps to correct those errors.

The common wisdom is that if you catch a reasonable number of an employee's mistakes, the employee will become more attentive and more careful. The more mistakes caught, the more careful the employee will become.

Debbie owns four dry-cleaning stores. Because of the demands on her time and the practical problems of supervising four stores, she cannot observe every employee all of the time.

Every night, Debbie goes through the financial records for each of the stores until she finds a mistake. The next morning, she leaves a note for the store manager and the responsible employee letting them know, in no uncertain terms, that she is aware of the mistake and of their carelessness in allowing it to occur.

In doing this, Debbie wants her employees to believe that she knows everything that goes on and that, if there is a mistake, she will catch it.

Debbie then gets on with her daily tasks, confident that she has impressed her employees with her managerial prowess.

The problem with Debbie's approach, and with that of the majority of business owners, is that it automatically turns you into a police force. You aren't interested in helping your employee understand their job or motivating them to do it better. You are only interested in catching errors and punishing employees. The entire approach conveys mistrust and a lack of confidence in your employees. More importantly, the approach is based upon an unspoken (and sometimes spoken) threat. If the employee gets caught making mistakes often enough he may be fired, demoted, or lose out on a raise.

What Debbie didn't consider when she was leaving her "poison pen letters" is that both the store manager and the employee were

> Training and motivating employees is both time consuming and requires a great deal of thought.

filling in for others who had called in sick. They were short-handed, but because of their loyalty to Debbie and their sense of responsibility to the job, they kept the store operating for the entire day.

As a direct result of her "managerial skill," Debbie has insulted and threatened (by implication) two excellent employees and left them both demoralized. (Don't expect either of them to show up to work on their day off again.)

Another problem Debbie faces is that some employees, insulted by being treated as children or incompetent, will turn her nightly inspections into a game, seeing how many mistakes they can make that go undetected (remember, Debbie stops after she finds the first mistake).

Finally, because of the fear of being discovered making mistakes, many employees will either delay, or fail altogether, in telling Debbie when a mistake has occurred.

Bob is one of Adam's store managers. One day, Bob realized that he made a mistake with a large cleaning order for a janitorial supply company, Adam's biggest customer.

Bob thinks that the problem can be fixed and he believes that Adam might have to get involved. But, Bob is afraid to tell Adam about his mistake for fear of losing his job. He decides to delay telling Adam while he tries to solve the problem himself. After all, what Adam doesn't know won't hurt him.

Ultimately, Bob is not able to correct the situation. By the time he tells Adam about the problem with his biggest customer it is too late for Adam to do anything about it.

Bob loses his job, and Adam loses both his biggest account as well as an experienced manager who was too afraid to be a responsible manager.

Catching errors made by employees may help eliminate errors in the future, but it will not motivate the employee into reaching for new heights. In short, you will have employees who follow an

> Catching errors made by employees may help eliminate errors in the future, but it will not motivate the employee into reaching for new heights.

approved pattern of behavior but none who will take a project, or an ad campaign, or a marketing plan, and ride it to the finish line.

You are paying full price for your employees, but because you have neglected to provide a work environment that motivates them, you are only getting half of what you are paying for. If you did that for the rest of your business, you would be out of business in no time.

Threats Are the Tool of an Ineffective Manager

Nothing is more counterproductive or demoralizing to employees than the use of threats.

Scott is the principal in a small law firm. When any new attorney is hired, Scott tells them that they have a quota that they must bill every month. He also tells them that their failure to reach this quota in any month will result in immediate termination.

Scott then turns the new attorneys over to the supervision of middle-level attorneys who are too busy trying to reach their own quotas to help the new and inexperienced attorneys develop the skills necessary to handle their work efficiently.

The new attorneys accept the job because they need the work experience in an overcrowded market. But, because of the constant fear of termination and the embarrassment it would cause, every one of the newly hired attorneys has continued to interview for a new job even after accepting Scott's offer of employment.

Because of their need to generate bills to Scott's clients, the new attorneys are more concerned with quantity than quality. Their work suffers, cases are lost, and the clients look elsewhere for legal services. But at least the new attorney has met his quota.

Even the attorneys who are able to meet their quotas continue to look for new jobs simply out of fear that they can't keep up the pace. Others leave out of sheer

> Nothing is more counterproductive or demoralizing to employees than the use of threats.

resentment of the stress and humiliation that they have endured.

Scott has found that he loses more money than he makes on the first year of any new attorney's employment. Understandably, he is upset and unable to understand why none of his attorneys stay with him for more than a year. Ultimately, it doesn't matter, because Scott has lost so many clients that he no longer needs to hire new attorneys.

Remember, motivation does more than encourage employees to excel. True motivation, that is, motivation coming from within the employee, is a result of job satisfaction; therefore, it also has a strong effect on your "bottom line" almost immediately.

Remember that your employees cost you both time and money. It takes both to interview job applicants and to train those employees to do the job for which they are hired. You provide them with benefits, insurance, and pay employment taxes. You pay for office space, a telephone, and maybe even a secretary.

Now, calculate how much profit you expect that new employee to generate during the first year of employment. Don't be surprised if you barely make any money at all on the new employee during the first year. And there's the problem: if the employee isn't satisfied with his job, if you don't motivate him, don't expect him to stay with you.

What is the point of spending all of that time and money training an employee for someone else?

This assumes you can even find an employee. In many parts of the country and in many different sectors of the economy, even semiskilled labor is hard to come by. Your inability to keep those employees and keep them producing, for you, may be the biggest obstacle you face.

Don't *Make* Employees Perform, *Let* Them Perform

While there is a motivational benefit in awards and incentives, the real motivation comes from allowing your employees to excel at a task that they find rewarding and satisfying. Don't think of it as motivating your employees, but as creating a workplace environment that allows them to be motivated.

> True motivation, that is, motivation coming from within the employee, is a result of job satisfaction; therefore, it also has a strong effect on your "bottom line" almost immediately.

Creating a Motivating Environment

1. *Make sure that your employees know what is expected of them.* Because most employees want to do well at their job, few things are more demoralizing that not knowing what is expected of them. They will sit at their desks, wander the office, shuffle paper, feel guilty watching the experienced employees work overtime, and wait for the time when you finally yell at them for not producing.

   Even if the employee has a general idea what the job entails, without a clear understanding of what your goals are for him, he will never meet your expectations.

2. *Make sure that your employees are adequately trained to perform their jobs.* Equally as demoralizing for an employee is not having the skills to do the job for which he has been hired. You don't have to think too hard to remember how frustrated and how badly you felt when you were unable to perform a task when you knew that others were counting on you. It's the same for your employees. If they feel good about their ability to do the job they will feel good about the job. More importantly, they will be ready for the bigger challenges that lie ahead for the truly motivated.

3. *Give your employees the means to gauge the success of their efforts.* Without feedback with respect to their efforts, your employees will be working in a vacuum. They won't know if they are doing well, poorly, or just average. How will they measure improvement?

   If how your employees are performing at their jobs isn't important enough for you to tell them about, don't expect them to think that it's important either.

4. *If you find it necessary to correct an employee, address the conduct and not the person.* Remember that you are not trying to destroy or demoralize the employee but to address and correct a behavior that is undesirable from the standpoint of your business.

   Explain what the conduct was that needs to be changed and why it needs to be changed. Suggest a different way

> Make sure that your employees are adequately trained to perform their jobs.

that the employee might have handled the situation and why it is a better approach, from the standpoint of the business.

If you take the time to explain your thought processes and your concerns, the employee will be better able to deal with a new situation in a way that is more compatible with the way you want things handled. Being insulting only causes the employee to become defensive. Once that occurs you may as well stop the lesson.

5. *Bring your employees "into the loop."* You can't expect your employees to go above and beyond the call of duty when you don't value them enough to tell them where you are going.

Peter owned a clothing manufacturing company. Each month the factory would change patterns to manufacture a different article of clothing. The employees in the plant who did the actual sewing and assembly were never consulted prior to any change of patterns. They were simply given the new patterns at the beginning of the month and told to start working.

As expected, production dropped sharply for the first week of every month while the employees accustomed themselves to the new pattern. Production then increased over the second week to meet the prior month's levels.

One month, Peter decided to call a meeting of the employees to show them the new pattern well in advance of the scheduled starting date. He asked for their comments and was pleasantly surprised when he received several good ideas for how to alter the pattern to make it easier or cheaper to produce.

The biggest surprise came when the new pattern went into production. The decline in production was nowhere as steep as in previous months and the production levels returned to normal within one week instead of the usual two.

> You can't expect your employees to go above and beyond the call of duty when you don't value them enough to tell them where you are going.

6. *Whenever possible, compliment your employees when they does something praiseworthy.* Don't just wait for the mistakes. Praise the good things your employees do and they will keep looking for ways to impress you.

Streetwise Reality Tour

1. Motivation will not permit you to put a "square peg into a round hole." All the motivation in the world will not fix the fact that you have hired the wrong person for the wrong job.
2. Cash rewards, bonuses, and incentives can motivate employees, but they are of minimal value when compared to finding a way for the employee to do what interests and excites him.
3. Some employees will resist efforts at motivation and will never seem to be satisfied with their jobs. Remember, you are not a social worker, you have a business to run. Sometimes you have to terminate employees who fail to respond to well-planned and effectively implemented motivation efforts.
4. Experienced employees have seen managers come and go and with them, all sorts of motivational programs. Be prepared for them to be suspicious and jaded by your efforts.

Cash rewards, bonuses, and incentives can motivate employees, but they are of minimal value when compared to finding a way for the employee to do what interests and excites him.

For more information on this topic, visit our Web site at www.businesstown.com

Chapter 12

Hiring New Employees

As you saw in the last chapter, the motivation of employees can achieve a great many benefits for your company. But there are also limitations on what motivation may accomplish. For example:

A person with a genius I.Q. may be able to handle the details of the company mailroom with ease. The lack of an intellectual challenge, however, may make the employee bored and frustrated.

A person with an introverted personality may fail as a commission salesman because there is nothing he hates more than meeting new people, having lunch with relative strangers, or making small talk.

An executive with years of successfully managing established businesses may not be the person to handle the turn-around of a financially troubled business.

In each case, motivation may get the best possible effort from the individual employees, but, in the final analysis, and for reasons personal to each individual, they are not the best people to hire for their specific jobs.

This is where hiring decisions come into play.

What Is the Job and What Are the Qualifications?

Before you hire any employee and before you even interview a job applicant, you should determine the following:

1. Exactly what job is being created or filled?
2. What are the work requirements of the job?
3. What personal characteristics are needed by an employee in such a position?
4. Is the position an entry-level position or a position for someone with some experience?
5. Will the successful applicant be working in a group or individually?

> What personal characteristics are needed by an employee in such a position?

6. Will the applicant be closely supervised or allowed a great deal of discretion in carrying out the job?
7. Are there specialized skills, licenses, or education required?

The Hiring Process

The Job Announcement

Once you decide to hire an employee and have decided what qualifications you are looking for, you will want to announce the job opening and receive job applications, or resumes.

In this respect you may wish to utilize the following services:

1. Newspaper want ads
2. Private employment agencies
3. Governmental employment assistance agencies
4. Job fairs
5. School placement offices
6. Word of mouth

The benefit of utilizing an employment agency or placement office is that you let that agency or office perform the initial screening of job applicants. Without this, you may find yourself inundated with applications that are simply too numerous to be reviewed effectively. And, even if you carefully review the applications, there is no guarantee that the finalists called in for a personal interview will be anywhere close to what you are looking for.

An employment agency can screen the applicants according to qualifications that you have already identified. Because the employment agency wants to retain your business, you can be fairly sure that you will not be flooded by applications from unsuitable job applicants. However, all of this will come at a cost of perhaps 80 percent of the first year's wages.

> An employment agency can screen the applicants according to qualifications that you have already identified.

Remember, you are hiring because you need the help. Will you really have the time to spend hours and even days poring over job applications and checking out references?

The Employment Application

You should utilize an employment application that requests the information you feel is important to the job. Forms are available from a variety of sources and the employment agency with which you work may even have one suitable for your business. Don't reinvent the wheel if you don't have to.

At the same time, be careful with the forms you use. The people who create forms are not unlike bureaucrats. They justify their own jobs by continually revising the forms they have created. The application becomes more and more detailed and requires the disclosure of more and more personal information. There are, undoubtedly, very qualified job applicants who you will never get to meet simply because they refuse to answer what they consider to be overly personal and irrelevant questions.

For example, one employment application for a claims adjuster position with an insurance company requested details on how the applicant financed his college education. How would you respond to a question like this?

The Interview

Once you have reviewed the employment applications (or had them reviewed for you) you will want to interview the applicants who appear to have the qualifications you seek. This is an area ripe with legal pitfalls. There probably isn't a week that goes by that you don't hear of an employer being sued over its hiring practices.

Title VII of the Civil Rights Act of 1964, the Age Discrimination in Employment Act, the Civil Rights Act of 1966, the Immigration Reform and Control Act of 1987, and the Americans with Disabilities Act are just some of the federal laws affecting hiring practices. Stated simply, you cannot discriminate against any job applicant on the basis of race, gender, age, or physical handicap. There are even

> You cannot discriminate against any job applicant on the basis of race, gender, age, or physical handicap.

more federal and state laws governing this area, which are too numerous to mention here.

When conducting the employment interview, your focus should be on asking questions relating to the applicant's ability to perform the job. If, for example, the job is for a salesman of machine parts, you may ask the following questions:

1. Does the applicant have a driver's license?
2. Does the applicant have a working knowledge of the industry?
3. Does the applicant have previous sales experience and, if so, what the nature of that experience?
4. Does the applicant have a compatible prior work history? For example, have the applicant changed jobs too frequently?
5. Does the applicant have the required educational background to discuss the product with potential customers?
6. Does the applicant have the personality necessary to carry on a conversation with potential customers with whom he have no prior experience?

Keeping these qualifications in mind, does it really matter whether the applicant is married, or has children, or is over the age of 41, or suffers from some type of physical disability?

As a general matter, stay away from questions dealing with the following areas:

- Religion
- Marital status
- Children
- Sexual orientation
- Age
- Arrest record (as opposed to convictions)

As a practical matter, however, when interviewing a number of applicants it is not difficult for a small business owner to inadvertently discriminate on the basis of age, or gender, or race, or physical

> When conducting the employment interview, your focus should be on asking questions relating to the applicant's ability to perform the job.

handicap. Because you, not one of your employees, will probably be making the ultimate decision, and, because hiring decisions almost always rely, to some extent, upon intuition and the personality of the applicant, almost any hiring decision can be explained or justified, even a discriminatory one.

Problems can occur, however, when it can be established that one candidate is clearly more qualified than the person who got the job and the rejected candidate can claim the protection of one of the legal statutes identified previously.

> Hiring decisions almost always rely, to some extent, upon intuition and the personality of the applicant, almost any hiring decision can be explained or justified, even a discriminatory one.

Ed, age 42, is applying for a job as a commission salesman. Ed has been in the business for years and has established relations with a number of potential customers. For some reason, however, Ed is passed over for the job in favor of Amy, a 22-year-old who recently graduated from college.

Because Ed is over the age of 41, he can claim the protections of the Age Discrimination in Employment Act (ADEA). Ed files a complaint with the state human relations commission or federal Equal Employment Opportunity Commission (EEOC), alleging that he was discriminated against because of his age.

Because he is over the age of 41, Ed does not have to prove that he was discriminated against because of his age. All he has to show is that he is over the age of 41 and that the job went to someone under the age of 41.

At that point the burden shifts to you, as the employer, to prove that Ed's age was not the reason for your decision not to hire him. If you cannot convince the hearing officer of this fact, he will win his case.

Problems can also develop when you hire employees with some frequency and it can be shown that a pattern exists because you never see fit to hire anyone in a certain age range or of a specific gender or a member of a racial or ethnic minority.

Checking References

Once you have completed the interview, do not hesitate to contact the applicant's references. You may think that the references are certain to say good things, otherwise they wouldn't be listed as references, but this is not always the case. You may also ask the applicant for permission to contact former employers, even if they have not been given as references.

Of course, even if the applicant consents, you may have trouble getting the former employer to give you any information. This is particularly the case if the applicant had a bad experience with that employer.

Remember, being given permission to speak with you does not give the former employer permission to slander the job applicant. And even though the former employer doesn't think what he is saying is slanderous, the applicant may think differently. As often as not, the former employer will decline to give any information on the applicant simply to avoid a possible lawsuit with a former employee. (You may want to keep this in mind when you are contacted about former employees).

Making the Offer

When you finally make the decision to hire the job applicant, you should put the offer into writing (Form 12-01 in the Appendix). The letter or contract should provide the following:

1. Name of applicant
2. Position and duties
3. Starting date
4. Hours
5. A stipulation that the employee will be considered "At Will" (unless, of course, the employee is being promised employment for a specific period of time). "At-Will" employees can be terminated by the employer at any time and for any reason, or for no reason at all. This may vary from state to state, however, and you should consult an attorney in your state to help you draft a form employment letter.

> "At-Will" employees can be terminated by the employer at any time and for any reason, or for no reason at all.

6. Salary
7. Vacation policy
8. Benefits, bonus plans, etc.
9. Any other material condition of employment
10. A statement to the effect that there are no other promises being made. (This will prevent the employee from saying that you promised him other things, such as a company car, country club membership, guaranteed employment, etc.)

Employment and Confidentiality Agreements

It is not uncommon for an employer to request that employees, particularly high-level employees, sign an employment agreement (Form 12-02 in the Appendix) that prevents the employee from disclosing such things as:

1. Trade secrets of the business;
2. Customer lists;
3. Price lists;
4. Any other proprietary information.

While various state and federal laws already protect employers from these types of disclosures, it is a far better practice to include them in the employment agreement.

Even if you, the employer, can prove that the employee violated the agreement, it is often difficult to place a dollar value on your damages. Consequently, the agreement may provide that your employee will have to pay a certain sum of money, as a penalty, if he is found to be disclosing this type of information.

Remember, however, that you cannot get blood from a stone. If the former employee has no assets, then your judgment against him may have little value.

You should know, however, that various state and federal statutes make the disclosure of various types of trade information a criminal offense.

> It is not uncommon for an employer to request that employees, particularly high-level employees, sign an employment agreement.

Agreements Not to Compete

In addition to the confidentiality agreement, you may want to have your employees sign an "agreement not to compete."

In the typical agreement the employee agrees that, if he leaves your employ at any time he will not compete with you or your company either by contacting your customers or by establishing a competing business within a certain geographical area. This can also include working as an employee for someone else who competes with you.

Regardless of what you have heard, these types of agreements are enforceable, so long as the terms are not overreaching and are reasonable with respect to protecting your interests. If the terms of the agreement are viewed as nothing but an attempt to restrain trade, prevent competition, or simply punish the employee, the court will limit their effect to only that which is reasonable.

> In the typical agreement the employee agrees that, if he leaves your employ at any time he will not compete with you or your company either by contacting your customers or by establishing a competing business within a certain geographical area.

After years of hard work, Dr. Smith, a chiropractor, finally decided to start his own practice. Because he signed an agreement not to compete with Dr. Jones, his current employer, he cannot contact any of the patients with whom he worked while employed by Dr. Jones. The agreement also stated that he will not open a chiropractic office within 100 miles of Dr. Jones's office.

When Dr. Smith opened his office 50 miles away from Dr. Jones, Dr. Jones filed a lawsuit in which he asked the judge to close Dr. Smith's practice and award him monetary damages.

Dr. Smith was able to establish that Dr. Jones neither advertises nor seeks patients more than 10 miles from his office. The prohibition of a competing office 50 miles away from Dr. Jones's office goes well beyond what Dr. Jones needs to protect his practice and his patients. Dr. Smith was allowed to stay open and was not forced to pay damages.

Employee Handbooks

Employee handbooks are essential for any business that employs more than one individual.

Handbooks contain a variety of provisions, including the following:

1. A statement that all employees are "At Will"
2. Vacation and leave policy
3. Health insurance information
4. Disciplinary policy
5. Methods of terminating employees
6. Rules of the workplace
7. Rules regarding seniority
8. Rules regarding the reporting of rules violations, work injuries, and other matters of importance
9. A statement to the effect that the handbook is for guidance only, and does not create any rights that the employee may use to sue you

> The handbook is for guidance only, and does not create any rights that the employee may use to sue you.

On a sunny Friday afternoon, Adam is called into Bob's office and notified that he is being terminated. Adam is told that the reason for his firing is because he is always late for work. This is the first time Adam has heard such a complaint.

With time on his hands, Adam decides to look through the employee handbook, which he had using to prop up a short leg on his desk.

There, in section 8, is the company policy for the termination of employees. Included is an entire system of notices, warnings, and informal hearings, all of which were to be utilized prior to termination.

With this in hand, Adam skipped along to his attorney's office to review the planned lawsuit against Bob for breach of contract and unlawful termination.

Too bad the handbook did not say that it was a guide for the employer, only, and did not confer any rights.

Streetwise Reality Tour

1. Even after weeks and months of interviewing employees, there is no guarantee that the person you hired will be able or willing to do the job.

2. Despite all of the language in an employment agreement prohibiting competition and prohibiting the disclosure of trade secrets, lawsuits are expensive to pursue and the former employee may be "judgment-proof" (remember that term from the section on structuring your business).

> Lawsuits are expensive to pursue and the former employee may be "judgment-proof."

For more information on this topic, visit our Web site at www.businesstown.com

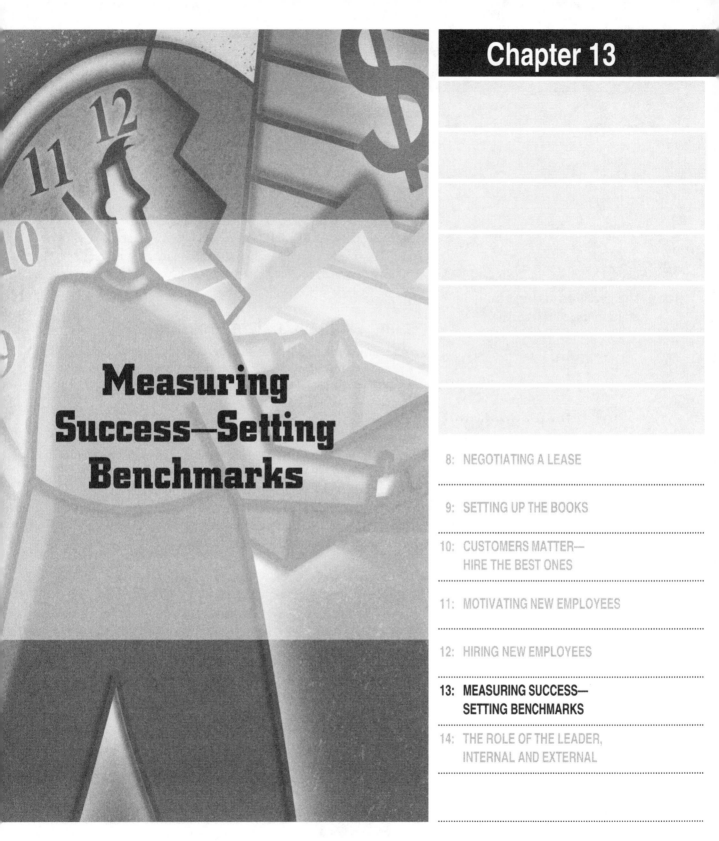

Chapter 13

Measuring Success—Setting Benchmarks

If you struggled with your business plan and breathed a sigh of relief when it was completed, think again. The best way to use a business plan is to make it into a changing document that is revisited and updated on a regular basis. What you expected to happen may not be what you experienced, and now you must adjust your numbers and reset your goals. You will do this at various times during the life of your company, but here we will take a look at the start-up phase. The time you spend analyzing your progress and making corrections may greatly influence your level of success.

How and When to Analyze Progress

After your business has been open for three months, you will want to take a close look at your results. Generate a profit-and-loss statement on a month-by-month basis, as well as a quarterly one. Both are needed to do your review.

You want to be looking at the percentages in your statement, not the raw numbers. Once you have a fix on your direct expenses (which rely completely on your volume), you will be able to accurately predict your break-even volume. And you can determine if you can realistically hit those numbers. For this number you will want to use the quarterly (three-month) statement, as you may have some variances due to opening sales, which have lowered prices, or some manufacturing glitches, or overstaffing as a result of your lack of experience.

> When Jeff opened his printing company, he thought that he knew exactly how to set up and staff the business. In his business plan, he projected that his gross profit would be 38%. At the end of his first three months, he was shocked to see the number was below 35%. When he looked at each month individually, he discovered that the first month had been at 31%, the second at 36% and the third at 38%. He decided that over the long run, he would meet his target because he was learning to staff more accurately and the number of printing mistakes that had to be redone had gone down since the first few weeks

> You want to be looking at the percentages in your statement, not the raw numbers.

when everyone was still learning how to use the new equipment.

If you have substantially underperformed in comparison to your expectations, look at the trend. If you see improvement in reaching the targets, you must decide whether there is improvement expected over the next months or whether you must rework your original projections. This may be based on one of two primary variances.

Your Volume Is Far Below Expectation

If you expected to do $30,000 per month by the end of the first year and at the end of the first quarter you are doing less than $10,000, you may have seriously overestimated sales potential. Most companies take the first year to reach their break-even volume, and now you realize that it will take you until the end of the second year to get there. Do you have enough working capital to fund this loss? If not, you are not very likely to survive long enough to pass the sales numbers you need. And if you do, you will be so short of capital that it will be almost impossible to operate on an ongoing basis. You may have funded these losses with debt (in most cases, unpaid bills) and additional credit will likely be tight.

As soon as you realize that this problem of lower volume exists, you must take steps to lower your break-even number by cutting your overhead. This will require a review of all fixed expense categories from rent through salaries and sales and marketing costs. Don't make across-the-board cuts without consideration to the impact on your existing operation. Be thoughtful and conservative.

John is operating a restaurant that has not produced the revenue he needs or expected. In a moment of panic, he fired his general manager and several servers and he and his wife have tried to fill the roles. The absence of a manager has resulted in costly disorganization and the loss of servers has resulted in poor service to customers who now complain. The restaurant will now likely have trouble ever reaching its goals with so many customers vowing never to come back.

As soon as you realize that this problem of lower volume exists, you must take steps to lower your break-even number by cutting your overhead.

Look at finding a balanced solution to your problem. Negotiate with your landlord to perhaps lower the rent temporarily and add the shortage to the later years of your lease. Rather than cut any necessary personnel, perhaps put a few on less than full time. Instead of hiring, use a temporary service to fill slots when needed. Maintain your sales and marketing efforts but do them less expensively.

The first step to finding a solution to this potential problem is to identify it. Always take a critical view of how you are doing in relation to what you projected.

> Your gross margins are the key to your break-even number.

Your Gross Profit Margins Are Far Below Expectation

If you are looking at actual results in gross profit margins that are substantially below your projections, you must correct this problem quickly. As you have seen earlier, your gross margins are the key to your break-even number. If the margin is lower, you will have to do substantially more volume to reach profitability.

There are two ways to raise your gross profit. The first is to lower your direct costs of material and labor. For a new company that is using only a small amount of material/product at a time, you may not be getting the quantity breaks that you need. The answer may be to use your capital, credit, or borrowing money to buy in a quantity break. You will have lower unit costs this way.

You may need to find lower cost suppliers or use less direct labor. Investigate all ways that you can reduce costs.

The other alternative to look at here is to raise prices, often not an easy task for a new company that is trying to grow and attract new customers.

Whatever choice you make, you must be sure that your gross profit margins are sufficient to provide capital to pay overhead.

Learn How to Budget

You must contain your costs in order to have a healthy bottom line. The best way to do this is to control costs going in, not just find out that you have exceeded your costs after the fact.

You must begin with a realistic number for sales revenue. Once you have seen how you've done in the real world of doing business, estimate your revenue on a quarterly basis for the next year. Budgeting is best done on a quarterly basis because there are often expenses that happen infrequently, such as a repair or a business trip, that will change the results in one month but be evened out over the quarter. There are months when your expenses will be extra low, as well.

Set up your budget as a percentage of sales. For example, sales are $20,000 per month and your gross profit is 40%. Your overhead expense must be less than 40% in order to show a profit. Begin with those numbers that have no room for movement—rent, utilities, interest, etc. Determine how much of the overhead they consume.

For example:

Sales	20,000	
Cost of sales	12,000	(60%)
Gross profit	8,000	(40%)

If your non-negotiable expenses are:

Rent	1,500	
Utilities	500	(average)
Interest	300	
Office salaries	1,200	
Phone	500	
	4,000	20% of sales is necessary

Then all other expenses must be kept at $4,000, or 20% of sales. If sales go up to $25,000, then your gross profit will be $10,000 and you will have $6,000, or 24% to allocate. Know these numbers, set your budgets, and stick to them.

> Budgeting is best done on a quarterly basis because there are often expenses that happen infrequently, such as a repair or a business trip.

Streetwise Reality Tour

1. You must take the time to do a complete analysis and comparison of your results after the first three months compared to your original projections.
2. Learn how to use your numbers to determine where any problems might be and how to correct them.
3. Don't just let things happen and learn after the fact. Set revenue goals and budgets for expenses. Then keep to them.

> Learn how to use your numbers to determine where any problems might be and how to correct them.

For more information on this topic, visit our Web site at www.businesstown.com

Chapter 14

The Role of the Leader, Internal and External

D epending on the extent of your small business experience, you may be very surprised by what it means to "be your own boss." If you expected to have great freedom and great rewards early in the game, you are likely to be engaged in a crash course in entrepreneurism. You no longer answer to one boss, now you answer to customers, vendors, bankers, and in many instances, employees as well. And the rewards you are expecting may be more long term than you hoped.

So what is the attraction in being an entrepreneur? It is a chance to be creative, to see the results of your hard work, and to learn more than you can imagine. And that is a major key to success. You must go beyond those aspects of the business that interest you and get up to speed on all phases of business management.

Many business owners come from a background of sales and marketing. It is a natural place to start. If you can sell a large quantity of products, why not do so for yourself and make the profit? A fair number come from a background of operations, and as of the last decade or so, a fair contingent with technology backgrounds who are product or software innovators have joined the ranks of the small business owners. Few come from the world of finance.

It is natural for you to have one or two skills that are more enhanced than the others, but that does not mean you can ignore or avoid learning all aspects of your business—especially finance. The single most likely cause of business failure is lack of financial planning, which results in shortage of capital. Whether it is knowing how to adjust prices or expenses to realize greater profit or how to understand pro formas in order to prepare for cash needs, the financial skills are critical. And you cannot just leave this work to an outside accountant because you may not get the information you require in time to take action. You must control the financial life of your company.

> The single most likely cause of business failure is lack of financial planning, which results in shortage of capital.

You Must Manage People and Resources

It would be wonderful to have all the material and personnel you needed all of the time so that all of your customers could be served well. That's not likely to be the case most of the time. You will have to balance the cost of labor and material to your expected volume and make adjustments as the situation requires. There is a learning curve in this skill.

The first part is in being able to predict the near-term business demands. You will get to know the rhythm of your company and have a reasonable idea, based on the current level of business and inquiries, what the sales level will be over the next months or quarter. Then you must be able to act on those ideas.

If you believe your business is in a growth mode, you must take the steps needed to prepare. Bringing in more material or products, even if it stretches financial resources, is one step. Finding and hiring additional workers is another. In a full-employment economy, this is not always easy. You should keep resumes on hand and always follow up on interested workers so you will have a pool of possible candidates available. The key here is to find the right time to increase staff so that they can be trained well enough to be productive. Throwing untrained employees into a situation they aren't prepared for is never productive.

You must also be willing to cut back when business gets soft. It is never easy to cut hours or reduce staff, but it is a necessary role for a bottom-line manager. Your job includes knowing when that should be done and taking appropriate action.

> You will be the person most closely associated with the company, and the rest of the business community will look to you for their impression of the company.

The Role of External Leader

You will be the person most closely associated with the company, and the rest of the business community will look to you for their impression of the company. Donald Trump is viewed as a glamorous man, and his company has that image as well.

If you are in a conservative field such as financial planning, you may want to keep a low public profile to encourage confidence. A restaurant owner should be gracious, outgoing, and give the impression of being a good host or hostess.

You want to be active in the business community in order to meet those who may become customers, vendors, or just good sounding boards. Places to look are chambers of commerce, service clubs, tip clubs, and trade associations. Get to meetings and events and meet as many people as you can—always carry business cards and information about your company.

The Need for Visionary Leadership

Nothing is static about the business environment.

Your job doesn't stop at day-to-day management, even though that may take more than 60 hours a week. You are the one who will be making the decisions about how you operate the company today and what changes you will make for the future. The need for these changes begins at almost the moment that you open the doors. Nothing is static about the business environment.

New products and technology are constantly being developed. New ways to market, sell, and distribute are coming on stream as well. Who knew the impact of e-commerce a decade ago? Markets change, sometimes shrinking and sometimes enlarging. Don't let this pass you by.

You should read local and national publications, take courses that are relevant, and attend industry seminars. Each day you should spend some time considering where your industry is headed and how your business can position itself. Then find out what it will take to get you there and begin to plan to make those moves. Keep future successes in your vision.

For more information on this topic, visit our Web site at www.businesstown.com

The Growing Business

In this section, you'll learn:

- **the ins and outs of contract negotiation**
- **what type of insurance you need and who can give it to you**
- **how to maximize profits most efficiently**
- **effective techniques for getting the money you're owed**
- **how to keep employees happy while keeping your business legally responsible**
- **which tax forms you'll need**
- **leadership tips that ensure success**

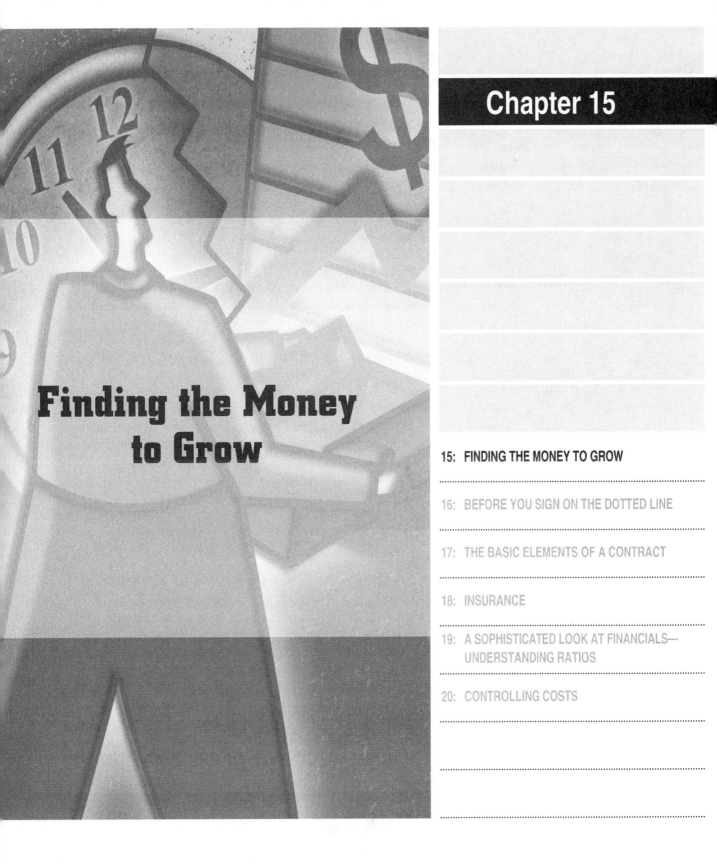

Chapter 15

Finding the Money to Grow

Getting a new business up to speed takes at least one year and often two. Your revenue must grow from zero to the break-even level. The capital you require to get to this point should be considered investment money, because it will not be returned quickly. The second phase of your business will be the growth phase. Revenues will have grown beyond the break-even phase, and profits are beginning to be realized. This increase in revenues and increase in profits will eventually provide you with the cash flow you need to operate the company easily.

However, during this growing phase, you will require working capital to fund your growth. There is always a lag in the cash cycle that requires capital. For example, if you make most of your sales on credit, you will not receive your money for 30 to 60 days after you provide the product/service to your customer. You may have to pay your supplier more quickly than you receive your money (vendor credit is one of the ways to fund growth). You will have to pay wages to your employees (and yourself), pay taxes and benefits, and cover your overhead expense—all while your capital is tied up in your growing receivables. And this does take into account the additional costs of growth, such as:

- Purchasing or leasing and preparing additional space;
- Additional equipment including auto or trucks;
- Increasing your inventory level;
- Advertising, travel, and promotional expense to sustain the growth.

Sue built a small plumbing company to a major plumbing contracting business over a period of three years. She accomplished this by taking on all of the work of a major real estate management company, including their repair work and new construction of bathrooms and kitchens. The volume of her business almost doubled in just one year. The size of her work force grew by 60%, from 20 to 32 employees; she rented more space; leased four new trucks, and inventoried twice as much material. Her new customer paid fairly promptly, but work couldn't be billed until it was complete. Sue tried to finance this growth

> During this growing phase, you will require working capital to fund your growth.

with vendor credit and existing cash flow. Three months into the big year, she found himself short of payroll–her check and a few trusted employees had to be held a few days. Then she failed to remit withheld taxes on time because the money wasn't available and she was hit with a big penalty. A month later, with vendor bills growing, a few suppliers cut off her credit. She almost let her success destroy the whole company until she and her accountant approached a willing bank and received a revolving line of credit to finance this phenomenal growth.

There are a number of sources of capital that can be tapped to finance profitable growth, but you must find them early enough that they will be in place when you need them.

First, Determine How Much You Need

When you wrote your plan, you included some pro forma statements. In Chapter 6, we discussed a cash flow statement, and this is what you will need to project how much capital you require and when. Now you have some operating data and you should be able to make fairly accurate predictions. Following are some things to consider.

Sales

Do not just take current sales numbers and make them grow by a chosen percentage (10 to 20% a year). Take this year's numbers, determine if you may lose some business (it is normal to do so) and then add new contracts or new customers that you are developing. If new business is likely but not guaranteed, then be conservative and plan for a part of it to become reality.

> If you plan substantial growth, you may be able to buy material at a higher quantity, and secure lower pricing. It may add to your profits by lowering your direct costs.

Direct Expense

If you plan substantial growth, you may be able to buy material at a higher quantity, and secure lower pricing. It may add to your profits by lowering your direct costs.

On the other hand, if you substantially increase your work force, you must be prepared that new workers are often less productive. This will raise costs, at least temporarily. The two changes may equalize themselves depending on whether material or labor is a higher percentage of your costs.

Fixed Costs

As previously stated, you may need more space to produce or sell your goods, and there are other costs that will accompany that expansion—utilities and insurance are among them. Overhead staffing requirements (secretary, billing clerks, warehouse men) may also be larger. You may need to become a more competitive employer by raising the benefits you offer. In the current full-employment economy, these items are important if you are trying to hire qualified people.

The reality is that you should not consider your fixed expense as cast in stone—as you grow, the costs will grow, but the goal is to keep it as the same or a lower percentage of your total revenue. This takes diligence.

> The loan you choose should be matched to the cash-flow realities of your business.

Borrowing the Capital You Need

Once you know how much you need, you can begin to seek out the right type of lending with the best payback terms that will support your growth. The loan you choose should be matched to the cash-flow realities of your business. For example, an investment in extra inventory may turn into cash in as little as 60 to 90 days. However, a newer or larger piece of equipment may take two or three or even more years to pay off in increased volume and productivity. You may choose the following terms:

- Short-term—less than one year.
- Intermediate-term—as long as three to five years.
- Long-term—in excess of five years (a mortgage may go as long as 15 to 20 years).

A short-term loan is likely to be a line of credit that you can draw on when you need it and pay back as your money comes in. For example, you have a $100,000 line of credit. Your receivables are building and your cash is low. You draw on the line to pay for payroll and to pay suppliers. Then, when your customers pay—you pay down the line. You may do this several times per year. You will pay interest only on the money you have drawn.

Most lines of credit are given on a year-to-year basis and require that the loan be paid to zero for up to 30 days annually. If all of the conditions are met, they likely will be renewed, as well as possibly increased if your needs have increased.

An intermediate-term loan is normally written as an installment loan, as opposed to a line of credit. This means you will pay a monthly payment of principal and interest until the amount is retired.

There is a hybrid type of loan called a nonrevolving line of credit, which is one that you draw incrementally, perhaps to pay for a project that will take some time to complete. Once the full amount is drawn, the loan terms out and regular payments are made.

> Andrew operates a restaurant that has been successful since its opening. He turns down private parties on a regular basis for lack of space. When additional space became available in his building, he jumped on the chance to develop a few new private dining rooms. He opened them one at a time over a period of six months using a line of credit to draw on as the space was completed. After the final space was done, the loan termed out and he began paying monthly payments over the next three years. The revenue increase easily paid for the loan.

Long-term loans, which extend beyond five years, are primarily used to fund major expansions, including the acquisition and improvements of property or purchase of major equipment. The return on this type of investment will come back over the years so you will need a longer term to pay back the funds.

Aside from granting a mortgage that is fully secured by the property, many banks are reluctant to lend money for equipment

> Most lines of credit are given on a year-to-year basis and require that the loan be paid to zero for up to 30 days annually.

and/or improvements on a long-term basis. The projections that can be made for any business beyond the three-year term are really speculative. Changes in technology, markets, and the business cycle itself are fairly unpredictable. This is a situation where an SBA guarantee or regional development authority participation is very useful.

There are times when the answer is to secure a package that includes both a mid-term installment loan and a line of credit, so that additional short terms are available when they are needed along the way.

Accounts Receivable Financing

You may be able to borrow directly against the value of your receivables with a line of credit based on their amount and secured by them. As your sales grow, you will have immediate access to capital, and as invoices are paid, your loan will be reduced.

Only a portion of your receivables will be eligible, normally around 80%, due to a number of conditions that will be imposed by your bank. Agings will be submitted on a regular basis, and accounts over 60 days will normally be disqualified. It will be your job to collect on these accounts and in your interest to do so aggressively.

You may also actually sell off your receivables to a business known as a factor. You sell your accounts at a discount and you receive immediate cash. The credit decision here is made based on the value of the customer. The higher the risk, the heavier the discount. You must also be aware that some factors use a heavy-handed collection approach that may offend your customers.

Inventory Lending

You may be able to specifically finance large-ticket items that you are selling, such as appliances and automobiles. When the item is sold, the bank is paid. This is a costly loan for a bank to maintain, as it requires a close amount of monitoring and your bank will charge accordingly. If your margins are small, this could eat away at your profits.

> You may be able to borrow directly against the value of your receivables with a line of credit based on their amount and secured by them.

Finding a Good Lender

All banks are not created equal, and one of your jobs as a business owner will be to find the best one for your company and develop a working relationship with it. You must decide between a branch of a large institution or a smaller community bank. The former will likely give you a broader range of services, but the smaller bank will give more personal attention. The interesting development in these days of bank consolidation, that has seen even large regional banks being swallowed up by the national megabanks, is that there are new boutique banks being opened. These serve a specific market and a number of them are meant to serve small business exclusively. If there is a bank like this in your community, you should talk to them.

Contrary to what many business owners claim, banks DO want to make loans to business customers. But they want to make good loans—where their collateral is secured and where the borrower has sufficient positive cash flow to pay the loan back. Remember that a bank will not help you fund losses; the negative cash flow will make it impossible to pay that back. But they are interested in providing capital to help you grow and become more profitable.

> All banks are not created equal, and one of your jobs as a business owner will be to find the best one for your company and develop a working relationship with it.

The Elements of a Loan Proposal

Many companies believe they can drop off their business plan at the bank and come back later to pick up the money. A business plan is not the same thing as a loan proposal, and the astute business owner must know the difference. You must ask your bank what they need and then provide all of the proper documentation.

Smaller loans (under $200,000) at many larger banks are approved by credit scoring, so all you may need to do is fill out a one- or two-page application and attach your current and historical financials (balance sheet and profit-and-loss statement). This will show what assets may be used for collateral and the extent of the available cash flow to meet debt service. Your relationship manager will help you prepare any documentation you may need. Then your information will be fed into a computer and using an established financial model, the decision will be made solely based on the data.

In the case of a smaller bank, however, the more complete and the more professional your loan proposal appears, the more likely you are to be successful. The decisions here are not made by a computer, rather they are made by a loan committee after the presentation of a loan officer. There is a more subjective approach at a smaller bank. Following are the elements of a loan proposal.

Purpose

A bank will lend money for the purchase of inventory and equipment that will increase revenue and profits. A bank will lend money to fund receivables until they are paid. A bank will lend money to develop new products or markets that have a good chance of future success.

A bank will not lend money to fund losses or pay back old debt except in circumstances where the change in interest or repayment terms will increase cash flow.

You must identify where the capital is to be used.

Payment

This will be focused on your pro forma, which shows that you will have sufficient cash flow to retire the debt. This section is where you show the growth and profitability that will come from the investment of the bank's capital.

Protection

What assets will you be using to secure the bank for its loan? Perhaps you do not have sufficient assets now, but the money you borrow will be purchasing hard assets such as equipment. Point this out in your loan proposals.

Other forms of protection are the pledging of personal assets as well as an SBA guarantee, which lowers the bank's exposure. You will likely sign a personal guarantee.

> A bank will not lend money to fund losses or pay back old debt except in circumstances where the change in interest or repayment terms will increase cash flow.

People

The skills, experience, and unique talents of your management team led by you also come into play. Blow your own horn and those of your associates. Your credibility and your track record will increase your bank's confidence in the fact that you can perform as you project.

Spend time researching before you need new funds to find an interested bank or banker and learn what they need when you do apply. Put together a well-researched and documented package and you will increase your chances of getting the funds you need.

Investment Capital

Perhaps you aren't quite eligible for a bank loan, or you need more than a bank is willing to lend, or the project is more speculative than a bank is comfortable with. This may be the time to consider an equity partner.

You will sell off an interest in the business for some cash that you will infuse into the operation, causing growth and increased profitability. This will increase the overall worth of the business and may well mean that your current equity is greater than it was, even if you now own less of the company.

> Adam started a printing company with an emphasis on a high level of graphic work and prepress expertise. The equipment is expensive and constantly changing. He has been profitable for years, but most of the money has been reinvested into equipment. He has a chance for some large new business but the cost far exceeds what he has or can borrow. One of his suppliers, Bob, is very interested, and they get together on a joint venture. Adam sells off 20% of his company, but in less than two years his volume increases dramatically, and with the value of his new equipment, the net worth of the company is up

Your credibility and your track record will increase your bank's confidence in the fact that you can perform as you project.

almost 40%. Adam once owned 100% of a business worth $300,000 and now he owns 80% of one worth $420,000. His interest is now valued at $336,000—10% higher than before. The growth would not have happened without Bob's investment.

Many business owners are reluctant to have any minority shareholders because they believe it lessens their control. The reality is that this is not much of a problem in a closely held company. Minority stockholders have voting rights, but the majority will control operation decisions. They will share in the outcome of the business, benefiting from any losses as a tax deduction and receiving their share of profits if a dividend is declared. And ultimately, if the business is sold, there may be a return to them for greater than their investment.

The benefit of raising money through investment is that the capital is considered at risk and does not have to be paid back unless you make a profit and declare a dividend.

This is not something a very sophisticated investor will do; they require a more controlled environment and a reasonable assurance of return. You are looking, instead, for individuals who are excited about your concept or have knowledge of the venture and its risks.

Successful high-tech entrepreneurs often invest speculatively in other technology because they know the potential for return. Some professionals earmark a portion of their investment dollars for a creative idea, even if the risk is higher. Restaurants are often able to raise money from investors who enjoy the thought of owning a piece of an "in" spot.

Family and friends are also possible investors in a going concern. You must take great care to point out all of the possibilities that a return will be less and longer in coming than you anticipate at this moment. The best policy is always to be candid with any investor. A disgruntled stockholder, even one with a very minority interest, can be a distraction, if not an out-and-out legal nightmare.

> Successful high-tech entrepreneurs often invest speculatively in other technology because they know the potential for return.

What About Venture Capital?

For those companies who need capital in excess of $250,000 and often $500,000 and expect to make a very high return on that investment, venture capital may be a possibility. The most likely candidates are high-tech firms where software development or patents or bioengineering discoveries come into play. Also, e-commerce businesses, Web site creators, and franchise potentials are interesting to venture capitalists. In all of these cases, there is a proprietary edge and the real chance for exceptional growth and return.

While venture capital is an investment and not a loan, it is a far more complicated deal to structure than a typical smaller investor. A venture firm will take a very strong position in overseeing operations and they will expect a major portion of the profit in return for their risk.

It takes substantial time and effort to find potential candidates and then attract the interest of one who is ready to make the deal. So if your need for capital is in the immediate future, this is not likely the place for you. Not only must you connect with just the right match, but both parties will want conduct a substantial due diligence.

You need to know what the firm's history is with reference to operational expertise as well as interference. Are they bringing something to the venture besides capital that will enhance the chance for success? Have they built other businesses into large and successful ventures? Or, do they have a history of acrimonious relationships with the companies they have been involved with? Your future is on the line—take time and check.

The venture firm will need to review all of your representations, historical financials, and any projections in great depth. They have a good bit at risk and they know how to pick a winner—it is by careful research and calculated risks.

If you have created a business venture with potential that is lacking only the financing to make it happen, do not despair. There are a number of ways to approach the challenge, so don't stop at just one. Look at both debt (bank loans) and equity (investment) capital.

> A venture firm will take a very strong position in overseeing operations and they will expect a major portion of the profit in return for their risk.

Streetwise Reality Tour

1. You will not find capital to fund losses nor to refinance old debt.
2. While collateral is important, cash flow sufficient to pay debt service is more important.
3. Minority stockholders in a closely held company can exert little influence.
4. Only a small number of new businesses are candidates for venture capital and it is a challenge to obtain.

> Only a small number of new businesses are candidates for venture capital and it is a challenge to obtain.

For more information on this topic, visit our Web site at www.businesstown.com

Chapter 16

Before You Sign on the Dotted Line

In the words of Benjamin Franklin, there are only two things of which a person can be certain, "death and taxes." Had Dr. Franklin been writing to small business owners, he would have added "contracts" to his list of the inevitable.

This often comes as a surprise to many business owners who view their business as too small to have to give much thought to the complexities of contracts. "After all," you say, "this isn't Microsoft. I run a small business that has a personal relationship with each of our customers and I do business on a handshake. Why do I need to worry about contracts?"

But, try as you might to avoid it, if you operate a business, sooner or later you are going to have to deal with contracts. Before you go too far with your business plans, you should have at least a basic understanding of what a contract is, what it does, and what happens when one of the parties to the contract doesn't do what he promises to do.

A Contract Is a Mutual Agreement

For starters, think of a contract in its simplest form. A contract is created when two people promise each other that they will do something.

> Jennifer is in the business of selling automotive parts to repair garages. Bob, of "Bob's Garage," is one of her best customers.
>
> One day, Jennifer called Bob on the telephone and told him about a new line of automotive paint she had just started carrying. Jennifer offered to sell Bob this new automotive paint for $10 per gallon (the "offer"). Bob agreed to buy 30 gallons of the paint at that price (the "acceptance").
>
> Jennifer and Bob have just entered into a contract.

There is nothing magical or even complicated about the creation of a contract. In fact, from the time in the first grade when you traded half of your peanut butter sandwich for half of your friend's

---

A contract is created when two people promise each other that they will do something.

bologna and cheese, you have been wheeling and dealing in the fast-paced world of contracts.

A contract is created when the following exist:

- An offer
- An acceptance
- A mutual promise (the concept of "consideration")

Let's look at each item separately.

The Offer

An offer must be sufficiently certain that it can be understood and, more importantly, enforced.

> Jennifer calls Bob and tells him, "I will sell you my new automotive paint." Bob, overwhelmed by Jennifer's friendship, agrees.

Is there a contract? No. Much more has to be agreed upon. For example, the price, the quantity, the color, the payment terms, and the delivery date. Without these, no one knows what the parties have really agreed to.

The Acceptance

The offer must be accepted and the acceptance must be understood as an acceptance.

Consideration

In order for a contract to be enforceable, there must be "consideration"; that is, a promise by each of the parties, not just one of them.

> Jennifer tells Bob that, because he has been such a good customer in the past, she's going to give him $500. Jennifer later changes her mind and decides not to part with her money.

In order for a contract to be enforceable, there must be "consideration"; that is, a promise by each of the parties, not just one of them.

Is there a contract to pay Bob $500? No. Jennifer made a promise but Bob made no promise in return.

If we change the facts slightly we obtain a different result.

Jennifer tells Bob that if he buys $5,000 worth of merchandise during the next year, Jennifer will give him $500.

Is there a contract? Yes. Jennifer promises to pay Bob $500 and Bob promises to buy $5,000 worth of merchandise in the next year. There is a mutual promise. There is "consideration."

A contract can be for almost anything.

- Agreements to buy or sell real estate
- Agreements to buy or sell equipment, inventory, or raw material
- Agreements to rent or lease office space
- Agreements to rent or lease equipment or an automobile
- Employment agreements
- Confidentiality agreements
- Loan agreements
- Contracts of insurance
- Investment agreements
- Purchase options and exclusivity agreements
- Guaranty agreements

Contract Clauses

Many people do not see the need for written contracts because they feel that a person's word is their bond. Others feel that it is an insult to ask someone to sign a written agreement because it shows that they are not to be trusted on their word alone.

Nothing could be further from the truth. Most people can be trusted and can be assumed to be honest. Most people do not enter into agreements with the intention to breach them and most people are not out to cheat you.

The fact remains, however, that even honest people can later disagree as to what they had agreed to. And, even honest people can

> Most people do not enter into agreements with the intention to breach them and most people are not out to cheat you.

alter their recollection of agreements, unintentionally, when they are faced with a substantial economic loss. A written contract requires that the parties sit down and commit to writing exactly what they are agreeing to. It signifies a clear meeting of minds and may unearth any misconceptions early in the game when they can be more easily solved.

> Adam owned a rental house that Frank wanted to buy and use as his residence. Frank, however, didn't have enough money to make a down payment and couldn't qualify for a bank loan.
>
> Adam and Frank agreed that Frank could lease the house for two years and then purchase the house outright (a "lease-purchase"). Because both Adam and Frank expect that Frank will be able to complete the deal, they don't go into any more detail.
>
> Over the next two years Frank pays all of his rental payments and, in addition, puts $10,000 of improvements into the property.
>
> At the end of the two years, Frank loses his job and cannot complete the purchase of the house.
>
> When Frank goes back to Adam for reimbursement for the cost of the improvements, he is told to "pound sand." Adam knows that he never agreed to reimburse those expenses even though he is now the beneficiary of those improvements. In fact, his rental house is now worth considerably more than it was when Frank moved in.
>
> Adam isn't being a cheat. He never agreed to pay for those improvements. In fact, Adam would never have agreed to pay for them for the simple reason that he couldn't afford them. If Frank wanted to fix up the property for his use, that was fine, but Adam can't afford it. That's the reason Adam was willing to sell the property in the first place.

In addition to forcing the parties to sit down and understand exactly what they are agreeing to, a written contract often fills in the

> A written contract requires that the parties sit down and commit to writing exactly what they are agreeing to.

"blanks" with generally accepted contract terms. These terms will assist in the interpretation of the contract and also help the parties understand exactly what their rights and liabilities are before they "sign on the dotted line."

Most business contracts contain some fairly uniform clauses, in addition to the more specialized ones, with which you should be familiar.

Identity of the Parties

Quite simply, the contract should identify the parties to the agreement. This has a very practical purpose if and when it becomes necessary to file suit to enforce the contract. It is amazing how many times a person will go to the trouble of putting together a detailed contract and then not include the correct name or entity of the parties (for example, a proprietorship, a partnership, a corporation, etc.).

> Jennifer reaches an agreement with "Bob's Garage" to sell 5,000 gallons of automotive paint. The contract identifies Jennifer as the seller and "Bob's Garage" as the buyer.
>
> What Jennifer didn't count on is the fact that "Bob's Garage" is the proprietorship of Bob Smith. The contract, however, is with a fictitious name, "Bob's Garage."

It may still be possible for Jennifer to successfully sue Bob Smith for breach of contract but it will be much more difficult than it has to be because Bob Smith, the real party, wasn't named as a party to the contract. The situation becomes much worse when Jennifer realizes that "Bob's Garage" is a partnership with no assets and she hasn't named the partners in the contract.

Bottom line, make sure you know who you are contracting with and name them correctly in the contract. Make sure the contract lists everyone who is a party to the contract.

Make sure you know who you are contracting with and name them correctly in the contract.

For more information on this topic, visit our Web site at www.businesstown.com

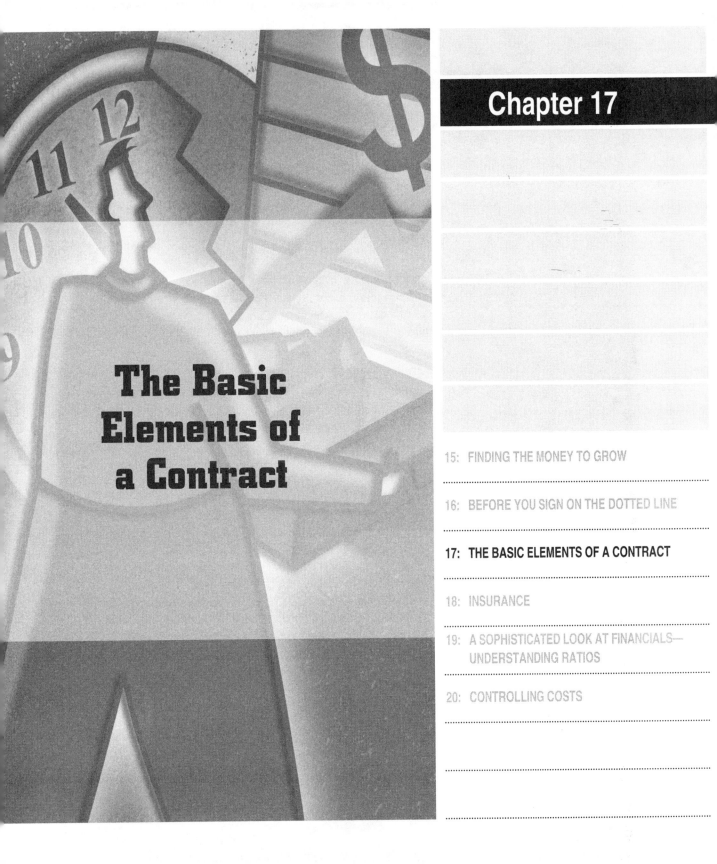

Chapter 17

The Basic Elements of a Contract

The Subject of the Contract

The contract should always describe the exact subject matter of the agreement. What is being bought, sold, or leased? Watch out for the "old switcheroo." If the contract says, simply, that you are buying a car, you may be without sufficient protection when the late model sedan you thought you were buying turns out to be a very used station wagon.

The Price and Payment Terms

You want to make certain that the contract states the total price, the dates of payment, and any penalty or interest rate that would be charged if a payment is not made.

Delivery Dates

If the contract is one for sale and delivery, specify exactly when you are required to deliver the goods. Watch out for the words "Time is of the essence." Once that term is included in your contract you can forget about flexibility and grace periods. The delivery date is a "drop dead" date and, if you miss it, you will be subject to sanctions or penalties.

> Adam agreed to manufacture and deliver laboratory counters for a new research facility being constructed by Bob. Because of the necessity of coordinating all of the other work going into the multimillion-dollar project Bob has required delivery for August 1. "Time is of the essence."
>
> Adam runs a small operation and has never been involved in a project of this size. When the purchase order comes in (yes, a purchase order can be a contract) with the drop dead date, he doesn't even read it and processes the order with all of the others.
>
> On August 5 Adam delivers $200,000 worth of counters. It's a shame, because they were much nicer that the ones Bob bought on August 3 at twice the price.

> You want to make certain that the contract states the total price, the dates of payment, and any penalty or interest rate that would be charged if a payment is not made.

Adam is out the cost of producing the counters and the profit he would have made. He has lost the cost of transporting them to Bob and he will incur storage charges for holding on to them until he can decide how to dispose of them.

More importantly, Bob has sued him for $200,000 to make up for the fact that he had to purchase replacement counters when Adam didn't meet his contractual deadline.

Adam files for bankruptcy two months later.

What Constitutes a Default Under the Contract by Either Party

Every contract should detail those things that are breaches under the contract. In a standard lease of commercial office space the "events of default" may include such things as:

- Failure to pay rent;
- Failure to pay common area maintenance;
- Failing to maintain insurance;
- Failing to keep the property properly maintained;
- Subleasing the property without the landlord's permission.

In fact, depending upon the type of transaction and the attorney drafting the contract, you may find that you will be in default of the contract from the very first day.

> Depending upon the type of transaction and the attorney drafting the contract, you may find that you will be in default of the contract from the very first day.

The Rights of the Nondefaulting Party

Once either party breaches the contract, what are the rights of the other "nonbreaching party"? Read this part carefully. Often, the contract simply specifies the rights that are available to the nonbreaching party anyway. Many times, however, the contract contains other, more dangerous terms, which may not even be enforceable in court. You won't know this, however, until you see a lawyer.

Some examples are:

- *Confession of Judgment.* Some states allow a nonbreaching party to enter a judgment against the other automatically upon breach and without going into court first.
- *Recovery of attorney's fees.* This clause allows the non-breaching party to recover whatever legal fees he incurs in enforcing the contract. The clause may also specify a percentage, as opposed to actual fees.
- *Liquidated damages.* While it may be easy to tell that the other party has breached the contract, it is not always easy to tell what your damages are as a result of that breach. A liquidated damages clause states exactly what the damages are, without the nonbreaching party having to prove them.

Jason has hired Bill to construct a shopping center for him. Jason is making plans for occupancy, negotiating with prospective tenants, and incurring other expenses in anticipation of an August 1 completion date.

If Bill does not complete in time, Jason can certainly figure out what some of his damages are, but many others are far too uncertain ("speculative") to ever recover in a lawsuit.

In the construction contract, Jason includes a liquidated damages clause. Now, if Bill is late in completing the project Jason will be able to charge him $1,000 per day without ever having to prove that his losses are actually $1,000 per day.

A Statement of What State Law Controls the Contract

Depending upon who you are dealing with and where they are located, you may want to include a clause that specifies which state's laws will control the dispute. While there may not be major differences, some state laws do differ and it may be advantageous,

> Some states allow a nonbreaching party to enter a judgment against the other automatically upon breach and without going into court first.

hypothetically, for one party to have the laws of New York followed rather than Pennsylvania.

A Statement That the Written Contract Is the Entire Agreement

This is extremely important. A statement to this effect will ensure that a contract is viewed as the complete agreement of the parties, and neither party is allowed to introduce any other terms. Regardless of what the seller may have told you, once you "sign on the dotted line," the contract controls and the court won't even listen to what the seller may have said in negotiations.

Adam is desperate to sell his new automotive paint. He presents Bob with a contract that requires Bob to purchase 10,000 gallons during the next year. He also assures Bob that the contract is a mere formality and that, if Bob later decides that he doesn't want that much paint, Adam will let him buy only 5,000 gallons.

During the trial in which Adam is trying to collect the money he would have made on 10,000 gallons of paint Bob tries to present evidence of Adam's assurances. He even has a letter from Adam saying the same thing.

Conclusion: the contract says what it says, and it says 10,000, not 5,000. Bob has painted himself into a corner.

Here's the rule: A party may not rely upon any discussions had prior to, or at the same time as, the written contract, if the purpose is to alter or vary the terms of the written contract.

Guaranty

Many times, one of the parties may want a third party to guaranty performance under the contract. This guaranty may be a separate document but it doesn't have to be. Watch where you are signing and make sure you know what you are signing.

> Regardless of what the seller may have told you, once you "sign on the dotted line," the contract controls and the court won't even listen to what the seller may have said in negotiations.

A Contract Does Not Always Have to Be in Writing—but It Doesn't Hurt

While a contract does not always have to be in writing in order to be enforceable, there is merit to the adage, "An oral contract isn't worth the paper it's written on." Legalities aside, if it isn't in writing, how are you going to prove that there was even a contract at all, much less the terms of the agreement?

Don't count on the other side to admit that they are wrong. It won't happen. Practicalities aside, there are legal requirements for contracts to be in writing.

Statute of Frauds

In all states there is something called the "Statute of Frauds." Put simply, certain types of contracts must be in writing in order for them to be enforceable. The most important ones are:

- Agreements for the sale of real estate;
- Agreements for the sale of personal property for an amount greater than $500;
- Contracts incapable of being completed within a year;
- Contracts to pay the debts of another.

> Certain types of contracts must be in writing in order for them to be enforceable.

Watch Out for Those Damages!

So, now you know what a contract is and what it can be used for. But what happens when one of you breaches the contract?

Remember that one of the purposes of a contract is to protect the expectations of the parties. Put another way, what did the non-breaching party expect to receive from the contract?

Lost Profits

Sarah and Carl entered into a contract in which Sarah agreed to sell (and Carl agreed to purchase) 5,000 gallons of automotive paint during the next year at a price of $10 per gallon. The total value of the contract is $50,000. Sarah's cost is $5 per gallon so she expects to make a $25,000 profit on the contract.

Two months into the contract Sarah has not heard from Carl, much less received an order for delivery. Sarah calls Carl and is told that Carl has decided to purchase his paint from a different supplier who has offered him a better price.

As far as Carl is concerned, Sarah has nothing to complain about. After all, Sarah is simply a sales rep. He has not yet ordered the product and doesn't carry an inventory. Sarah is no worse off than if the contract had never existed.

Sarah hires an attorney, files suit, and receives a judgment against Carl for her lost profit of $25,000.

Sarah's profit was guaranteed under the terms of the contract and she is entitled to that amount of money.

Cost of Goods

Assume, in the previous example, that Sarah, in anticipation of filling the contract with Carl, actually orders and pays $25,000 for the automotive paint. Now when she sues Carl she will be asking for $50,000 (Sarah's actual cost of $25,000 plus her lost profit of $25,000).

Consequential Damages

Consequential damages are damages that go beyond the basic contract losses of lost profit and cost of goods. Consequential damages are other losses sustained by the nonbreaching party, which are directly related to the breach of the contract.

Adam and Bob entered into a contract in which Adam agreed to sell (and Bob agreed to purchase) 5,000 gallons of automotive paint during the next year at a price

> Consequential damages are damages that go beyond the basic contract losses of lost profit and cost of goods.

of $10 per gallon. The total value of the contract is $50,000. Adam's cost is $5 per gallon so he expects to make a $25,000 profit on the contract.

The contract requires that Adam have the product in inventory and ready for delivery within 24 hours after an order is received. As a result, Adam pays $25,000 for the product and rents a storage facility to hold the product until an order is received. Adam is required to pay $1,000 per month for the storage facility.

Two years later, Adam is out his $25,000 purchase price for the paint, $25,000 in lost profit, interest on the $50,000 that he should have had by the end of the contract year, as well as the $1,000 per month he has had to pay for the storage facility for the additional year.

Using these facts, assume that Adam had invested his life savings in his automotive supply business. The contract with Bob is the largest contract he has ever had. Because of it, he has had to invest $49,000 in the order ($25,000 to buy the paint and $24,000 for storage charges). Adam cannot absorb the loss and goes out of business. Now, when he sues, he will claim money for the loss of his business.

Attorney's Fees

When Jim started his business he was smart enough to see a lawyer who provided him with a form contract suited to his particular type of business. Sure, Jim could have bought a form contract at a legal supply store, but that's a little like wearing someone else's shoes. The fit just isn't quite right. (In addition to his statement about "death and taxes," Benjamin Franklin also cautioned against being "penny-wise and pound foolish").

In the contract Jim uses he included a clause stating that he could collect legal expenses in the event that he had to file suit to collect his money. Now, in addition to everything else, Jim claims an additional $5,000 in legal expenses.

> Benjamin Franklin also cautioned against being "penny-wise and pound foolish"

Specific Performance

In certain circumstances, money just doesn't make things right.

After months of searching, Adam finally found the piece of real estate on which to construct his new warehouse. It was an ideal location.

After he and the seller, Joan, signed a sales agreement, Joan got cold feet and decided not to sell the property after all.

Adam sat down with his attorney to discuss the lawsuit and discovered, to his surprise, that he couldn't identify any specific losses. He had not yet incurred any expenses, he had no lost profit, and it simply isn't possible to calculate losses that he might incur from building his warehouse someplace else.

Even if he could come up with a hard number for damages, the fact is that he doesn't want money, he wants the property.

Adam and his attorney decide to sue for specific performance. They will ask the court to order Joan to complete the sale of the property to Adam.

Duty to Mitigate Damages

Just because the other party to the contract has defaulted doesn't mean that you can simply sit there and let your damages build.

Sam and Dan entered into a contract in which Sam agreed to sell (and Dan agreed to purchase) 5,000 gallons of automotive paint during the next year at a price of $10 per gallon. The total value of the contract is $50,000. Sam's cost is $5 per gallon so he expects to make a $25,000 profit on the contract.

In order to meet his contract commitment Sam must have the product in inventory and ready for delivery within 24 hours after an order is received. As a result, Sam pays $25,000 for the product and rents a

> Just because the other party to the contract has defaulted doesn't mean that you can simply sit there and let your damages build.

storage facility to hold the product until an order is received. Sam is required to pay $1,000 per month for the storage facility.

Two months into the contract year Dan advises Sam that he will not be purchasing any product from him.

Sam cannot just sit there and do nothing while his storage charges are growing at the rate of $1,000 per month. Instead, Sam must attempt to reduce his losses. He may do this by finding a buyer for the product, or by finding a cheaper storage facility.

The problem here is that Sam is in the business of selling automotive paint. If he resells Dan's paint to another customer it may reduce his claim against Dan, but it still leaves Sam with that much less in sales.

Bob desperately needs automotive paint. He thinks that he has finally found a reliable supplier in Adam. Even better, he believes that he has tied down Adam with a contract that ensures a source of paint, at a reasonable price, for a full year.

Unfortunately, two months into the contract, Adam advises Bob that he cannot obtain the paint necessary to meet the contract.

Bob is now obligated to mitigate his damages. He goes to another supplier, Carl, to obtain his paint. Carl, however, charges $5 more per gallon than the contract with Adam provided for. Bob signs the contract with Carl and sues Adam for the $25,000 difference between what he has to pay Carl and what he was supposed to pay Adam.

> Having a contract doesn't necessarily guarantee that you won't become involved in litigation over who was wrong.

Streetwise Reality Tour

1. Having a contract doesn't necessarily guarantee that you won't become involved in litigation over who was wrong.

2. Even a winning argument and a good contract do not guarantee that you will be able to collect for your losses.

3. A written contract can be altered, orally, after the contract is signed. The best contract can be defeated if the breaching party convinces the court that you had orally agreed to different terms after the contract was signed. Document your conversations, send confirming memos (nothing fancy required), and periodically remind the other side that no oral modifications will be honored.

4. Remember, verbal agreements may be contractually binding, so keep notes of dates and times of any meetings or calls where deals are negotiated. Write down the specific terms agreed to and send your notes to the other party.

> Remember, verbal agreements may be contractually binding, so keep notes of dates and times of any meetings or calls where deals are negotiated.

For more information on this topic, visit our Web site at www.businesstown.com

Chapter 18

Insurance

For many business owners, the very word insurance conjures up images of boring and unintelligible contracts and annoying sales calls. And who hasn't had that uncomfortable feeling that you were paying for something you don't understand and may never receive? Let's face it, the only way you are going to benefit from your insurance is when a disaster strikes. It's too easy to try to ignore the need because of the expense. Despite this, insurance is an important aspect of business planning and operations. In some cases, it is a legal requirement.

> Often, it is better to look for an agent or a brokerage firm who is able to write insurance with a number of different companies.

Start with a Reputable Insurance Agent

As in choosing other professionals (lawyers, accountants, etc.), it is important that you find an insurance agent who you are comfortable with, who will be responsive to your needs, and who is knowledgeable about his product.

Often, it is better to look for an agent or a brokerage firm who is able to write insurance with a number of different companies. No one company can handle all of your needs and, even if they could, you would not necessarily receive the best prices. A broker who sells for a variety of carriers can shop around and get you the best deal. They may also be better able to tell you which coverage is best for your specific business.

Types of Insurance

Personal Protection

For the sake of your business you should take the time to understand the various types of insurance and how each may impact upon your business. We will begin with the ones you are most familiar with and those that may concern you personally.

Life Insurance

Most people understand that life insurance is intended to provide a cash benefit to your family or estate upon your death. It is intended to cover the costs of funeral, burial, and, ideally, to provide your heirs with enough money to tide them over until they can replace the income lost as a result of your death.

From a business standpoint, life insurance can also be used to provide your estate with enough money to pay the federal estate taxes on your estate. After all, your company has a value that will be included in your estate.

> After years of hard work, Adam had built a successful company with a net worth of over one million dollars. Adam's wife died several years prior so his entire estate will go to his children. Because of federal estate taxes (as well as state inheritance taxes) his estate will be taxed at between 50 to 75% of all assets in excess of $600,000.00.
>
> Because Adam always plowed his earnings right back into the company, all of his assets are tied up in the business. Consequently, there is no cash available to pay the estate taxes. His estate is "cash-poor."
>
> The only options to deal with Adam's estate taxes is to liquidate the business, borrow against it at a time that may not be advantageous (and perhaps not even possible), or not pay Uncle Sam when the tax is due. (Don't go there!)
>
> Fortunately, Adam purchased life insurance in an amount sufficient to pay the estate taxes, thereby preserving the business for the benefit of his children.

Life insurance can also be used to fund a "buy-sell agreement" between partners.

> Tim and Linda were 50/50 shareholders in a corporation that manufactured engine parts. As an operating entity the corporation is worth over $2 million.
>
> Upon Tim's death his estate takes over his shares in the corporation but, without a market for the shares (and there really is none for this type of close corporation) the shares are valueless. Consequently, Tim's estate and family

> Life insurance can also be used to fund a "buy-sell agreement" between partners.

cannot realize any value from the business that he spent his life building.

If they had no other options, Tim's family could utilize his 50% interest in the company and attempt to liquidate the corporation in an effort to realize some value through a sale. Unfortunately, the value of the business is not in its pieces, but as an operating entity managed by either Tim or Linda.

Linda would like to see Tim's family taken care of, but while the business has provided both she and Tim with a good living, it cannot support the type of cash payment that Tim's family needs. In fact, it cannot even afford payments spread out over time.

Fortunately, Tim and Linda had executed a buy-sell agreement which gave the survivor the right and obligation to purchase the shares of the first to die (in this case, Tim). In addition, they had the corporation take out life insurance policies on each of their lives.

Now, upon Tim's death the monies exist to allow Linda to purchase Tim's interest in the business. Linda can continue to make a living with her business and Tim's family has the money it needs to live.

Life insurance can also be used to pay business debts that you have guaranteed, such as bank loans or auto leases. This may be called "credit life" or "decreasing term" because the benefit decreases over time to match the reduced amount of the financial obligation. Some lenders may require you to secure this type of insurance.

Disability Insurance

One type of insurance that is commonly overlooked is disability insurance. One reason may be that disability insurance, when purchased individually, is quite expensive. It may also be due to the fact that most people do not believe that they can be disabled to the point of being unable to perform their job.

> Life insurance can also be used to pay business debts that you have guaranteed, such as bank loans or auto leases.

Disability insurance is designed to provide you with a certain percentage of your current income in the event that you become disabled and unable to work.

The benefits are obvious. But you must shop for the right coverage.

Scott is an attorney who practices law by himself with no partners or associates. Due to a recent serious illness he is unable to work.

Scott had purchased a disability policy that pays 50% of his prior income after the first six months of disability. The coverage continues for two years.

What Scott did not consider is the fact that, if his illness continues beyond two years, he will have no income. If he returns after two years there will be no practice to return to, his clients will have, understandably, gone elsewhere. In essence, he will have to start over.

Some factors to consider in purchasing disability insurance are as follows:

- How long do you have to be disabled before the coverage goes into effect?
- How long will the insurance continue?
- What is the definition of disability? For example, some policies define disability as the inability to do any job, not just yours. You may not be able to perform your job as the manager and owner of a construction company, but you can perform the duties of a telemarketer.

You may think that you are protected by workers' compensation or Social Security disability but, for a variety of reasons, neither may be the savior you were hoping it would be.

Workers' compensation only covers work-related injuries and diseases. If your disability is caused by a motor vehicle accident on your off-hours or an illness unrelated to the job, workers' compensation is no help.

> Disability insurance is designed to provide you with a certain percentage of your current income in the event that you become disabled and unable to work.

In addition, in most states, workers' compensation has a maximum weekly or monthly payout that may be significantly less than you need, and less than you would receive with a disability policy.

Also, in many states, a business owner is not protected by workers' compensation. Even if he is, he may have the option to opt out of coverage and if so, usually does so in an effort to hold down costs.

Social Security is usually harder to qualify for than disability insurance. To qualify for Social Security the disabled individual has to establish that he cannot perform any job that exists in the national economy. It doesn't matter whether that job is available in the state where he resides, it is only important that the job exists somewhere.

If you decide to purchase a disability policy, consider whether the disability insurance you purchase is intended to pay your living expenses or whether it is intended to preserve your business until you can return to work. Then, purchase your policy accordingly.

Distinguish between disability insurance and business overhead expenses ("BOE") insurance.

Disability insurance is intended to replace a portion of your lost income. "BOE" is intended to pay the bills of your business when you, the owner, are unable to work. The types of expenses covered include the following:

- Rent
- Utilities
- Wages for employees
- Professional fees

Unlike disability insurance, which pays a portion of your lost income, BOE usually pays for all of the expenses that your business needs to operate.

BOE will not last forever, but it will give you the breathing room to decide what to do about your business if your disability continues longer than expected. For example, you may decide that you cannot return to work and that it is best to sell the business. If, however, the lease has been lost due to nonpayment of rent, or, if your

> To qualify for Social Security the disabled individual has to establish that he cannot perform any job that exists in the national economy.

key employees have left because there have been no paychecks, you will have nothing to sell.

Key-Man Insurance

You may also find it useful to obtain life insurance and/or disability insurance on any key employees ("key-man" insurance). This will compensate the company for the loss, temporarily or permanently, of any important employee.

Adam has a small but successful graphics business. Adam is the businessman but his employee, Lisa, is the creative genius.

Years before, Adam had the foresight to enter into an employment agreement with Lisa. He sleeps soundly, now, comfortable in the knowledge that Lisa cannot take another job or leave his company without appropriate notice.

One day, Lisa is involved in an automobile accident, which leaves her unable to work for over a year. Adam's employment contract cannot help him here.

Had Adam taken out a "key-man" disability policy on Lisa, things still would be difficult but, at least, there would be some cash flow to carry the company until Adam can figure out what to do about Lisa's absence.

Health Insurance

You will need to have health coverage for yourself and your family. And in the current full-employment economy, most qualified candidates expect at least partial coverage. You will have to offer a plan to be competitive. And the coverage you can get will be cheaper and more comprehensive if you are part of a group as opposed to a single subscriber.

Talk to a benefits coordinator to make sure you are providing the opportunity to all eligible people in an equitable manner. And investigate plans that are offered by larger organizations such as Chambers of Commerce and trade associations. They spread the risk over a wider group and the fees are often lower and the coverage more complete.

> Investigate plans that are offered by larger organizations such as Chambers of Commerce and trade associations.

Workers' Compensation Insurance

Most states require that employers maintain workers' compensation insurance. In some cases, not having this coverage is a criminal offense.

The purpose of workers' compensation insurance is to provide for medical care and lost wages in the event that an employee becomes injured or disabled as a result of a work-related activity.

Workers' compensation rates are usually established by state-established standards. Consequently, there is little an employer can do to change his rates going into a policy year. However, there are rebates offered for companies that have a good safety record, and if your premium is very large, you may be able to get back a dividend. At the end of the year, a portion of your premium will be returned. In some cases, this may exceed 30%.

To the extent the employer can do anything, those efforts are usually limited to ensuring a safe work environment, making sure that all claims of injury are documented and investigated on a timely basis, and coordinating efforts with the insurance carrier so as to provide "light duty" to injured employees in an effort to return the injured employee to work at the earliest possible date. Each incident affects your rates, so you must be diligent about your policies.

A Package Policy

Naturally, if you own the building in which you conduct business you will want to obtain insurance for such things as fire, flood, and liability. You will also want to make sure that the amount of coverage is sufficient to rebuild the structure (remember, the building may appraise for $100,000 but it may cost you $120,000 to rebuild it).

The same problems exist even if you simply rent your business space. Your landlord may still want you to obtain insurance for what happens in your designated leased space as well as coverage protecting him from injured individuals who might go looking to establish liability against him. This will be covered under an umbrella liability policy.

You will also want to make certain that the contents of your business space are insured. What would it cost you to replace all of your office furniture, equipment, customer lists, catalogues, and business

> The purpose of workers' compensation insurance is to provide for medical care and lost wages in the event that an employee becomes injured or disabled as a result of a work-related activity.

records? This loss will not be covered at all unless you have your own insurance. Don't expect the landlord's insurance to protect you.

Product Liability Insurance

Regardless of the type of business you own, you will want to obtain liability insurance. Make sure your umbrella policy has this specific coverage.

- Lawyers, doctors, accountants, architects, and other professionals should carry professional liability insurance.
- Bar owners should have liability protection for injuries caused by customers who may have been over-served with alcohol while at their establishment.
- Manufacturers will want to be protected from injuries sustained by the users of the products they have manufactured.
- Restaurants and caterers will want coverage for customers who become ill from improperly prepared food.
- Store owners will want protection from the customer who slips on snow in the parking lot.

Remember all the thought that went into deciding what business form to use (corporation, LLC, partnership) and how one of the biggest factors to consider is whether you are personally protected from debts incurred by the business.

Remember, also, that tort lawsuits (suits for personal injuries or property loss) may still be brought against you, as owner, simply because you made the decision that resulted in the harm. Corporation or not, you may be liable.

Insurance provides the protection when the form of business entity you select simply can't.

> Insurance provides the protection when the form of business entity you select simply can't.

Business Interruption Insurance

In addition to the contents and assets of the business, consider what loss you would suffer if no work could be done for at least two weeks.

This is easy to imagine if all of your business records have been destroyed or if your computer melted in a fire. Ask those who have suffered this type of loss—the disruption can easily destroy your company.

You will want to ask your agent about business interruption insurance. This type of coverage will pay you for a certain portion of your established loss of income to the business in the event that the business cannot operate and generate income. This type of coverage can mean the difference between inconvenience and disaster.

Your expenses will not stop—rent, leases, and loans will still need to be paid even if you are not up and operational. And you will have no cash flow to pay those expenses.

> As much as insurance can help, it can be expensive and may not be affordable for you. Consider your needs and risks carefully.

Streetwise Reality Tour

1. All the insurance in the world will not completely protect you from the disasters life may throw your way.
2. As much as insurance can help, it can be expensive and may not be affordable for you. Consider your needs and risks carefully. Ask the advice of a reliable insurance agent.
3. If it looks like your agent is pushing too hard or is trying to sell policies with amounts much greater than you think necessary, get a second quote.
4. Periodically take bids to make sure that you are getting competitive pricing.

For more information on this topic, visit our Web site at www.businesstown.com

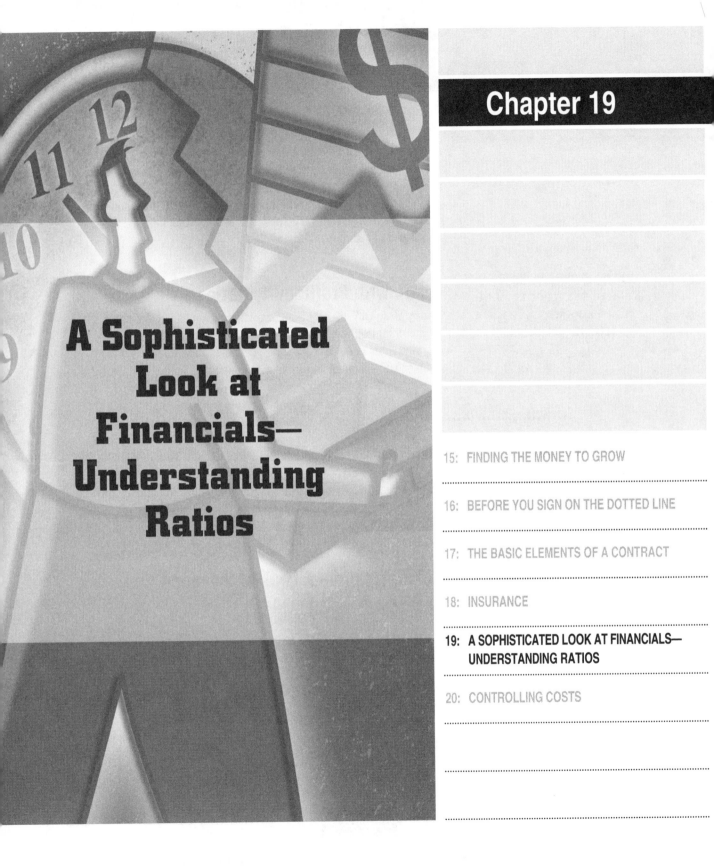

Chapter 19

A Sophisticated Look at Financials— Understanding Ratios

Y ou must learn to read the financial reports of your company on a regular basis and understand what they show you about the current results of your business activities, as well as the trends you watch for the future (Forms 19-01, 19-02, 19-04, 19-05, 19-06, 19-07, and 19-08 in the Appendix). Ratios are determined by extracting certain numbers from your balance sheet as well as your profit-and-loss statement.

> If the gross margin is going down, your pricing is not keeping up with your direct costs.

Begin with Profitability Ratios

Your gross profit margin is as important a number as the net profit of the operation. Begin there and watch the trend of profit as a percentage of revenue over a period of time. Compare same periods, such as third quarter of this year as contrasted with third quarter of last, as that will give you a picture not influenced by seasonal changes. You are looking at the percentage, not the total dollars.

If the gross margin is going down, your pricing is not keeping up with your direct costs. You must find lower-priced material, increase productivity to lower costs, or raise prices to cover your direct expense.

Net profit percentages will trend downward as a result of several events. First, gross margins are down. If they are steady, then the reason is lower total revenue or increasing overhead expense. Use these numbers to troubleshoot the problem and correct it.

Current Ratio—A Look at Solvency

There is a quick way to determine the liquidity of your company, which represents your ability to pay current liabilities as they become due. You will find the numbers in your balance sheet. Look at current assets:

Cash
Inventory
Accounts receivable

And your current liabilities:

Accounts payable
Portions of loans due over next 12 months

Divide your assets by your liabilities. For example, if you have $200,000 of assets and $100,000 of current liabilities, then you have a ratio of 2 to 1, which is a figure in the normal range. Those businesses that have little inventory and few receivables, such as a service business or a restaurant, can have a lower ratio and still be in a good liquidity position.

You must watch the trends here, as they show the amount of working capital and a decline in that number is an indication of potential cash problems that must be corrected.

Quick Ratios

There is a variation of the current ratio that may be more accurate for companies carrying large inventories, some of which may be obsolete. Here, you will use the current assets (cash and accounts receivable) without the inventory number. Your 2 to 1 ratio may go down to as low as 1.3 to 1 (meaning $130 in assets for every $100 of liabilities).

What matters when you set the goals for your own company is what is standard in the type of industry you are in. These numbers are available from RMA (Robert Morris Associates), and your accountant or banker can help you find them.

Receivable Turnover Ratio

Determining this number will give you insight on how your cash flows, as it will tell you how many days it takes your company to collect once a bill has been issued to a customer. You will calculate this ratio by dividing annual sales by total current receivables. Sales of

CENTER FOR FAMILY BUSINESS HUSSON COLLEGE

> There is a variation of the current ratio that may be more accurate for companies carrying large inventories, some of which may be obsolete.

$500,000 and receivables of $100,000 will give you a turnover of five times a year. Divide this number (5) into 365 (total number of days). A bill issued today will become cash in 73 days.

You must look at the trends in this ratio because increasing number of days means that cash is getting tighter. It may also mean that some accounts may not be paying at all and your money is at risk. This ratio should be monitored on a constant, ongoing basis.

Payable Turnover Ratio

Similar to the receivable ratio, this number will tell you how many days, on average, it is taking for your company to pay an invoice to a vendor. You determine this ratio the same way, by dividing your total purchases by your current payables. For example, your annual purchases are $300,000 and you currently owe vendors $50,000. Your turn is six times per year and if you divide that into 365, you will come up with 61, meaning that you typically pay a bill 61 days after you receive it.

This is another important trend to watch because you need vendor credit as a source of low- or no-cost financing. A deterioration in this ratio could be an indication of cash crunch and may jeopardize these relationships. Your goal should be to time the receivable and payable turnover as close as you can so that cash inflow will be able to meet outflow.

Inventory Turnover Ratio

Managing your inventory is critical to the success of any business. You need to turn (sell) that inventory quickly so that your money is not tied up and your cash flow is adequate. You determine this number by taking the total purchases of material and dividing it by the value of your current inventory. For example, you have purchased $280,000 of inventory throughout the year and now have $70,000 of

> Your goal should be to time the receivable and payable turnover as close as you can so that cash inflow will be able to meet outflow.

that inventory in stock, your turnover ratio is 4. Divide that into 365 and you find that your turn in days is 91. Remember that this number is an average so if half of your inventory is old and almost never sells, that will influence this figure. It is a number to be monitored to show trends and predict cash needs.

Debt-to-Worth Ratio

During the growth phase of any business, the company will need to leverage its equity and make money on borrowed money. You will determine this ratio by dividing all debt (current and long term) by the total amount of equity (net worth). For example, if your debts are $500,000 and your worth is $250,000, then your debt-to-worth ratio is 2 to 1. Most lenders see a 3 to 1 ratio as the upward limit, and lower numbers are a good sign.

The age of a company and the stability of its assets will determine where the target of this number should be. The safer the assets (such as real estate and cash instruments vs. raw material), the higher the number can go. The older the company, the lower the number should be.

Again, watch the trends.

> During the growth phase of any business, the company will need to leverage its equity and make money on borrowed money.

Return on Equity Ratio

This number helps you determine if the return is adequate for the risk. You can compare the return on your money invested in the company vs. an investment in another vehicle.

You divide the net equity (worth) by the net profit. Assume you have $150,000 in equity in your business and you earn $15,000 in profits, then your return is 10%. You must determine how high the risk is (has your profit remained stable, grown, or been erratic?) and whether or not you can earn more by investing in the market or even bonds or safe cash instruments. Of course, your ability to earn a living should be a part of this consideration.

Streetwise Reality Tour

1. If you want to win, your must be able to read the score. Understand your financials.
2. Don't ignore the trends. If they are going down, consider that a warning and take action.
3. You are in business to be creative and earn a living. But any business must also pay a dividend on the investment. Look realistically at your return.

Don't ignore the trends. If they are going down, consider that a warning and take action.

For more information on this topic, visit our Web site at www.businesstown.com

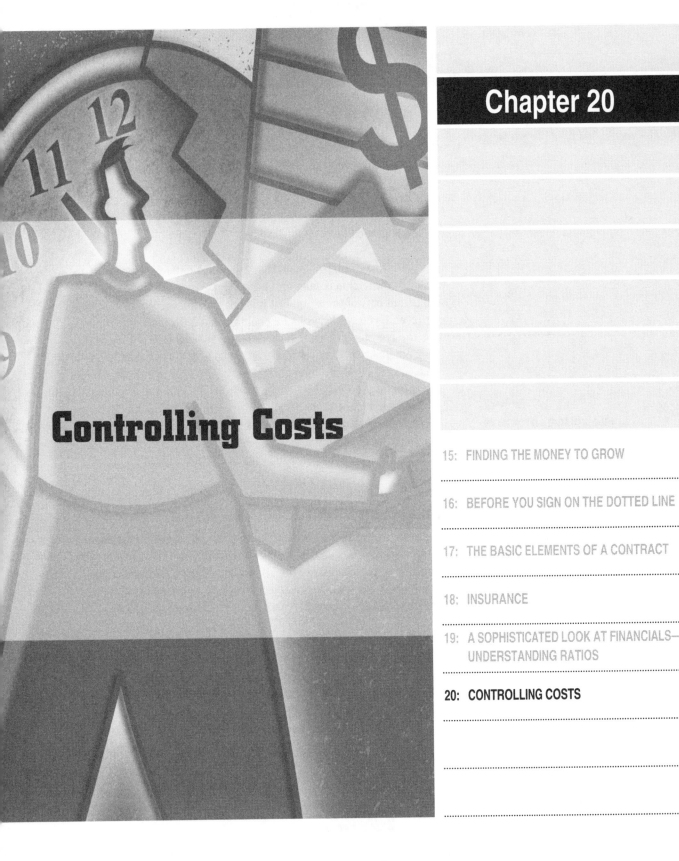

Chapter 20

Controlling Costs

Mark operated his printing company for two years and was happy with his growth. Sales had topped the half-million mark the first year, although profits were nonexistent. By year two, revenue increased an amazing 35% and sales now topped $700,000, yet profits were still very small. His marketing plan was working fine but his bottom-line strategy needed help.

Many new entrepreneurs think the most important aspect of business ownership is sales and marketing. No doubt that is an important part of the story. But it is not the gross revenues that matter (even if you've always had a goal to run a million-dollar business), it is the bottom line that determines your success and, at times, even your possibility of survival. You must be able to service debt, build financial reserves, and fund at least part of your growth from profits if you are to prosper.

So what is the secret to a healthy bottom line? Simple, the way to get there is to plan for it and stick to that plan by using a budget. Set goals for the cost of everything from direct expense to overhead and then monitor how you are doing on a regular basis.

> It is the bottom line that determines your success and, at times, even your possibility of survival.

Budgeting Direct Expense—Labor

For a service business, labor is the primary direct cost. In manufacturing, the cost may still be high. In sales organizations such as retail stores or wholesale distribution, direct wages are a fairly small portion of total costs. But in all cases, it is important to control them, and in some cases such as a restaurant, it is absolutely critical.

Sandy had a fairly popular Italian restaurant that was open from 11 A.M. to 11 P.M. six days a week. Lunches were unpredictable, mid-afternoon always slow, and dinner good to excellent Thursday through Saturday. Profits were always thin and money often scarce. Sandy realized that she was overstaffing but didn't know how to cut it back. She wanted to give the best service always, so she made sure a full staff was always on hand.

What Sandy needs is a firm number to use as a goal for labor costs and to use to make her scheduling decisions. You need them also, and here is how you do it. Use your pro forma income statement to determine your goals of labor as a percentage of revenue. Now, look realistically at your sales over the past quarter. Do you expect them to grow, stay the same, or perhaps be lower because of seasonal changes? Project them on a month-to-month basis for the next six months. Now, insert the labor percentage into the gross number and you have the money available for direct payroll.

For example, Sandy has sales of $10,000/week and projects that they will stay the same over the next two months and then rise to $12,500/week during a holiday month. She wants her direct labor to stay at 30%, so she budgets $3,000/week for the first two months and $3,750/week for the third. She schedules staff accordingly. There will be times that she is a bit short-handed but that can be handled with some charm and perhaps a free glass of wine as an apology. The other alternative is to overstaff, just in case, which will at the very least lower your profit or worse yet, absorb your entire bottom line.

Don't Forget Benefits and Taxes

Your payroll carries a cost beyond just the actual dollars paid, and you must keep that in mind as well. You should know that you have an employer's contribution to FICA tax of almost 8%, but you must also make a contribution to the unemployment tax to both the state and federal governments. You have workers' compensation insurance that is based on the wages of your employees to consider, and you may also be carrying all or part of a health insurance package. Remember all of these costs as you create your budget for labor—keep the total number within your projections.

Perhaps the toughest part of this exercise is reducing your labor force when business is soft, whether it is expected due to seasonal changes or due to a problem such as losing a big customer or contract. As soon as you are aware that your revenue will go down and by how much, you must make the same cuts in personnel. No

> Your payroll carries a cost beyond just the actual dollars paid.

one likes to lay off employees, but not to do so may endanger the entire operation and the jobs of everyone.

Monitor Inventory Budgets Too

The other direct expense is material—whether it is raw material or finished products that you resell. In this category as well, you are looking at percentages and not fixed numbers (they will come into play in the overhead category). Here you may want to budget quarterly because you must take a physical inventory to get an actual count, even if you are maintaining some inventory control on your computer accounting system. There are two reasons to take a physical count or at least a spot check—the first is for accuracy and the second is to see whether or not any of the material is damaged, unusable, or obsolete. If you are in the retail business, you will need to put merchandise on sale, and that will dramatically change your direct cost percentage. But you must continue to monitor your cost percentages so you can be alerted to when they begin a drift upward on a longer-term basis. At that point, you must take some action, either finding more economical suppliers or raising your prices.

> Budgeting and monitoring direct costs means that you can keep your gross profit margins stable.

Budgeting and monitoring direct costs means that you can keep your gross profit margins stable. That is the first part of operating a profitable company. Next, you must set up a system to monitor your overhead budget as well.

Review Your Overhead Budget

Your overhead costs are often described in accounting terms as "fixed" because they remain steady regardless of the level of your sales. In reality, that is only partially true, because some of them will need to grow as your volume does. Costs such as sales and marketing expense, including travel, advertising, and promotional costs, will go up as your sales go up although the percentage of increase will be less. These are important items to budget.

Your overhead budget is based on total dollars spent, and you can allocate those dollars any way you want. After you have established your sales projections for the next year (you want to work on annual overhead budgets and revisit them every quarter to see how you have done)—then determine the overhead dollars available. For example, your projected sales for next year are $700,000 and your direct expense is 65%. This means that your gross profit is 35% or $245,000. As a part of your budget, you will need to determine how much net profit you will need to manage debt service (the principal payments are not expensed) and provide sufficient cash to pay investors, fund growth, and provide a cash cushion. For the sake of discussion, you need a 10% bottom line or $70,000. You will then have $175,000 to fund the overhead of the business.

Start with the Most Necessary Costs

There are overhead items that must be paid on an ongoing basis simply to keep the doors open such as rent, utilities, insurance, telephone, and any interest on loans. Not paying these expenses on time could result in serious problems. Then you have the staff required to do administrative (and therefore overhead) tasks such as secretarial and record keeping. Inside and outside sales functions will be expensed here as well. Allocate these expenses first in your budget.

What is left will be used to pay the owner's salary—no, you're not first on the list; get used to it. Of course you are entitled to the value of your work, and you should be getting a return for your investment, but this may not happen in the early stages of your business. And there also may be times when cash is tight and expenses must be cut, including your salary. Make budget decisions based on the projected results of your company and you will have a better chance of long-term success and prosperity.

Other discretionary budget items must be established and adhered to as well. Benefits offered to you and your employees are a good example. It may be legally permissible to have the company pay for a car for you and perhaps a generous allowance for entertainment, but if the cash flow can't sustain it, you could be damaging your entire company.

> Make budget decisions based on the projected results of your company and you will have a better chance of long-term success and prosperity.

You must use the same reasoning about any new expenditure, be it company cars, employee benefits, or marketing expense. Is there room in your budget for the added items while still maintaining adequate cash flow to pay your ongoing expenses? A pro forma budget will give you those answers.

Streetwise Reality Tour

Budgets are living documents, they must be revisited from time to time.

1. Strong overall revenues are an admirable goal for a business, but it is the bottom line that counts.
2. Labor costs must be kept under control even when the answer is to cut back employment.
3. Budgets are living documents, they must be revisited from time to time.
4. The owners' salaries and perks must be a part of the budget process.

For more information on this topic, visit our Web site at www.businesstown.com

Chapter 21

Pricing for Profit

There are two criteria that must be the major considerations in pricing, and it is the balance of these two that determines the success of your strategy. The first is internal, the understanding of exactly what it costs you to produce your product, sell your merchandise, or provide your service. The second is external, it requires an understanding of the market you are serving and the competition that already exists in that market. A blend of the knowledge of these two factors will give you your pricing levels.

Adam started his restaurant in a busy, high-traffic area that would provide many customers for lunch as well as dinner. There were a number of other establishments in the area but Adam decided his would be a "fine dining" establishment with a high level of service and prices that reflected that strategy. After the first two months in business, he realized that his plan had been too ambitious.

The restaurant was seldom busy enough at lunch, and at dinner, traffic was light except for weekend nights. Adam saw the traffic at his competition and realized that the customers in this area were interested in "family type" dining.

He quickly created a new menu and spent money on advertising to promote his new game plan. The results were mixed. The traffic was up a bit but the revenue was down even more because prices were lower. The future didn't look very good. First impressions stuck and few new customers came in the doors.

In the end, Adam had to hire a restaurant consultant to rename the business, redesign the menu, and develop the marketing strategy. After some serious losses and expenses, the business began to grow and prosper.

You can avoid this mistake by doing your homework well in advance and understanding where to look and what to change if you haven't seen the results you want. Your pricing strategy will determine how quickly you get to your break-even point. The larger the margins, the less total revenue you will require. On the other hand, the lower your prices are compared to your competition, the more customers you may attract.

> Your pricing strategy will determine how quickly you get to your break-even point.

Understanding the Cost Factor

Your direct costs include all of the labor and material that are "directly" involved in producing your product or service. These are also referred to as variable costs because they are linked to the volume of your sales, going up as sales go up and down as revenues drop. Only the labor and material that are "directly" related to your product or service are included in this category—you must know what your costs are in order to price effectively.

Your labor costs can be gotten directly from your payroll, but don't neglect to add taxes, insurance, and benefits such as vacation. They can raise labor by as much as 30%. Divide your current payroll into your volume and that will tell you what percentage you are spending on labor.

Material costs may be a bit harder to capture in some, but not all, cases. In a restaurant, for example, a constant physical inventory must be taken to establish how much food has been used. And in that business, a certain amount of unused food may spoil, so that must be added into the costs as well.

In the end, many businesses have a "hidden" cost of material. For retail businesses, it may be product that goes unsold and is put out at drastic discounts simply to turn some money. In manufacturing, there may be production mistakes that spoil some amount of material, and that must be factored in the cost. And you must also include any inbound freight that is charged, as that is an element of the costs.

It is extremely important that you know as closely as possible how much any product or service that you sell costs you. This is the first step to profitable pricing.

> Your direct costs include all of the labor and material that are "directly" involved in producing your product or service.

What Gross Margin Do You Need?

You must now deal with the economics of your established business. Once you have grown to a reasonable size, how much gross profit do you require to be a viable business?

Tom's printing company has three presses and he projects that he can do $800,000 of gross sales annually. His overhead cost, including loans, rent on his building, insurance, advertising, and his own salary is about $250,000, so he must earn over 32% on sales. To do so means marking up his printing about 40%–what costs him $1.00 is sold for $1.40.

Now, What About Competition?

In some cases your prices are set by manufacturers, such as with branded clothing and other retail items. If there is little you can do on the price side, you must be clever on the cost side. But the most creative small businesses are those that have some latitude in how they position themselves by their pricing. You want your product or service to distinguish itself in the market so that you can show good value to potential customers and they will be willing to meet your asking price.

There are many ways to do this, and to be what is often referred to as a niche marketer. Following are some of the characteristics of such a company:

- Products that are hard to find elsewhere
- Convenient location
- Free delivery and home service
- Easy credit terms (not necessarily good for buyer but good for seller)
- Extended hours
- Customized products

Control your costs if you are selling a generic product, and then position that product high on a value-added scale, and your profit margins are likely to be healthy.

Not the Biggest, but the Best

At some point in the growth of your business, you will be making decisions about growth. Are you building a megacompany or a

> In some cases your prices are set by manufacturers, such as with branded clothing and other retail items.

mid-size venture? The pricing strategy you choose may have a great influence on your growth.

There are always one or two innovators that have grown extremely large and have been very profitable creating great wealth for their funders. Just remember that for every one that has scored big, there are thousands that have not, many having not made it at all.

Your challenge will be to develop a profitable strategy and plan for growth that maintains that bottom line. There are many aspects of this goal, but pricing is one of the key ones.

Lowering Prices to Spur Growth

There are a number of reasons to reduce prices, the main one being to move merchandise that is out of season or obsolete or even damaged in some way. Introducing a new product or service might require a short-term pricing incentive, but it is wise to limit the time you offer the discounts. Make it clear that your normal pricing structure will go into effect reasonably soon.

What you must not do without great analysis and consideration is to lower prices across the board with the idea that you will create sufficient increase in volume to maintain your profitability. You may be very surprised to learn how much of an increase you will require. Consider the following.

Assume you have an item that sells for $100 and costs you $60. If you sell 100, you will gross $4,000 in profit.

100 units at $100	$10,000
Cost of $60 × 100	$6,000
Gross profit	$4,000

A price decrease of 10% means you will perform as follows:

100 units at $90	$9,000
Cost of $60 × 100	$6,000
Gross profit	$3,000

> Introducing a new product or service might require a short-term pricing incentive, but it is wise to limit the time you offer the discounts.

You will need a growth of almost 35% in order to achieve the same gross profit dollars:

135 units at $90	$12,150
Cost of $60 × 135	$8,100
Gross profit	$4,050

In the end you will likely have an increase in fixed costs to sustain the increased traffic and volume. You may need more space, more billing clerks or salespeople, and your phone bills and postage will be higher as well. In the end, you will be doing more work for less money.

The Effect of a Price Increase

In some cases, your customers will be price sensitive, but it may be less so than you think. Clients get used to shopping or doing business in the same place with the same individuals, and are not as likely as you think to leave just because you are charging a bit more. The fact is that you can afford to lose a bit of volume and still keep the same or higher profitability.

For example:
Original pricing

100 units at $100	$10,000
Cost of $60 × 100	$6,000
Gross profit	$4,000

Price increase of 10% with a 20% decrease in sales

80 units at $110	$8,800
cost of $60 × 80	$4,800
Gross profit	$4,000

In addition, your overhead cost may actually go down because you are handling fewer units. Fewer employees and less space may be needed.

> Clients get used to shopping or doing business in the same place with the same individuals, and are not as likely as you think to leave just because you are charging a bit more.

It is very seldom the case that volume will go down by as much as 20% as a result of a price increase. If you maintain your current level, your profits will increase substantially. So you see, pricing is a critical part of profitability.

Streetwise Reality Tour

1. You must know all of your costs before you can see pricing strategies.
2. Don't forget the hidden cost of labor, which is benefits, and material, which is shrinkage.
3. Know what your competition is doing but dare to be different.
4. Lowering prices may create a profit drop in greater number than your growth.

> Know what your competition is doing but dare to be different.

For more information on this topic, visit our Web site at www.businesstown.com

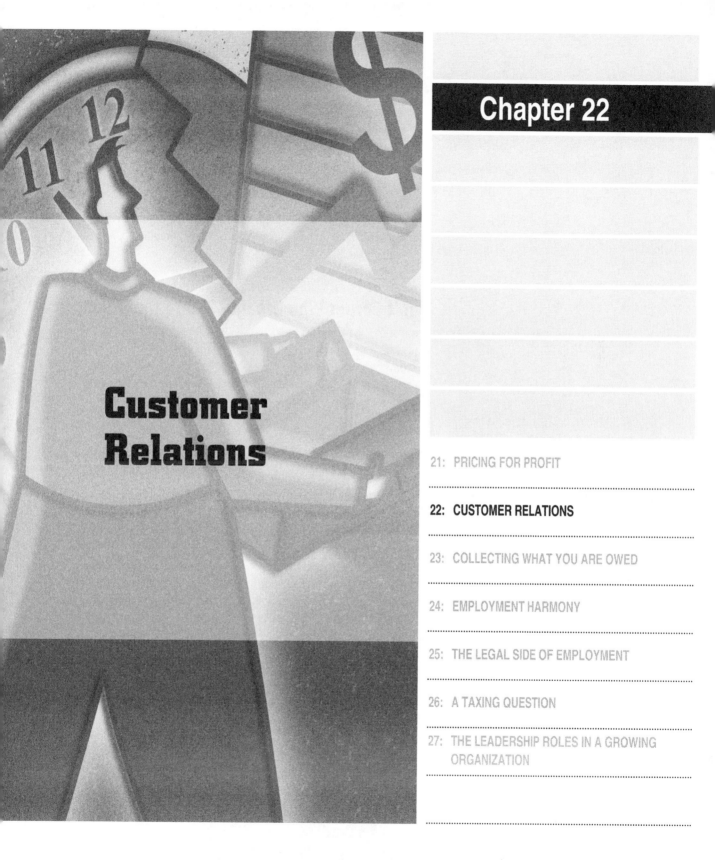

Chapter 22

Customer Relations

When you opened your doors and the first customer walked through, you were thrilled. Your pride in your product or service was that of a parent with a new child and you were looking for approval. A sale is just that, proof that someone values what you do.

But then your customers grew in numbers and not everyone was pleasant. Some made demands, and some complained, and some even demanded their money back.

Don't Forget Who Brought You to the Dance

It's ironic that the more successful your business becomes, the less time you spend with your established customers—the very customers on whom your success was based. Instead, you go off on a hunt for new prospects, the wealthier customer, thinking that many customers are better than a few (and sometimes they are).

Why can't we just be grateful for what we have? Some of the reasons may be as follows.

Your Strength Has Been in Marketing, Not Servicing Customer Accounts

Many business owners are great when it comes to marketing, (also known as "rain-making" or "schmoozing"). They are terrific at selling themselves and the business. They always have an amusing story or joke to tell, they are up on the latest sports score, and they just have a way of getting people to like them. Unfortunately, and perhaps because they are not detail oriented or service oriented, as soon as the "sale" is made they are off to the next potential customer, the next conquest.

When the business was just starting, the owner took care of everything, including service. But, as soon as he found a reason for leaving the detail-oriented aspects of customer relations to others, he did.

> It's ironic that the more successful your business becomes, the less time you spend with your established customers—the very customers on whom your success was based.

You Like Customer Service, but You Can't Do Everything

As the business grows, you realize that you can't be everywhere at once. You find that you must delegate at least some customer service to your employees. Unfortunately, what you may also find is that your employees do not care as much as you do about whether the customer is satisfied.

Be careful, though, because there are also dangers in having employees who are too good at customer service and who, because you are so busy, have unrestricted access to your customers.

Adam has built a successful manufacturing business. He has always been the "front man" and is so completely identified with the business and its product that no new customer is "brought aboard" without Adam personally "closing the deal."

Over the years Adam has turned over more and more responsibility to his employees, Elizabeth and Carl, to deal with his established customers. Elizabeth and Carl are sharp, detail oriented, and ambitious. They also feel unappreciated and underpaid.

As a result of their frequent contact with Elizabeth and Carl, Adam's customers have developed a personal relationship with each.

One day, Elizabeth and Carl enter Adam's office and tender their resignations. It turns out that Elizabeth and Carl have decided to start their own business and, by the way, they will be taking most of Adam's established customers with them.

The Luster and Excitement Have Gone

The fact of the matter is, you have become complacent, even bored, with your long-time established customers. You want to take your company in new directions, to play in the "big leagues." The

> You must delegate at least some customer service to your employees.

problem is that the little customers on whom you have based your success don't quite fit into your new image.

These reasons are not exclusive and, in your case, there may be others. And the fact is that the reasons are not always invalid. Sometimes, a change in customers is necessary. In fact, sometimes a change is essential to survival, for both you and the business. But when you are making any change that may affect customer satisfaction, make sure that you are doing it for the right reasons, and not simply because you are bored, or overworked, or hate dealing with the details of customer service. Remember, a good customer is too good to lose.

> Remember, a good customer is too good to lose.

Your Highest Rate of Return May Come from Your Established Customers

John has allocated $10,000 per year to identifying, locating, and making a sale to one prospective customer. He has determined that, for every $10,000 he spends, he locates ten good leads. Of those ten leads, two actually place an order for equipment. Each customer purchases $25,000 per year in equipment orders. So, with two new customers placing $25,000 in orders, John breaks even on his $10,000 investment in the first year.

John also allocates $1,000 per year in promotional items, dinners, and service calls on established customers, who also spend $25,000 per year in equipment orders. (So, for every customer that John keeps after the first year, he makes $6,500 in gross profit after reducing the actual gross of 30% by the $1,000 in promotional costs per year.) His old customers mean profits, his new ones are only potential.

It's Easier to Service Customers with Whom You Are Familiar

Remember, despite all of the excitement of new faces, new territories, and new markets, you will have an easier time servicing your established customers than the new ones.

Knowledge of the Business

Over the years you gain a knowledge of your client that is essential to servicing the account. You may know that the customer likes deliveries on a certain day of the week. Or, you may know that the customer wants invoices monthly as opposed to on the date of delivery. You may even get to know who the weak employees of your customer are and then compensate for them.

Cathy has been selling machine parts to "Bob's Automotive Warehouse" for years. Cathy was annoyed by the fact that Bob's son ("Bobby Jr."), who happened to be in charge of inventory control, never got it together enough to place an order more than 24 hours in advance of when it was needed. The order was always a rush and it always cost Cathy more (in time, money, and aggravation) to fill the order than with her other customers.

Cathy knows that Bobby Jr. is a weak link. She also knows that the chances of Bobby Jr. being fired are nonexistent and that Bobby Jr. will probably end up owning the company after his father retires.

Because she knows all of this, Cathy places a telephone call to Bobby Jr.'s secretary, Carla, every week just to see what "Bob's Automotive Warehouse" anticipates needing. Carla is efficient (she has to be to cover up for Bobby Jr.) and lets Cathy know exactly what "Bob's" needs that week.

Conclusion: Bobby Jr. looks good. Bobby Sr. appreciates the fact that Bobby Jr. looks good. Carla appreciates the fact that she doesn't have to deal with a daily ordering emergency. Cathy gets the order and avoids the aggravation and additional cost of selling to "Bob's." Cathy also ends up with most of "Bob's" business because no other supplier knows just how weak Bobby Jr. is (or how competent Carla is).

If you are efficient, you have taken what you know about your customers and placed it into a file. (There are even software programs available that provide a format for the organization of this

> If you are efficient, you have taken what you know about your customers and placed it into a file.

type of information, including dates of service calls, memos of previous conversations, and additional matters of importance.)

Knowledge of Key People

Sometimes, knowing your customer's employees can be as important as knowing the customer. Over the years you learn which employees have influence within the customer's organization. You may want to record their birthdays or anniversaries so that you can send a card. You may also learn their personal interests so that you can establish a personal relationship unrelated to business. (In the end, it's all related to business.)

Emotional Attachment (Customer Loyalty)

Don't kid yourself, emotional attachments are everywhere, including business. In the end, emotional attachment may not help when your competitor is offering product at half your cost, but it is what will keep you in "the game" and viable even during bad times.

Emotional attachments are not automatic and they do not arise from one or two orders over a year. They are built over many years, and many conversations, and many shared interests. Try doing that with a brand new customer!

Servicing the Customer

There are literally hundreds of ways to service a customer, depending upon the type of business, industry, employees, etc. The one thing that is essential is that you "know the customer."

> If you promise to do something by a certain day, do it by that day. Few things irritate people more than waiting for things that were promised to be done.

- *Follow up on every delivery with a telephone call to make sure that everything was alright.* Did the order arrive on time, was there damage, was the order correct and, if not, what can be done to correct it?
- *If you promise to do something by a certain day, do it by that day.* Few things irritate people more than waiting for things that were promised to be done.

Be realistic, this is probably not your only customer and you probably have other things to do. Correcting an incorrect delivery or checking into a special order may only take you four hours but, depending upon your workload, it may not be realistic to think that it can be done in less than two days.

Your customers will often understand that certain things take time. If something is likely to take two days, then tell the customer it will take two days. And then, make sure you do it in two days!

Better yet, see if the customer will be satisfied with three days and then do it in two. The customer will love the fact that it was done early.

• *Keep the lines of communication open.* You may find that the loud mouthed, overbearing, customer who you can barely tolerate is the customer you will keep the longest. Why? Because you never have to wonder where you stand. If he has a problem, he tells you. After all, you can't fix something if you don't know it's broken.

What you have to be careful of is the customer who never complains. (Remember, no one is that good. At some point every customer will have a problem.) For any number of different reasons, however, the customer may not tell you.

Adam has sold material to "Roberta's Sewing Barn" for three years. Adam likes Roberta because she is pleasant to deal with, never complains, and pays all invoices within twenty days.

Roberta, however, has always been irritated by the invoices sent by Adam. It seems that Adam has been burned by nonpaying customers in the past. As a result, Adam has inserted certain language in his invoices regarding late payments, which Roberta finds somewhat insulting; particularly when she has never been a problem and had always paid on time.

One day, Adam realizes that he hasn't received any orders from Roberta in three weeks. He calls her,

> Better yet, see if the customer will be satisfied with three days and then do it in two. The customer will love the fact that it was done early.

only to be advised by a secretary that Roberta is purchasing from another supplier.

Had Adam known about the invoices, he could have changed the ones sent to Roberta in less than five minutes, and would have gladly done so. As it is, Roberta is gone and Adam is still left wondering why.

- *Communication is a two-way street.* Communication is more than simply learning about your client's needs and wants. Communication allows you to let the client learn about you.

  Sometimes there are simple, honest misunderstandings between people. Business relationships are no different.

  Jason received an order from Helen, which, because of a transit strike in the Midwest, could not be filled on time.

  Not wanting to disappoint Helen, a long-time customer, Jason went "above and beyond the call of duty," calling in favors from around the industry just so that Helen could have her order within three days after the planned delivery date.

  Unless Jason says something, Helen only knows that Jason was late and that, as a result, he is going to have problems with his customers.

  Helen is one of those customers who does not always complain and Jason, because he was trying to be a "can-do" kind of guy, never told her about his efforts. Unfortunately, the relationship has never been more strained.

  When Helen pays Jason's invoice late (to make up for the late delivery) Jason tells her to find another supplier.

> Communication is more than simply learning about your client's needs and wants. Communication allows you to let the client learn about you.

For more information on this topic, visit our Web site at www.businesstown.com

Collecting What You Are Owed

Remember, not all of the problems you face with your customer will be your fault. The problem is not always something that can be fixed and is not always something that should be fixed.

One problem you will undoubtedly face will be when your customer is more than a little slow at paying your bill.

Debt collection is something you had better be prepared to deal with, because one nonpaying customer can be enough to wipe out the profit you earned on all of your other customers put together. Remember, when a customer doesn't pay, you lose not only the profit you would have earned but also the money that went into the product that was sold to the nonpaying customer.

> One nonpaying customer can be enough to wipe out the profit you earned on all of your other customers put together.

Adam's company produced detergent specifically for use in cleaning automobiles. Competition is fierce and the profit is "razor-thin." Adam sells a gallon of detergent for $10 and makes $1 of profit on each gallon.

Bob has been a client of Adam's for five years. He is not the fastest-paying client, but all of his invoices are eventually paid.

Last year, Bob purchased 5,000 gallons of detergent in the largest single order Adam has ever received. Three months later, Adam has received nothing on Bob's $50,000 account balance. At month six, Adam hears about Bob's bankruptcy.

Forget about Adam's lost profit of $5,000. He is out the $45,000 that it cost him to produce the product. That is not something that he is going to be able to recover from without great difficulty, if he can recover at all.

What Could Adam Have Done? What Can You Do?

Get a Credit Application

Before you start doing business with a customer you should have that customer complete and submit a credit application. The credit application should include information such as the type of the customer's business (that is, whether it is a corporation, a partnership, a proprietorship, etc.), and, if it is a partnership, the names and addresses of each of the partners. (This will make your job a lot easier if you have to file a lawsuit to collect your money.)

The credit application should also list various trade or credit references (and remember that it is useless to ask for references if you are not going to check them out).

The credit application should set a limit on the dollar amount of credit. And then make sure that you do not go over that limit without either a very good reason or added security.

Get a Guaranty

Remember that one of the biggest reasons that people choose to operate as corporations is to protect themselves from personal liability for business debts. Consequently, the fact that you insist upon a personal guaranty makes your chances of collecting your invoices that much better. Guaranties come in a variety of shapes and forms, and very simple guaranties can be included in a one-page credit application. It is amazing what people will sign when they see nothing but success on the horizon. Years later, when they are the verge of bankruptcy, they will be shocked to see that they personally guaranteed the corporation's obligation to your business.

Correspondence

Make sure that you periodically correspond with the customer and commit to writing the fact that there are no problems with past deliveries or the quality of goods sold. This will be invaluable if you have to file suit to collect the debt. (More on this later.)

Establish a Credit Policy

One of the most difficult decisions you will have to make is when to finally "pull the plug" on a customer.

If you were to speak with 100 individuals whose businesses were in dire financial circumstances and about to fail, almost all

> The fact that you insist upon a personal guaranty makes your chances of collecting your invoices that much better.

would tell you that they were "on the road to recovery," that their "ship was coming in," that they were "turning the corner," or that they could see the "light at the end of the tunnel."

You want to help. You want to believe. And because you are either soft-hearted or soft-headed, you extend the credit even though you know better.

A well-considered credit policy will give you some anchorage when the customer pleads for more credit. It will also allow you to make a reasoned decision as to how you want to balance the risks of bad debt with the benefits of sales.

Learn About the Customer

Learning about the customer does more than allow you to make the sale and service the account. Knowing about the customer allows you to get a handle on the customer and his business, to understand how his business and his industry are doing financially. Make sure that your salespeople are attentive to the warning signs of a troubled business. Talk with other suppliers.

Keep Copies of Customer Checks

If you do win in court, the easiest place to get money is directly from their bank.

Review Accounts Receivable on a Monthly Basis

Computer billing programs offer much more than simply invoicing. Use that capability. You can generate reports by customer, by date, by age, by product, by almost anything you want. And in so doing, you may be able to spot the danger signs. For example:

- Has there been a change in the amount or type of purchases? An increase in the volume of purchases may suggest that other suppliers have stopped doing business with the customer. The same is true if the customer suddenly starts purchasing product from you that he always used to purchase from someone else. Find out why.

> Knowing about the customer allows you to get a handle on the customer and his business, to understand how his business and his industry are doing financially.

- Has the customer who has always paid within 30 days now going 90 days before paying the bill? One of the first things a business in trouble will do is slow down on payables.
- Periodically obtain an updated credit report on the customer. See if the credit report is listing any problems such as new and numerous lawsuits, judgments, or tax filing.
- Watch out for the "Swan Song." A business in trouble may try to make a one-time profit on a large credit purchase.

William is in trouble and he knows it. He is having trouble making payroll, and don't even ask him about the IRS. He is fast approaching the point where he will not be able to purchase the inventory he needs to sell to his customers.

William decides to place an order with Mike for 5,000 gallons of detergent. It is the largest order he has ever placed at one time. William figures that, with this order filled, he will be able to generate enough cash to "keep the wolves away"; at least for the time being. The cash he generates will allow him to make payroll and keep the lights on. The one thing it will not be used for is to pay Mike.

William knows that Mike's business is competitive and that, even after Mike stops selling to him, he will be able to buy from another supplier.

> Periodically obtain an updated credit report on the customer. See if the credit report is listing any problems such as new and numerous lawsuits, judgments, or tax filing.

The Party's Over

At some point in time you are going to have to take a customer's statement of account and mark it as a bad debt. You may still sell product to the customer, but all sales will be cash on delivery. There will be no more credit. With this simple act, the relationship has changed, perhaps irrevocably. You are now a creditor, and worse, your customer is now a debtor.

Now, you have to figure out how to collect the money owed to you.

Make a Collection File for Each Customer

If suit becomes necessary, your memory, scribbled memos, and computer-generated reports will be of limited use to your attorneys.

In the collection file, make sure that you have placed the credit application, any credit reports, and copies of the unpaid invoices, along with information as to the merchandise ordered, the date ordered, the date delivered, and the unit prices of the merchandise. Include any delivery receipts and any correspondence with the customer. (Remember we told you to periodically correspond with the customer to confirm that there were no problems.) It will surprise you when the customer who had never complained of anything now claims that he won't pay you because the merchandise was junk or wasn't delivered at all.

Send a Demand Letter

Make sure the letter details the amount of the debt and makes demand for full payment within a reasonably short period of time. Make sure that the customer is told that you will be charging interest on the debt.

If you are willing to accept installment payments, tell the customer that. But remember, never step back, never retreat. You have gone this far. You didn't want to do it, but it was necessary. Do not declare a victory and go home just because the customer promised that he would pay the bill. If you say that you are going to file suit within ten days, make sure that you do. Do not make any threats that you cannot back up. At this point in the relationship credibility is crucial.

If you enter into a payment arrangement, try to include as many of the following terms as possible:

- Establish payment terms—the amount of payment and the day of the month when due.
- Have the customer admit to the debt. This will help considerably if the customer stops making the payments and a lawsuit becomes necessary.
- Have the customer agree to let judgment be entered in your favor to protect you in the event that he fails to make the payments promised.

> In the collection file, make sure that you have placed the credit application, any credit reports, and copies of the unpaid invoices, along with information as to the merchandise ordered, the date ordered, the date delivered, and the unit prices of the merchandise.

Collection Agencies

Depending upon where your customer is located, you may find it useful to engage a collection agency. The benefits are as follows:

- They are created and operated solely for the purpose of collecting money. Because it is all that they do, they will probably be better at it than you are.
- Because of the number of their clients and their contacts in the commercial community, they may already have information on the debtor that will allow them to move quickly to collect your money.
- Collection agencies have access to a large number of collection attorneys in the geographical area where the debtor is located. This is particularly useful if the customer is located across the country.
- Agencies know which of the collection attorneys in an area are best for a certain job.
- Because of the number of collection cases they handle, they have considerably more influence over the collection attorney than you will ever have.
- Collection agencies usually work on commission. You don't pay unless they collect.
- Collection agencies can refer your case to attorneys who also work on commission.

Get to an Attorney

In collection matters, time is money!

Understand, collection law is not brain surgery. But this does not mean that just any attorney will do. You want a collection attorney. You want someone who understands that collection is a matter of applying pressure and keeping up that pressure until the debtor pays. You want someone who understands not just the time value of money, but also that you are being hurt, perhaps irreparably, by the delay in payment.

It may be possible for you to handle your own legal work, but because your business is something other than law, you will not

> Collection agencies usually work on commission. You don't pay unless they collect.

be nearly as effective or as efficient as an attorney. It will also take time away from that which you are most profitable at, running your business.

Streetwise Reality Tour

1. Sometimes, and despite your best efforts, customers want to go to someone else.
2. "The customer is always right" may be a nifty slogan but, in fact, the customer is not always right and sometimes you are better off without him.
3. For all of your efforts you are going to have customers who won't pay you.
4. Don't be fooled into thinking that your business is successful just because you are busy. If you are not being paid or don't expect to be paid, your activity is just wasted time. Better to dump the nonpaying customer and go home early to see your family.
5. Is it our imagination or are nonpaying customers also the biggest complainers and the customers who make the most demands on your time? Oh, let's not forget that the time you spend with nonpaying customers is time taken away from paying customers. Kill three birds with one stone, get rid of them!

> If you are not being paid or don't expect to be paid, your activity is just wasted time.

For more information on this topic, visit our Web site at www.businesstown.com

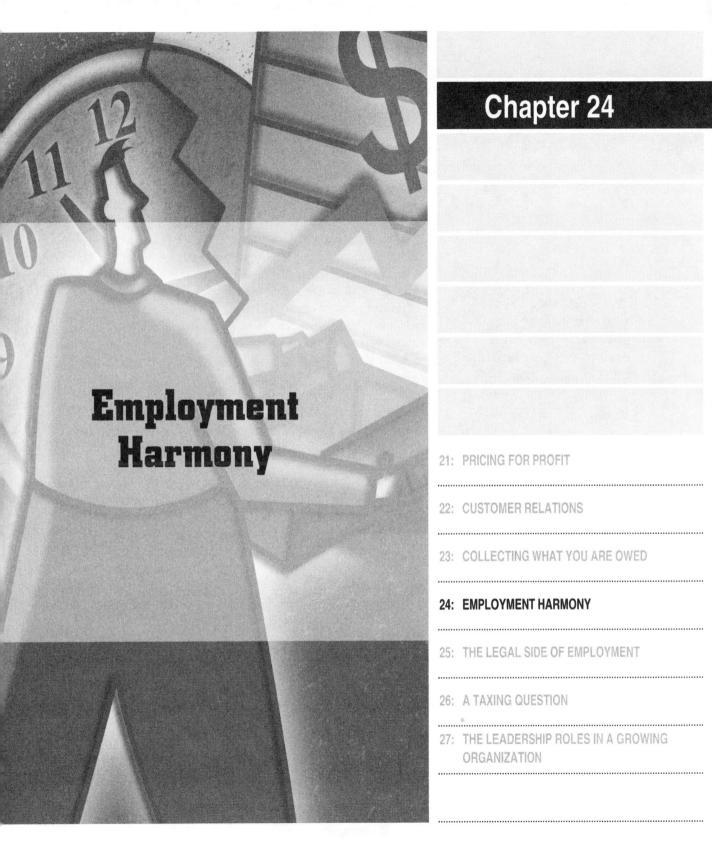

Chapter 24

Employment Harmony

A dam has finally arrived. After years of struggle his business is humming like a well-oiled machine. Why would he ever look back, why would he ever long for those days when he worked at a desk in his basement and was responsible for everything from sales calls, to manufacturing, to stuffing envelopes? Why? Employees, that's why!

When you think about starting a business it is easy to underestimate the complexities inherent in having employees. After all, you hire people, you tell them what to do, you pay them to do it, and they do it. What's so hard about that?

Nothing is hard about it, so long as the employees you hire have no intelligence, no independent motivation, no personality, no emotional baggage, no petty jealousies, no spouses, no children, no time conflicts, no illnesses—do we have to go on, or are you getting the idea?

The world is made up of all kinds of people. Some are team players, some are complainers, some seem to think that the world owes them a living, and others, still, think that they should be able to do whatever they want, whenever they want, regardless of what you want them to do.

> Employees come to you with a whole range of issues that have been derived from a whole lifetime of experiences—all different experiences.

The fact is that employees come to you with a whole range of issues that have been derived from a whole lifetime of experiences—all different experiences. These employees will be spending anywhere from one-third to one-half of their waking hours with you and your business, doing your work, or getting to or going home from your business. And, even after they are home, they often deal with the stresses of the job.

Whether you like it or not you are going to have to figure out a way to take these very diverse individuals and make them work together as a team. And, like it or not, you had better be prepared to protect yourself in the event that you can't.

Some of the concepts discussed in this chapter were first touched upon in Chapter 11, Motivating New Employees. Why is this? Because, as you might expect, many of the issues that affect employee motivation are also crucial to keeping employee harmony within the workplace.

Employee Handbooks

It is amazing how flexible you can be when you have just one employee and how drastically that changes when you add the second.

With two employees you need to treat each equally. Even if there were no laws that required an employer to treat all employees equally, just see what happens when you start favoring one employee over another.

The fact is, if you have any employees, and certainly if you have more than one employee, you had better have an employee handbook. An employee handbook is a written statement of the terms and conditions of employment as well as the rules that apply to employee conduct.

One issue you must pay careful attention to is whether the employee handbook is simply a statement of goals and policies or whether it acts like a contract, in effect, giving your employees rights which can be enforced in court. Let's look at an example from Chapter 12.

> On a sunny Friday afternoon, Adam is called into Bob's office and notified that he is being terminated. Adam is told that the reason for his firing is because he is always late for work. This is the first time Adam has heard such a complaint.
>
> With time on his hands, Adam decides to look through the employee handbook, which he had using to prop up a short leg on his desk.
>
> There, in section 8, is the company policy for the termination of employees. Included is an entire system of notices, warnings, and informal hearings, all of which were to be utilized prior to termination.
>
> With this in hand, Adam skipped along to his attorney's office to review the planned lawsuit against Bob for breach of contract and unlawful termination.
>
> Too bad the handbook did not say that it was a guide for the employer, only, and did not confer any rights.

> One issue you must pay careful attention to is whether the employee handbook is simply a statement of goals and policies or whether it acts like a contract.

As a result of the language of the employee handbook the jury found that a contract existed between Adam and his employer. The jury also found that the employer had breached the contract when it fired Adam without following the procedures established in the employee handbook.

You want to make sure that you have the flexibility to deviate from the policies contained in the employee handbook, if that is in the best interests of the company.

At a minimum then, your employee handbook should contain your company's policies on the following:

- Working hours
- Holidays
- Overtime (including how it is allocated among employees)
- Vacation
- Illness
- Personal Time
- Performance Reviews
- Discipline and Discharge
- Policies regarding acceptable behavior with respect to such matters as sexual discrimination, harassment, drugs and alcohol, employee safety, and the personal use of company equipment, (telephones, e-mail, etc.)
- The employee handbook should also make clear that every employee is considered an "At-Will" employee who can be discharged at any time and for any reason, or for no reason at all. (Most states still recognize the "At-Will" employee, although more and more exceptions seem to be created every year.)

With a well-thought-out employee handbook, you will always have something to which you can refer to guide your actions. It may never seem fair to the employee who is asking for the extra time off, but, at the very least, it will allow you to apply the rules uniformly to all employees; and there is a certain fairness in that which will help to prevent problems.

> With a well-thought-out employee handbook, you will always have something to which you can refer to guide your actions.

The Performance Review

Few things seem to be as dreaded (by either the employer or the employee) as the performance review. At the same time, few things you do can serve as many useful goals.

A performance review facilitates the following:

- *It requires you to sit down and think about what the job requires and what a successful employee needs to do in the job.*

    This is extremely important. Few things are more unfair to an employee than being criticized for not doing work, or doing work poorly, that he didn't even know he was required to do. Don't leave your employees in limbo. Know what the job entails and make sure that the employee knows what is expected of him.

- *It requires you to sit down and take the time to assess the skills or accomplishments of a particular employee.*

    If you haven't already realized it, as the owner of a business you are going to be extremely busy. It is practically a certainty that you will be too busy, on almost any given day, to sit down and consider the accomplishments of a particular employee. Your life will be a blur and your memory of a particular employee will consist of the fact that on one day, you were pleased with his performance or on another, you were disappointed.

    More likely than not, your pleasure or disappointment with the employee will have to do more with the fact that he made your life easier or more difficult on a particular day.

> Few things are more unfair to an employee than being criticized for not doing work, or doing work poorly, that he didn't even know he was required to do.

Sean was swamped. He had three meetings scheduled before 10:00 A.M. and hadn't even started preparing the financial reports that the bank needed to see before the end of the day. Sean could feel his stomach churn and his head pound.

When Sean found out that Bob, one of his salesmen, had already taken care of two of his meetings for him, he was thrilled.

"Thank God for Bob," muttered Sean. "I don't know what I would do without him."

Without a formal performance review, Bob can't expect to receive a bonus. The problem is that Bob is supposed to be a salesman, not a manager. Bob's job has nothing to do with what Sean was happy about. Bob will be rewarded for doing something that has nothing to do with his job. And what about the other salesmen who are doing well at their jobs? What type of signal does this send to Bob and his fellow salesmen?

The performance review requires Sean to sit down and assess Bob's performance as a salesman in comparison with other salesmen. Sean can still reward Bob for his initiative on that terrible day, but it will be only one factor to consider along with the others.

- *It gives you the opportunity to motivate your employees.*

Many supervisors use the performance review to comment upon the failings of an employee and to detail the manner and times the employee has fallen short of the goals set for him. Even those supervisors who attempt to praise an employee do so mostly because they are told that they should, or they are trying to make the employee feel better about a less-than-stellar review.

A performance review is a perfect time to engage the employee in a discussion about the job. Let the employee know that you are interested enough to offer several examples of his accomplishments. Solicit the employee's comments. Not only does this type of exchange positively affect morale, but it motivates the employee to do better.

- *It creates a record for an adverse employment action.*

The performance review may be the one place where you can establish a record of employee problems and the efforts to deal with them. It may set the stage for disciplinary action or a discharge of the employee.

> A performance review is a perfect time to engage the employee in a discussion about the job.

Too many times, an employee is discharged from a job without ever previously being told that his work was, in some way, deficient. Without any warning of a possible adverse action, the employee may well suspect that there is "more to the firing than meets the eye."

On a Friday afternoon, Adam was summoned to his boss's office and was told that he was being fired. His boss told Adam that his work was careless and that there was no sign of improvement in the last year.

Adam was in shock. He had no idea that his job was even in jeopardy. He started to think that there was more to his firing than the lame excuses given by his former boss.

Adam's attorney tells him that, because Adam is over 40 years old, he may be protected by the federal "Age Discrimination in Employment Act." Because of that federal law, the employer must prove that the firing was unrelated to Adam's age.

Unfortunately for Adam's former boss, Adam has always received good comments in his annual performance reviews. The jury will not believe that Adam's firing had anything to do with the quality of his work when there is nothing in his employment file that reflects any problems.

Adam spends the next several months lying on the beach counting the money from his lucrative jury verdict.

> Too many times, an employee is discharged from a job without ever previously being told that his work was, in some way, deficient.

For more information on this topic, visit our Web site at www.businesstown.com

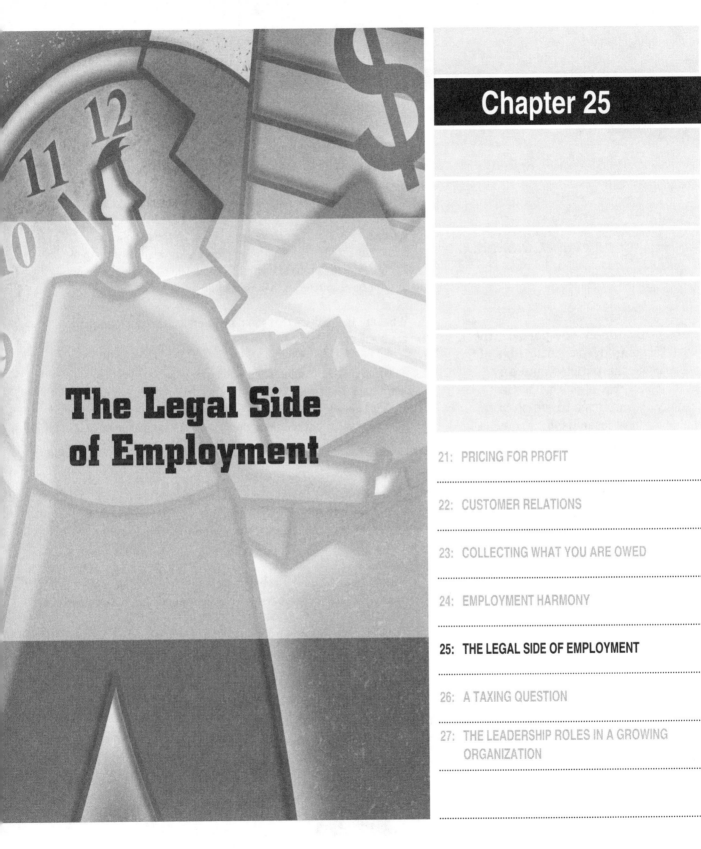

Chapter 25

The Legal Side of Employment

A s you have probably deduced, the key to avoiding, or at least minimizing, legal problems with your employees is to:

- Establish rational policies that are applied equally to all employees;
- Ensure that your employees are aware of those policies;
- Document the policies, the employee's knowledge of the policies, and any problems with the employee to which you may later have to refer in the event of litigation.

What are the policies that should be understood and followed? Here are some examples:

- The employee handbook does not create any contractual rights in the employee;
- Employees are "At-Will" employees and can, therefore, be discharged at any time, for any reason, or for no reason at all;
- Employees are to be on the job during the official work hours;
- Employees are to be suitably dressed for the particular job, including protective clothing, if warranted;
- Any personal use of business property, telephones, or accrual of long distance charges (even postage stamps, and office supplies) may be grounds for disciplinary action;
- The use of drugs or alcohol, or being under the effects of either, while at the work site, may be grounds for disciplinary action;
- Policy regarding nondiscrimination (for any reason);
- Policy regarding sexual harassment.

Some of these policies, and particularly those dealing with discrimination and sexual harassment should be contained in a separate disclosure statement, which the employee is required to sign and return to you.

> Document the policies, the employee's knowledge of the policies, and any problems with the employee to which you may later have to refer in the event of litigation.

In addition, you may also want to go so far as to offer short seminars to employees as to what constitutes discrimination or harassment.

For all of your efforts it is still possible that, for example, an employee can be harassed sexually while on the job. Should that happen, the employee can sue both the offending employee and the company. But, if you can demonstrate that the company was unaware of the specific situation and, in addition, had implemented measures to prevent such conduct, it has a good chance of avoiding an adverse verdict.

Investigation

In addition to the documentation of problems discussed previously, you must be prepared to investigate any of the following:

- *Reports of discrimination or harassment.* In the event of litigation, you must be prepared to show that you investigated the allegations and took appropriate action.
- *Reports of Injuries.* Employees can become hurt while on the job. Unfortunately, on many occasions employees can exaggerate the extent of their injuries or claim that a non-work injury occurred while on the job. You should be prepared to investigate and document the claim of injury, as well as how it occurred.

  The last thing you want is to be perceived as a "patsy" for employees looking to live off of workers' compensation. Consequently, you will want to coordinate the handling of compensation claims with your insurance carrier.

- *Reports of hazardous conditions at the work site.* If suit is brought, whether by an employee or someone else (a visitor to the site or even a trespasser), you always want to be in the position of appearing willing to investigate and acting responsibly with respect to potential hazards. Even if you lose the lawsuit, the damages may be limited because the company was perceived as willing to assume responsibility for attempting to avoid the injury.

> You will want to coordinate the handling of compensation claims with your insurance carrier.

At a minimum, be prepared to document the following:

- The day and time of the report
- The details of the complaint
- Who made the complaint
- The findings of the investigation
- The conclusion, as well as any disciplinary action

Ready, Aim, Fired!

Sooner or later you are going to have to fire someone. There are many ways to do it, and suggestions for how best to do it. Consider the following:

- *If a firing becomes necessary, do not let it become fodder for office gossip.*

  It is between the company and the employee and no one else. Letting the matter become "public" invites the employee to engage in "face-saving" denials and lawsuits. You may also find that you have opened the door to allegations of slander and disparagement. Remember, in most states, you do not need a reason to fire an "At-Will" employee. So, don't feel compelled to give anyone a reason. It's nobody else's business.

- *Notify the employee of his discharge at the end of the day on a Friday afternoon.*

  You want to avoid a situation where the fired employee returns to his office and attempts to work for the rest of the day. You also want to avoid the inevitable discussions and work disruptions that will occur as word of the firing spreads through the office.

  By waiting until the end of the day, the office will be quiet, and some employees will have already left the office for the weekend. The discharged employee can immediately leave the office without attracting attention, and you have the weekend to go through the employee's work folders and make plans for completing his work the following Monday morning.

> If a firing becomes necessary, do not let it become fodder for office gossip. It is between the company and the employee and no one else.

- *Avoid the employee's efforts at negotiating the firing. The decision has to be final.*

  Expect that the employee will try to negotiate the firing, to promise that he will improve. If you have done everything right, the employee is already aware of the problem and has already been given the opportunity to improve.

  After the shock has passed, and assuming that the employee is not without some redeeming characteristics, suggest that the company can assist with job placement or an appropriate recommendation for future employment. Depending upon the circumstances, you may offer to continue medical or pension benefits for a reasonable amount of time or grant him a severance payment.

  In exchange for this assistance, you will want the employee to sign a release whereby he agrees that he has no claim against you or the company for any improper or unlawful conduct.
- *Have the employee escorted from the office.*

  This may seem like kicking a person when he is down, but remember that disgruntled employees can wreak havoc if unattended and they are of a mind to do so. Just consider how easy it might be for a knowledgeable employee to damage the office computer system, delete irreplaceable customer records, or possibly even copy confidential trade information for later use or sale to a competitor.
- *Notify the building security that the employee has left the company and ensure that his access to the office is terminated.*

  This is self-explanatory: once the employee is out, he's out.
- *Make sure that the employee's supervisors are aware of the situation so they can handle work flow and customer inquiries.*

> Avoid the employee's efforts at negotiating the firing. The decision has to be final.

Unemployment Compensation

Most states provide for unemployment compensation. The idea is to provide the employee for some income when he becomes unemployed through no fault of his own.

Lay-offs, seasonal slow-downs, or simple realignments all allow the employee to file for compensation. In fact, compensation is usually payable even when the dismissal was the result of the employee not being very good at his job. The key here is to distinguish between not being good at the job and "willful misconduct."

Willful misconduct requires that the employee actually violate some company rule or directive and is fired because of it. (Another reason you want to investigate and document employee problems.)

An employee can also be entitled to unemployment compensation even though he quits the job.

Liz has worked for the same company for three years. One day the company announces that it is moving its offices 40 miles away. Because she is such a good worker, however, Liz is told that she still has his job and will be given a small raise for the inconvenience.

Liz quits the job because the extra drive is just too much for her on a daily basis.

Because the condition of her employment has changed so much, Liz's resignation is considered as a discharge entitling her to unemployment compensation.

Independent Contractors

One of the things that you may find useful is the "independent contractor."

Quite simply, an independent contractor is not an employee of the company but is hired by the company to perform certain types of duties or for a limited period of time.

The benefit of the independent contractor is that you pay him the agreed salary and don't have to worry about such things as withholding for taxes, pension contributions, health insurance, or workers' compensation. And, when the job is finished, you face no problems regarding unlawful firings or even unemployment compensation.

> Willful misconduct requires that the employee actually violate some company rule or directive and is fired because of it.

It is a perfect answer for those times when you may need a specialized expertise on a short-term basis or you need services that are typically beyond what your company offers.

If it sounds too good to be true, maybe it is too good to be true. There are two big problems with independent contractors.

- Many businesses hire independent contractors to do the work of its regular employees.

  They think that it is a great way to avoid all of the various obligations that come with employees, like the employer taxes, unemployment compensation premiums, etc. The problem is that the Internal Revenue Service is aware of this type of abuse and has set very strict rules on the use of independent contractors.

  The long and short of it is, if the independent contractor 1) does the work of your usual employees, even on a short term basis; or 2) is told how to do the work and must complete the work in the manner directed by you, the chances are that the IRS will say that they are employees, and not independent contractors.

- If you have a union it will be very upset when it sees work going to nonunion employees.

  Not only does the use of independent contractors take work away from the union members, but it also reduces the contributions that will be made to such things as union pension and benefit plans.

> If it sounds too good to be true, maybe it is too good to be true.

Fair Labor Standards Act

A full discussion of the Fair Labor Standards Act (FLSA) is beyond the scope of this book. Nevertheless, the FLSA is what requires the following:

- *Minimum Wage.* Applicable to all employees (four major exceptions being the "executive" exemption, the "administrative" exemption, the "professional" exemption, and the "outside salesperson" exemption). There are a number of other exemptions, however, and you will want to discuss this with your attorney or accountant to make sure whether you are exempt.

Be aware that there are also a variety of minimum wage laws applicable to particular industries (Davis-Bacon for federal works projects; the Walsh-Healy Act for work on government contracts for supplies exceeding $10,000).

- *Overtime.* The FLSA requires that an employer pay overtime to employees at the rate of one and one-half times the employees' regular rate for hours in excess of forty hours in a "workweek."
- *Child Labor.* The FLSA also restricts the use of child labor unless otherwise exempt under the statute. In addition, certain jobs and industries are totally prohibited to individuals of certain ages (14, 16, and 18).
- *Record Keeping, Posters Display, Inspections.* The FLSA requires that various records be maintained so as to allow its inspectors to determine whether you are complying with the Act. In addition, you may be required to post various signs required by the "Wage and Hour Division" of the Department of Labor.

Health and Safety

The federal government and most states have laws that govern safety in the workplace.

- Occupational Safety and Health Act (OSHA)
- Mine Safety and Health Act (MSHA)
- National Environmental Policy Act
- Federal Clean Air Act
- Federal Water Pollution Control Act
- Hazardous Waste Control Laws
- Migrant Health Act

> Be aware that there are also a variety of minimum wage laws applicable to particular industries (Davis-Bacon for federal works projects; the Walsh-Healy Act for work on government contracts for supplies exceeding $10,000).

A Plague on Society or the Protector of the Worker?

We're not going to go into any discussion about the merits of a union. The fact is that they exist, and the day may come when you have to deal with one. Even before you deal with a union, however, you will have to deal with efforts to have your business unionized.

This is a complex area and well beyond the scope of this book. If there is one piece of information you get from this chapter, it is that at the first serious word about unionization, you should see an attorney experienced in labor law. Do not try to prevent unionization on your own, and do not attempt to do anything without competent legal advice.

Be aware that certain efforts at discouraging employees from unionizing, or discriminating against those employees who try to bring in a union, will start litigation, including possible investigations and monetary penalties by the National Labor Relations Board (NLRB).

Do not try to prevent unionization on your own, and do not attempt to do anything without competent legal advice.

Streetwise Reality Tour

1. If an employee is mad enough he will sue you, no matter what you do, say, or can document.
2. The person most likely to disregard an employee handbook is you.
3. An employee handbook that you disregard is worthless.
4. It costs money to lose employees.

For more information on this topic, visit our Web site at www.businesstown.com

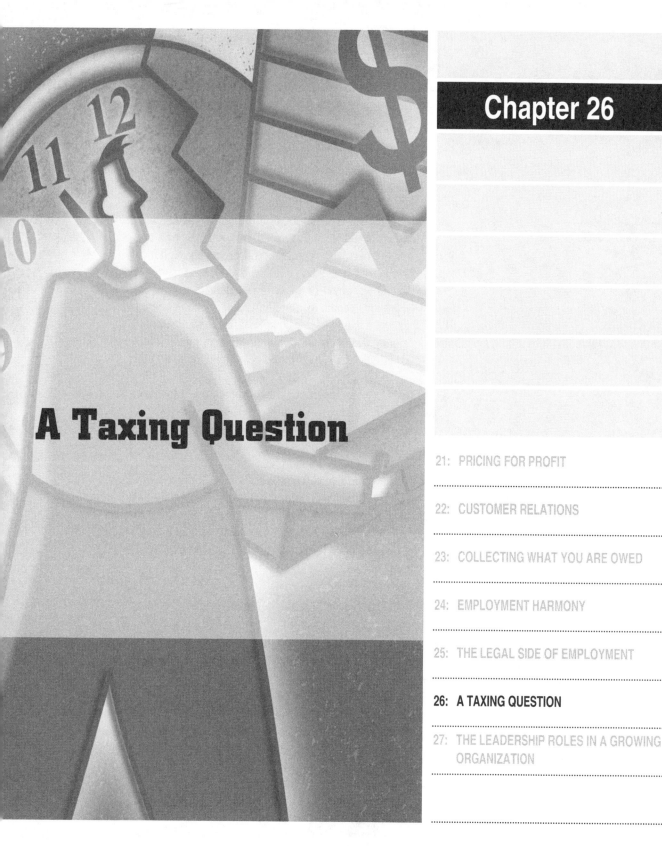

Chapter 26

A Taxing Question

Frank opened his restaurant and even he was surprised at the success. It became the "in" place and was crowded much of the time. He hardly had time to do all of his day-to-day tasks much less keep his books up to date. Cash came in and was deposited and credit card money went directly to his account. All through the day, he was into the cash register to pay small bills–$40 for produce, $55 for the beer distributor, and other equally seemingly inconsequential amounts. He put slips in the register, planning to transfer them to a ledger. But that time never came and the slips became lost. At the end of the year, there was $36,000 worth of small expenditures untracked. The money was spent for business, but now the problem was creating a tax return that would stand up to scrutiny.

It may be possible for Frank to reconstruct his records enough to fill out his income tax return, but this oversight should be avoided. Every businessperson must understand that they have a silent partner in their operation; the government–local, state, and federal. Part of your job is to be a tax collector for these bodies in the form of sales tax and employment tax. And once you have worked and earned your profit, they want their share of those profits. In the first case, you need to give them everything they are entitled to, but in the second case, you don't want to pay any more or any less personal or corporate tax than you have to.

> It is usually cost effective to engage a payroll service not only to compute your correct payroll obligations but to remit all of the withholding taxes properly and in a timely manner.

The Employer's Obligation

It is usually cost effective to engage a payroll service not only to compute your correct payroll obligations but to remit all of the withholding taxes properly and in a timely manner. If you only have a few employees, you might find it easier to do the payroll in-house, but remember the time it will take to track and file all of the necessary returns. If you still intend to do so, make sure you are communicating regularly with your accountant and being reminded what must be filed when. Of great importance as well is the depositing of withholding tax in a timely manner according to the government requirement, so that you do not incur a penalty. Some are due concurrent with payroll, some on a monthly basis, and some on a quarterly basis. You or your controller must track all of these dates.

A Serious Matter

There are times when it may be difficult to make a payroll—every small business goes through it. Money that you expected doesn't come in and you're a bit short. Hold paychecks (your own or everyone's), but don't use the money that belongs to the taxing bodies! It is costly and it is a very bad habit to get into. You may well find yourself with a bill for penalty and interest that doubles the original tax! And to make matters more difficult, the IRS has powers to levy your bank account, and even money due you from your customers. Although any other creditor can do this as well (but only after a long court proceeding), the IRS has far greater administrative powers to take such action. Don't borrow money from them!

Employment Taxes

You will withhold and remit income tax to federal, state, and local authorities (Forms 26-01 and 26-02 in the Appendix). You will also withhold the FICA (Social Security and Medicare) tax and pay an equal share as the employer as well. At the end of each quarter you will file a return showing what was due and what was paid.

In addition, as the employer, you will pay a percentage of your payroll to the state and federal government for your unemployment compensation coverage. It is likely you will file and pay these amounts on a quarterly basis. You can actually save money on these taxes by keeping your claims as low as possible. Be careful about hiring for the short term and then laying off, which increases the number of claims. And if someone is fired "for cause," document as much as you can and fight the charge. Letting an employee "quit and collect," for whatever reason, does have a cost to you. You are rated by how much of the money is paid out on benefits: the lower the claims, the lower your rate.

> The IRS has powers to levy your bank account, and even money due you from your customers.

Sales Tax Collection

Here, the amount is clear and the rules very straightforward—you will collect this tax and pay it monthly to your state. Some items, such as food, and in some states, clothing, are nontaxable. If you wholesale to others for resale, you will not collect the tax, they will. And some services are not taxable either. Know the rules and keep your records up to date.

But when you do collect the tax, you must send it in on a timely basis. This is a situation where there is the greatest likelihood of prosecution if you do otherwise. You have collected the money under the authority of your state, it belongs to them, not to you. Don't forget that!

> If you have not incorporated, you will report business income and expense on a schedule C, which will be included with your personal return.

Income Tax—Schedule C

If you have not incorporated, you will report business income and expense on a schedule C, which will be included with your personal return. This type of reporting works best for consultants or other independent professionals. Salespeople who work on a commission-only basis may file this type of schedule in order to deduct any of their business expenses that are not reimbursed. You should meet with your accountant to discuss whether this is applicable to your situation and learn each of the categories of expense you can deduct. Keep a ledger of those items and always keep any back-up receipts. Some valid expenses are as follows:

- Office space—if you rent a separate office, its costs and all of the utilities can be deducted. If you use a home office, make sure you follow all of the rules about the space and the percentages that apply. This can be a red flag for an audit.
- Equipment and supplies—any computers, phones, faxes, and general office supplies are fully deductible.
- Vehicle usage—any business use of a car or truck is eligible—keep careful records of business-only use.
- Books, publications, and memberships in professional organizations also may be used.

- Travel and entertainment—there are rules and limitations that must be followed to make sure you will pass any scrutiny.

The better day-to-day records you keep, the more likely you are to be able to recapture all of your deductions come tax time. Track them on an easy software package such as Quickbooks and keep a file for the actual paper receipts.

The Corporate Return

From the first day you begin to create a new venture, you are acquiring start-up costs that are deductible on your tax return. Any research you do, lawyers and accountants you hire, and expenses of any type you incur can be used as a business expense—even if your company does not even begin doing business in the year you were spending the money. The critical issue here is making sure you have recorded and documented all of the expenses.

You can take up to 60 months to amortize the costs of a start-up. The decision will be based on how much profit you have that needs an offset in deductions. Discuss this at length with your accountant.

Plan the Timing

Adam's print shop just received a very large order in December and it was likely to be shipped right around the last day of the year. This additional revenue was likely to raise his profits so his taxable income would be quite high. Since his customer didn't need the goods until early January, Adam suggested that they ship and bill the day they returned from New Year's break. Everyone's needs were met by this action and Adam was able to lower his taxes.

You should schedule an end-of-the-year review of your company's performance that is done by mid-November (assuming you are

> You can take up to 60 months to amortize the costs of a start-up. The decision will be based on how much profit you have that needs an offset in deductions.

on a calendar year). Determine whether you need income or expense from a tax perspective. If you need additional revenue, perhaps you can pre-bill an order or shipment that is not quite scheduled to go out. If you don't, you may want to do what Adam did and bill a large order right after the first of the year.

The expense side allows for flexibility as well. You can schedule end-of-the-year expenses to occur in the tax period that would benefit you the most. Accelerate a project to the current year or postpone one to the next. Make extra purchases or schedule repairs for the most favorable periods as well.

Using Depreciation to Save Tax

Most tangible business assets, such as machinery, equipment, motor vehicles, and computers, can be depreciated and that amount deducted as expense. What this accomplishes is to account for the decrease in market value of these items. The tax laws govern the length of time you can use to "write off" the value of your assets. Your accountant will be able to give you the details and create a schedule that will be followed for your taxes.

Any buildings that are owned (not leased) and used for business may also be depreciated. This is not true of land since it does not become devalued over a period of time.

Depreciation is a noncash expense that may be used to shelter some profits from taxes. But remember, it is meant to account for the need to replace those items when they are no longer serviceable.

Spend Money to Save Money

Every business files a number of different tax forms, from employment tax (Federal form 94) to corporate tax (Federal Form 1120) to property and usage taxes. The services of a qualified accountant are vital in this area, but there is one additional tip as well. If you meet with your accountant to plan tax strategy at least twice a year—after the first quarter and early in the fourth quarter—to review how you

> Any buildings that are owned (not leased) and used for business may also be depreciated. This is not true of land since it does not become devalued over a period of time.

are doing and plan ways to minimize your taxes, you will pay for the advice but it will be well worth it.

Streetwise Reality Tour

1. Understand all of the taxes you are required to file and make sure they are done in a timely manner.
2. Never borrow money from the IRS—remit all withheld taxes immediately.
3. Failure to pay sales tax may be treated as a criminal offense.
4. The timing of revenue or expense may make a substantial difference in the taxes due.
5. A good accountant should make his fee in the taxes he can save.

> The timing of revenue or expense may make a substantial difference in the taxes due.

For more information on this topic, visit our Web site at www.businesstown.com

Chapter 27

The Leadership Roles in a Growing Organization

Leadership is a very familiar word, but it is a concept that is often misunderstood, particularly in the context of work.

Adam started his business five years ago. He now has ten employees and annual gross sales in excess of $1,000,000.

Adam is the owner of the business and is a very skilled operating guy. By virtue of his title as president and his position as owner, Adam leads his company and directs his employees.

But does "leading" make Adam a "leader"?

> A leader creates the mission for the organization.

What Is a "Leader"?

Vision

A leader creates the mission for the organization. He has a vision of what the organization should become and the place it should hold in the community, the industry of which it is a part, and the lives of its employees. The leader's vision answers the question, "Why are we here?"

In addition to his personal understanding of the vision, the leader, by virtue of his energy, commitment, and interpersonal skills is able to share that vision with his associates and employees. In so doing, the leader motivates, inspires, and energizes the employees to work to their fullest potential.

A leader is never satisfied with the way things are and always looks toward the future. Without the leader's vision the business becomes a job, and the employees merely parts of a machine. The business exists, it functions, but it has no goals, it is adrift.

Leader Is Not the Same as Manager

Being a leader is not the same as being a manager. In its simplest form, a leader sets goals and direction for the managers to implement.

John is a leader. After careful thought and after analyzing the strength of his product as well as that of the competition, he has decided that in ten years his company will sell its product nationwide, will expand its product line to make maximum use of its marketing effort, and have annual gross sales of $10,000,000. John wants his company to become a "player" in the industry. At the same time, John wants his product and the name of his company to be associated with quality, even if it means slower growth.

Despite his best intentions, and while he is great at seeing the "big picture," John is simply not a detail-oriented person.

In addition, while John was competent to manage the company in the early years when he had one employee and worked out of his garage, John realizes that he does not have the business skills, experience, or knowledge necessary to plan and carry out a nationwide marketing campaign. Nor is he capable of planning the purchasing, manufacture, and delivery of the product on a multimillion-dollar scale.

For those reasons John has hired Bob and Carl to be his principal managers. Bob is the engineer who can keep the production line moving and Carl is a "whiz-kid" when it comes to marketing, branding, and sales.

In the course of their staff meetings John will share his vision with Bob and Carl and they will then design the plan for ensuring that the founder's vision (and now theirs) is carried out.

Perceives and Understands the Feelings of Others

The leader in a growing organization is attuned to the thoughts, feelings, and concerns of those with whom he works. His is a "people-centered" point of view.

> The leader in a growing organization is attuned to the thoughts, feelings, and concerns of those with whom he works.

Adam is the President of Adamco, Inc., a company with over 1,000 employees. He is also the youngest of the three shareholders.

The corporation has departments for personnel, engineering, sales, manufacturing, plant safety, and research and development. In addition, the company has an active employees' union with which he must deal.

As might be expected, each department has developed its own identity and goals.

One day, word spreads through the company that Adamco may be awarded a contract which will put it on the "ground floor" of a construction project that will generate a significant profit for the next four years. The contract will, however, require a considerable expense and commitment of resources, which will keep Adamco from diversifying during the term of the contract.

> High volume at a low price per unit will mean very busy days but will not likely bring increased wages.

- The sales department knows that the income of its salesmen is dependent upon the amount of sales. In order to help boost their incomes, as well as their prestige within the company, they want Adamco to get the contract and they want to be as competitive as possible so that they can undercut the other bidders. They also want engineering to assure them a rapid manufacture and delivery.
- The employees' union realizes that the income of its members is based almost entirely upon an hourly wage. High volume at a low price per unit will mean very busy days but will not likely bring increased wages.
- The union employees might be happy if the contract meant more overtime for them, but there is talk of adding an additional shift and actually reducing the amount of overtime available to the current employees.
- The union officials see additional shifts as meaning more union employees, more union dues, and more contributions to the union pension funds.
- Research and development believes that the real future of the company depends upon new and better products. It also knows that when the plant is focused almost entirely upon maximum production of a single item, there is little money or attention given to research and development.

- Of the three shareholders, two are ready for retirement and would like Adamco to get the contract so as to bolster the company's balance sheet. They will then sell their stock to Adam, who, under a buy-sell agreement, is obligated to purchase their shares for a set price based upon the balance sheet.
- The personnel and engineering departments don't have a feeling for or against the contract. They just want to know that they will have jobs ten years down the road and they are concerned that devoting all available resources to one contract may leave the company unable to compete once the contract is over.

Adamco has very good managers in each of its departments. The problem is that they are so busy protecting their own departments, their own staff, and managing their respective duties that there is no coordination of effort. They are competing over funding, profits, resources, and prestige. Because they are good managers, they are doing their respective jobs very efficiently. Unfortunately, the company is in total "gridlock."

Fortunately, Adam is a leader. He also happens to believe that the future of the company is not to be found in a short-term contract.

Because he is a leader with a vision for the company, he takes the time to share his vision of the future with his employees.

He also listens and understands their feelings and concerns. Just as importantly, he makes sure that the employees know that he is concerned about their thoughts and feelings. He explains how his vision addresses their concerns.

Adam knows that he will not convince everyone that his vision is best or that it will fit perfectly into their personal plans and ambitions. Yet, he will encourage them, he will influence them, and he will inspire them to work together as a team.

Ability to Influence Others

The ability of the leader to influence those around him or her is crucial. We often think of a leader as a person with power and authority. Adam might be thought of as a leader because he has the

> The ability of the leader to influence those around him or her is crucial.

power to hire and fire employees. In truth, in many situations, a leader does not have any authority over others, other than his ability to persuade and influence.

Think back to your junior high school civics class. You learned that the United States has three branches of government and that they are supposed to be equal in power: the Executive Branch (President), the Legislative Branch (Senate/House of Representatives), and the Judicial Branch (the Courts). Yet, despite this, most people, when asked, would say that the president is the most powerful of the three branches. But why?

The president can't declare war. He doesn't make the laws. He doesn't create the federal budget. He doesn't decide how much tax to collect or where the tax monies are to be spent. In appointing judges and cabinet officers he must seek the "advice and consent" of the Senate (the "Legislative Branch"). By today's standards of executive compensation, he is not even terribly well paid.

How can a person with so little constitutional power be viewed as the most powerful person in the country?

Think about any president whom you consider a great leader. He will invariably have had the following characteristics:

- A vision for where he wants the country to be, politically, economically, and morally
- Compassion for the thoughts and feelings of others, yet unwavering in his pursuit of his vision
- Decisiveness
- Unafraid to stand against the crowd, when necessary
- Influences others by force of personality and charisma
- Able to communicate his vision, thoughts, and feelings to those around him
- Accountability

> Leadership requires the willingness to accept responsibility for what happens to the organization.

Leadership requires the willingness to accept responsibility for what happens to the organization. They face the challenges and take the risks. They deal with the failures and enjoy the successes. They understand that the troops have followed them, and the strategy, motivation, and follow-through was their responsibility.

A good leader is there when he or she is needed and is prepared to do "whatever it takes." He never expects others to do things he wouldn't do, regardless of the reason.

Whether you are the President of the United States or the president of a corporation, or the member of the football team that everyone looks up to as a team leader, leadership skills remain the same.

Are Leaders Born or Are They Made?

There is a great deal of disagreement about whether a person is born with leadership skills or if he learns to be a leader. As with most things in life, the truth probably lies somewhere in between.

Over the years, various psychological studies have identified different personality types and the managerial/leadership skills and deficiencies of each.

What has evolved is a recognition of the fact that, while every personality type has its own set of leadership skills, those skills are not always appropriate for every stage of an organization's life.

Quite simply, the leader of a business during its growth years is not the same person to lead the business once it has reached its full maturity. And the leader during periods of financial crises and "turnaround" may not be the right person to lead the business when finances are stable, and slow sustainable growth is desired.

Mike is known for being a "troubleshooter." He loves the opportunity to go into a financially strapped business, seize control, motivate the employees to deal with the looming crises, and bring the company back to financial stability.

Once the danger has passed, however, Mike becomes bored. He is not a "people person" and, without a crisis, he finds it difficult to relate to the employees or to convey any sense of purpose or urgency to them. He does not have a vision for the company's future other than getting it past the current problems. Instead, he adopts and tries to implement the visions of others.

Mike is a leader with a preference for management.

> The leader of a business during its growth years is not the same person to lead the business once it has reached its full maturity.

Joe, on the other hand, is a visionary. He has taken his company from a garage workshop into its first small assembly facility.

He genuinely cares about his employees and wants them to be with him at the "finish line." He is loyal to his employees and they are loyal to him. They know his vision and take comfort in the fact that the boss is there.

Joe sees the possibilities. He is creative, and is anxious to see the change occur.

Joe is a leader who might benefit from having a strong manager working for him to implement the plan that Joe has laid out.

> Fortunately, leadership skills can be learned regardless of your personality type.

If you are like most small businesses, you cannot afford to go out and hire a "leader." The truth is, you do not want another leader for your business. Maybe there are others with better leadership skills but, after all, you started the business, you nursed it along, you want it to achieve your vision. Regardless of your personality type, you are it! You are the leader! Now, here's what you are going to do.

Fortunately, leadership skills can be learned regardless of your personality type. Following is a list of some of the goals you should strive for as a leader of your organization:

- Understand the nature and purpose of the organization (its role in the community, in the lives of its employees, and within the industry);
- Take time to analyze the product or service the company offers (know its strengths and weaknesses and the role it fills for the customer);
- If you are not a "visionary," meet with others who are to "brainstorm" as to the possibilities of growth, product uses, improved products, new associated products or services, new markets or customers, and employee relations (you may even have a different group of consultants depending upon the type of issue);

- Take time to understand your coworkers' concerns and viewpoints (you can't make them share your vision unless you know how to present it in a way that addresses their concerns);
- Continually update your knowledge by attending seminars, continuing education, and reading about strategic planning and management;
- Decide upon your company's long-range goals: where you want your business to be in five, ten, and fifteen years (do you see a small business with a single, quality product or a large company with gross sales in the millions of dollars and nationwide marketing?);
- Determine your short-range objectives, the steps you will take to reach the long-range goals (for example, what employees will you need to hire? What facilities will you need to have? What type of sales force and commission structure will facilitate the sale of your particular product or service?);
- Set time tables for reaching each objective and goal (this may be changed as circumstances warrant, but not setting a time table is a little like going on a car trip without a map);
- Share your vision with your employees and coworkers;
- Make sure that your employees and coworkers understand their role in the future of the company. Let them know that they have a stake in the future;
- As the leader, be prepared to stand alone. Accept the responsibility for failing to meet your goals, but be big enough to share the credit for success;
- Be loyal to your employees;
- Convey the sense that every minute is important. A sense of purpose, like personal energy, is self-perpetuating;
- Don't ask anyone to do anything that you would not do yourself (sometimes, you might even help someone with their job to show them that the job is important and that you do not consider it beneath you);
- Stress the importance of a job well done and be prepared to practice what you preach;

> Determine your short-range objectives, the steps you will take to reach the long-range goals.

- Be fair and consistent in your handling of employees (and yes, sometimes it is fair to reprimand and even fire employees);
- Don't engage in petty office politics or unnecessary criticism of others.

Streetwise Reality Tour

1. As your business grows you may find that you do not have the leadership or managerial skills to successfully control that growth. This isn't a crime and it isn't a personal failure. Failing to recognize it, however, is! Play to your strengths and hire employees with the skills necessary to supplement yours.
2. Don't think that employees will accept you as a leader just because of your title. Leadership creates power, power doesn't create leadership.
3. Leading by consensus (in effect, giving everyone a vote in the vision) may sound good, but, in reality, it leads to plans of action that are ineffective and without a unified thought. A plan of action or a vision that satisfies 100 people is nothing but a collection of compromises.
4. Employees may deny this, but they want a strong leader. They want to know that the boss is in the building. (Remember, a leader is not a tyrant.)

> Leading by consensus (in effect, giving everyone a vote in the vision) may sound good, but, in reality, it leads to plans of action that are ineffective and without a unified thought.

For more information on this topic, visit our Web site at www.businesstown.com

Taking Your Venture to the Next Level

In this section, you'll learn:

- **how and where to invest your business's money**
- **how to ally with other businesses to increase profits**
- **the legal aspects of copyrights and trademarks**
- **strategies to make the most of a merger**
- **the correct ways to reward your employees**
- **how to keep your successes coming**

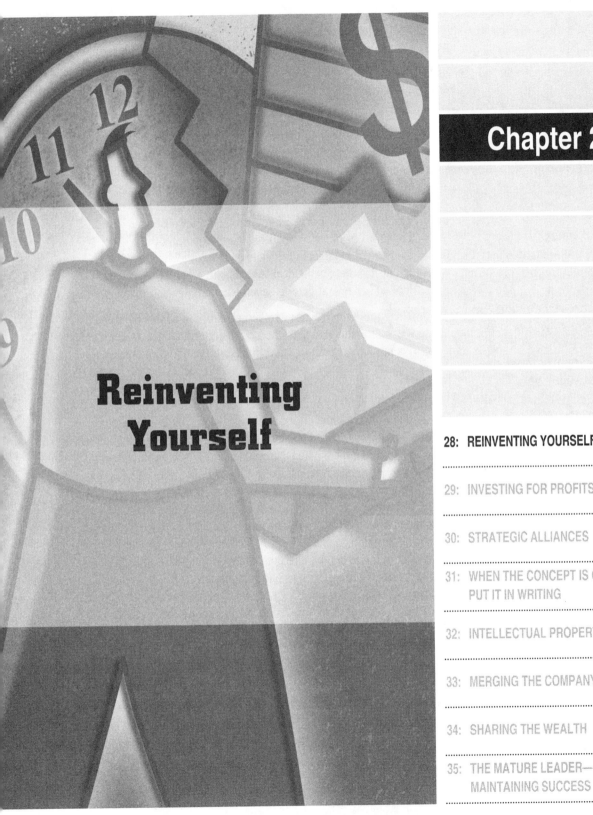

Chapter 28

Reinventing Yourself

Dawn started her printing company in the late 1980s with very cutting-edge equipment. It represented quite an investment at the time and made her shop efficient and cost effective. Within five years, most of what she was operating was almost obsolete and her prepress department could not keep up with the latest methods to transfer files from graphic designers and other customers. Her customer base began to shrink as competitors were promoting their investment in latest in technology. Dawn watched her sales fall by 15% before she decided that she needed to take a look at her operation and develop a strategy for change.

There are many reasons why companies have to step back and take a look at themselves with the knowledge that change is in the offing. This has always been the case in business, but in recent years, the pace of change has increased dramatically. Product cycles are shorter, markets have become global, and through technology, you can service a wide area. The tools of operation have become more and more sophisticated and the amount of information that is available to help run a business is enormous and readily accessible through the Internet. Every aspect of your business may be impacted by these changes, and you must keep up with the trends. Just as the early vision for the business was yours, the future direction of your company must be yours as well.

The answer for Dawn is not to spend money and chase down the latest in new equipment. The cost of doing so would likely be a major financial burden and in the end, her prices could well become prohibitive just to service the debt. Dawn should have been keeping aware of the technology on an ongoing basis, which would have minimized the impact. Now, the best bet for Dawn is use new communication technology to develop a larger market area in which to grow and to become specialized in a niche that will give her a higher level of expertise to market.

> Just as the early vision for the business was yours, the future direction of your company must be yours as well.

The Internal Audit—A Look at Your Operations

When you started your business, you probably completed many tasks with few people. You probably wore a number of hats, as did most of your employees. As the company grew, you hired new employees to perform specific tasks. For example, you may have had a one-person office with the same employee answering the phone, keeping the financial book, and doing the correspondence. As you grew, perhaps you hired a full-time bookkeeper and a full-time secretary.

The same increase in the number of personnel is likely in a retail operation or a restaurant where the owner began as the manager and eventually hired others to handle those roles. Manufacturing plants may require supervisors as well as managers, and service businesses may be adding field managers. Bottom line is that few companies grow in a pre-planned way with an organizational chart in hand. Most see the workload increase in the growth phase and begin hiring to meet urgent needs. At some point you will need to revisit your structure to determine your level of productivity.

On the face of it, it may make sense to you that your company had 10 employees when it was grossing a half a million dollars of sales and now has 50 employees to handle almost three million. But the true test of your productivity is the percentage cost of sales that your labor requires. On a direct basis—the actual cost to produce or provide your goods/services—that number should remain about even. Restaurants, for example, often have labor costs that run between 28 and 32% of sales. Service business may exceed 40%. Once your best cost level has been established, you need to make sure you keep within your goal.

The second tool of productivity is utilizing the technology that is available to either automate some of the tasks or to create a more effective scheduling of jobs to increase efficiency. In the case of a printing company, the scheduling is very critical. The "make ready" time involved in any job is a major cost of the production. Use effective tracking software to assure that all elements of the job are complete and that it fits the equipment being used. You can shave 10 to 15% off production costs by upgrading the software used to plan production, and even more by upgrading the technology of all levels of equipment.

Your administrative technology is another critical area for review. Is your accounting system up to date and operating efficiently? Work that had been done by several accounting clerks may be more completed quickly, using fewer employees, with the latest

> The "make ready" time involved in any job is a major cost of the production.

version of your current accounting software or a more sophisticated program. But cost control (in terms of lower employment) is only one of the stories of an effective accounting and administrative system (order entry, inventory control, etc.). There are other benefits that are equally important.

One of the most powerful and profitable results of accurate, timely, and detailed information is that your management decisions are far more effective. Excess inventory ties up cash and increases the chance that goods will be left over and ultimately discounted. Knowing exactly what is selling and exactly what you have in stock will allow you to order the right quantity faster and create more profit in the end.

Knowing exactly what product or service is selling the best and generating the greatest profit is a powerful tool in running your business. You will be able to determine the areas that have the best growth potential and those that have the best profit margins. Hopefully they are the same. But if you should find that the profit margin is less than desirable on a high-volume item, you will be able to target the costs on that product to improve its margin and subsequently, your overall profit. This is managing by numbers—accuracy and detail is critical.

Internal Communication

The most productive companies (and therefore the most profitable) are the ones that utilize an above-average teamwork approach. Everyone must be on the same page moving toward a common goal. Certainly, an element in this is clear, ongoing communication. The systems to facilitate this are easily put into place with a company e-mail system. If sales gets a request for a quick delivery, there is a need to get that information quickly and accurately to production. An internal company communication system is an effective tool for this purpose. General company information is posted as needed and department-to-department communication is quick, easy, and verifiable. This sort of "in-house" system is almost mandatory for any company expecting to develop and sustain a high level of profitability.

> One of the most powerful and profitable results of accurate, timely, and detailed information is that your management decisions are far more effective.

The External Audit—Are You Utilizing All Available Resources?

Entire books are being written about e-commerce, and every business owner should be reading the available material and learning how the Internet will affect the future of their business, because inevitably, it will. In some way, all businesses will be impacted by what is currently developing with the Internet and information technology.

No, everyone will not be doing all of their selling on the Web. The Internet is an additional outlet for many businesses, just as catalogs and television shopping have grown as alternatives to in-store shopping. There is room for all methods of sales. Some industries, such as the travel industry, are facing very major competition. Travel Web sites offer complete packages including air, hotel, and car rentals, often at very competitive prices. Virtually all airlines have sites offering incentives for making reservations directly and saving them the commission cost. Hotels and car rental companies also have sites, and bargaining sites such as Priceline are available as well. This is one industry that is changing dramatically. It may be far less for yours now but you must keep up to date.

> The Internet is an additional outlet for many businesses, just as catalogs and television shopping have grown as alternatives to in-store shopping.

Enlarge Your Market Area

Virtually every company can improve their sales by reaching a wider market, and the Web may be a good way to accomplish this goal in a cost-effective way. This serves as another type of advertising, and as in all forms of advertising and promotions, you should base your decisions on what will be most cost effective. A presence on the Web does not represent substantial cost, but you must make the effort to be responsive. If you set up a system for customers to contact you, make sure that you react in a timely way. The information on your site must be current and updated. Your site is a representation of how you operate your business. Make the effort to put your best foot forward.

Customers you may never have been able to reach through traditional methods of marketing may well find out about you through the Internet, which gives you ample opportunity to enlarge the area you cover. The key is how easily you can be found—i.e., are you available through the major search engines or are you hyperlinked to other associated sites? If you distribute a product, does the manufacturer have you linked to their site? Are you a member of a trade or professional association and linked to their site? Having a presence on the Web is a necessity these days but it seldom is sufficient to just throw up a page or two and think that you have met your goals.

An Informational Resource

New product developments, new industry standards, changing buying patterns, and data on cutting-edge technology—all of this is available on the Internet. Keeping up with the rapidly changing business environment is a critical task for any entrepreneur. Many industries are changing radically as a result of the power of information that is now available to virtually anyone. You can either utilize the information or you can allow your business to be overcome with it.

Put the tools into the hands of many of your key people and allow them to act on the information they can access. It will energize the entire business.

> You can access your bank account to verify balances, move money from one account to another, and make payments through the use of automatic funds transfers.

The Money Exchange

The use of high-speed and secure networks has changed the business of banking dramatically over the last few years. The use of debit cards is an efficient way to transfer funds without handling paper transactions. If you sell to the public, you certainly want to be able to handle debit card transactions.

Other on-line banking services are also valuable to your business. You can access your bank account to verify balances, move money from one account to another, and make payments through the use of automatic funds transfers. You can also encourage customers to pay their bills through bank transfers. You will likely need to engage a processing agent, but the increase in your cash flow will be well worth any cost.

When you think of the time required to have a paper check issued, then mailed, and then the time required to deposit and clear the funds from the originating bank—it makes good sense to encourage the use of the technology available. You can speed up cash flow by almost a week and find your business much easier to run.

The time is approaching when you will be doing most of your billing electronically, saving the time it takes to mail bills to customers and keeping paper down to a minimum.

Purchasing is already being done via linkage from the buyer's system to the seller. It is possible to check inventory on-line and to enter orders directly into a supplier's computer. This speeds up the ordering and delivery process and allows many businesses to carry far less inventory and therefore be more cost effective as well as efficient.

The Future Is Now—Be Online

The possibilities are endless for becoming far more cost effective and efficient by the use of existing technology. Learn what is available in your industry.

> Purchasing is already being done via linkage from the buyer's system to the seller. It is possible to check inventory on-line and to enter orders directly into a supplier's computer.

Streetwise Reality Tour

1. Internal operations should be automated to provide accurate and almost instantaneous information.
2. The flow of information within a company can increase with simple communication software.
3. Marketing opportunities increase with a presence on the World Wide Web, but you must have a current, informational, and responsive site.
4. The transactional possibilities on-line are substantial. You can purchase, transmit bills, and transfer funds quickly and accurately. Learn to use this tool.

For more information on this topic, visit our Web site at www.businesstown.com

Chapter 29

Investing for Profits

The primary way your business will earn money is through its sale of products/services. During the start-up phase and the growth cycle, there is unlikely to be any excess cash and when there is, you will need it to pay bills or fund the purchase of equipment or inventory. However, there should come a time when profits are stable and cash is available. Then your financial decisions will involve putting that cash to use so it increases the profits of your company. There are a number of ways to do this and a number of issues to consider. The primary one is whether you will you need to reconvert your investment back into cash. If it may be soon (less than a year), you will have to keep your financial instrument one which is liquid. Using excess profit to lower overhead may also work because it will increase ongoing cash flow to lessen the need for additional working capital.

> You can earn money on your money by keeping all excess cash in an interest-bearing account.

The First Place to Look Is Your Bank

You can earn money on your money by keeping all excess cash in an interest-bearing account. It makes no sense to have money you aren't using sit idle in a checking account. Depending on how high your balances may get and how long you may be able to invest the money, your bank should be able to manage this for you.

The first thing you must do is to maximize the cash in your account by billing promptly and using electronic transfers that deposit payments directly into your account or using the bank lock box address so the money goes directly to your bank and thereby saving several days in transit. The more cash in your account to invest, the higher the return.

If your excess cash exceeds $100,000, it is likely your bank will be willing to manage transfers between your investment account and your checking account. Otherwise you can do it yourself. Open an alternative money market account and keep all cash in that account until needed to cover checks written on your normal business account. Then you can make the transfer (or the bank will) as the funds are needed. You can only draw limited checks on an interest-bearing account, but you can make as many funds transfers as you need to.

Longer-Term Investments

If you have excess funds that will not be needed in the next 90 days to one year, there are other possibilities available, such as Treasury Bills or Certificates of Deposit. Keep in mind that any earlier withdrawal will result in a penalty.

Investing in Your Ongoing Business

Perhaps the best investment you can make in the future of your company is in areas that will make it easier to operate, such as lowering the overhead. If you have been renting space and have been seeing the cost go up, it may be time to buy your building or move to one you can purchase. You can purchase the right-sized space at a fixed price, and chances are that your mortgage costs will be less than your current rent and you will not have any increases over the years, except in the area of property taxes.

You can design the space to be efficient and effective, saving you money on utilities and earning money due to your increased productivity. Landlords may not be willing to make these types of changes and as a renter, you may not have been willing to spend the money either. Once the property is yours, it makes sense to maximize the value.

Owning property has another benefit to your company, it strengthens your balance sheet and may protect some of your profits from taxes. The value of the building will go on your balance sheet and the equity you build in it will be reflected there. However, you will also have an allowance for depreciation, which may be used as an expense to shelter some of your taxable income. Buying real estate may well be the best use of your profits at a certain time in your business life. Your location and the cost of your space will be fixed over the long term.

Taking Advantage of Deals

If you are a manufacturer or retailer and buy raw material or finished products, making opportune purchases may be one way to use

> Owning property has another benefit to your company, it strengthens your balance sheet and may protect some of your profits from taxes.

your excess capital to increase profits. Even if your purchases are limited to services, you still may be able to do a deal. How about requesting a discount on invoices for prompt payment? While this benefit is more frequently available in times of high-interest ratio, if your vendors have occasional cash flow problems, the chance to get immediate cash may be attractive to them.

Many suppliers offer quantity breaks, which give you a lower unit price. If you are buying an item you use on an ongoing basis this may make sense. Perhaps a higher quantity will also give you prepaid shipping, saving even more money on your goods.

Keep in touch with your suppliers and let them know you are in the market for overstocked items that they may be offering at discount. The end of a selling season may bring these offers or, in states where inventory is taxed at the end of the year, that is the time you will find them.

The deepest discounts you will find will be in close-out merchandise, often sold by brokers as opposed to the original source of supply. You may find them in industry specialized groups such as apparel, electronic equipment, gift items, etc.

There is usually nothing wrong with the merchandise with the exception that it is no longer the latest model or color or style. Many businesses have made great profits selling this type of merchandise. A number of e-commerce companies specialize in it. Your task is to make sure that your customer base will be interested in the goods and that you have the talent to merchandise them. It makes no sense to buy something, however low the price, that you can't sell.

Invest in Something Entirely New

Perhaps it is time to take the money you have made in one venture and invest it in another. There are two ways to go with this idea. You can begin a joint venture or alliance with another company (which will be covered fully in the next chapter) or purchase another company outright.

One way to grow your existing business is to get a larger share of the market. If you purchase one of your competitors, you will have

> Many suppliers offer quantity breaks, which give you a lower unit price.

their customer base to add to your own and your revenue will increase. The best case scenario is when you can do higher volume with your existing organization. This will substantially increase your gross operating profits and if your general expense stays the same or goes up only slightly, your bottom line should be very healthy.

The caution here is what you pay for the other business. You are buying customers, so make sure you don't pay for other assets that you do not need, such as property and equipment. Inventory should be heavily discounted and you must be sure it is saleable to your existing or newly acquired customers.

Be very sure that your market image and customer base is compatible. A top-of-the-line store is not likely to attract and hold discount-type customers. Unless you are buying iron clad contracts (and few really are) you will only retain customers who feel you meet their needs and are satisfied with your services. So make sure the mix is good or you will pay for customers that you never sell.

On the other hand, buying upscale customers when you don't have the level of service or personnel to handle their needs is risky as well. Perhaps there are employees in the other company that could come to work for you to help. If not, your entire operation may be stressed and you risk losing your existing customers.

How Much to Pay

If you are purchasing the assets of another company (property, equipment, and inventory) because you can use them—the value is fairly easy to establish. To make it all worthwhile for you, the discount on the purchase must be substantial. You can have an appraisal done of what is included and negotiate from that number. Don't forget to reduce your offer by what is included that is of no use to you.

Buying intangibles such as a name, a trademark, or a customer list is far trickier. The key question to ask yourself is how much your net profit will increase by this purchase, and make an offer based on a percentage of that prediction. Or even better, make the offer contingent on the volume that you generate from the customers you

> If you are purchasing the assets of another company (property, equipment, and inventory) because you can use them—the value is fairly easy to establish.

have acquired. Your job will be to make sure the costs are in hand and that the volume increase produces profits, but the risk of paying for something that may not happen is reduced.

If you have been successful at the business you have, there is every reason to believe that you can enhance that success with an expanded operation. Buying an existing one may be the best deal.

> You can grow by purchasing a competitor but you must be careful about making the deal.

Streetwise Reality Tour

1. A good banker should be able to help you manage your cash to increase your profits.
2. Consider buying the property you use instead of renting. You fix the cost and build equity.
3. Discounted merchandise can be profitable if you can sell it.
4. You can grow by purchasing a competitor but you must be careful about making the deal.

For more information on this topic, visit our Web site at www.businesstown.com

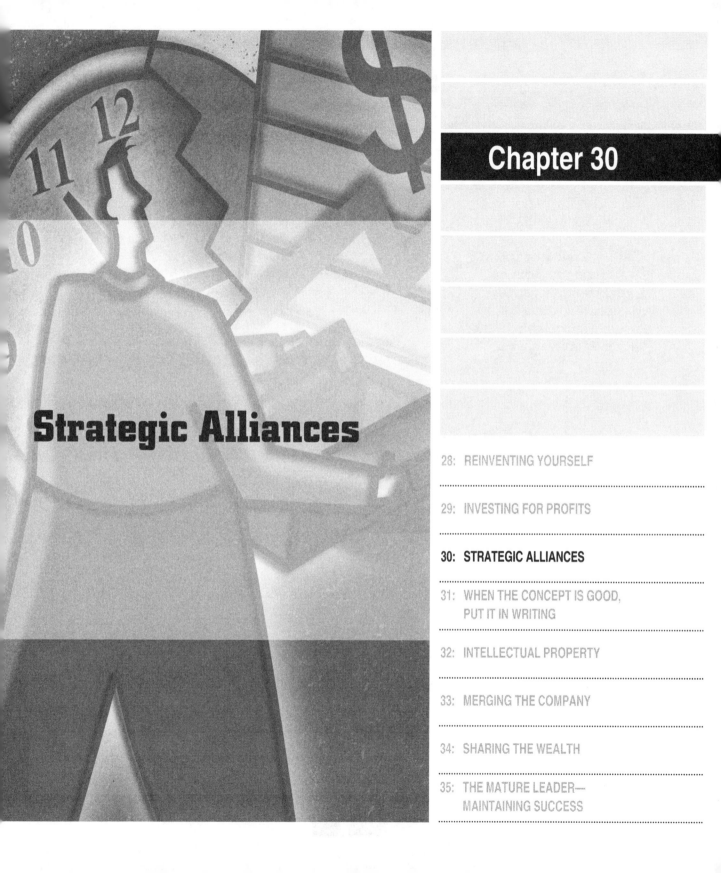

Chapter 30

Strategic Alliances

To compete in an ever-changing business climate, today's business owner must be more creative than ever before. This is an age of specialization, global competition, and rapidly changing technology. At the same time, interesting opportunities are opening up that will allow small companies to compete in arenas they may not have approached years ago. Larger companies have abandoned products and markets, and smaller entities can use this as an opening to expand their own business.

These changes are not simply passing trends, but are the result of technological advances that have opened up a range of options as to how business will be conducted in the future.

Whether you are a one-man business or a multinational corporation, the needs and opportunities for the formation of strategic alliances has never been greater.

What Is a Strategic Alliance?

In its simplest form, a strategic alliance occurs any time you form an understanding and a relationship with another person or business to work for your "mutual benefit."

> A strategic alliance occurs any time you form an understanding and a relationship with another person or business to work for your "mutual benefit."

Adam is a painting contractor. Over the last ten years he has been engaged entirely in residential jobs and small commercial projects, but has never broken into the large industrial or structural jobs that could mean a big payday for his company and for himself.

Time after time Adam receives notices soliciting bids for industrial projects and realizes that he is simply too small to compete effectively with the larger contractors who are bidding on those jobs. He also knows that there is a greater risk in jobs of that size and that he does not have the capital to absorb a delay in payment or a missed payment, altogether.

One day Adam is approached by Bob, one of his competitors in the residential painting business. Bob suggests that the two of them form a joint venture, along with Carl, another residential painting contractor, and submit a bid for a painting job on a large municipal project.

With their combined resources, Adam, Bob, and Carl have three times the capital, three times the labor force, and three times the supervisory capability. More importantly, none of the three takes the risk for the entire expense or loss.

Reasons to Form Strategic Alliances

There are many reasons to form a strategic alliance with another business.

Access to New Customers and Markets

When you ally yourself with another business, you automatically come into contact with new people, new suppliers, new customers, and new ways of doing things.

Take the previous example: for 20 years, Adam did nothing but residential and some small commercial painting jobs. He had an ad in both the yellow pages and the local merchant's magazine that is handed out free at the local supermarket. Other than that, his business comes from word-of-mouth.

Once Adam enters into a joint venture with Bob and Carl, however, his name goes on a large sign in front of the project, he attends numerous meetings with architects, prime contractors, city officials, and bonding agencies, as well as other tradespeople and suppliers.

On this single municipal job Adam has made more new contacts (and contacts in the type of work that results in large profitability), than he has in the last 20 years.

At the same time Adam "learns the ropes" for handling the large municipal and industrial job, including the contract, the procedures for payment, bonding requirements, arbitration of disputes, etc.

> When you ally yourself with another business, you automatically come into contact with new people, new suppliers, new customers, and new ways of doing things.

Reduces the "Peaks and Valleys" of the Workload

If yours is like most businesses, it has busy times and it has slow times. This occurs for a number of reasons, but the one that is the most common comes from the fact that while you are busy doing the work you don't have the time to look for new work.

Adam has a small graphic design business but no employees or other support staff.

Because of the nature of his business, when a project comes in to the shop it is almost always a rush and requires that he work 12- to 15-hour days, including weekends, to get the project done on schedule.

The money is great for the four weeks that it keeps Adam busy, but once the project is finished, he has nothing else to work on.

It's possible that Adam could accept smaller jobs in the meantime in the hope of starting them once the larger job has been completed, but more than likely even small jobs have deadlines and no client wants to wait for Adam's more important job to be completed. Most customers also don't want to be thought of as a secondary customer, anyway.

Consequently, when Adam is finished with his big job, he spends the next four weeks trying to line up new work. The "peaks and valleys" of his workload wreak havoc with his cash flow and his blood pressure.

Adam has considered hiring an employee to help handle the busy times. The problem is that he will either have to pay that employee's salary during the time when no income is coming into the office, or he will have to lay off the employee approximately every other month. Neither of these options is desirable or feasible.

What Adam needs is a strategic alliance with another business in the same industry. Let's call it a "strategic associate." Now, when Adam has the large project with the short deadline, he has the assistance of another experienced graphic designer to help with the job. Adam shares some of the income from the job, but the extra help makes his life much more tolerable. The extra help also gives Adam time to continue developing new business for those slow periods. It

> While you are busy doing the work you don't have the time to look for new work.

also means that, when Adam's strategic associate is busy, he will ask Adam to assist him in much the same way.

Access to Bigger and More Profitable Contracts

On many occasions, a job or contract is simply too large for a small business like yours to handle. It may be that the initial cash requirements are more than you can afford, or that the progress payments are spaced too far apart for you to carry. It may also be that, if something goes wrong with the job, you would simply not be able to absorb the loss, thereby destroying what you have been able to build over the years. Your arm just isn't quite long enough to "reach the brass ring."

In the first example, when Adam formed an alliance with Bob and Carl, the three small residential painting contractors had access to the bigger more lucrative contracts, which they never would have had any other way.

> On many occasions, a job or contract is simply too large for a small business like yours to handle.

Receive the Benefits of Involvement in Larger Projects While Spreading out the Risks

When Adam forms his strategic alliance with Bob and Carl, he understands that he will not get all of the profit from the job but that it will be divided between he, Bob, and Carl. But that's alright for Adam because even one-third of the contract has more profit than any dozen of the small residential jobs he normally handles. And, because the work is spread among three contractors, he is not responsible for all the capital, he does not have to carry the account totally on his own between progress payments, and, if things go wrong, he only has to worry about his one-third of the loss.

Enlarge Your Knowledge About Another Facet of the Industry

When Adam gets into the municipal project with Bob and Carl, he is learning a whole new facet of his business, one that will place him in good stead for obtaining other large projects, either with others or by himself.

Adam learns about bonding, commercial arbitration, pricing the job, insurance, and a range of other things that he never had to give any thought to in his residential business. He knew some of it, however, and what Adam did not know, Bob and Carl have a good handle on.

Learn from the Experiences of Those with Whom You Ally Yourself

With any luck, when Adam teams up with Bob and Carl, one or both of them will have had some experience in this area and Adam can learn from them while working to their mutual advantage (not all strategic alliances are between people of equal knowledge, experience, or resources). There are a number of reasons why Adam might be selected as a strategic associate for the project.

You Become a "Player" in the Industry Within Which You Do Business

Take our example several steps further. After a successful completion of the municipal project, Adam, Bob, and Carl bid on several more large municipal and industrial projects as strategic associates. After five years, all three of them have developed a reputation within the community as being knowledgeable, dependable, and quality contractors.

Success builds on itself, and so long as Adam, Bob, and Carl do not trip themselves up, they stand to become a powerhouse in the local community. People will try to form strategic associations with them because of their experience, and private contractors may seek them out because of who they know and what they know.

Obtain Access to Only Those Employees, Facilities, and Equipment That Are Necessary for You to Operate

When you form a strategic alliance you can acquire assets and capital on an "as needed" basis. If the municipal project requires thirty painters, Adam does not have to worry about hiring that many painters. He simply needs to know that his painters, plus Bob's and Carl's, are available. And when the job is finished, Adam does not

> People will try to form strategic associations with them because of their experience, and private contractors may seek them out because of who they know and what they know.

have to worry about unnecessary overhead, unemployment compensation claims, or other employee problems that come with lay-offs. Adam will be paying for just what he gets and nothing more.

Examples of Strategic Alliances

Strategic alliances can take many forms. In addition, they can allow for as much, or as little, involvement in the business of the other as the parties want.

Some of the types of strategic alliances are listed as follows.

Networking and Marketing

A networking group can be anything from a civic organization, like the Kiwanas; to a business organization, like the Chamber of Commerce; to a professional association, like the Society of Engineers; to a marketing group, which is formed specifically for the purpose of referring business among its members.

While each of these groups may have different purposes, they all offer benefits to the small business owner. The organization may hold seminars and workshops on matters of common interest. Or, it may engage in lobbying. Or it may provide health insurance at affordable group rates.

Whether or not they intend to, networking groups all offer opportunities for their members to meet new people, meet new prospective clients, obtain leads to new business, and share in ideas and information relating to business; both locally and nationally.

In a marketing group, the sole purpose is the making of business referrals. The members of the marketing group do not involve themselves in the operations of the other members' businesses. Instead, the members simply refer business to other members of the networking group.

In most organized marketing groups one member from each type of business or industry is allowed (for example, one lawyer, one accountant, one car dealer). In this way, the accountant receives all of the referrals from the members for accounting services, the lawyer receives all of the referrals for legal work, and so on.

> Networking groups all offer opportunities for their members to meet new people, meet new prospective clients, obtain leads to new business, and share in ideas and information relating to business; both locally and nationally.

Sometimes the networking goes beyond mere referrals of business to a sharing of the income from that business or the payment of a referral fee. When businesses engage in mutual referrals there is an agreement to make the referral of business and an agreement to share, in some manner, in the income generated from the business.

After seeing the success of his recent municipal painting project Adam decides that he wants to continue doing residential painting, but not commercial. Bob decides that he wants to do commercial, but not residential.

Both Adam and Bob have a wealth of contacts among potential residential and commercial customers.

Adam and Bob reach an agreement that Adam will refer all of his commercial leads to Bob and Bob will refer all of his residential leads to Adam. They will then pay the other either a referral fee or a share of the profit from that particular job.

> At some time you may find it beneficial to become associated with a consortium. A consortium is a loose association where the members provide their respective services to customers.

At some time you may find it beneficial to become associated with a consortium. A consortium is a loose association where the members provide their respective services to customers.

Adam is an accountant who, because of his experience working with small businesses, has seen a need to make available a variety of services to small businesses, such as accounting, legal, personnel, etc.

Adam reaches an agreement with Bob (an attorney), Lindsay (a computer expert), Dave (a media consultant), and Ed (a graphic designer). They will work together to offer clients a complete business service that none of them could offer separately.

They still have their own businesses, but they can now sell something more, a new entity. The income will be distributed in accordance with the work done by each and as agreed to by each.

Joint Ventures

A joint venture is very much like the partnership discussed in Chapter 2, with one exception. Unlike a partnership, a joint venture is limited to a specific project, a specific time period, or a specific type of business.

Tony and Sue both have established painting businesses and both expect that their children will step into the business at some time in the future. Whether or not the children come into the business, neither Tony nor Sue (maybe because they read Chapter 2) want to deal with a partner on a daily basis. And they certainly don't want to deal with a partner's children.

Tony and Sue have seen, however, just how much money they made on the municipal project and decide that they want to stay together just for that type of work. In all other respects, the businesses will be separate.

Tony and Sue form a joint venture with the agreement that it will be limited to municipal projects. There is no requirement that the joint venture has to do any projects in a given year. In fact, it doesn't have to, because it has no employees and no overhead.

> Unlike a partnership, a joint venture is limited to a specific project, a specific time period, or a specific type of business.

Subcontracting

Sometimes, because the work will not be of a continuous nature, or you don't want to develop the longer-term relationship required of a joint venture, or for any number of other reasons, you may find it beneficial to subcontract a part of your work to another. Remember the second example of this chapter? Adam subcontracted graphic design work to Bob and Bob, in turn, subcontracted work to Adam.

There was no formal agreement that Adam and Bob subcontract to one another; it simply developed. Also, because they are neither partners nor joint venturers, they have no duty to one another and may, in fact, bid independently on the same work.

While subcontracting can be relatively informal it can just as often be very structured, with written subcontracts, payment terms, work assignments, insurance requirements, etc. This is particularly the case in the construction industry, where a general contractor may hire subcontractors for such things as electrical, heating and air conditioning, and plumbing.

Franchising, Licensing, and Distributorships

Another way to expand your business is to offer others a chance to acquire a franchise.

> Another way to expand your business is to offer others a chance to acquire a franchise.

After years of hard work Sam has gotten his restaurant business "down to a science." He has a great concept, a catchy name, a good menu, and he has worked out all of the problems with portion control, pricing, hiring, and training practices.

But, because people will only travel so far when they go out to eat, there is a limit on the size to which Sam's restaurant can grow.

Sam has considered opening a second restaurant about an hour's drive away but he realizes that he doesn't have the time, or the energy, to handle two locations up to an hour apart. Sam could also hire a manager, but he isn't comfortable with placing too much trust in someone other than himself.

Sam has decided to offer franchises. For a sizeable fee, Sam will use what he has learned to identify possible business locations, and put together a list of necessary equipment, inventory, recipes, logos, concepts, etc. He will then sell the rights to all of his information, in addition to future set-up and management advice, to others.

Five years later, Sam still has his original restaurant and, in addition, receives income in franchise fees from the five franchise locations he has sold to others.

Licenses work in much the same way. Assume that you develop a formula, a concept, a method, or other idea (called intellectual property). You can sell another business the right (license) to use your idea.

David, a chemist, has developed a new product for home insulation. David has no interest in running a company and dealing with the details of production, sales, installation, etc. He also knows that he will make more than enough money from licensing others to use the formula.

If David wants to keep a little more of the pie, he may control production, but establish distributorships around the country to whom he will sell the product. He then lets the distributors handle the sales calls, oversee installation, handle problems, and assume the risk of not being able to sell the product. David gets paid by the distributors, whether or not they sell the product.

What to Look for in a Strategic Ally

Analyze Your Needs

As with any partnership or business venture, you must be careful to analyze your needs. For example:

1. Do you really need to establish a subcontractor relationship or is it time for you to consider hiring an employee? Sure, the added overhead may be frightening but you may be giving away more in profits to a subcontractor than what you would pay an employee.
2. By subcontracting, are you contracting away most of the profit?

> As with any partnership or business venture, you must be careful to analyze your needs.

Judy is a graphic designer. Because she has limited actual experience and little capital for equipment she finds that she is subcontracting to others such things as copying, layout, and photography.

When all is said and done, Judy ends up with only about 10% of the profit on the job because she has had to pay the rest to her subcontractors.

The work Judy actually does is worth the 10% but Judy receives nothing extra for assuming the responsibility for coordinating and managing the work of all of the subcontractors. So, in effect, Judy is losing money on every job.

3. Does your strategic associate really have something to offer or are you simply more comfortable having someone else in the boat with you?
4. Do you need to establish a long-term relationship or will a short-term agreement be sufficient?

Analyze What Type of Person You Need or Want to Ally Yourself With

Once you decide that you want to form a strategic alliance and figure out what you expect from that alliance, you need to make a determination about whether the person you have selected is compatible with your goals.

For example, do you share common goals and do you have similar work habits and work philosophy? Will you both insist on calling the shots, will you be supportive of each other, and will you be able to equitably divide the responsibilities?

Most importantly, can the potential ally be trusted to handle the work assigned to him, to satisfy your customers, to not overbill your customers, and to not try to steal your customers? Remember, a partnership (and that's really what a strategic alliance is) is like a marriage. It isn't something that should be done strictly for convenience or by looking at a balance sheet. Even short-term relations can have long-term consequences.

Protect Yourself

When considering a strategic alliance, you should consider how to protect your trade secrets, your methods of operation, and even your customers, from an ally who may one day be a competitor.

> Does your strategic associate really have something to offer or are you simply more comfortable having someone else in the boat with you?

If yours is the type of business that relies upon specialized methods, procedures, and other confidential information, your best protection is to formalize your relationships with others by a written agreement.

The agreement should contain details as to what information each is bringing to the alliance and what each is not bringing to the alliance. It should also identify that information that the parties consider to be confidential.

The agreement should contain provisions that prohibit the ally from utilizing the information which has been classified as "confidential." It can also contain noncompete provisions, which prevent the ally from contacting or doing business with any of your customers for several years after the conclusion of the alliance. It might also contain a liquidated damages clause, where you can recover a specific sum of money if you can prove that your former ally violated the agreement. (Many times, proving your damages may be next to impossible. A liquidated damages clause will avoid this problem.)

Streetwise Reality Tour

1. A strategic alliance is a two-way street. You may meet new people and customers through your strategic associate. You may also learn new information and methods of operation. But remember that your ally has the same access to your customers, contacts, and information.
2. A strategic alliance may be a good way to test the waters of a new undertaking but it may also keep you from moving your business into that new and more profitable undertaking. Why split the profit on a type of work or job that you are capable of handling yourself?
3. There may be no really effective way to prevent a former ally from utilizing your confidential information. Enforcing these agreements can be expensive and time consuming. And, as often as not, the recovery will not be worth the trouble.

A strategic alliance may be a good way to test the waters of a new undertaking but it may also keep you from moving your business into that new and more profitable undertaking.

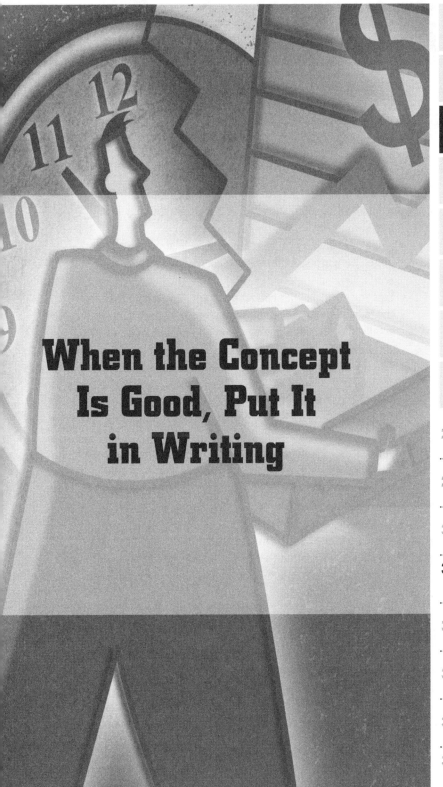

Chapter 31

When the Concept Is Good, Put It in Writing

O .K., you've analyzed your business's needs, you've searched for the perfect strategic partner, and you've found the ideal match. Now what?

Well, first, you put your agreement with your perfect partner to the real test. You put it in writing. Or at least you try to. If your agreement with your prospective strategic partner can withstand being put into writing then there is a chance that you may have really found something.

Why is it so hard to put an agreement for a strategic alliance into writing? There are several simple reasons.

- You and your partner can agree to the "concept" of the strategic alliance, but there was never any agreement on the details, like who will manage, how the profit will be divided, and how expenses will be shared.
- When you and your strategic partner see your agreement in writing, one or both of you gets "cold feet." Before, there was a certain comfort in just talking about the alliance. But seeing it in writing, with legal consequences, is a different matter altogether.
- Your attorney reviews the agreement and he puts such a fear into you about all of the things that can go wrong that you run back to the security of your little one-man business, never again to venture forth.

As you sit down to draft your agreement there are a number of things that should be included in the agreement. Some of them were discussed in "Before You Sign on the Dotted Line." Following are the key points to consider.

Identity of the Parties

Remember to identify exactly who is entering into the agreement. Adam wants to reach an agreement with Bob. Bob, however, is not a proprietor but owns, and is employed by, BOBCO, INC., a corporation. So, does Adam want the agreement to be with Bob, or with BOBCO? If he's smart, Adam wants both to sign the agreement.

> If your agreement with your prospective strategic partner can withstand being put into writing then there is a chance that you may have really found something.

When you are considering who you want your agreement to be with, make sure to consider anyone else who may be critical to the alliance. If Carl, who is employed by BOBCO, INC, is essential to the success of the project, make certain that Carl is obligated to the project. Bob and BOBCO may be willing to make Carl available but, if Carl quits one day, what will Adam or Bob do about it?

Either make Carl a party to the contract or make sure that Carl is subject to an employment agreement with either Bob or the strategic alliance.

What Are the Parties Trying to Accomplish?

Don't be coy! And don't load up on the "legalese." State simply and plainly what it is you hope to accomplish through the strategic alliance.

For example, is the strategic alliance a test for what you hope may develop? If so, then say in the agreement that the parties are interested in putting together a strategic alliance in order to explore new business opportunities.

If, on the other hand, the purpose of the alliance is simply to allow the parties to pool their resources in order to bid on certain types of work, then say that.

This may seem unnecessary but you'd be surprised by how many prospective partners got as far as drafting an agreement only to find out that they weren't in agreement on the purposes or the goals of the alliance. Not only is it better to find this out at the outset, but it will be easier to resolve disputes in the future if your objectives are clearly stated in the original agreement.

How Long Will the Strategic Alliance Last?

As part of your planning and part of the agreement, figure out how long you want the alliance to last. Will it be for only a single project, for a period of years, or will it be for an indefinite period, handling anything that the strategic partners want to get involved in?

Why do you want to specify the time period anyway?

> If the purpose of the alliance is simply to allow the parties to pool their resources in order to bid on certain types of work, then say that.

- First, setting the time period, like explaining the goals of the alliance, will help in clarifying the parties' intentions and interpreting the agreement.
- Second, knowing how long the alliance will last will allow the parties to make decisions as to labor, equipment, and capital needs over the period of the alliance. After all, you don't want to take on the expense of employees or equipment in anticipation of a job three years in the future if your strategic partners are planning to wind things up in one year.
- Third, you want to make sure that you are not committed to the alliance for any longer than you want to be.

Remember, if the alliance works successfully and everyone is making money, the parties will probably have no problem in agreeing to extend the strategic alliance. So, it may not be beneficial to obligate the strategic partners for an unreasonably long period of time.

On the other hand, you want to make certain that, once you have invested time, effort, and money in a strategic alliance, it stays in existence long enough to recoup your expenses if not a substantial profit.

How will a final accounting be done? How will assets and profits be distributed among partners?

Termination

Will the agreement simply expire at the end of the time period or at the end of the project? Be specific. Or will it continue to renew itself until a formal termination is requested? Can one side terminate for any reason with notice?

How will a final accounting be done? How will assets and profits be distributed among partners? Can one side begin the project again without paying royalties or commission to prior partners?

If any unforeseen liability arises after dissolution (or any dispute), how will it be resolved?

In short, consider the end as well as the beginning and the middle. And commit your agreement to writing.

Contributions

As with any business, you will have to decide how the alliance is to be funded. This means that the partners in the strategic alliance will have to agree on how much money each will contribute to the alliance, and what form that contribution will take.

The contribution can be in the form of cash, equipment, office space, or anything else of value, if that is agreed to by the partners.

With cash, keeping track of contributions is fairly easy. A bigger problem occurs, however, when one party is contributing cash and another is contributing equipment or office space. If that is the case, the partners have to agree as to how the noncash contributions, such as equipment, will be valued for purposes of determining the amount of the contribution.

For example, if an automobile is contributed to the alliance, will you treat the entire value of the car as the contribution or only a lease value? Will insurance, maintenance, expenses, and other incidentals be included as a contribution?

Profits

While you may think that profits will be distributed to each of the partners equally, this does not have to be the case. If the parties agree, the profits can be divided in any proportion that they choose. For example, if Adam has much more experience and contributes more capital than Bob or Carl, then he may take an increased share of the profits.

This is an issue that must be resolved before the alliance gets under way. It is also an area which, more than any other, will result in disputes, litigation, or liquidation of the alliance.

> The partners have to agree as to how the noncash contributions, such as equipment, will be valued for purposes of determining the amount of the contribution.

Management and Decision Making

One of the touchiest areas you will have to deal with is what role each of the principals will play in the management of the alliance.

Remember that each of the strategic partners will, more likely than not, have their own businesses and be used to giving the orders. And, like most people, you will think that yours is the best way of doing things. Think of how uncomfortable you would be turning over control of the alliance to someone else. Well, your strategic partner is not going to feel any better about turning control over to you.

You have got to come up with a way where both of you can have input in, and control over, the project without getting in each other's way.

Depending upon the type of project, you may want to designate one of the partners to be primarily responsible for the project, but with the approval of all the partners being necessary to incur certain types of expenses or to alter, in any way, the original plan of action. This may be easier with an odd number of partners because you could then require a majority vote (although an odd number of principals may only result in an odd number of decisions).

Another way to approach the situation would be to assign each of the strategic partners responsibility for a certain area of the business or project. You can supplement this by giving each partner veto power over any decision.

Another solution may be to name a third person (financial advisor, attorney, etc.) to act as a tie-breaker in the event you and your strategic partners reach an impasse in decision making.

The most important thing is to avoid having the alliance immobilized by disputes and indecision. Remember, disputes are unavoidable and can occur even when the parties are acting with the best of intentions. The best thing that you can do is plan for those disputes and try to resolve them as quickly and inexpensively as possible.

Resolving Disputes

Sometimes, disputes with your strategic partners go beyond details of management. And sometimes they can't be resolved by agreement of the partners. What do you do when a dispute threatens not only the future of the alliance but threatens your own business and assets?

You could hire a lawyer, file a lawsuit, and go to court, but that will cost you a substantial amount of money and at least several

> The most important thing is to avoid having the alliance immobilized by disputes and indecision.

years. In the meantime, your capital is tied up in an alliance that is doing nothing.

The better choice is to agree, in your initial contract, to arbitrate any disputes. In arbitration, the parties agree that any dispute will be submitted to an impartial panel of arbitrators who will be presented with the facts and make a decision as to which of the parties is correct. The parties agree, in advance, that the decision of the arbitrators will be binding.

A clause in the contract that requires arbitration will generally be enforced in the courts, as will the decision of the arbitrators.

Protection of Trade Secrets and Confidential Information

Depending upon the type of business the alliance engages in, you may find that you are sharing, with your strategic partners, your trade secrets and confidential information such as customer names, pricing, services rendered, etc. Once a strategic alliance ends, what is to stop your former partners from using that information to steal your business and customers?

First, in any agreement you are going to specifically designate what each partner is bringing to the alliance and what he is not bringing to the alliance. You should also have each partner designate what material he feels is confidential or a trade secret (Form 31-01 in the Appendix). If you don't do this you can expect that, after a dispute arises, there will be all sorts of allegations that one or more of the partners have stolen protected information.

By putting this in writing up front, you will know exactly what should or should not be treated as confidential. It takes away the ability of any former partner to allege that something is confidential when he never said it was confidential in the first place.

You may also want to implement other safekeeping measures such as coding or numbering of customer lists, equipment, supplies, etc., which were provided by you to the alliance, so that there is no dispute as to what you contributed.

The agreement should also be very clear that no former partner may use your protected information in any way or for any reason.

> Once a strategic alliance ends, what is to stop your former partners from using that information to steal your business and customers?

Ultimately, and because it is difficult to establish damages, even if you can prove a use of your protected information, you may want to include a liquidated damages clause, whereby upon a showing that a former partner is using protected information, a money judgement will be entered for a sum certain.

Wrap-Up

A written agreement is essential for refining your ideas before entering into any alliance, for clarifying the rights and liabilities of the parties, for planning purposes, for preventing disputes, and for avoiding costly litigation expenses should disputes arise. A written agreement: "Don't leave home without it!"

A written agreement: "Don't leave home without it!"

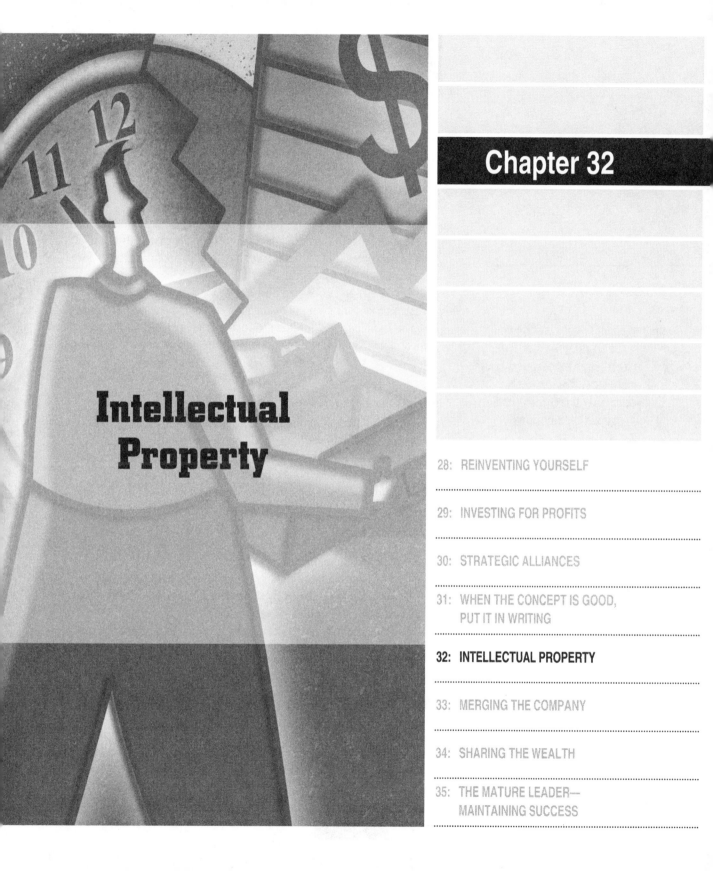

Chapter 32

Intellectual Property

With the spread of the computer and the growth of virtual offices and e-businesses, the most valuable asset of many companies will be their ideas, concepts, inventions, and other creative processes. These types of assets are known as "intellectual property."

If you take the time to think about it, is it your computer that is valuable, or is it the software? Is it the cost of the materials to build your photocopier that makes it valuable, or is it the invention of the photocopier, itself, that is valuable?

If you buy an established business you may find that its not the desks and chairs, or even the manufacturing equipment, that gives the business its value; but the ideas it owns, its trade name, its company logo, and the manufacturing processes owned uniquely by the business.

> Generally speaking, intellectual property has certain features that separate it from all other types of property.

What Is Intellectual Property?

The term "intellectual property" refers to many different types of property, including inventions (and improvements to existing inventions), formulas, recipes, machines, manufacturing processes, artwork, writings (articles, books, advertising), cartoon characters, designs, movies, computer software, symbols, and logos.

Generally speaking, intellectual property has certain features that separate it from all other types of property:

- It is an original creation or idea;
- After creation, the rights in the property have been preserved and protected by the owner (who may be the creator or someone who employed the creator);
- It has, or may have, a commercial value to the owner or others now or in the future.

Why Is Intellectual Property So Valuable?

Most of his neighbors knew Pete to be a salesman for a national hand tool manufacturer. What they didn't know was that he was also a frustrated inventor.

Almost every night for five years Pete would go out to his garage and work on a design for a new hand tool, something that would find a use in every workshop in the country.

Pete's wife and family have put up with his absences as well as the fact that he has used all of their savings for development costs, prototypes, etc.

When Pete finally perfects his design he starts to show it to people in and around the industry, partly to look for marketing leads and partly out of pride.

Six months after he finishes his design, but before he finds a distributor, Pete finds an exact duplicate of his hand-tool at "Cheatems" a local branch of a national hardware store. Pete remembers when he showed his design to the sales people at Cheatems and their lack of interest in the tool. Now, they are making a fortune on his design and he is still months away from generating his first sale.

The examples are endless, and by no means are limited to thoughts of Pete and his garage workshop. Multinational companies spend hundreds of billions of dollars every year on research and development of new products, inventions, and processes.

The bottom line is that no one will spend the money, take the risk, or waste the time to develop important new ideas, inventions, medicines, or anything else unless there is protection for the results of their hard work.

The importance of preserving intellectual property has become so pronounced that new laws are being generated at both the state and federal levels mandating criminal prosecution for the theft of trade secrets and other intellectual property.

If your business exists solely to produce and sell a certain piece of machinery to which you hold the patent, think of what would happen if others took your design and started mass-producing it.

> The importance of preserving intellectual property has become so pronounced that new laws are being generated at both the state and federal levels mandating criminal prosecution for the theft of trade secrets and other intellectual property.

How Do You Protect Intellectual Property?

Intellectual property is generally protected by means of patents, trademarks, or copyrights.

Patents

There are two principal types of patents:

- *Utility Patent.* A utility patent protects new, useful processes, machines, compositions of matter, or any new and useful improvement thereof. This protection prevents someone other than the patent holder from making, using, or selling the patented invention for a period of 20 years.
- *Design Patent.* A design patent is issued for new, original, and ornamental design of an article of manufacture. This protection prevents someone other than the patent holder from making, using, or selling the patented invention for a period of 14 years.

The Application Process

Applying for a patent can be a long (three- to five-year) process than can cost thousands of dollars in legal and consulting fees.

As much as you may want to do the work yourself (in order to hold down costs), the patent application process usually begins with the hiring of an attorney who specializes in patents and other intellectual property. Most attorneys who perform patent work have technical backgrounds (and many even have graduate degrees in areas such as civil engineering, electrical engineering, chemical engineering, computer science, chemistry, physics, etc.).

Once an attorney is selected, a patent application is completed, which will be submitted to the United States Patent and Trademark Office in Washington, D.C.

You will also have to conduct a search of the patents on file at the Patent Office to determine what patents already exist and how they may affect your application. (Having an attorney with a technical background can be of enormous value in reviewing the patents on file, understanding the impact of similar or related patents, appreciating the economic benefit (or lack thereof) of previously filed patents upon your patent, refining the scope of the patent application, and even suggesting improvements to the idea or invention).

> Once an attorney is selected, a patent application is completed, which will be submitted to the United States Patent and Trademark Office in Washington, D.C.

The Patent Office will have an examiner review the application to determine whether the idea is something that:

- Is capable of being patented (that is, new and useful, processes, machines, compositions of matter, or any new and useful improvement thereof);
- Is owned by the applicant, who is the original inventor or creator;
- Is novel and original;
- Is useful; and
- Is not obvious to others in the trade or industry.

Protection of the Patent

Successfully registering the patent is only half the battle. Whether you are the inventor or someone who acquired rights in the patent through assignment, licensing, or purchase, you are going to have to take steps to protect your rights in the invention, even after you register the patent.

- Make sure that you use all of the warning notices and labeling required by statute (for example, U.S. Patent # 350056).
- Monitor the activities of employees, licensees, and all others who come in contact with the patented invention to make sure that the invention is not being circulated without proper notices or that it is being circulated carelessly;
- Take immediate and decisive legal action against any people or companies who may be infringing upon your patent;
- Continue to watch the industry and maintain aggressive research and development so that you can continue to obtain new patents on all potential improvements to the invention.

In short, if you aren't going to protect your invention, don't expect the courts to. In fact, failing to take immediate and decisive action to prevent the unauthorized use of your idea or invention may result in a loss of your patent. Years of time and money in

> In short, if you aren't going to protect your invention, don't expect the courts to.

development and patent application costs will all be for nothing because you thought that there was nothing else that you had to do to protect your invention.

Trademarks

A "trademark" is any name, symbol, logo, or device used to identify the origin and ownership of products and services and to distinguish them from those owned and sold by others. A "service mark" is any name, symbol, logo, or device relating to a service, as opposed to goods. The owner of a trademark can prevent others from using his trademark or one that is confusingly similar.

Remember, a trademark is your identification. It is your symbol with which potential customers will identify. Assuming that your product is well made and desired by the public, it will be the focus of good will among consumers. (The goal behind trademark protection is to prevent consumers and potential customers from purchasing someone else's product on the mistaken belief that it is yours.)

Trademarks do not have to be registered in order to confer rights on you. Without registration it is still possible to take legal action to prevent others from using your trademark. Your protection, however, will be limited to where you currently conduct business. And this can be a problem.

If, one day, you decide to branch out your business into another state, you may find that a trademark similar to yours is already in use in that state. You may have spent a lot of money developing your trademark. You may have even built an advertising campaign around it and your established customers will be looking for it. But, without registration, you are either going to have purchase the other person's rights (if they are for sale) or select another trademark to operate in that state.

For those who do not feel that this is enough protection (and you should be one of them) there is federal trademark protection.

The process for registration of a trademark is similar to that for obtaining a patent; that is, submit an application for trademark registration to the United States Patent and Trademark Office (Form 32-15 in the Appendix).

> Trademarks do not have to be registered in order to confer rights on you. Without registration it is still possible to take legal action to prevent others from using your trademark.

Once you record you trademark you have the right to:

- Sue in federal court to prevent the use of your trademark;
- Sue to prevent anyone, nationwide, from using your trademark, not just the immediate geographic area;
- Sue to recover for all damages, including profits, triple damages, and attorney's fees.

Registration is good for ten years but may be renewed for additional ten-year terms. It is important, however, that you continue to use the trademark during the period of registration. Remember, registration is not intended to reserve a name "just for the fun of it." You must actually be using the trademark or intend to use the trademark within six months after registration.

Not all trademarks are entitled to registration. There are three general categories of trademark protection:

- Arbitrary, coined, or fanciful marks. This is considered the strongest category of trademark protection. An arbitrary trademark is one that has nothing to do with the product or service and a consumer is not likely to know, just by looking at it, what the product is. (For example, "Seven Seas" for salad dressing, or "Apple" for computers.)

This is the strongest level of protection because it is truly unique when applied to the product. What are the chances of someone else accidentally using a similar trade name for the same product unless they are attempting to infringe on someone else's trademark?

- Suggestive Marks. A suggestive trademark is just that. It suggests a relationship to the product or service. At the same time, a consumer would not necessarily know what the product is just be seeing the trademark. (For example, "Second Hand Rose" for a second hand store, or "Ever-Brite" for a light bulb.)
- Descriptive Marks. A descriptive mark cannot usually be registered unless the owner can establish some distinctiveness or

> You must actually be using the trademark or intend to use the trademark within six months after registration.

consumer association between the trademark and the product. (For example, "Bobo's Cola" or "Cool-Whip" whipped cream.) Cola and whipped cream are in common usage. Trademarks cannot be granted with respect to words or terms in common usage. If, however, you can establish that the public can identify your product "Bobo's Cola" as separate and distinct from cola, generally, you may still qualify.

Your best bet when selecting a trademark is to pick one which is unrelated to the product and, therefore, unlikely to be infringed upon, even accidentally.

Protection of the Trademark

As with a patent, you are going to have to take steps to protect your rights in the trademark, even after registration.

- Make sure that you use all of the warning notices and labeling required by statute. (For example, use of the notation TM (Trademark), or SM (Service mark), or R (Registered) after the mark).
- Monitor the activities of employees, licensees, and all others who come in contact with the patented invention to make sure that the trademark is not being utilized without proper notices or that it is being circulated carelessly.
- Take immediate and decisive legal action against any people or companies who may be infringing upon your trademark.

Copyrights

Copyrights protect original works of authorship in the areas of "literary, dramatic, musical, artistic, graphical, sculptural, architectural, which are fixed in any tangible medium of expression."

As with a trademark, the author or creator of a visual work obtains various rights as soon as the work is created and fixed in a tangible medium. But, as with a trademark, the rights you obtain by registration make it worth the time and effort. (If your business relies upon the exclusive use of the copyrightable material, why wouldn't you want

> Copyrights protect original works of authorship in the areas of "literary, dramatic, musical, artistic, graphical, sculptural, architectural, which are fixed in any tangible medium of expression."

to obtain as much protection as possible? Would you leave your office unlocked or your keys in the ignition of your delivery truck?)

The Application Process

Unlike patents and trademarks, copyrights are submitted to the Copyright Office. There, the examiners will determine whether the submitted material is an appropriate work of original authorship.

Unlike patents and trademarks, copyrights are intended only to prevent the copying of registered material. But, if someone else comes up with the same material or idea, totally independent of the copyright holder, there is no right to sue for infringement.

Protection of the Copyright

As with patents and trademarks, you are going to have to take steps to protect your rights in the copyright, even after registration.

- Make sure that you use all of the warning notices and labeling required by statute (Copyright © 1999 by Wingpro, Inc. All Rights Reserved).
- Monitor the activities of employees, licensees, and all others who come in contact with the copyright to make sure that it is not being utilized without proper notices or that it is being circulated carelessly.
- Take immediate and decisive legal action against any people or companies who may be infringing upon your copyright.

> Unlike patents and trademarks, copyrights are intended only to prevent the copying of registered material.

Trade Secrets

A business's trade secrets can consist of any number of different materials and information, including the following:

- Customer lists
- Computer programs
- Methods of operation
- Formulas
- Recipes
- Data compilations relating to the business

In determining whether information rises to the level of a trade secret the courts will usually look at:

- Whether the information has an economic or commercial value;
- The amount of time and/or money spent by the owner to develop or gather the information;
- The effort made by the owner to keep the information confidential;
- The success of the owner at keeping the information confidential;
- Whether the information is generally known outside of the owner's business.

While trade secrets are usually discussed in conjunction with intellectual property, they are generally not protected by patents, trademarks, or copyrights. Instead, state law relating to unfair competition generally provides the protection for trade secrets. And, unlike patents or trademarks, laws protecting trade secrets generally do not prevent another person from developing and using the same information independently of yours.

As with other intellectual property, it is essential that you take all necessary and reasonable steps to protect your confidential information.

> As with other intellectual property, it is essential that you take all necessary and reasonable steps to protect your confidential information.

Over the last ten years Adam has built his business selling and installing computer networking software.

In the course of his business Adam has spent considerable effort and money gathering extensive information on not just his customers, but on prospective customers.

One day, Bob, Adam's most senior employee, resigned to take a job with one of Adam's competitors. When he leaves, Bob makes a full computer back-up of Adam's data-base including customer names, addresses, contact persons, purchases, prices, and everything else Adam has worked to gather over the years.

Adam hires a lawyer but the damage has been done. Adam's lawsuit will cost him thousands of dollars, three years of his time, and, even if he wins, damages will be too hard to prove, much less collect.

Confidentiality Agreements

What could Adam have done to protect himself?

If Adam wants to protect himself, and his trade secrets, he should, at a minimum:

- Have all employees sign contracts agreeing that various materials are confidential and agreeing to keep them that way;
- Talk with his computer specialist about restricting access to computer files that contain confidential information;
- Place "red flags" within data files so that he can determine whether his lists or data are being used by others;
- Have employees sign noncompete agreements. If employees cannot compete with him, his trade secrets will be of little value to them;
- Make numbered copies of all printed materials and have the employees to whom they are assigned sign for their receipt and return them at the end of the day or before leaving the company.

Streetwise Reality Tour

1. Having a patent does not guarantee financial success. Many times, there are simply no markets for the product or no one willing to manufacture or distribute the product.
2. Just because you have a patent or a trademark or a copyright doesn't mean that a competitor cannot or will not come up with a very similar invention, idea, or design based upon yours (and maybe even a little better) that your registration will not protect against.
3. Even if someone infringes on your patent, trademark, or copyright, the costs of litigating infringement lawsuits may take all of the money you have.

> Even if someone infringes on your patent, trademark, or copyright, the costs of litigating infringement lawsuits may take all of the money you have.

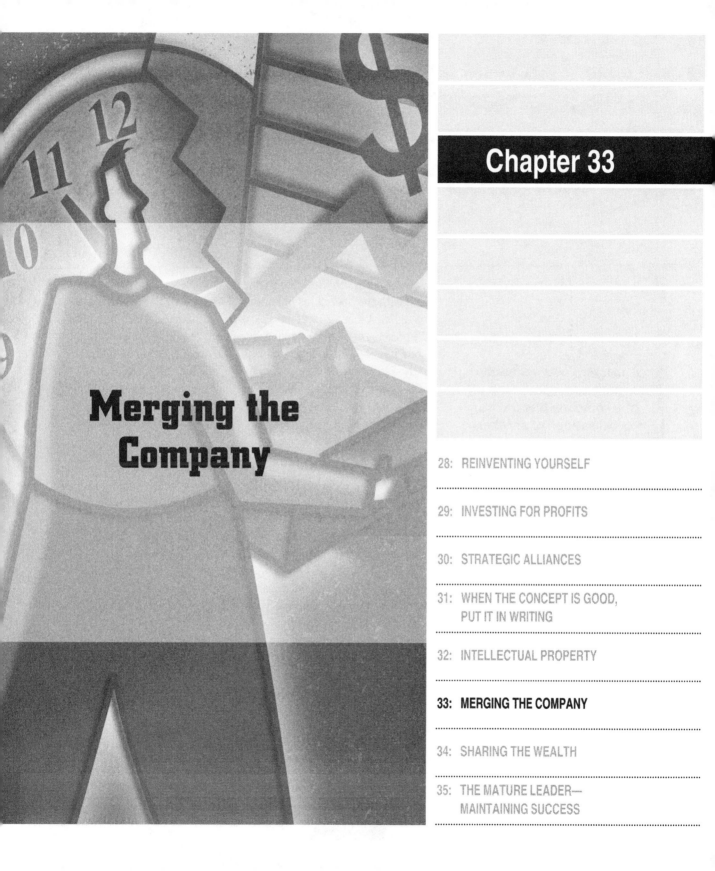

Chapter 33

Merging the Company

Perhaps you are not able to purchase another company outright but instead the best deal for your company will be a merger with another. A number of benefits can occur from this step—adding new customers, new product lines, and new territories. This may serve as a strategic way to grow.

What Is a Merger?

A merger occurs anytime the business operations of one company blend with the operations of another (Forms 33-01 and 33-02 in the Appendix). A merger can take a number of different forms, from one that preserves the separate identity of each of the original entities; to one in which the identity of one of the original entities significantly disappears, or is absorbed; to one in which an altogether new entity is formed and the identities of the original participants disappear. Some examples to help you understand this distinction are provided as follows:

> A merger occurs anytime the business operations of one company blend with the operations of another.

Retained Independence

Robin's corporation manufactures air filters for sale to commercial and some residential customers. Robin's company engages in the simple assembly of components, purchased from suppliers, into the final unit, the air filter itself.

Neither Robin nor her staff has any experience in manufacturing the component parts that go into the air filters. Robin, however, would very much like to secure a guaranteed source of supply for the blowers, which are central to her air filters. She would also like to diversify her business operations so that she is not so reliant on her air filter business.

Fifty miles away is Bobco, Inc., which manufactures the blowers used in Robin's air filters. Bob, the president of Bobco, Inc., knows that his blowers are not particularly unique and that his customers can easily switch to another supplier if he cannot consistently quote the lowest prices. He also sees a big future in the manufacture and sale of commercial air filters. Unfortunately, Bob also knows that Bobco, Inc., is not equipped to get into the air filter market.

Robin and Bobco, Inc., decide to merge their operations. Shares certificates are transferred and property is retitled. Now, Robin has a guaranteed source for the major component of her air filters and Bobco, Inc., gets a "foot in the door" of the potentially lucrative market of air filters. Both companies remain separate and distinct companies and, in fact, Bobco, Inc., can sell blowers to other customers in addition to Robin, and Robin can purchase blowers from another source.

Despite the merger, both companies maintain their previous locations, including staff, business premises, equipment, etc. In effect, nothing changes. Because these are different types of businesses there should be very little overlap between the functions of the various employees. So, there is no reason why there should be lay-offs or significant changes in management structure.

Merger in the Nature of a Sale

Many mergers look very much like the purchase of a business, with the purchasing entity merging the assets or operations of the seller into its own.

Using the Bobco example discussed previously:

Robin wants to secure a source of blowers for her air filters and looks in the direction of her major supplier, Bobco, Inc.

Bob, the president and sole shareholder of Robco, Inc., is reaching retirement age. Bob doesn't have the drive he once had, he has no children who are interested in taking over the business, and even if they were, Bob sees a bleak future in being solely engaged in the production of blowers.

As part of their merger, Bobco, Inc., agrees to be consumed by Robin's company.

Robin could keep the two companies separate but, with Bob approaching retirement and hoping to get out of

> Many mergers look very much like the purchase of a business, with the purchasing entity merging the assets or operations of the seller into its own.

the business altogether, Robin may decide to merge the two operations at the most beneficial location.

Robin will probably have her accounting department handle all accounting matters for both divisions, her payroll department can handle all employees with minimal extra effort, her personnel department can handle the hiring and employee benefits for all employees, and her collection department can handle all collection issues.

A New Company Is Formed

Many times, with mergers of larger organizations, companies neither remain as separate entities nor as one consumed by the other. Instead, the identity of both disappears and shows up in an entirely new entity.

Under the same set of facts discussed previously:

Robin's company and Bobco, Inc., are both small regional companies and do not have much name recognition outside of their own geographic areas.

Neither Robin nor Bob wants to leave the business, and both realize that they could each bring something different and unique to a new business enterprise.

Robin and Bob get together and create a new corporation, Robbob, Inc. Bob, because he is older and has a certain talent for overall planning, will become chairman of the board of directors. Robin, with a special expertise in the details of manufacturing, will become chief executive officer.

Because they are close to each other in terms of distance and because neither owns their particular facility, Robin and Bob decide to merge operations in an entirely new facility to be leased by the new company. They will now pool their advertising dollars into new "catchy" product names and will market themselves as an entirely new enterprise.

> Many times, with mergers of larger organizations, companies neither remain as separate entities nor as one consumed by the other.

Reasons to Merge

There are a number of different reasons why one company would want to merge with another.

Access to Trade Secrets or Patented Inventions

When Bob looks at Robin's company, he sees that Robin has designed a unique air filter that has features possessed by no other. Bob would like to move into the air filter market but he knows that he could not create a better design than what he sees in Robin's air filters.

By merging with Robin, Bob gains access not only to a new product line and market, but to the patented features of Robin's air filter, as well.

Economies of Scale

Sometimes a merger makes sense because, for a little additional effort, one of the companies can take over all of the functions of the second.

For example, Robin's company could take over all billing, payroll, advertising, debt collection, and personnel functions of both companies. So, where both companies had a total of twenty employees working in these areas, once combined, they need only ten. So, right off the bat, the merger has saved anywhere from $300,000 to $500,000 in salaries, employment taxes, insurances, and pension benefits.

Allows One Company to Move Into a New Geographic Area

If Robin wants to sell her air filters in a market 500 miles away from her headquarters she is going to face significant problems. To do business that far away, Robin is going to have to establish a sales force familiar with the customers in that area, offer prices better than those of her competitors, and overcome customer loyalties (and this may be difficult if Robin has to absorb the costs of shipping to this new market). In addition, Robin will face the problem of lack of name recognition and the fact that she does not have a regular interaction with customers in those areas.

> Sometimes a merger makes sense because, for a little additional effort, one of the companies can take over all of the functions of the second.

If, instead, Robin merges with a company similar to her own, and with operations already established in that geographic area, she reduces her risks considerably. She now acquires access to a sales force already established in the area, established trade names, familiarity with the customers, and she can utilize production capability in that distant market to hold down her delivery costs.

Access to New Product Lines (the Vertical Merger)

At the beginning of this chapter we told about Robin looking to acquire Robco, Inc., so as to guarantee a source of supply. This is a vertical merger. It is not a case of a manufacturer of air filters merging with the manufacturer of another type of air filter, but the manufacturer of an air filter merging with a supplier or even a consumer of the air filter.

Diversification

We have all been taught the importance of not "putting all your eggs in one basket." For Rob, who engages solely in the manufacture of blowers, and for Robin, who simply assembles the component parts into new air filters, the risk is that their particular industry might be hurt by a slump in the economy, or a loss of sales to new and better products. By merging, they diversify.

So now, if the market for air filters were to suddenly "nose-dive," the new merged company could focus its attention on the manufacture and sale of blowers to either other customers or in new uses altogether. If, on the other hand, the market for blowers suddenly diminishes, all attention can be directed toward air filters, modifications, and new uses.

Preparatory Steps for a Merger

Assess Needs

The very first thing you are going to have to do is assess your own business for any weaknesses. You don't consider a merger

> The very first thing you are going to have to do is assess your own business for any weaknesses.

simply because its possible! You consider a merger for what it provides your business!

Reasons to Consider a Merger

- You have a limited number of products and/or services and you cannot expand with your current organizational structure or capital;
- You and your staff have a lack of expertise in manufacturing or sales, which would restrict your ability to move into new areas;
- The competition for your product or services is so great in your area of operation that profits have almost disappeared;
- Your particular product is becoming obsolete;
- The size of your company makes it impossible to acquire bank loans to significantly expand or to assure prospective larger customers that you are able to meet their supply needs.

These are just some of the things that you should consider, but they are by no means the only things to consider. It is important to periodically sit down and assess your business, where you want it to go and, if it can't get there, to determine why not. The answer to many of your problems may be a merger.

Look for Businesses to Supplement Yours

Once you uncover a particular weakness in your business (and determine that it is not feasible to deal with it internally), you need to start searching for the business that will address those needs. Don't simply look for a merger partner that is successful, because it may be successful for a number of reasons unrelated to what you are looking for. (And, if the merger target is that successful, are you really going to have any bargaining strengths when you sit down to hammer out the details of the merger?)

Success aside, if the other business mirrors your own business's strengths, does it really have anything to offer you?

In either event, there may be no logical reason to merge with that particular business, no matter how successful it is.

> It is important to periodically sit down and assess your business, where you want it to go and, if it can't get there, to determine why not. The answer to many of your problems may be a merger.

If you are looking to expand your product line, does the merger target provide that type of expanded product line? Is its product line significantly different from yours? Is it protected by patent or copyright? Is there a future market for the target company's products? These are all things to consider.

If you have a good product but you can't quite seem to "get your foot in the door" of your target market, you may be looking for a merger partner with an established name, an established sales force, trademarks, and other intellectual property that people automatically think of when they think of the particular type of product you manufacture.

Initial Discussions

Once you determine your needs and have located prospective parties who offer what you believe your company needs to have, you have to start focusing your efforts. If possible, narrow your search to the top five.

Create a chart showing your specific needs and how each of the prospective candidates meets those needs.

The next step is to make introductions and discuss the benefits of a merger. Some potential targets will be immediately resistant, while others will be quick sells, and others still may need a little time to see the benefits of a merger. As with any negotiation, you've got to present the proposal as a "win-win" situation.

The Work Begins

Once you have found a target who is interested in pursuing merger discussions the real work begins.

Assessment Team

The first step is to put together your assessment team. The team will consist of your lawyer, your accountant, your top managers, a business consultant, and, possibly, your banker. Each will be assigned a separate issue to consider from the standpoint of whether

> Create a chart showing your specific needs and how each of the prospective candidates meets those needs.

the target is really a good target and how the merger will affect the long- and short-term operations of the business.

Confidentiality Agreements

Before you even get started, you want to have confidentiality agreements executed by everyone involved. Remember, in many mergers, it is not simply a one-way street. Many mergers are true mergers, and not simply purchases of the target company. So you may be sharing information on your sales, customers, product design, and manufacturing processes the same as the target company. (Does Bobco, Inc., really need Robin's company or would it do just as well to learn the details of Robin's operations so that it can do manufacture the same air filters in its own plant? Without a confidentiality agreement, you may find out the hard way.)

As we have discussed in previous chapters, the confidentiality agreement should identify what each party is supplying in terms of information, identify the confidential information to the greatest extent possible, and stipulate that neither party may use that information for any reason other than for the conduct of the review.

Due Diligence

Due diligence is the term used by bankers, lawyers, and business people to describe the review of the business, financial, and legal aspects of a business.

Due diligence is often expensive, and it is usually time consuming. If the merger does not go through, it is a lot of wasted time and money. But, there is nothing more important to a successful merger than due diligence. It is what allows you to "pull back the curtains" and examine, in minute detail, the operations of the other party and to determine whether it is as good as you had thought or if there are "skeletons in the closet."

Remember, for all the good reasons to merge there are also some bad ones, and some merger targets will make their financial statements look a whole lot better than they are in the hopes that it will be bailed out by the strength of your business in a merger.

> The confidentiality agreement should identify what each party is supplying in terms of information, identify the confidential information to the greatest extent possible, and stipulate that neither party may use that information for any reason other than for the conduct of the review.

Things to Look for During Your Due Diligence

Generally, the amount of information you will be looking for during your due diligence will vary depending upon the type of businesses involved, the length of time the parties have been in existence, and their legal structure. Preliminarily, however, you will want to see the following:

- Corporate minute book with articles of incorporation, bylaws, and minutes of previously held directors and shareholders meetings
- Current list of shareholders, as reflected on the books of the corporation
- Any shareholder agreements whereby a shareholder agrees not to transfer shares or agrees to sell them at set prices to the corporation or to other shareholders
- Balance sheets and financial statements
- Reports of any audits during the preceding five years
- Copies of federal, state and local income tax returns
- Any correspondence with regard to those returns or amendments of those returns
- Monthly balance sheets, financial projections, budgets, accounts receivables
- Any employment agreements, and independent contractor agreements
- Any union contracts
- Any employee benefit plans (pension, retirement, health, stock option plans, all other benefit or incentive plans)
- List of all property owned by the parties
- List of all property leased by the parties
- Fair market value for all property owned by the parties
- An explanation of operations

While technically not part of the due diligence, you can't consider a merger without giving serious thought as to how the merged companies will operate in the future.

For example, one of the first things you are going to have to consider is who will be calling the shots with regard to the new

> While technically not part of the due diligence, you can't consider a merger without giving serious thought as to how the merged companies will operate in the future.

entity. This is made more difficult if the merger is not a buy-out of another entity but is a true merger of two or more entities into a new organization. For example:

- Will the president of the target entity play a key role in the new entity and, if so, what will be his responsibilities?
- What is going to happen to the shareholders of the previous company?
- Will the shareholders have the same number of shares in the new entity or will their shares be discounted based upon the valuations set on the entities themselves?
- How will the sales and marketing strategies of the two companies come together in the new entity?
- Will the new entity retain the trade name of the previous companies and/or their products, thereby capitalizing on good will, or will entirely new marketing strategies be established?

Negotiation–Setting the Price

Once you have decided that a merger is not only feasible, but desirable, you have got to decide how to merge the two companies while giving value to the shareholders or owners of each.

If the value of Robin's company is $500,000 but the value of Robco, Inc. is $2,000,000, will you give the owners of each an equal share of the new entity? If current value is the only consideration, you undoubtedly will not give equal shares. But, if you don't give equal shares of ownership to each of the two factions, won't the management that controls the new entity be in the hands of the larger more valuable partner?

This is where negotiation comes in.

Structuring the Transaction

Once you have decided that you want the merger to go forward and have valued the entities participating in the merger, you have to decide whether the legal entities (e.g., corporations) will be acquired or just the assets of those corporations.

> Will the shareholders have the same number of shares in the new entity or will their shares be discounted based upon the valuations set on the entities themselves?

Purchase of Assets

In most cases, a merger that is in the nature of a purchase is best structured as a purchase of assets. The acquiring entity wants to take over the value of the acquired company, including employees, equipment, assets, etc., but it specifically does not want the liabilities that may go with that old company, such as, pension obligations, environmental problems, tax problems, etc.

At the same time, the acquiring entity avoids problems with the shareholders of the acquired entity. In essence, the acquiring business pays a certain monetary value for the assets of the acquired corporation and that payment is distributed among the shareholders of that corporation in proportion to their ownership interest.

Purchase of Shares

Depending upon the circumstances, it may be useful to purchase the stock of the target business. This is particularly true where the acquired entity has licenses, permits, or contracts that are nontransferable.

Due diligence is particularly important in this type of situation because you are going to be taking on any debt of the acquired business, and some of it may be substantial (for example, environmental liability, pension liability, tort liability).

Noncompete Agreements

Once the merger is completed, there may be former owners, shareholders, and managers who will be looking for work. If they start up a new business, identical to the one that just merged with yours, you may find that you just paid a lot of money for nothing.

For example, the former managers have the knowledge of the production process, sales plans, sales projections, and may have the customer's loyalty. Your purchase of the "good will" means nothing if it walks out the door with the former owners or managers.

As part of any merger or purchase, make sure that noncompete agreements are signed by all former officers, shareholders, and management. It may cost you a little more to obtain this, but without it the next sound you hear may be the sound of your money going down the drain.

> Depending upon the circumstances, it may be useful to purchase the stock of the target business. This is particularly true where the acquired entity has licenses, permits, or contracts that are nontransferable.

Streetwise Reality Tour

1. A merger is not a "cure-all." Sometimes it just opens the door to a new set of problems.
2. A merger may make business sense, but it may end up defeating why you really wanted to have your own business in the first place: independence.
3. Just because you can grow and merge doesn't mean that you have to grow and merge. Take the time to reassess your personal goals. Does a merger make sense from a personal perspective?
4. While a partnership has been described as a marriage, a merger is more. Partners can always "divorce." If a merger doesn't work, you may find that there is no way to undo it, at least not without destroying your original business.

> Just because you can grow and merge doesn't mean that you have to grow and merge. Take the time to reassess your personal goals. Does a merger make sense from a personal perspective?

For more information on this topic, visit our Web site at www.businesstown.com

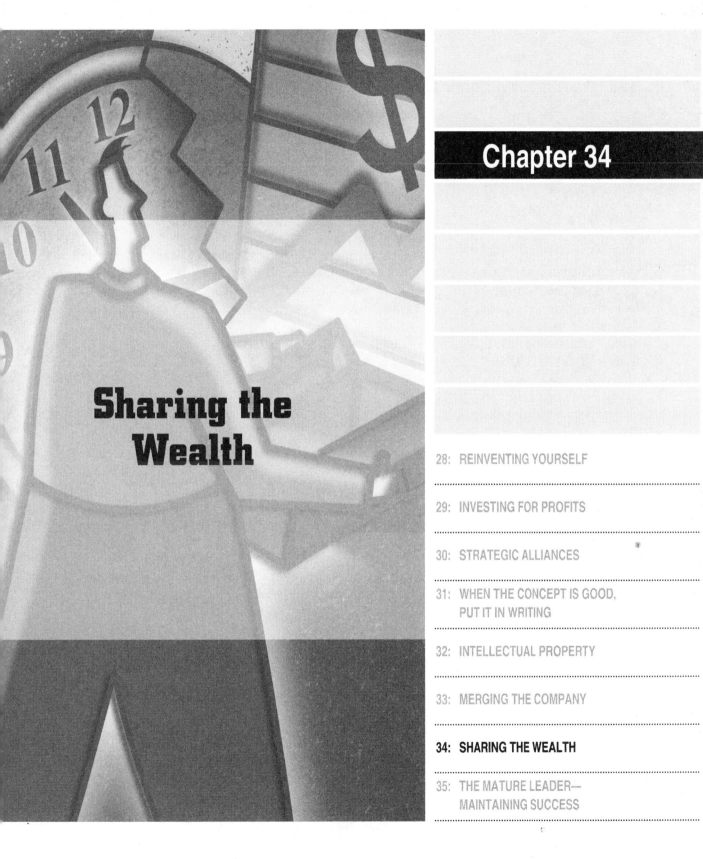

Chapter 34

Sharing the Wealth

At some point, and for any number of different reasons, you may decide that its time to share the wealth (or future wealth) of the business.

For many of you this may seem a totally foreign concept. After all, you are the one who took the risks, you are the one who mortgaged your home, and you are the one who put in 80-hour weeks building the business into the success it is.

Sure, you've had some very good employees and they have contributed to the company, but they have always been paid for their time and, if they didn't like it, they were free to leave. They got something and you got something, so why should they get more?

There are several reasons why a savvy business owner would want to share the profits of the business.

To Motivate Employees

You may want to review the chapter of this book that deals with motivating employees.

There are many things you can do to motivate an employee and to reap the benefits of his or her work. And, while money is not always the tool for motivating employees, "it ain't bad." More importantly, if you want your employees to be as concerned about the long-term health and success of the company, what better way to do so than to give them a small piece of what they have been working for?

> If you want your employees to be as concerned about the long-term health and success of the company, what better way to do so than to give them a small piece of what they have been working for?

Matt owns a small but successful restaurant. Because he can't be there every day, and because many of the jobs are minimum wage jobs, he often employs college students in such capacities as hostess, waiters, bus boys, etc.

What Matt doesn't know is that, on Friday evenings, when he is taking a much-deserved rest, customers are actually leaving the restaurant because they are not being seated quickly enough, the food is not being served quickly enough, and the orders are often incorrectly taken and delivered.

For those employees who do not even look to tips, the mindset is simply "so what?"

If, on the other hand, that employee knew that his paycheck would be based upon the night's profits and the profits of every weekend after that, then you may well see a vastly different attitude toward customer satisfaction.

To Reward Employees

When an employee does a good job for you, you want that employee to be rewarded. The reward not only serves to acknowledge the superior effort by the employee (remember that encouragement and recognition are two key factors in employee motivation), but the word spreads to other employees that their hard work may also be recognized and rewarded. How often does good employee work go unrewarded or unrecognized? The fact that a program is in place to reward employees, and that system for reward is not simply at the whim of the manager or owner but is part of a program or benefit plan, will greatly enhance the benefits.

To Show Appreciation

While examples of this are few and far between, very often a business owner will establish a benefit program for the sake of his employees just because he is grateful for their efforts over the years, which have led to his success.

In one recent real-life situation, a paving company, started 40 years before, was sold to a large corporation for $400,000,000. The man who started and ran the company decided to pay out approximately $150,000,000 to his employees to thank them and to show recognition of their contribution to his success.

> Stock option plans have attracted a great deal of attention within the last few years, particularly with respect to Internet-based companies.

Ways in Which to Share the Wealth

Stock Option Plans

Stock option plans have attracted a great deal of attention within the last few years, particularly with respect to Internet-based companies. Stock option plans are a great way to repay employees.

Adam has started a small e-business and needs a staff of trained software engineers to get the whole thing up and running.

Unfortunately, software engineers are in high demand and they can easily find businesses willing to pay $100,000 a year as a guaranteed salary for their services.

Adam knows he cannot compete with those hard cash offers so, instead, offers his employees $50,000 per year with stock options in the company.

In essence, what Adam tells his employees is that if they stay with the company and work hard and if the company succeeds they will be able to turn those stock options into ownership worth, sometimes, thousands of times more than the original stock option.

In Adam's case, after the first year of their employment he gives each employee a grant to purchase 1,000 shares in the corporation at $.10 per share. That continues each and every year for five years.

In year six of the corporation Adam is doing so well that he takes the company public and the value of the initial shares is $200. At that point, each of the employees will exercise their option to purchase shares at 10 cents per share, making them now the owner of 5,000 shares apiece for a total investment of $500. Because the shares are now worth $200 a share, they merely run to their brokerage house and sell the shares on the market for a total of $500,000; a clear profit of $499,500. Their total compensation for each year is now $150,000.

> In a profit sharing plan, the business owner decides that a certain percentage of its profits will be placed into a fund and divided, according to some formula, among the employees.

Profit Sharing

In a profit sharing plan, the business owner decides that a certain percentage of its profits (usually profits over a said dollar amount) will be placed into a fund and divided, according to some formula, among the employees.

Bonus Plans

A bonus can be anything valued by the employee, but what seems to be more important is the fact that there is an actual bonus program. Bonuses can be a double-edge sword. The fact that the boss is feeling generous on one day and rewards an employee could have a disastrous effect if the equally good work of other employees is ignored altogether.

To be effective, a bonus program has got to be uniformly applied and must, as much as possible, reward each employee equally when their efforts benefit the company.

Cafeteria Plan

Cafeteria plans are sponsored by the employer, who sets a fixed amount for each employee to access. The company then offers employees a list of benefits that they can receive, such as life insurance, health insurance, dental and vision coverage, as well as disability insurance. An employee not needing any or all of these benefits could increase their cash compensation by the unused portion.

401(k) Plans

401(k) plans are retirement plans set up by the employer in accordance with strict guidelines under federal law. The key benefit of a 401(k) plan is that it allows both the employer and employee to contribute money to the plan without immediate income tax consequences.

In most cases, the money that the employee builds up in the plan is completely safe and cannot be touched by creditors. It is invested and the value grows tax free, until such time as the employee starts drawing against the fund during his retirement years.

Perks

In addition to the larger items discussed previously, an employer can provide any number of different benefits to employees, sometimes of great value and sometimes of smaller monetary value, which will still have an impact in improving productivity and morale. Sometimes the perks do nothing more than show the appreciation of the owner, and sometimes they provide a real benefit to employees, providing them with peace of mind and relieving some of the stress of their daily lives, giving them a clear head for

> The key benefit of a 401(k) plan is that it allows both the employer and employee to contribute money to the plan without immediate income tax consequences.

the business affairs of the owner. Some of these perks can include the following:

- Day care facilities
- Health club memberships
- Taxi service when working late
- Education benefits
- Attendance at seminars and conferences
- Company cafeteria

The list could go on, but the concept is clear. Give some time and thought to what might be of service to your employees, and when the profits allow for it, share the wealth you have created together.

Streetwise Reality Tour

1. No company ever made it to great success on the efforts of just one. Know the contribution of your employees and reward it.
2. In the competition for the best work force, total compensation including benefits is often considered.
3. You can also participate in some of the plans such as 401(k) and it will shelter some of your compensation until you retire. It is a win/win opportunity.

> You can also participate in some of the plans such as 401(k) and it will shelter some of your compensation until you retire. It is a win/win opportunity.

For more information on this topic, visit our Web site at www.businesstown.com

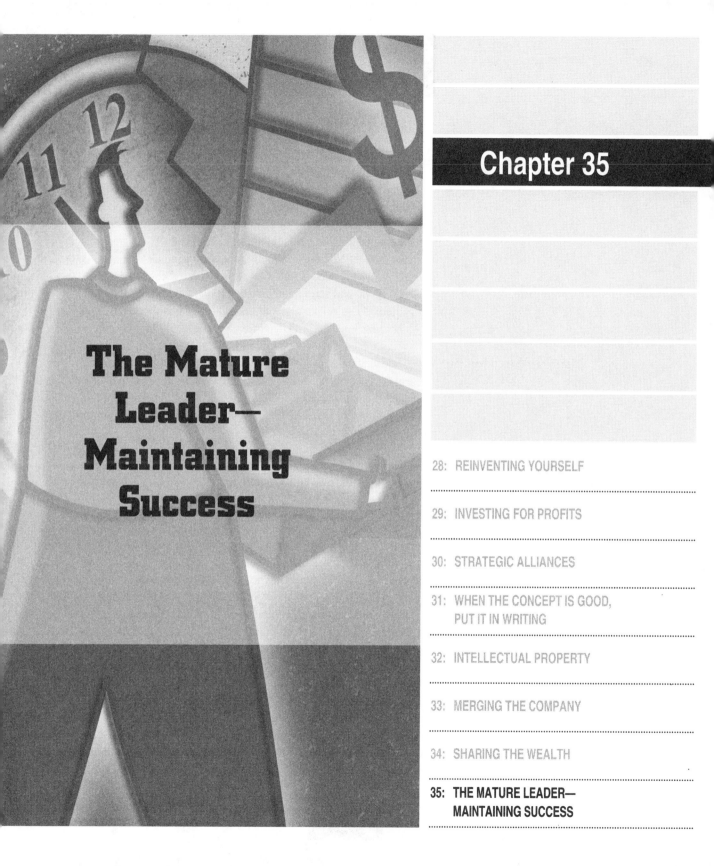

Chapter 35

The Mature Leader— Maintaining Success

The early days of Carl's distributing business involved many 16-hour days and 6- to 7-day weeks. There wasn't any role in the organization that he didn't fill. From the warehouse to delivery to the office, Carl did whatever was needed. As soon as was possible, he hired others, taught them well, and built a successful company. During the rapid growth phase, he spent much of his time meeting with accountants and bankers, and romancing customers. Volume and profit grew and his employees handled the day-to-day tasks well. Carl walked around checking up on everyone and soon he became bored. He began spending more time on the golf course and taking longer vacations. Why not? He wasn't really needed. Or was he?

The leadership role changes during the life of a business, and it isn't always easy to know what is expected and how to change. But an important skill is to be sensitive to the needs of your company and committed to learning the new skills required to maintain and build on the success you have achieved.

Your Attention Is Required

Regardless of whether you have work to do or not, your presence and your interest are necessary. After all, you are the one everyone looks to as the ultimate decision maker, and you must be up to speed on what is happening inside the company, in the marketplace you serve, and in the general business community. You won't learn this on the golf course. Much about your company and your industry will be changing, with cycles becoming shorter and shorter. Any gap in your knowledge could prove very costly.

When the day comes that you are no longer enthusiastic about your business, that is the day you must think about getting out. If you have a successor, put him or her on the fast track. If not, prepare to find a buyer. Nothing destroys a company faster than the indifference of the owner.

Employees lose their motivation, needed decisions get postponed or not made at all, and the investment of time and money

> The leadership role changes during the life of a business, and it isn't always easy to know what is expected and how to change.

for the future seldom gets made. If you are not interested, find
someone who is.

Learn How to Macromanage

You started as a worker, and chances are, when you hired employees,
you acted as a micromanager. That is, you oversaw everyone's activity and discussed all decisions, some of them very inconsequential.
This was your creation and you felt you needed to know everything.
Then you learned how to delegate work, but have you really learned
to delegate authority?

Do you have an organizational chart? If not, you should—and it
should be specific as to who reports to what department, and if at all
possible, keep the number of managers reporting directly to you at a
minimum. If you can have an effective general manager to field all
but the most essential questions, that makes a good buffer zone.
Having a number of line managers report to you takes time and may
cause some confusion.

Empower Your Managers

Allow people to make decisions, and allow them to make mistakes.
Chances are you have in the past and will do so in the future—but
the important issue is that you corrected the mistake before it
caused any damage. Now is the time to allow others that privilege.
No one is perfect, but few of us would be willing to make many creative decisions in an environment where we were graded on every
misstep. If you have hired competent folks and trained them well,
you can expect that they will act prudently and work to minimize any
effect of their miscalculations. Back them up.

Put Money Where the Authority Is

The best way to add real accountability to managers is to give them a
budget to spend or a financial goal to meet and judge them by their

> Do you have an
> organizational chart?
> If not, you should—and
> it should be specific as
> to who reports to what
> department, and if at all
> possible, keep the number
> of managers reporting
> directly to you at a
> minimum.

effectiveness. If they work in the revenue side (sales), the goal is perhaps to increase in income. On the production side, it may be reduction in costs. The budgetary authority shows confidence, and the specific, outcome-based goal is a way to encourage others to use their effort and creativity and benefit from its successful outcome.

Instead of overseeing day-to-day minutia, you will meet with your top managers and review the results of their work. You may also convene or attend larger managers' meetings. You will need to find benchmark numbers to review and make sure you collect and analyze them regularly. Act like a professional executive, and your company will benefit from it.

Be Visible as a Representative

Your company will always be very connected to you, and people will closely associate the two—you and the company. If your name is on the marquee, this is even more true. The higher the profile that you keep, the more your name and the company will be in front of potential customers. It really is a part of your role.

Customers like to know that "the boss" is concerned with how they are being treated, and they like special attention. You can do that by making appearances at conferences, trade shows, and conventions. Perhaps you can host a cocktail party or a dinner. Take some special clients to lunch. Make calls to ask how they are doing. Send letters to mark special occasions, or say thanks for a new order or a contract renewal. In short, be an ambassador, telling the company story and winning new friends whenever you can.

Your Place in the Community

Building a successful business is quite an achievement, and it is likely that you have had some luck and some help along the way. Some of the help may have been local—your community banker, your local professionals (lawyer, accountant, insurance broker, etc.), and perhaps a local customer base. You have benefited from your

> Customers like to know that "the boss" is concerned with how they are being treated, and they like special attention.

community, and now it is time for you to make a contribution. It can be fun, even beneficial.

There are a number of local organizations that give you a way to do this, starting with the local Chamber of Commerce. They are interested in promoting the business community as well as the look, safety, and desirability of the area. Service organizations such as Rotary, Lions, and Kiwanis are always worthwhile because of their charitable deeds. Then there are nonprofit boards that could benefit from your expertise and the skills you have acquired. Join one or take part in several activities—it's the right thing to do and you will enjoy it as well.

Streetwise Reality Tour

1. As long as the business is yours, you must give it the attention it needs.
2. Empower your managers and encourage them to make decisions and impact operations.
3. Remember to return a bit of the good fortune you have received.

> Empower your managers and encourage them to make decisions and impact operations.

For more information on this topic, visit our Web site at www.businesstown.com

Appendix

Form 01-01
Business Plan—Imago Press

1. The Concept

With a combined experience of almost four decades in small business management and a shared love of the written word, Vera A and Suzanne C have founded a new venture to leverage this synergy. A's background and knowledge of the printing industry and C's experience as a speaker, seminar leader, and published author comprise the formula for success as a niche market subsidy publisher. Focusing on projects in several specifics genres such as business, politics, biographies, and modern cultural topics, the founders believe that they can offer clients a professional level of support in services such as writing, editing, design, and marketing, as well as quality printing.

This venture will benefit from Vera's ownership of Imago Press, which offers a cost advantage in the printing side of the publishing. This will differentiate this company with their ability to offer a higher level of service at competitive pricing.

Subsidy publishing is a consistently growing business. The economics of the commercial publishing industry are very top-loaded on a few high-profile projects, and many well written books with good market potential are not accepted by the traditional publishers. Writers in greater numbers have determined that it is in their creative as well as financial self-interest to retain their own copyright and self-publish their work. Imago Press expects to become a respected player in this business.

II. The Market

In 1994, there were approximately 154,000 books published, of which 18%, or over 27,000, were self-published. A quarter of these are written, edited, printed, and distributed by specific interest organizations. The balance of almost 20,000 are individual works self-published by their authors. These are the individuals to whom Imago Press will market their services. Our projections are based on capturing one-half of 1% of this market (100 books) by the second year of operation, although reaching the 1% or 200-book level could well be within reach.

III. Operating Strategies

Imago Press will operate as a virtual corporation with no full-time employees and the principal working on a part-time basis. All editors, graphic designers, and marketing professionals will be independent contractors brought in on an as-needed basis. Once fully operational, a small administrative staff will be added as needed. At present, it is our intention to operate from the headquarters of Imago Press. This will be a low-overhead operation.

We will position ourselves as one of the more sophisticated subsidy publishers as we will not accept any manuscript submitted that we are unable to publish and promote with full commitment. In order to produce the high quality from both the literary and production that we desire, it will be critical to accept only the work that we believe we can give the best presentation. We will create an editorial board to review all submissions, make suggestions as to content and style, and provide insights into the distribution strategies. We are currently forming this group.

The other significant difference between Imago Press and the average subsidy publisher is the way in which we will market our services. While most subsidy publishers use advertising in magazines and newspapers, both those directed to writers and general interest, Imago Press will be more directed in its approach.

First will be direct solicitation at writers' conferences. C has been attending a number of these over the past few years, making presentations at a few of them. She will continue this effort, and A will begin to attend others during 2000. Both Vera and Suzanne have been approached by people looking to self-publish, and these opportunities will now be fully developed in one-to-one meetings.

A direct mail solicitation will be made to literary agents who often see works that should be published but for many reasons can't be sold. We will ask for referrals, and, if it is appropriate, we will offer a finder's fee. There are other professionals within publishing such as freelance editors, etc. whom we intend to solicit.

Finally, there are a number of professional organizations whose members are interested in the possibility of self-publishing, primary among these are speakers groups. Many speakers create books as a product to sell after their presentations as a source of additional revenue. Academics, scholars, and professional consultants are also likely candidates for self-publishing.

IV. Sources of Revenue

Primary source of revenue will be the value-added services we add to the book printing to making it full-service publishing. These will include writing services, editing, typesetting, cover design, and marketing and promotional advice. Freelance professionals will be utilized and their services will be marked up by 25-40% depending on the level of coordination required. In addition, all printing will be commissioned by Imago Press at the rate of 15%.

The average project value is expected to be $12,000 with $6,500 in printing costs and the balance in additional services. The average will result in revenues to the publishing group of $6,475. At the level of 100 books/year, the company will have total revenues of $647,000 and could reach the 200 book/year level and revenues of $1,294,000.

V. Capital Required

Legal and Accounting	$1,000
Promotional Materials	$7,500
Travel and Conference Fees	$3,500
Marketing Seminars	$3,000
Working Capital	$15,000
Total	$30,000

VI. Capitalization Plan

1. *2,000 Shares Issued Upon Incorporation*

Shareholders	Shares Issued	Price Per Share	Capitalization This Issue	% Interest
V.	1,000	$1	$1,000	33%
S.	1,000	$1	$1,000	33%

2. *750 Shares to Board Members*

Shareholders	Shares Issued	Price Per Share	Capitalization This Issue	% Interest
Insiders	750	$25	$18,750	24%

3. *250 Shares to Investors Shareholders*

Shareholders	Shares Issued	Price Per Share	Capitalization This Issue	% Interest
Outside Investors	250	$50	$12,500	8%

Form 02-01
Partnership Agreement

AGREEMENT by and between the Undersigned ('Partners').

1.   **Name.** The name of the partnership is: _____

2.   **Partners.** The names of the initial partners are: _____

3.   **Place of Business.** The principal place of business of the partnership is: _____.

4.   **Nature of Business.** The partnership shall generally engage in the following business: _____.

5.   **Duration.** The partnership shall commence business on: _____ and shall continue until terminated by this agreement, or by operation of law.

6.   **Contribution of Capital.** The partners shall contribute capital in proportionate shares as follows:

     Partner   Capital   Partnership Shares

7.   **Allocation of Depreciation or Gain or Loss on Contributed Property.** The partners understand that, for income tax purposes, the partnership's adjusted basis of some of the contributed property differs from fair market value at which the property was accepted by the partnership. However the partners intend that the general allocation rule of the Internal Revenue Code shall apply, and that the depreciation or gain or loss arising with respect to this property shall be allocated proportionately between the partners, as allocated in Paragraph 5 above, in determining the taxable income or loss of the partnership and the distributive share of each partner in the same manner as if such property had been purchased by the partnership at a cost equal to the adjusted tax basis.

8.   **Capital Accounts.** An individual capital account shall be maintained for each partner, the capital of each partner shall consist of that partner's original contribution of capital, as described in Paragraph 6, and increased by additional capital contributions and decreased by distributions in reduction of partnership capital and reduced by his/her share of partnership losses, if these losses are charge to the capital accounts.

9.   **Drawing Accounts.** An individual drawing account shall be maintained for each partner. All withdrawals by a partner shall be charged to his/her drawing account. Withdrawals shall be limited to amounts unanimously agreed to by the partners.

10. **Salaries.** No partner shall receive any salary for services rendered to the partnership except as specifically and first approved by each of the partners.

11. **Loan by Partners.** If a majority of partners consent, any partner may lend money to the partnership at an interest and terms rate agreed in writing, at the time said loan is made.

12. **Profits and Losses.** Net profits of the partnership shall be divided proportionately between the partners, and the net losses shall be borne proportionately as follows:

     Partner   Proportion

13. **Management.** The partners shall have equal rights and control in the management of the partnership.

14. **Books of Accounts.** The partnership shall maintain adequate accounting records. All books, records, and accounts of the partnership shall be open at all times to inspection by all partners, or their designated representatives.

15. **Accounting Basis.** The books of account shall be kept on a cash basis.

16. **Fiscal Year.** The books of account shall be kept on a fiscal/calendar year basis, commencing January 1st and ending December 31st, and shall be closed and balanced at the end of each year.

17. **Annual Audit.** The books of account shall be audited as of the close of each fiscal year by an accountant chosen by the partners.

18. **Banking.** All funds of the partnership shall be deposited in the name of the partnership into such checking or savings accounts as designated by the partners.

19. **Death or Incapacity.** The death or incapacity of a partner shall cause an immediate dissolution of the partnership.

20. **Election of Remaining Partner to Continue Business.** In the event of the retirement, death, incapacity, or insanity of a partner, the remaining partners shall have the right to continue the business of the partnership, either by themselves or in conjunction with any other person or persons they may select, but they shall pay to the retiring partner, or to the legal representatives of the deceased or incapacitated partner, the value of his or her interest in the partnership.

21. **Valuation of Partner's Interest.** The value of the interest of a retiring, incapacitated, deceased, or insane partner shall be the sum of (a) the partner's capital account, (b) any unpaid loans due the partner, and (c) the partner's proportionate share if the accrued net profits remaining undistributed in his drawing account. No value for goodwill shall be included in determining the value of a partner's interest, unless specifically agreed in advance by the partners.

22. **Payment of Purchase Price.** The value of the partner's interest shall be paid, without interest, to the retiring partner, or to the legal representative of the deceased, incapacitated or insane partner, in twelve (12) monthly installments, commencing on the first day of the second month after the effective date of the purchase.

23. **Termination.** In the event that the remaining partner does not elect to purchase the interest of the retiring, deceased, incapacitate, or insane partner, or in the event the partners mutually agree to dissolve, the partnership shall terminate, and the partners shall proceed with reasonable promptness to liquidate the business of the partnership. The assets of the partnership shall first be used to pay or provide for all debts of the partnership. Thereafter, all money remaining undistributed in the drawing accounts shall be paid to the partners. Then the remaining assets shall be divided proportionately as follows:

Partner   Proportion

24. **Binding upon Successors.** This agreement shall be binding upon and inure to the benefit of the parties, their successors, assigns and personal representatives.

Signed under seal this _____ day of _____, 20__.

_____

_____

_____

Form 03-01
Bylaws of a Statutory Close Corporation

ARTICLE I

Offices and Fiscal Year

Section 1.01.   Registered office. The registered office of the corporation in Pennsylvania shall be at _____, _____, until otherwise established by an amendment of the articles or by the board of directors and a record of such change is filed with the Department of State in the manner provided by law.

Section 1.02.   Other offices. The corporation may also have offices at such other places within or without Pennsylvania as the board of directors may from time to time appoint or the business of the corporation may require.

ARTICLE II

Notice–Waivers–Meetings Generally

Section 2.01.   Manner of giving notice.

(a) General rule. Whenever written notice is required to be given to any person under the provisions of the Pennsylvania Business Corporation Law of 1988 ('Business Corporation Law') or by the articles or these bylaws, it may be given to the person either personally or by sending a copy thereof by first class or express mail, postage prepaid, or by telecopier, to the address of the person appearing on the books of the corporation or, in the case of directors, supplied by the director to the corporation for the purpose of notice. The notice of meeting shall specify the place, day, and hour of the meeting and any other information required by any other provision of the Business Corporation Law, the articles, or these bylaws.

Section 2.02   Notice of meetings of board of directors. Notice of a regular meeting of the board of directors need not be given. Notice of every special meeting of the board of directors shall be given to each director by telephone or in writing at least five days before the time at which the meeting is to be held. Every such notice shall state the time and place of the meeting. Neither the business to be transacted at, nor the purpose of, any regular or special meeting of the board need be specified in a notice of the meeting.

Section 2.03   Notice of meetings of shareholders.

(a) General rule. Written notice of every meeting of the shareholders shall be given by, or at the direction of, the secretary to each shareholder of record entitled to vote at the meeting at least:

(1) ten days prior to the day named for a meeting called to consider a fundamental transaction under 15 Pa.C.S. Chapter 19; or

(2) five days prior to the day named for the meeting in any other case.

If the secretary neglects or refuses to give notice of a meeting, the person or persons calling the meeting may do so. In the case of a special meeting of shareholders, the notice shall specify the general nature of the business to be transacted.

(b) Notice of action by shareholders on bylaws. In the case of a meeting of shareholders that has as one of its purposes action on the bylaws, written notice shall be given to each shareholder that the purpose, or one of the purposes, of the meeting is to consider the adoption, amendment or repeal of the bylaws. There shall be included in, or enclosed with, the notice a copy of the proposed amendment or a summary of the changes to be effected thereby.

Section 2.04.   Waiver of Notice.

(a) Written waiver. Whenever any written notice is required to be given under the provisions of the Business Corporation Law, the articles or these bylaws, a waiver thereof in writing, signed by the person or persons entitled to the notice, whether before or after the time stated therein, shall be deemed equivalent to the giving of the notice. Except as otherwise required by this subsection, neither the business to be transacted at, nor the purpose of, a meeting need be specified in the waiver of notice of the meeting. In the case of a special meeting of shareholders, the waiver of notice shall specify the general nature of the business to be transacted.

(b) Waiver by attendance. Attendance of a person at any meeting shall constitute a waiver of notice of the meeting except where a person attends a meeting for the express purpose of objecting, at the beginning of the meeting, to the transaction of any business because the meeting was not lawfully called or convened.

Section 2.05   Use of conference telephone and similar equipment. One or more persons may participate in a meeting of the board of directors or the shareholders of the corporation by means of conference telephone or similar communications equipment by means of which all persons participating in the meeting can hear each other. Participation in a meeting pursuant to this section shall constitute presence in person at the meeting.

ARTICLE III

Shareholders

Section 3.01.   Place of meeting. All meetings of the shareholders of the corporation shall be held at the registered office of the corporation unless another place is designated by the board of directors in the notice of a meeting.

Section 3.02   Annual meeting. The board of directors may fix the date and time of the annual meeting of the shareholders, but if no such date and time is fixed by the board, the meeting for any calendar year shall be held on February 15 of each such year, if not a legal holiday under the laws of the Commonwealth of Pennsylvania and, if a legal holiday, then on the next succeeding business day, not a Saturday, at 10:00 o'clock a.m. and at said meeting the shareholders then entitled to vote shall elect directors and shall transact such other business as may properly be brought before the meeting. If the annual meeting shall not have been called and held within six months after the designated time, any shareholder may call the meeting at any time thereafter.

Section 3.03   Special meetings.

(a) Call of special meetings. Special meetings of the shareholders may be called at any time:

(1) by the board of directors; or

(2) unless otherwise provided in the articles, by shareholders entitled to cast at least 20% of the votes that all shareholders are entitled to cast at the particular meeting.

(b) Fixing of time for meeting. At any time, upon written request of any person who has called a special meeting, it shall be the duty of the secretary to fix the time of the meeting which shall by held not more than 60 days after the receipt of the request. If the secretary neglects or refuses to fix the time of the meeting, the person or persons calling the meeting may do so.

Section 3.04   Quorum.

(a) General rule. A meeting of shareholders of the corporation duly called shall not be organized for the transaction of business unless a quorum is present. The presence of shareholders entitled to cast at least a majority of the votes that all shareholders are entitled to cast on a particular matter to be acted upon at the meeting shall constitute a quorum for the purposes of consideration and action on the matter.

Section 3.05   Action by shareholders.

(a) General rule. Except as otherwise provided in the Business Corporation Law or the articles or these bylaws, whenever any corporate action is to be taken by vote of the shareholders of the corporation, it shall be authorized by a majority of the votes cast at a duly organized meeting of shareholders by the holders of shares entitled to vote thereon.

Section 3.06   Organization. At every meeting of the shareholders, the chairman of the board, if there be one, or, in the case of vacancy in office or absence of the chairman of the board, one of the following officers present in the order stated: the vice chairman of the board, if there be one, the president, the vice presidents in their order of rank and seniority, or a person chosen by vote of the shareholders present, shall act as chairman of the meeting. The secretary or, in the absence of the secretary, an assistant secretary, or in the absence of both the secretary and assistant secretaries, a person appointed by the chairman of the
meeting, shall act as secretary.

Section 3.07.   Voting rights of shareholders. Unless otherwise provided in the articles, every shareholder of the corporation shall be entitled to one vote for every share standing in the name of the shareholder on the books of the corporation.

Section 3.08   Voting and other action by proxy.

(a) General rule.

(1) Every shareholder entitled to vote at a meeting of shareholders or to express consent or dissent to corporate action in writing without a meeting may authorize another person to act for the shareholder by proxy.

(2) The presence of, or vote or other action at a meeting of shareholders, or the expression of consent or dissent to corporate action in writing, by a proxy of a shareholder shall constitute the presence of, or vote or action by, or written consent or dissent of the shareholder.

(b) Minimum requirements. Every proxy shall be executed in writing by the shareholder or by the duly authorized attorney-in-fact of the shareholder and filed with the secretary of the corporation. A proxy, unless coupled with an interest, shall be revocable at will, notwithstanding any other agreement or any provision in the proxy to the contrary, but the revocation of a proxy shall not be effective until written notice thereof has been given to the secretary of the corporation. An unrevoked proxy shall not be valid after three years from the date of its execution unless a longer time is expressly provided therein. A proxy shall not be revoked by the death or incapacity is given to the secretary of the corporation.

Section 3.09.   Voting by corporations.

(a) Voting by corporate shareholders. Any corporation that is a shareholder of this corporation may vote by any of its officers or agents, or by proxy appointed by any officer or agent, unless some other person, by resolution of the board of directors of the corporation or a provision of its articles or these bylaws, a copy of which resolution or provision certified to be correct by one of its officers has been filed with the secretary of this corporation, is appointed its general or special proxy in which case that person shall be entitled to vote the shares.

(b) Controlled shares. Shares of this corporation owned, directly or indirectly, by it and controlled, directly or indirectly, by the board of directors of this corporation, as such, shall not be voted at any meeting and shall not be counted in determining the total number of outstanding shares for voting purposes at any given time.

Section 3.10   Consent of shareholders in lieu of meeting.

(a) Unanimous written consent. Any action required or permitted to be taken at a meeting of the shareholders or of a class of shareholders may be taken without a meeting if, prior or subsequent to the action, a consent or consents thereto by all of the shareholders who would be entitled to vote at a meeting for such purposes shall be filed with the secretary of the corporation.

(b) Partial written consent. Any action required or permitted to be taken at a meeting of the shareholders or of a class of shareholders may be taken without a meeting upon the written consent of shareholders who would have been entitled to cast the minimum number of votes that would be necessary to authorize the action at a meeting at which all shareholders entitled to vote thereon were present and voting. The consents shall be filed with the secretary of the corporation. The action shall not become effective until after at least ten days' written notice of the action has been given to each shareholder entitled to vote thereon who has not consented thereto.

ARTICLE IV

Board of Directors

Section 4.01.   Powers; personal liability.

(a) General rule. Pursuant to 15 Pa.C.S. §2332, the business and affairs of the corporation shall be managed by or under the direction of the shareholders of the corporation, rather than by or under the direction of a board of directors. When acting in such a capacity, the remainder of this Article IV shall apply as if, and to the extent that said shareholders, were directors.

(b) Standard of care; justifiable reliance. A director shall stand in a fiduciary relation to the corporation and shall perform his or her duties as a director, including duties as a member of any committee of the board upon which the director may serve, in good faith, in a manner the director reasonable believes to be in the best interests of the corporation and with such care, including reasonable inquire, skill, and diligence, as a person of ordinary prudence would use under similar circumstances. In performing his or her duties, a director shall be entitled to rely in good faith on information, opinions, reports, or statements, including financial statements and other financial data, in each case prepared or presented by any of the following:

(1) One or more officers or employees of the corporation whom the director reasonable believes to be reliable and competent in the matters presented.

(2) Counsel, public accountants, or other persons as to matters which the director reasonably believes to be within the professional or expert competence of such person.

(3) A committee of the board upon which the director does not serve, duly designated in accordance with law, as to matters within its designated authority, which committee the director reasonable believes to merit confidence.

A director shall not be considered to be acting in good faith if the director has knowledge concerning the matter in question that would cause his or her reliance to be unwarranted.

(c) Consideration of factors. In discharging the duties of their respective positions, the board of directors, committees of the board, and individual directors may, in considering the best interests of the corporation, consider the effects of any action upon employees, upon suppliers and customers of the corporation and upon committees in which offices or other establishments of the corporation are located, and all other pertinent factors. The consideration of those factors shall not constitute a violation of subsection (b).

(d) Presumption. Absent breach of fiduciary duty, lack of good faith or self-dealing, actions taken as a director or any failure to take any action shall be presumed to be in the best interests of the corporation.

(e) Personal liability of directors.

(1) A director shall not be personally liable, as such, for monetary damages for any action taken, or any failure to take any action, unless:

(i) the director has breached or failed to perform the duties of his or her office under this section; and

(ii) the breach or failure to perform constitutes self-dealing, willful misconduct or recklessness.

(2) The provisions of paragraph (1) shall not apply to the responsibility or liability of a director pursuant to any criminal statute, or the liability of a director for the payment of taxes pursuant to local, state, or federal law.

(f) Notation of dissent. A director who is present at a meeting of the board of directors, or of a committee of the board, at which action on any corporate matter is taken shall be presumed to have assented to the action taken unless his or her dissent is entered in the minutes of the meeting or unless the director files a written dissent to the action with the secretary of the meeting before the adjournment thereof or transmits the dissent in writing to the secretary of the corporation immediately after the adjournment of the meeting. The right to dissent shall not apply to a director who voted in favor of the action. Nothing in this section shall bar a director from asserting that minutes of the meeting incorrectly omitted his or her dissent if, promptly upon receipt of a copy of such minutes, the director notifies the secretary, in writing, of the asserted omission or inaccuracy.

Section 4.02.   Qualifications and selection of directors.

(a) Qualifications. Each director of the corporation shall be a natural person of full age who need not be a resident of Pennsylvania or a shareholder of the corporation.

(b) Election of directors. Except as otherwise provided in these bylaws, directors of the corporation shall be elected by the shareholders. In elections for directors, voting need not be by ballot, except upon demand made by a shareholder entitled to vote at the election and before the voting begins.

Section 4.03.   Number and term of office.

(a) Number. The board of directors shall consist of such number of directors, not less than one no more than five, as may be determined from time to time by resolution of the board of directors.

(b) Term of office. Each director shall hold office until the expiration of the term for which he or she was selected and until a successor has been selected and qualified or until his or her earlier death, resignation or removal. A decrease in the number of directors shall not have the effect of shortening the term of any incumbent director.

(c) Resignation. Any director may resign at any time upon written notice to the corporation. The resignation shall be effective upon receipt thereof by the corporation or at such subsequent time as shall be specified in the notice of resignation.

Section 4.04   Vacancies.

(a) General rule. Vacancies in the board of directors, including vacancies resulting from an increase in the number of directors, may be filled by a majority vote of the remaining members of the board though less than a quorum, or by a sole remaining director, and each person so selected shall be a director to serve for the balance of the unexpired term, and until a successor has been selected and qualified or until his or her earlier death, resignation, or removal.

(b) Action by resigned directors. When one or more directors resign from the board effective at a future date, the directors then in office, including those who have so resigned, shall have power by the applicable vote to fill the vacancies, the vote thereon to take effect when the resignations become effective.

Section 4.05.   Removal of directors.

(a) Removal by the shareholders. The entire board of directors or any individual director may be removed from office without assigning any cause by the vote of shareholders. In case the board or any one or more directors are so removed, new directors may be elected at the same meeting. The board of directors may be removed at any time with or without cause by the unanimous vote or consent of shareholders entitled to vote thereon.

Section 4.06.   Place of meetings. Meetings of the board of directors may be held at such place or without Pennsylvania as the board of directors may from time to time appoint or as may be designated in the notice of the meeting.

Section 4.07.   Organization of meetings. At every meeting of the board of directors, the chairman of the board, if there be one, or, in the case of a vacancy in the office or absence of the chairman of the board, one of the following officers present in the order stated: the vice chairman of the board, if there is one; the president; the vice presidents in their order of rank and seniority; or a person chosen by a majority of the directors present, shall act as chairman of the meeting. The secretary or, in the absence of the secretary, an assistant secretary, or, in the absence of the secretary and the assistant secretaries, any person appointed by the chairman of the meeting, shall act as secretary.

Section 4.08.   Regular meetings. Regular meetings of the board of directors shall be held at such time and place as shall be designated from time to time by resolution of the board of directors.

Section 4.09.   Special meetings. Special meetings of the board of directors shall be held whenever called by the chairman or by two or more of the directors.

Section 4.10. Quorum of and action by directors.

(a) General rule. A majority of the directors in office of the corporation shall be necessary to constitute a quorum for the transaction of business and the acts of a majority of the directors present and voting at a meeting at which a quorum is present shall be the acts of the board of directors.

(b) Action by written consent. Any action required or permitted to be taken at a meeting of the directors may be taken without a meeting if, prior or subsequent to the action, a consent or consents thereto by all of the directors in office is filed with the secretary of the corporation.

ARTICLE V

Officers

Section 5.01. Officers generally.

(a) Number, qualifications and designation. The officers of the corporation shall be a president, a secretary, a treasurer, and such other officers as may be elected in accordance with the provisions of Section 5.03. Officers may but need not be directors or shareholders of the corporation.

(b) Resignations. Any officer may resign at any time upon written notice to the corporation. The resignation shall be effective upon receipt thereof by the corporation or at such subsequent time as may be specified in the notice of resignation.

(c) Bonding. The corporation may secure the fidelity of any or all of its officers by bond or otherwise.

(d) Standard of care. Except as otherwise provided in the articles, an officer shall perform his or her duties as an officer in good faith, in a manner he or she reasonably believes to be in the best interests of the corporation and with such care, including reasonable inquiry, skill and diligence, as a person of ordinary prudence would use under similar circumstances. A person who so performs his or her duties shall not be liable by reason of having been an officer of the corporation.

Section 5.02. Election and term of office. The officers of the corporation, except those elected annually by the board of directors, and each such officer shall hold office for a term of one year and until a successor has been selected and qualified or until his or her earlier death, resignation, or removal.

Section 5.03. Subordinate officers, committees, and agents.
The board of directors may from time to time elect such other officers and appoint such committees, employees or other agents as the business of the corporation may require.

Section 5.04. Removal of officers and agents. Any officer or agent of the corporation may be removed by the board of directors with or without cause. The removal shall be without prejudice to the contract rights, if any, of any person so removed. Election or appointment of an officer or agent shall not of itself create contract rights.

Section 5.05. Vacancies. A vacancy in any office because of death, resignation, removal, disqualification, or any other cause, shall be filled by the board of directors or by the officer or committee to which the power to fill such office has been delegated pursuant to Section 5.03, as the case may be, and, if the office is one for which these bylaws prescribe a term, shall be filled for the unexpired portion of the term.

Section 5.06. Authority. All officers of the corporation, as between themselves and the corporation, shall have such authority and perform such duties in the management of the corporation as may be provided by or pursuant to resolutions or orders of the board of directors or in the absence of controlling provisions in the resolutions or orders of the board of directors, as may be determined by or pursuant to these bylaws.

Section 5.07. The chairman and vice chairman of the board.
The chairman of the board or in the absence of the chairman, the vice chairman of the board, shall preside at all meetings of the shareholders and of the board of directors and shall perform such other duties as may from time to time be requested by the board of directors.

Section 5.08. The president. The president shall be the chief executive officer of the corporation and shall have general supervision over the business and operations of the corporation, subject, however, to the control of the board of directors. The president shall sign, execute, and acknowledge in the name of the corporation deeds, mortgages, bonds, contracts, or other instruments authorized by the board of directors, except in cases where the signing and execution thereof shall be expressly delegated by the board of directors, or by these bylaws, to some other officer or agent of the corporation; and, in general, shall perform all duties incident to the office of president and such other duties as from time to time may be assigned by the board of directors.

Section 5.09. The secretary. The secretary or an assistant secretary shall attend all meetings of the shareholders and of the board of directors and shall record all the votes of the shareholders and of the directors and the minutes of the meetings of the shareholders and of the board of directors and o committees of the board in a book or books to be kept for that purpose; shall see that the notices are given and records and reports properly kept and filed by the corporation as required by law; shall be the custodian of the seal of the corporation and see that it is affixed to all documents to be executed on behalf of the corporation under its seal; and, in general, shall perform all duties incident to the office of secretary, and such other duties as may from time to time be assigned by the board of directors or the president.

Section 5.10.   The treasurer. The treasurer or an assistant treasurer shall have or provide for the custody of the funds or other property of the corporation; shall collect and receive or provide for the collection and receipt of moneys earned by or in any manner due to or received by the corporation; shall deposit all funds in his or her custody as treasurer in such banks or other place of deposit as the board of directors may from time to time designate; shall, whenever so required by the board of directors, render an account showing all transactions as treasurer and the financial condition of the corporation; and, in general, shall discharge such other duties as may from time to time be assigned by the board of directors or the president.

Section 5.11.   Salaries. The salaries of the officers elected by the board of directors shall be fixed from time to time by the board of directors or by such officer as may be designated by resolution of the board. The salaries or other compensation of any other officers, employees, and other agents shall be fixed from time to time by the officer of committee to which the power to elect such officers or to retain or appoint such employees or other agents has been delegated pursuant to Section 5.03. No officer shall be prevented from receiving such salary or other compensation by reason of the fact that the officer is also a director of the corporation.

ARTICLE VI

Certificates of Stock, Transfer, Etc.

Section 6.01.   Share certificates. Certificates for shares of the corporation shall be in such forms as approved by the board of directors, and shall state that the corporation is incorporated under the laws of Pennsylvania, the name of the person to whom issued, and the number and class of shares and the designation of the series (if any) that the certificate represents. The share register or transfer books and blank share certificates shall be kept by the secretary or by any transfer agent or registrar designated by the board of directors for that purpose.

Section 6.02.   Issuance. The share certificates of the corporation shall be numbered and registered in the share register or transfer books of the corporation as they are issued. They shall be signed by the president or a vice president and by the secretary or an assistant secretary or the treasurer or an assistant treasurer, and shall bear the corporate seal, which may be a facsimile, engraved or printed. In case any officer who has signed, or whose facsimile signature has been placed upon, any share certificates shall have ceased to such officer because of death, resignation or otherwise, before the certificate is issued, it may be issued with the same effect as if the officer had not ceased to be such at the date of its issue. The provisions of this Section 6.02 shall be subject to any inconsistent or contrary agreement at the time between the corporation and any transfer agent or registrar.

Section 6.03.   Transfer. Transfers of shares shall be made on the share register or transfer books of the corporation upon surrender of the certificate therefor, endorsed by the person named in the certificate or by an attorney lawfully constituted in writing. No transfer shall be made inconsistent with the provisions of the Uniform Commercial Code, 13 Pa. C.S. §8101 et seq., and its amendments and supplements.

Section 6.04.   Record holder of shares. The corporation shall be entitled to treat the person in whose name any share of shares of the corporation stand on the books of the corporation as the absolute owner thereof, and shall not be bound to recognize any equitable or other claims to, or interest in, such share or shares on the part of any other person.

Section 6.05.   Lost, destroyed or mutilated certificates. The holder of any shares of the corporation shall immediately notify the corporation of any loss, destruction, or mutilation of the certificate therefor, and the board of directors may, in its discretion, cause a new certificate or certificates to be issued to such holder, in case of mutilation of the certificate, upon the surrender of the mutilated certificate or, in case of loss or destruction of the certificate, upon satisfactory proof of such loss or destruction and, if the board or directors shall so determine, the deposit of a bond in such form and in such sum, and with such surety or sureties, as it may direct.

Section 6.06.   Share transfer restrictions. The provisions of 15 Pa.C.S. §2322 (b)(2),(3), and (4) do not apply and no transfer of an interest in shares of the corporation, whether voluntary or involuntary, shall be effective under those provisions; except that a shareholder's interest may pass to his executor or administrator upon the death of the shareholder, as provided by 15 Pa.C.S. §2322(4).

ARTICLE VII

Miscellaneous

Section 7.01.   Corporate Seal. The corporation shall have a corporate seal in the form of a circle containing the name of the corporation, the year of incorporation, and such other details as may be approved by the board of directors.

Section 7.02.   Checks. All checks, notes, bills of exchange, or other orders in writing shall be signed by such person or persons as the board of directors or any person authorized by resolution of the board of directors may from time to time designate.

Section 7.03.   Amendment of bylaws. These bylaws may be amended or repealed, or new bylaws may be adopted, either, (i) by vote of the shareholders at any duly organized annual or special meeting of shareholders; or (ii) with respect to those matters that are not by statute committed expressly to the shareholders and regardless of whether the shareholders have previously adopted or approved the bylaw being amended or repealed, by vote of a majority of the board of directors of the corporation in office at any regular or special meeting of directors. Any change in these bylaws shall take effect when adopted unless otherwise provided in the resolution effecting the change.

Form 03-33

Form **2553**
(Rev. September 1997)

Department of the Treasury
Internal Revenue Service

Election by a Small Business Corporation
(Under section 1362 of the Internal Revenue Code)
▶ For Paperwork Reduction Act Notice, see page 2 of instructions.
▶ See separate instructions.

OMB No. 1545-0146

Notes: 1. This election to be an S corporation can be accepted only if all the tests are met under **Who May Elect** on page 1 of the instructions; all signatures in Parts I and III are originals (no photocopies); and the exact name and address of the corporation and other required form information are provided.

2. Do not file **Form 1120S**, U.S. Income Tax Return for an S Corporation, for any tax year before the year the election takes effect.

3. If the corporation was in existence before the effective date of this election, see **Taxes an S Corporation May Owe** on page 1 of the instructions.

Part I	**Election Information**		

Please Type or Print

	A Employer identification number
Name of corporation (see instructions)	
Number, street, and room or suite no. (If a P.O. box, see instructions.)	**B** Date incorporated
City or town, state, and ZIP code	**C** State of incorporation

D Election is to be effective for tax year beginning (month, day, year) . . . . ▶   /   /

E Name and title of officer or legal representative who the IRS may call for more information

F Telephone number of officer or legal representative
( )

G If the corporation changed its name or address after applying for the EIN shown in **A** above, check this box . . . . ▶ ☐

H If this election takes effect for the first tax year the corporation exists, enter month, day, and year of the **earliest** of the following: (1) date the corporation first had shareholders, (2) date the corporation first had assets, or (3) date the corporation began doing business . . . . ▶   /   /

I Selected tax year: Annual return will be filed for tax year ending (month and day) ▶ . . . .

If the tax year ends on any date other than December 31, except for an automatic 52-53-week tax year ending with reference to the month of December, you **must** complete Part II on the back. If the date you enter is the ending date of an automatic 52-53-week tax year, write "52-53-week year" to the right of the date. See Temporary Regulations section 1.441-2T(e)(3).

J Name and address of each shareholder; shareholder's spouse having a community property interest in the corporation's stock; and each tenant in common, joint tenant, and tenant by the entirety. (A husband and wife (and their estates) are counted as one shareholder in determining the number of shareholders without regard to the manner in which the stock is owned.)	**K** Shareholders' Consent Statement. Under penalties of perjury, we declare that we consent to the election of the above-named corporation to be an S corporation under section 1362(a) and that we have examined this consent statement, including accompanying schedules and statements, and to the best of our knowledge and belief, it is true, correct, and complete. We understand our consent is binding and may not be withdrawn after the corporation has made a valid election. (Shareholders sign and date below.)		**L** Stock owned		**M** Social security number or employer identification number (see instructions)	**N** Shareholder's tax year ends (month and day)
	Signature	Date	Number of shares	Dates acquired		

Under penalties of perjury, I declare that I have examined this election, including accompanying schedules and statements, and to the best of my knowledge and belief, it is true, correct, and complete.

Signature of officer ▶   Title ▶   Date ▶

See Parts II and III on back.   Cat. No. 18629R   Form **2553** (Rev. 9-97)

Part II **Selection of Fiscal Tax Year** (All corporations using this part must complete item O and item P, Q, or R.)

O Check the applicable box to indicate whether the corporation is:

1. ☐ A new corporation adopting the tax year entered in item I, Part I.

2. ☐ An existing corporation retaining the tax year entered in item I, Part I.

3. ☐ An existing corporation changing to the tax year entered in item I, Part I.

P Complete item P if the corporation is using the expeditious approval provisions of Rev. Proc. 87-32, 1987-2 C.B. 396, to request **(1)** a natural business year (as defined in section 4.01(1) of Rev. Proc. 87-32) or **(2)** a year that satisfies the ownership tax year test in section 4.01(2) of Rev. Proc. 87-32. Check the applicable box below to indicate the representation statement the corporation is making as required under section 4 of Rev. Proc. 87-32.

1. Natural Business Year ► ☐ I represent that the corporation is retaining or changing to a tax year that coincides with its natural business year as defined in section 4.01(1) of Rev. Proc. 87-32 and as verified by its satisfaction of the requirements of section 4.02(1) of Rev. Proc. 87-32. In addition, if the corporation is changing to a natural business year as defined in section 4.01(1), I further represent that such tax year results in less deferral of income to the owners than the corporation's present tax year. I also represent that the corporation is not described in section 3.01(2) of Rev. Proc. 87-32. (See instructions for additional information that must be attached.)

2. Ownership Tax Year ► ☐ I represent that shareholders holding more than half of the shares of the stock (as of the first day of the tax year to which the request relates) of the corporation have the same tax year or are concurrently changing to the tax year that the corporation adopts, retains, or changes to per item I, Part I. I also represent that the corporation is not described in section 3.01(2) of Rev. Proc. 87-32.

Note: *If you do not use item P and the corporation wants a fiscal tax year, complete either item Q or R below. Item Q is used to request a fiscal tax year based on a business purpose and to make a back-up section 444 election. Item R is used to make a regular section 444 election.*

Q Business Purpose—To request a fiscal tax year based on a business purpose, you must check box Q1 and pay a user fee. See instructions for details. You may also check box Q2 and/or box Q3.

1. Check here ► ☐ if the fiscal year entered in item I, Part I, is requested under the provisions of section 6.03 of Rev. Proc. 87-32. Attach to Form 2553 a statement showing the business purpose for the requested fiscal year. See instructions for additional information that must be attached.

2. Check here ► ☐ to show that the corporation intends to make a back-up section 444 election in the event the corporation's business purpose request is not approved by the IRS. (See instructions for more information.)

3. Check here ► ☐ to show that the corporation agrees to adopt or change to a tax year ending December 31 if necessary for the IRS to accept this election for S corporation status in the event (1) the corporation's business purpose request is not approved and the corporation makes a back-up section 444 election, but is ultimately not qualified to make a section 444 election, or (2) the corporation's business purpose request is not approved and the corporation did not make a back-up section 444 election.

R Section 444 Election—To make a section 444 election, you must check box R1 and you may also check box R2.

1. Check here ► ☐ to show the corporation will make, if qualified, a section 444 election to have the fiscal tax year shown in item I, Part I. To make the election, you must complete **Form 8716,** Election To Have a Tax Year Other Than a Required Tax Year, and either attach it to Form 2553 or file it separately.

2. Check here ► ☐ to show that the corporation agrees to adopt or change to a tax year ending December 31 if necessary for the IRS to accept this election for S corporation status in the event the corporation is ultimately not qualified to make a section 444 election.

Part III **Qualified Subchapter S Trust (QSST) Election Under Section 1361(d)(2)***

Income beneficiary's name and address	Social security number
Trust's name and address	Employer identification number

Date on which stock of the corporation was transferred to the trust (month, day, year) . . . . ► / /

In order for the trust named above to be a QSST and thus a qualifying shareholder of the S corporation for which this Form 2553 is filed, I hereby make the election under section 1361(d)(2). Under penalties of perjury, I certify that the trust meets the definitional requirements of section 1361(d)(3) and that all other information provided in Part III is true, correct, and complete.

_____   _____
Signature of income beneficiary or signature and title of legal representative or other qualified person making the election   Date

*Use Part III to make the QSST election only if stock of the corporation has been transferred to the trust on or before the date on which the corporation makes its election to be an S corporation. The QSST election must be made and filed separately if stock of the corporation is transferred to the trust after the date on which the corporation makes the S election.

✪

Form 03-34
Resolution Approving S Corporation Election

WHEREAS, it is determined to be in the best interests of the corporation and its shareholders to elect to be treated as an S Corporation, pursuant to the Internal Revenue Code and under the comparable state tax laws.

RESOLVED, that the officers of this corporation are hereby authorized and directed to execute all documents and to take such action as they may deem necessary or appropriate in order to elect for S Corporation treatment, including but not limited to the submission of necessary corporation election documents to the Internal Revenue Service and the state taxing authority.

Form 03-35
Cover Letter for Resolution Approving S Corporation Election

June 13, 2000

<u>CERTIFIED MAIL</u>
<u>RETURN RECEIPT REQUESTED</u>

Internal Revenue Service

RE: Form 2553 – S Corporation Election
    For _____

Dear Sir/Madam:

Enclosed please find Form 2553 – 'S Corporation Election' for _____.

Please time stamp and return the enclosed copy in the enclosed stamped self-addressed envelope.

Very truly yours,

_____

Enclosure

Form 03-36
Limited Liability Company Agreement

THIS LIMITED LIABILITY COMPANY AGREEMENT, dated as of _____, is entered into by and among _____, a _____corporation ('_'), as the Class A Member, and _____, a _____l ('_'), as the Class B Member.

Preamble

The parties hereto desire to become associated in a Limited Liability Company under the Act for the purposes and on the terms herein set forth. Therefore, in consideration of the mutual promises made herein, the parties hereto, intending to be legally bound, do hereby agree as follows:

1. Certain Definitions.

When used herein, the following terms shall have the meanings set forth below:

a. 'Act' means the Pennsylvania Limited Liability Company Act of 1994, 15 PA C.S.A.§8901 et seq. as amended from time to time.

b. 'Adjusted Capital Account Deficit' means, with respect to any Member, the deficit balance, if any, in such Member's Capital Account after giving effect to the following adjustments:

(i) Credit to such Capital Account the sum of (A) any amount which such Member is obligated to restore pursuant to any provisions of this Agreement, (B) an amount equal to such Member's share of Company Minimum Gain and of Member Nonrecourse Debt Minimum Gain as determined under Treas. Regs. 1.704-2(g) and 1.704-2(i)(5), respectively, and (C) any amount which such Member is deemed to be obligated to restore pursuant to Treas. Reg. 1.704-1(b)(2)(ii)(c); and

(ii) Debit to such Capital Account the items described in subclauses (4),(5),and(6) of Treas. Reg. 1.704-1(b)(2)(ii)(d).

The foregoing definition of Adjusted Capital Account Deficit is intended to comply with the provisions of Treas. Reg. 1.704-1(b)(2)(ii)(d) and shall be interpreted consistently therewith.

c. 'Affiliate' means, with respect to any Person, any Person directly or indirectly controlling, controlled by or under common control with such Person. As used in the immediately preceding sentence, the term 'control' means, with respect to a Person, the right to exercise, directly or indirectly, a majority of the voting rights attributable to such Person, and the term 'majority' means more than fifty percent (50%).

d. 'Agreement' means this Limited Liability Company Agreement as the same may be amended and supplemented from time to time.

e. 'Capital Account' means the capital account of each Member established and maintained in accordance with Section 7.1.

f. 'Capital Commitment', in respect of any Member, means that which is agreed to be contributed to the capital of the Company by such Member without regard to such Member's Capital Contribution.

g. 'Capital Contribution' means, with respect to any Member, the amount of cash and/or the fair market value of the property or services actually contributed to or performed on behalf of the Company by such Member.

h. 'Certificate' means the certificate of formation, and all amendments thereto, executed and filed pursuant to the Act and the terms of this Agreement.

i. 'Code' means the Internal Revenue Code of 1986, as amended. All references herein to specific Sections of the Code shall be deemed to refer also to the corresponding provisions of succeeding law.

j. 'Company' means the Limited Liability Company formed pursuant to this Agreement.

k. 'Company Minimum Gain' has the same meaning as the phrase 'partnership minimum gain' as set forth in Treas. Regs. 1.704-2(d).

l. 'Deadlock Procedure' means that deadlock procedure established under Section 10.2(a)(i) of this Agreement.

m. 'Excess Capital Contribution' means, with respect to any Member, the amount of such Member's Capital Contributions (if any) in excess of such Member's Capital Commitment as set forth in Section 6.1.

n. 'Fiscal Year' means the Company's fiscal year, which shall commence on October 1 and end on September 30 (unless otherwise required by the Code) of each year, except that (i) the Company's first fiscal year shall commence on the date of the filing of the Certificate and (ii) such term shall also include any period for which the Company is required to allocate Net profits, Net Losses and other items of income, gain, loss or deduction pursuant to Section 7.

o. 'Liquidation Trustee' means the trustee selected by the Members pursuant to Section 15.2.

p. 'Majority-in-Interest of the Members' means Members holding Member Interests representing greater than fifty percent (50%) of the total of the Capital Accounts of all Members.

q. 'Management Committee' means the Management Committee formed pursuant to Section 10.2.

r. 'Member Debt' shall mean any loan made by a Member to the Company.

s. 'Member Interest' means an ownership interest in the Company representing the Capital Account of a Member and including such Member's share of Net Profits and Net Losses, such Member's right to receive distributions hereunder and any and all other rights and interests to which such Member may be entitled as provided in this Agreement.

t. 'Member Nonrecourse Debt Minimum Gain' has the same meaning as the phrase 'partner nonrecourse debt minimum gain' as set forth in Treas. Reg. 1.704-2(i).

u. 'Member Nonrecourse Deduction' has the same meaning as the phrase 'partner nonrecourse deduction' as set forth in Treas. Reg. 1.704-2(i).

v. 'Member Nonrecourse Loan' means a loan made to , or credit arrangement for the benefit of, the Company by a Member or by a person related to a Member (as defined in Treas. Reg. 1.752-4(b)), which by its terms (or by operation of law) exculpates the Members from personal liability on the debt, but under which such Member or related person bears the ultimate economic risk of loss within the meaning of Treas. Reg. 1.752-2.

w. 'Members' means the Class A Member and the Class B Member, and each of them individually, and any other Person who becomes a Member in accordance with this Agreement.

x. 'Net Losses' for any Fiscal year means the excess, if any, of the items of loss and deduction over the items of income and gain of the Company as recorded on its financial accounting books and records for such Fiscal Year.

y. 'Net Profits' for any Fiscal Year means the excess, if any, of the items of income and gain over the items of loss and deduction of the Company as recorded on its financial accounting books and records for such Fiscal Year.

z. 'Nonrecourse Deductions' has the meaning set forth in Treas. Reg. 1.704-2(b).

aa. 'Organizational Expenses' means the fees, costs, and expenses of, and incidental to, the organization of the Company. Such expenses shall include any and all amounts categorized as 'organizational expenditures' under the Code.

bb. 'Person' means any individual, partnership, corporation, trust or other entity.

cc. 'Pre-Operating Expenses' means the investigation fees, costs, and expenses incidental to the creation of the Company and the fees, costs, and expenses incurred in connection with the commencement of operations of the Company. Such expenses shall include any and all amounts categorized as 'start-up expenditures' under the Code.

dd. 'Property' means all of the property, real, personal, or mixed, tangible or intangible, owned by the company or in or to which the Company has any interest of any nature or description.

ee. 'Tax Matters Member' means the Member of the Company so designated pursuant to Section 10.6.

ff. 'Treas. Reg.' and 'Regulations' mean the Income Tax Regulations promulgated under the Code, as such regulations may be amended from time to time (including corresponding provisions of succeeding regulations).

2. Organization.

2.1 Formation. The Members hereby ratify and confirm the filing of the Certificate with the Office of the Secretary of the Commonwealth of Pennsylvania on _____ and agree to organize and continue the Company as a limited liability company pursuant to the provisions of the Act and upon the terms and conditions set forth in this Agreement.

2.2 Name. The name of the Company is '____, L.L.C.'.

3. Principal Place of Business: Registered Office and Agent.

(a) The principal place of business of the Company will be located at _____, or at such other place as the Members may determine from time to time.

(b)   The address of the Company's registered office in Pennsylvania is _____, and its initial registered agent for service of process is _____. The Members may designate a different address of its registered office and a different registered agent by amending the Certificate in accordance with the Act.

4.   Purposes and Powers of the Company.

4.1   General Purposes and Powers. The Company is organized for the purposes of acquiring, owning, designing, developing, constructing, improving, financing, managing, operating, selling, exchanging, or otherwise disposing of _____and other related goods and services, and the Company shall have the power to do all things as the Members from time to time may deem necessary or advisable in connection therewith or as otherwise contemplated by this Agreement.

4.2   Additional Powers. The Company shall have and may exercise all of the powers that may be possessed and exercised by limited liability companies under the Act.

5.   Term. Except as otherwise set forth in this Agreement, the Company shall terminate on December 31, 2025.

6.   Capital Contributions and Related Matters.

6.1   Capital Contributions.

(a)   As its Capital Commitment, A shall contribute $ in cash to the capital of the Company, payable upon the execution hereof (of which $____has been expended by A for the benefit of the Company and shall be credited against such Capital Commitment).

(b)   As its Capital Commitment, BC shall contribute $ in cash to the capital of the Company, payable upon the execution hereof.

(c)   Organizational Expenses and Pre-Operating Expenses incurred and paid by any Member on behalf of the Company shall not be deemed to be Capital Contributions. Upon the execution hereof, each Member shall be reimbursed for any such Organizational Expenses and Pre-Operating Expenses.

6.2   Additional Capital Contributions. Except as expressly provided in this Agreement and except as the Members may otherwise unanimously agree, no Member shall be required or permitted to make any additional contributions to the capital of the Company, it being understood, however, that the parties contemplate that A may, at its discretion, make Excess Capital Contributions.

6.3   Repayment of Capital Contributions. Except as expressly provided in this Agreement, no specific time has been agreed upon for the repayment of Capital Contributions, and no Member (or its successor in interest) shall have the right to withdraw any capital contributed to the Company.

6.4   No Priorities Among Members. Except as expressly provided in this Agreement, no Member shall have the right to receive property other than cash in return for its Capital Contribution, nor shall any Member have priority over any other Member either as to the return of its Capital Account or as to profits, losses, or distributions.

7.   Capital Accounts: Allocations

7.1   Capital Accounts.

(a)   There shall be established and maintained for each Member on the books of the Company a Capital Account initially reflecting an amount equal to its Capital Contribution. The Capital Accounts shall be adjusted from time to time to reflect the Members' additional Capital Contributions, allocable shares of Net profits or Net Losses or any item thereof, distributions pursuant to Section 8 and as otherwise required by the provisions of this Agreement and the Code and Regulations including, but not limited to, the rules of Treas. Reg 1.704-1(b)(2)(iv).

(b)   If allocations for tax purposes are required to be made pursuant to Sections 7.5(b) or (c), then the adjustments to the Capital Accounts of the Members in respect of the property described therein shall be made in accordance with Treas. Reg. 1.704-1(b)(2)(iv)(g) for allocation to them of items of income, gain, loss, and deduction (including items of depreciation, depletion, amortization, or other cost recovery) as computed for book purposes, and no further adjustments shall be made to the Capital Accounts to reflect the Members' shares of the corresponding tax items. In computing such adjustments to the Capital Accounts, the Company shall utilize the method of computing such items as is utilized for federal income tax purposes except that the property's value for book purposes will be used rather than its adjusted tax basis.

7.2   Allocations of Net Profits. Net Profits for any Fiscal Year, and upon liquidation of the Company's assets pursuant to Section 15, shall be allocated, subject to Section 7.3(e), as follows:

(a)   first, to the Class A Member to the extent of the cumulative Net Losses previously allocated to the Class A Member pursuant to Section 7.3(d) (less cumulative Net Profits previously allocated to the Class A Member pursuant to this Section 7.2(a)

(b) second, to all of the Members to the extent of, and in proposition to, the cumulative Net Losses previously allocated to such Members pursuant to Section 7.3(c) (less cumulative Net Profits previously allocated to such Members pursuant to this Section 7.2(b));

(c) third, to all of the Members to the extent of, and in proportion to, the cumulative Net Losses previously allocated to such Members pursuant to Section 7.3(b) (less cumulative Net Profits previously allocated to such Members pursuant to this Section 7.2(c)); and

(d) thereafter:

    (A) seventy-five(75%) percent to the Class A Member; and

    (B) twenty-five(25%) percent to the Class B Member;

7.3   <u>Allocations of Net Losses.</u> Net Losses for any Fiscal Year, and upon liquidation of the Company's assets pursuant to Section 15, shall be allocated as follows:

(a) first, to all of the Members to the extent of, and in proportion to, the cumulative Net Profits previously allocated to such Members pursuant to Section 7.2(d) (less cumulative Net Losses previously allocated to such Members pursuant to this Section 7.3(a));

(b) second, to all of the Members to the extent of, and in proportion to, their respective Excess Capital Contributions (less cumulative Net Losses previously allocated to such Members pursuant to this Section 7.3(b));

(c) third, to all of the Members to the extent of, and in proportion to, their respective Capital Contributions (excluding their respective Excess Capital Contributions) (less cumulative Net Losses previously allocated to such Members pursuant to this Section 7.3(c)); and

(d) thereafter, to the Class A Member.

(e) Net Losses allocated to the Class B Member pursuant to the foregoing subsections of this Section 7.3 shall not exceed the maximum amount that can be so allocated without causing such Member to have an Adjusted Capital Account Deficit at the end of any Fiscal Year. All Net Losses in excess of the limitation ('Excess Losses') set forth in the preceding sentence shall be reallocated to the Class A Member. In the event of any such reallocation of Excess Losses, subsequent allocations of Net Profits (or any item thereof) in an amount sufficient to offset the allocation of such Excess Losses shall be made to the Class A Member prior to any other allocations being made pursuant to Section 7.2.

7.4   <u>Special Allocation.</u> Notwithstanding any other provision of this Agreement, the following special allocations shall be made for each Fiscal Year prior to the making of any allocations under this Agreement and, in the following order and priority:

(a) <u>Minimum Gain Chargeback.</u>

    (i) If there is a net decrease in Company Minimum Gain during any Fiscal Year so that an allocation is required by Treas. Reg. §1.704-2(f)(1), items of income and gain shall be allocated to the Members in the manner and to the extent required by such Regulation. This provision is intended to be a minimum gain chargeback within the meaning of Treas. Reg. § 1.704-2(f)(1) and shall be interpreted and applied consistently therewith.

    (ii) If there is a net decrease in Member Nonrecourse Debt Minimum Gain during any Fiscal Year so that an allocation is required by Treas. Reg. § 1.704-2(i)(4) (minimum gain chargeback attributable to a partner nonrecourse debt), items of income and gain shall be allocated in the manner and to the extent required by such Regulation.

(b) Qualified Income Offset. In the event any Member receives any adjustment, allocation, or distribution described in subclause (4), (5) or in (6) of Treas. Reg. §1.704-1(b)(2)(ii)(d), items of Company income and gain shall be specially allocated to such Member in an amount and manner sufficient to eliminate, to the extent required by the Regulations, the deficit balance in such Member's Capital Account as quickly as possible, provided that an allocation pursuant to this Section 7.4 (b) shall be made only if and to the extent that such Member would have such deficit balance after all other allocations provided for in Section 7.2 have been tentatively made as if this Section 7.4(b) were not in this Agreement.

(c) Member Nonrecourse Deduction. Any Member Nonrecourse Deduction shall be allocated to the Member who bears the economic risk of loss with respect to the Member Nonrecourse Loan giving rise to such deduction within the meaning of Treas. Reg. §1.752-2.

(d) Section 754 Adjustments. To the extent an adjustment to the adjusted tax basis of any Company asset pursuant to Section 734(b) of the Code or Section 743(b) of the Code is required pursuant to Treas. Reg 1.704-1(b)(2)(iv)(m)(2) or with respect to a distribution to a Member in liquidation of such Member's interest in the Company, pursuant to Treas. Reg. 1.704-1(b)(2)(iv)(m)(4) to be taken into account in determining Capital Accounts, the amount of such adjustment shall be treated as an item of gain (if the adjustment increases the basis of the asset) or loss (if the adjustment decreases such basis), and such gain or loss shall be allocated to the Members in accordance with their interests in the Company, in the event Treas. Reg. 1.704-1(b)(2)(iv)(m)(2) applies, or to the Member to whom such distribution is made, in the event Treas. Reg. 1.704-1(b)(2)(iv)(m)(4) applies.

7.5 Tax Allocations.

(a) General. For federal, state, and local income tax purposes, all items of taxable income, gain, loss, and deduction for each Fiscal Year shall, except as provided in Sections 7.5(b) and (c), be allocated among the Members in accordance with the manner in which the corresponding items were allocated under Section 7.2, 7.3, and 7.4.

(b) Contributed property. If property is contributed to the Company by a Member and if there is a difference between the basis of such property to the Company for federal income tax purposes and the fair market value at the time of its contribution, then items of income, deduction, gain, and loss with respect to such property as computed for federal income tax purposes (but not for book purposes) shall be shared among the Members so as to take account of such difference as required by Section 704(c) of the Code.

(c) Revalued property. If property (other than property described in Section 7.5(b)) of the Company is reflected in the Capital Accounts of the Members and on the books of the Company at a book value that differs from the adjusted basis of such property for federal income tax purposes by reason of a revaluation of such property, then items of income, deduction, gain, and loss with respect to such property for federal income tax purposes (but not for book purposes) shall be shared among the Members in a manner that takes account of the difference between the adjusted basis of such property for federal income tax purposes and its book value in the same manner as differences between adjusted basis and fair market value are taken into account in determining the Members' shares of tax items under Section 704(c) of the Code.

8. Distributions.

(a) The Company may (subject to Section 12.3(b)) make distributions to the Members from time to time. All distributions hereunder, whether in cash or other property (or a combination thereof) shall be made to the Members in the following order of priority:

(i) first, to the Members in proportion, and in an aggregate amount equal, to their respective Excess Capital Contributions;

(ii) second, to the Members in proportion, and in an aggregate amount equal, to their respective Capital Contributions (excluding their respective Excess Capital Contributions); and

(iii) thereafter,

(A) seventy-five (75%) percent to the Class A Member; and

(B) twenty-five (25%) percent to the Class B Member.

(b)   Distributions shall not be authorized or made hereunder if and to the extent that such distributions would render the Company insolvent or impair its ability to discharge its obligations, whether or not accrued, absolute, fixed or contingent, would interfere with its ability to carry out the purposes of the Company or otherwise would be in violation of the Act.

(c)   Notwithstanding the provisions of Section 8(a) hereof, to the extent possible (taking into account Section 8(b) hereof) the Company shall distribute annually, to the extent requested by a Member and permissible under this Section 8(c), to each Member in cash, no later than 90 days after the close of each Fiscal Year, an amount equal to the actual tax liability (inclusive of tax liabilities in respect of federal, state and local income taxes) of the Member (or equity owner of a Member if such Member is a conduit tax entity) attributable to its Member Interest. Distributions pursuant to this Section 8(c) shall only be made from the Company's Net Operating Income Available for Tax Distributions (as hereinafter defined). For purposes of this Section 8(c), the term Company's Net Operating Income Available for Tax Distributions shall mean that amount so designated by the Management Committee each year as the Company's Net Operating Income Available for Distribution. Notwithstanding any provisions herein to the contrary, the term Company's Net Operating Income Available for Distribution shall not include the proceeds of the Member Debt or the Members' Capital Contributions. Any distributions made pursuant to this Section 8(c) shall be treated as advances against distributions made pursuant to Section 8(a) hereof.

9.   Books of Account: Reports.

9.1   Books of Account. The Company's books and records shall be maintained at the principal office of the Company or at any other location designated by the Members, and all Members shall have access thereto at all reasonable times. The books and records shall be kept on the basis of accounting used for federal income tax purposes, reflect all Company transactions and shall be otherwise appropriate and adequate for the conduct of the Company's business.

9.2   Reports.

(a)   Within seventy-five (75) days after the end of each Fiscal Year, the company shall prepare and submit to each Member an annual report of the Company for such Fiscal Year. The annual report shall include the balance sheet of the Company as of the last day of such Fiscal Year and statements of profit or loss and cash flows of the Company for such Fiscal Year. The report shall be accompanied by a supplementary schedule showing the entries to the Members' (separately and in the aggregate) Capital Accounts in respect of such Fiscal Year, together with the appropriate Internal Revenue Service forms showing entries required to be made on each such Member's federal income tax return with respect to the Company's Net Profits or Net Losses.

(b)   In connection with the liquidation and dissolution of the Company, the Members of the Liquidation Trustee (as the case may be) shall prepare and submit to the Members a termination report containing the financial statements of the Company as of and for the period ended upon the substantial completion of liquidation.

10.   Management of the Company.

10.1   Management by Members. The management, operation, and control of the company and its business and affairs shall rest exclusively with the Members.

10.2   Management Committee.

(a)   The management of the company by and on behalf of the Members shall be effectuated by a Management Committee comprised of four individuals, two (2) of whom shall be designated at any time and from time to time by A, and two (2) of whom shall be designated at any time and from time to time by BC. Each individual serving on the Management Committee (i) shall serve at the pleasure of, (ii) may be removed at any time and for any reason by, (iii) shall be the agent of, and (iv) shall cast any votes as may be taken hereunder on behalf of the Member who shall have designated such individual in accordance with this Section. All actions taken and all determinations and decisions made by (x) a majority in number of the members of the Management Committee shall be deemed for all purposes to be the actions taken by the Members and (y) all of the members of the Management Committee shall be deemed for all purposes to be the actions taken by all of the Members. Any action, determination, or decision as to which a majority in number of the members of the Management Committee cannot agree shall be taken or made pursuant to the following Deadlock Procedure.

(i) In the event the Management Committee cannot agree in respect of a decision on behalf of the Company, such decision shall be made by a three-person panel (the 'Deadlock Panel'). One member of the Deadlock Panel shall be appointed by A, one member of the Deadlock Panel shall be appointed by BC, and the third member shall be appointed by the panelists appointed by the Members (the 'Panelists'). The Panelists shall appoint the third member of the Deadlock Panel by a blind drawing of the name of the third member from a pool of six potential candidates, three of which shall be provided by A and approved by BC and three of which shall be provided by BC and approved by A. The recommendation of the Deadlock Panel shall be binding on the Members and the Company when two of the three members of the Deadlock Panel agree on the decision necessitating the implementation of this Section 10.2(a)(i).

(b) In furtherance of (and subject to) subsection (a) of this Section 10.2, the following individuals are hereby designated as the initial members of the Management Committee.

By A: _____; and

_____;

By BC: _____; and

_____;

(c) The Management Committee may adopt and amend such by-laws, rules, regulations, policies, and procedures as it may determine to be in the best interest of the Company (but not inconsistent with this Agreement) for the conduct of the business of the Management Committee and the business and affairs of the Company.

(d) Notwithstanding the foregoing provisions of this Section 10.2, the Management Committee shall not have the power to take the following actions without the consent of a Majority-in-Interest of the Members:

(i) The issuance, sale, or other disposition by the Company of any debt or equity securities of or similar interests in the Company;

(ii) The sale, lease, or transfer of a material portion of the assets of the Company or the sale, transfer, or assignment of any material governmental permit or license relating to the business of the Company;

(iii) The adoption of operating, capital, and other budgets;

(iv) The modification to a then-current approved budget or the approval of any expenditure in excess of amounts previously included in a then-current approved budget;

(v) Any action which would cause the Company to (A) guaranty or otherwise become liable for any indebtedness of any other person, (B) extend credit (other than as required in the ordinary course of business) to any person, (C) incur any indebtedness (other than trade payable incurred in the ordinary course of business and as included in a then-current approved budget), or (D) pledge, encumber, or create a lien in any assets of the Company;

(vi) The employment of management personnel and the discharge or a material modification of the duties of such personnel;

(vii) The authorization or payment of any compensation to an employee of the Company or any other person engaged by the Company if the expected annual compensation payable to such employee or other person exceeds $ _____;

(viii) The authorization, approval, or execution of any contract or other agreement on behalf of the Company under which the Company would be obligated for amounts in excess of $ _____;

(ix) The authorization or payment of any bonus to an employee of the Company or any other person engaged by the Company;

(x) Any change to the Company's existing employee benefit structure;

(xi) Transactions with affiliates.

10.3 Management in the Event of Default Under Member Debt. A has agreed to loan the Company up to $2,000,000 under the XYZ Credit Agreement. The XYZ Credit Agreement and its Exhibits contain certain events of default ('Events of Default'). If any Event of Default occurs, A has the right, but not the obligation, to take immediate control of the Management Committee by appointing additional members to the Management Committee so that the total number of Management Committee members appointed by A is sufficient to approve or disapprove any and all actions the Company may, from time to time, take or abstain from taking until such time as the Company cures the Event of Default or discharges its obligations under the Line of Credit Agreement.

10.4 Title Designations. The Management Committee shall have the power to create such employee or officer-type designations (such as president, vice president, and the like) as it shall determine to be in the best interests of the Company, to designate the powers, authorities, and responsibilities as shall be deemed to have been granted to and undertaken by those individuals to whom such designations are assigned, and to determine those individuals(s) to whom such designations (and the accompanying powers, authorities, and responsibilities) shall be assigned. Except as may be limited by contract, each individual to whom is assigned any such designation shall serve at the pleasure of the Management Committee, and any such designation (and the accompanying powers, authorities, and responsibilities) may be modified or terminated at any time in the sole discretion of the Management Committee.

10.5 Liability and Indemnification.

(a) No Member, and no member of the Management Committee, shall be liable to the Company or to any other Member for any debts owed by the Company to any such Member, or for any actions taken or omissions made in good faith and reasonably believed by such Member (or member of the Management Committee) to be in the best interests of the Company, or for errors of judgment, except to the extent such acts or omissions constitute gross negligence, recklessness, or willful misconduct.

(b) To the fullest extent permitted by law, the Company shall indemnify each Member, each member of the Management Committee, and the Company's and each Member's (and member of the Management Committee's) partners, employees, agents, and Affiliates (where acting for or as agent of the Company or the Member (or the member of the Management Committee) in its capacity as such) (any of the foregoing Persons being hereinafter an 'Indemnified Person') and save and hold them and each of them harmless from and in respect of (i) all fees, costs, and expenses, including attorneys' fees, incurred in connection with, or resulting from, any claim, action, or demand

against any such Indemnified Person or the Company that arise out of, or in any way relate to, the Company, its properties, business, or affairs, and (ii) all such claims, actions, and demands and any losses, liabilities, or damages resulting therefrom, including amounts paid by such Indemnified Person with the prior written consent of the Company in settlement or compromise of any such claim, action, or demand; provided, however, that this indemnity shall not extend to any such Indemnified Person to the extent that its acts and omissions shall have been adjudged to constitute a breach of this Agreement or gross negligence, recklessness, or willful misconduct.

10.6 Banking. All funds of the Company shall be deposited in such bank account or accounts of federally insured bank(s) as shall be determined by the Members. Such funds shall not be commingled with any of the funds of any Member. All withdrawals therefrom shall be made upon written authorization signed by any Person authorized to do so by the Members.

10.7 Tax Matters Member. The Class A Member shall be the 'tax matters partner' (as defined in Section 6231(a)(7) of the Code) to act on behalf of the Company in connection with Company income tax matters.

11. Other Activities of the Members. Nothing in this Agreement shall preclude any Member or its Affiliates from engaging in other transactions and possessing interests and making investments in and loans to other business ventures of any nature or description (whether or not competitive with the business of the Company), independently or with other, whether existing as of the date hereof or hereafter coming into existence, and neither the Company nor any other Member shall have any rights in or to any such other transactions, investments, or ventures or the income or profits derived therefrom.

12. Expenses and Fees.

12.1 Initial Expenses. Pre-Operating Expenses and Organizational Expenses will be amortized as permitted by the Code.

12.2 Operating Expenses. The Company shall be obligated to pay or reimburse the expenses of operating and maintaining the Company and its Properties, which expenses shall include, without limitation, legal, accounting and auditing fees, and expenses of the Company and the costs of the acquisition, maintenance, repair, and disposition of the Company's Properties and taxes and assessments with respect thereto.

12.3 Compensation.

(a) No Member shall receive any salary, fee, or draw for services rendered to or on behalf of the Company.

(b) The Company shall pay to the Members for the use of their capital any accrued and unpaid Guaranteed Return prior to the making of any distributions to the Members under Sections 8 or 15.3. The payments to be made to the Members pursuant to this Section 12.3(b) are intended to, and to the greatest extent permitted by the Regulations shall, be treated as 'guaranteed payments' as described in Section 707(c) of the Code. All payments under this Section shall be made in proportion to each Member's accrued and unpaid Guaranteed Return.

13. Transfers of Interests: Admission

13.1 Transfer Restrictions.

(a) No Member may sell, transfer, encumber, or otherwise dispose of (collectively, 'transfer') his Member Interest, or any interest therein, unless the transfer is permitted by Section 13.1(b) or unless such Member shall have first complied with the provisions of Section 13.1(c). Any transfer of any Member Interest, or any interest therein, in violation of this Agreement shall be void and of no effect.

(b) Compliance with Section 13.1(c) shall not be required for the transfer or retransfer of any Member Interest, or any interest therein, by a Member to the following individuals and/or entities:

(i) transfers to the spouse or any one or more of the issue, or in trust for the benefit of any one or more of the spouse and issue, of such Member;

(ii) transfers to an Affiliate of the Member; provided, however, that such Affiliate and the Persons holding the ownership and beneficial interests therein shall have entered into an agreement with the Members and the company providing for restrictions on the transfer, and rights of the Members in respect, of such interests substantially as set forth in this Section 13.1;

(iii) transfers by a Member which is an entity to the Persons holding the equity interests in such entity;

(iv) transfers to any successor in interest upon the sale of substantially all of the assets or the merger, consolidation, or dissolution of the Member;

(v) transfers to the estate of an individual Member; or

(vi) transfers by the estate of a deceased individual Member to any Person described in clauses (i) and (ii) of this Section 13.1(b).

(c) Right of First Refusal.

(i) If a Member receives a bona fide offer (the 'Offer') which such Member (the 'Selling Member') proposes to accept, whether or not solicited, to sell or otherwise dispose of all or any portion of its Member Interest, then, except as provided in Section 13.1(b), the Selling Member shall furnish to the other Members written notice (the 'Notice') of the receipt of the Offer together with the principal terms and conditions of the proposed sale, including the minimum price (the 'Sale Price') at which such Member Interest, or interest therein, is proposed to be sold, and a statement as to the identity of each real party in interest making the offer, and the other Members shall then have the right to purchase all, but not less than all, of the Member Interest, or interest therein, (the 'Offered Interest') proposed to be sold by the Selling Member upon and subject to the terms and conditions as set forth in this Section 13.1(c). In the event more than one of the other Members wishes to purchase the Offered Interest, the right to purchase shall be allocated among them in proportion to their relative interests in that portion of Net Profits as are allocable pursuant to Section 7.2(d).

(ii) The price and terms at which the Offered Interest may be purchased pursuant to Section 13.1(c)(i) shall be the price and terms contained in the Offer. If the price contained in the Offer shall consist (in whole or in part) of consideration other than cash, payable at the closing thereof or at a later date, the cash equivalent fair market value of such other consideration shall be included in the price at which the offered Interest may be so purchased.

(iii) The other Members shall have sixty (60) days after receipt of the Notice to elect to purchase the Offered Interest. The purchase transaction shall be consummated at a closing to be held at the principal executive offices of the Company, or at such other location as may be agreed by the parties, with 30 days following the date of the other Members' election to purchase the Offered Interest. At the closing, unless otherwise stipulated in the Offer, the purchasing Members shall deliver to the Selling Member the full purchase price, against delivery of an instrument appropriately transferring the Offered Interest sold thereby.

(iv) If the other Members do not elect to purchase the Offered Interest, or if there shall be any default in the making of payment in full for all the Offered Interest, then the Selling Member may accept the Offer and, pursuant thereto, sell the Offered Interest. However, if the Selling Member does not sell the Offered Interest pursuant to the Offer within 60 days after the termination (by passage of time or otherwise) of the rights of first refusal created under this Section 13.1(c), the Selling Member may not thereafter transfer the Offered Interest (or any part thereof) without again complying with the provisions of this Section 13.1(c).

13.2 Admissions

(a) All transfers by a Member of its Member Interest, or any interest therein, shall entitle the transferee only to receive the allocations and distributions to which the transferring Member would otherwise be entitled, and such transferee shall become a Member, and shall have the right to participate in the Management of the business and affairs of the Company, only upon compliance with the requirements of Section 13.2(b) and (c) and only with the advance written consent of all of the Members other than the Member making such transfer, which consent shall be given in the sole and absolute discretion of the other Members.

(b) No Person to whom a transferring Member has transferred its Member Interest, or any interest therein, shall become a Member of the Company or have the right to participate in the management of the business and affairs of the Company unless (i) provision therefor is made by the instrument of assignment, (ii) such Person executes and acknowledges such instruments as the Members (other than the Member making such transfer) reasonably deem necessary or advisable to permit such person to

become a Member, (iii) in the opinion of counsel for the Company, (A) neither the assignment of such Member Interest, or any interest therein, nor the becoming of a Member by such Person will adversely affect the Company's classification as a partnership for federal income tax purposes and (B) neither the offering nor the proposed transfer of such Member Interest, or interest therein, will violate, or cause the original issue thereof to be in violation of, the securities laws, rules or regulations of the United States, any state thereof or any other jurisdiction, (iv) all other steps are taken which, in the opinion of the Members, are reasonably necessary to permit such Person to become a Member, and (v) such person pays for all expenses incurred by the Company in connection with such Person's becoming a Member.

(c) Any Person becoming a Member pursuant to this Section 13 will succeed to all rights and be subject to all the obligations of the assigning Member with respect to the Member Interest, or interest therein, assigned to such Person.

13.3 <u>Distributions and Allocations in Respect to Transferred Interests.</u> If any Member Interest, or any interest therein, is sold, assigned, or transferred, or any Person otherwise becomes a Member during any Fiscal Year in compliance with the provisions of this Section 13, Net Profits, Net Losses, each item thereof, and all other items attributable to such Member Interest, or interest therein, for such Fiscal Year shall be allocated among the Members by taking into account their varying interests during such Fiscal Year in accordance with Section 706(d) of the Code. Unless otherwise required by the Regulations, such sale, assignment, transfer, or admission shall be deemed to have occurred at the end of the calendar month during which such event shall have actually occurred, and such allocations shall be determined and made pursuant to a <u>pro forma</u> closing of the books of the Company as of the end of such month. With respect to a transferred Member Interest, or any interest therein, all distributions on or before the deemed date of such transfer shall be made to the transferor and all distributions thereafter shall be made to the transferee. Neither the Company nor any Member shall incur any liability for making allocations and distributions in accordance with the provisions of this Section 13.3.

14. <u>Dissolution of Company.</u>

(a) The Company shall dissolve upon the occurrence of any of the following events:

(i) the expiration of the term of the Company as provided in Section 5 unless such term is extended by the unanimous agreement of the Members;

(ii) the written agreement of all of the Members;

(iii) subject to Section 14(b), the death, retirement, resignation, expulsion, bankruptcy, or dissolution of a Member or the occurrence of any other event that terminates the continued membership of a Member in the Company;

(iv) the sale of all or substantially all the assets of the Company;

(v) the entry of an order of judicial dissolution under the Act; or

(vi) the entry of a final judgment, order, or decree of a court with competent jurisdiction adjudicating the Company to be bankrupt, and the expiration of the period, if any, allowed by applicable law in which appeal therefrom.

(b) An event described in clause (iii) of Section 14(a) shall not cause the Company to dissolve if the business of the Company is continued with the consent of all of the remaining Members within ninety (90) days after the date of such event.

15. Winding Up of the Company.

15.1 Termination of Company Business. Upon dissolution of the Company as provided in Section 14, the Company shall cease to conduct its activities, and its business and affairs shall be wound up as promptly as practicable in conformity with the procedures herein set forth and the requirements of the Act.

15.2 Liquidation of Assets. Upon dissolution of the Company, the Members or a Liquidation Trustee selected by a Majority-in-Interest of the Members shall arrange for liquidation of the Company's assets and cause such liquidation to be carried out as promptly as is consistent with realization of maximum value. The Members or the Liquidation Trustee, as the case may be, shall have full power and authority to:

(a) sell, at such prices and upon such terms as they or it in their or its sole discretion may deem appropriate, any or all of the Company's assets, provided that such sales shall be made for cash to the fullest extent practicable;

(b) incur such fees, costs, and expenses for the account of the Company as may be reasonable and necessary or advisable to accomplish such liquidation;

(c) defer and withhold from liquidation Company assets if, in their or its best judgment, such action is in the best interests of Company's creditors and the Members; and

(d) take any and all other actions as may be permitted under the Act.

Pending the liquidation provided for herein, the Members or the Liquidation Trustee, as the case may be, shall have the power and authority to operate, manage, and otherwise deal with Company Property and to pay or provide for payment and discharge of the Company's debts, obligations, and liabilities, whether or not accrued, absolute, fixed, or contingent.

15.3 Distribution of Assets.

(a) Gain or loss realized upon the sale or exchange of Company assets pursuant to Section 15.2 shall be allocated to the Members' Capital Accounts in accordance with the provisions of Section 7.

(b) Prior to any distribution relating to liquidation of the Company, the Members or the Liquidation Trustee, as the case may be, shall also adjust each Member's Capital Account to reflect the manner in which the unrealized income, gain, loss, and deduction inherent in the Company's Property (that has not been reflected in the Members' Capital Accounts previously) would be allocated among the Members if there were a taxable disposition of such Property for the fair market value of such Property (taking Section 7701(g) of the Code into account) on the date of distribution.

(c) Distributions relating to liquidation may be made in cash or other property (or a combination thereof).

(d) Distribution of the Company assets upon liquidation shall be made in the following order:

(i) To the payment and discharge of all debts, liabilities, and obligations of the Company to Company creditors (including Members and former Members) in the order of priority as provided by law.

(ii) To the establishment of any reserves for any contingent or unforeseen liabilities or obligations of the Company; provided, however, that if such reserves are established, the Capital Accounts of the Members shall be adjusted pursuant to Section 15.3(b) and upon the determination that it is no longer necessary to maintain any particular portion of such reserves, such portion shall be immediately distributed in accordance with Section 15.3(d)(iii).

(iii) To the Members in accordance with the net credit balances of their respective Capital Accounts, as determined after taking into account all Capital Account adjustments for the Company's taxable year during which such liquidation occurs (other than those made pursuant to this clause(iii) and subsection(e)), by the end of such taxable year (or, if later, within 90 days after the date of the Company's liquidation).

(e) If any Member has a deficit balance in its Capital Account following the distribution of Company assets upon dissolution, as determined after taking into account all Capital Account adjustments for the taxable year during which such dissolution occurs (other than those made pursuant to this subsection(e)), such Member shall be required to restore the amount of such deficit to the Company as soon as practicable but in no event later than the end of such taxable year (or, if later, within 90 days after the date of the Company's liquidation), which amount shall be paid to the Company's creditors or distributed to the Members in accordance with their respective positive Capital Account balances in accordance with clause (d)(ii) of this Section 15.3; provided, however, that no Company creditor may rely upon this sentence in order to create an obligation of any Member to pay a Company debt that such Member is not otherwise personally obligated to pay.

(f) Upon the completion of the winding up of the affairs of the Company and the distribution of its assets as provided for herein and in the Act, the Members shall cause the Certificate to be canceled in accordance with the Act.

16. **Amendment of Agreement.** This Agreement may be amended in whole or in part only with the written consent of all of the Members.

17. **Action by and Meetings of the Members.**

17.1 **Action by the Members.** Any vote, consent, approval, determination, election, or agreement in regard to any action required of or permitted by a Member (including on behalf of a Member by the members of the Management Committee which are designated by such Member) by any provision of this Agreement or by law may be expressed as follows:

(a) by the written consent of the Member at or prior to the time of the action for which the consent is intended, provided that such consent is not nullified by written notice thereof by such member to the Company at or prior to, or the negative vote by such Member at, any meeting that may be held to consider the action;

(b) by the Member's failure to respond to a written request for consent sent by another Member to such Member, which failure to respond continues for at least 30 days after the date upon which such request was received by such member (which date shall be determined with reference to the date set forth in the return receipt with respect to the mailing of such request by the Member seeking such consent); or

(c) by the affirmative vote of the Member as to the action for which the vote is taken at any meeting which may be called and held to consider such action pursuant to Section 17.2.

17.2 **Meeting of Members.**

(a) Any matter requiring the vote, consent, approval, determination, election, or agreement of the Members or any class of Members pursuant to any Section of this Agreement or by law may be considered at a meeting held not fewer than fifteen (15) days nor greater than sixty (60) days after written notice thereof shall have been given by any Member.

(b) Such meeting may be held at the principal office of the Company or may be held by means of conference telephone or similar methods of communication during which all persons participating may be heard simultaneously.

18. **Members' Covenants: Breach.**

18.1 **Covenant Not to Dissolve.** Notwithstanding any provision of the Act or Section 14, each Member hereby covenants and agrees that the members have entered into this Agreement based on their mutual expectation that all Members will continue as Members and carry out the duties and obligations undertaken by them hereunder and that, except as otherwise permitted by Section 13, no Member shall cease to be a Member, be entitled to demand or receive any distributions, a return of such member's Capital Contributions or profits (or a bond or other security for the return of such Capital Contributions or profits), or exercise any power under the Act to dissolve the Company, without the unanimous consent of the Members.

18.2 **Consequences of Violation of Covenant.** Notwithstanding anything to the contrary in the Act, if a Member (a 'Breaching Member') attempts to cease being a Member or dissolve the Company in breach of Section 18.1, the Company shall (subject to the requirements of Section 14(b)) continue and such Breaching Member shall be subject to this Section 18.2. In such event, the following shall occur:

(a) the Breaching Member shall immediately cease to be a Member and shall have no further power to participate in the business or affairs of the Company or to otherwise act for or bind the Company;

(b) the other Members shall continue to have the right to possess the Company's assets and goodwill and to conduct its business and affairs;

(c) the Breaching Member shall be liable in damages, without requirement of a prior accounting, to the Company for all costs and liabilities that the Company or the other Members may incur as a result of such breach;

(d) the Company shall have no obligation to pay to the Breaching Member any distributions or its Capital Contribution or profits, but may, by notice to the Breaching member within 30 days of such breach, elect to make Breach payments (as defined in Section 18.3) to the Breaching Member in complete satisfaction of the Breaching Member's interest in the Company;

(e) if the Company does not elect to make Breach Payments pursuant to Section 18.2(d), the Company shall treat the Breaching Member as if it were an assignee of the Member Interest of the Breaching Member and shall make allocations and distributions to the Breaching Member only of those amounts otherwise allocable and distributable with respect to such Member Interest hereunder;

(f) the Company may apply any distributions otherwise payable with respect to such Breaching Member's Member Interest (including Breach Payments) to satisfy any claims it may have against the Breaching Member;

(g) the Breaching member shall have no right to inspect the Company's books or records or obtain other information concerning the Company's operations;

(h) the Breaching member shall continue to be liable to the Company for any unfulfilled Capital Commitment hereunder with respect to its Member Interest; and

(i) notwithstanding anything to the contrary herein above provided, unless the Company has elected to make Breach Payments to the Breaching Member in satisfaction of his Member Interest, the Company may offer and sell (on any terms that are not manifestly unreasonable) the Member Interest of the Breaching Member to the other Members or other Persons on the Breaching Member's behalf, provided that any Person acquiring such Member Interest becomes a Member with respect to such Member Interest in accordance with Section 13.

18.3 Breach Payments. For purposes hereof, Breach Payments shall be made in four installments, each equal to one-fourth of

the Breach Amount, payable on the next four consecutive anniversaries following the breach by the Breaching Member, plus interest accrued from the date of such breach through the date each such installment on the unpaid balance of such Breach Amount at the lowest rate permitted under Section 1274 of the Code so as to avoid the imputation of interest income. The Breach Amount shall be an amount equal to the lesser of (i) the balance in such Breaching Member's Capital Account on the date of such breach or (ii) the fair market value of such Breaching Member's Member Interest in the Company determined by appraisal, the cost of which shall be borne entirely by the Breaching Member. The Company may, at its sole election, prepay all or any portion of the Breach Payments and interest accrued thereon at any time without penalty.

18.4 No Bonding. Notwithstanding anything to the contrary as may be provided by law, if, under Section 18.2(e), the Company treats a Breaching Member as an assignee of a Member Interest in the Company, the Company shall not be obligated to secure the value of the Breaching Member's Member Interest by bond or otherwise; provided, however, that if a court of competent jurisdiction determines that, in order to continue the business of the Company such value must be so secured, the Company may provide such security. If the Company provides such security, the Breaching Member shall not have any right to participate in Company profits or distributions during the remaining term of the Company, or to receive any interest on the value of such Member Interest.

19. Disputes. In the event of any dispute with respect to any matter arising out of this Agreement, as the same may be amended or supplemented, such dispute shall be submitted to arbitration upon request of any one or more of the disputants, who shall notify each of the other disputants in writing of such request. Each of the disputants shall promptly designate one person to serve as an arbitrator and the arbitrators so designated shall within 30 days select another person as Chairman of the Board of Arbitration by agreement or, if they are unable to agree, then through the services and facilities of the Pittsburgh, Pennsylvania regional office of the American Arbitration Associates and in accordance with the rules thereof. The parties hereto agree that in any such arbitration proceeding (i) discovery in accordance with the Federal Rules of Civil Procedure shall be available to each of the disputants, and (ii) the Federal Rules of Evidence shall govern the admissibility of all evidence. The decision and award of a majority of the Board of Arbitration shall be final and binding upon the disputants, and judgment may be entered thereon in accordance with applicable law in any court having jurisdiction thereof. The agreement herein to arbitrate shall be specifically enforceable under applicable law in any court having jurisdiction thereof. The cost of any arbitration shall be borne by the nonprevailing party or in such other manner as the Board of Arbitration may determine.

20. Miscellaneous.

20.1 Notices. Any notice, payment, demand, request, or other communication required or permitted to be given by any provision of this Agreement or by law shall be in writing and shall be delivered in person, by overnight air courier, by certified mail, by facsimile transmission, or by telegram. Any such communication shall be deemed to have been effectively delivered or given, whether or not the same is actually received (except in the case of payments), (i) if mailed, upon the earlier of actual receipt or five days after deposit in the United States mail by certified mail, postage prepaid, to the proper address, (ii) when delivered in person or by overnight air courier, (iii) when receipt of a facsimile transmission is confirmed by telephone, or (iv) when a telegram is received.

Notices shall be addressed as follows or to such other address or addresses as may be specified by written notice to the Members:

If to the
Company: ABC
              _____
              _____
              Attention: _____
              Fax No.: _____

If to A: _____
              _____
              _____
              Attention: _____
              Fax No.: _____

With a copy to: _____
              _____
              _____
              Attention: _____
              Fax No.: _____

If to BC   _____
              _____
              _____
              Attention: _____
              Fax No.: _____

and   _____
              _____
              _____
              Attention: _____
              Fax No.: _____

20.2 <u>Section Headings.</u> Section and other headings contained in this Agreement are for reference purposes only and are in no way intended to describe, interpret, define or limit the scope, extent or intent of this Agreement or any provision hereof.

20.3 <u>Severability.</u> The provisions of this Agreement shall be deemed severable, and the invalidity or unenforceability of any provision shall not affect the validity or enforceability of the remainder of this Agreement or any valid clause of any invalid portion.

20.4 <u>Governing Law.</u> The laws of the Commonwealth of Pennsylvania, excluding its choice of law provisions, shall govern this Agreement. All references herein to statutes, regulations and governmental agencies are deemed to refer to their corresponding provisions of succeeding statutes or regulations or to successor agencies, as the case may be.

20.5 <u>Counterpart Execution.</u> This Agreement may be executed in any number of counterparts with the same effect as if all parties hereto had signed the same document. All counterparts shall be construed together and shall constitute one Agreement.

20.6 <u>Parties in Interest.</u> Each and every covenant, term, provision, and agreement herein contained shall be binding upon, and inure to the benefit of, the parties hereto and their respective heirs, personal representatives, successors, and assigns.

20.7 <u>Gender and Number.</u> As the context requires, all words used herein in the singular shall extend to and include the plural; all words used in the plural shall extend to and include the singular; and all words used in either gender shall extend to and include the other gender or be neutral.

20.8 <u>Section References.</u> Except as otherwise specifically noted or required in the context, all references herein to Sections shall refer to Sections of this Agreement.

20.9 <u>Entire Agreement.</u> This Agreement sets forth the entire agreement and understanding among the parties as to the specific subject matter hereof and supersedes all prior discussions, agreements and understandings between the parties.

IN WITNESS WHEREOF, this Limited Company Agreement has been executed as of the date first above written.

ATTEST:

_____   By:_____
                               Title: _____

ATTEST:

_____   By:_____
                               Title: _____

Form 06-02

Filed with the Department of State on _____

_____

Secretary of the Commonwealth

Articles of Incorporations—For Profit

Indicate type of domestic corporation (check one):

__Business-stock (15 Pa. C.S. §1306) __Management (15 Pa. C.S. §2702)

__Business-nonstock (15 Pa. C.S. §2102) __Professional (15 Pa. C.S. §2903)

__Business-statutory close (15 Pa. C.S. §2303) __Cooperative (15 Pa. C.S. §7102A)

In compliance with the requirements of the applicable provisions of 15 Pa. C.S. (relating to corporations and unincorporated associations) the undersigned, desiring to incorporate a corporation for profit hereby state(s) that:

1. The name of the corporation is:

2. The (a) address of this corporation's initial registered office in this Commonwealth or (b) name of its commercial registered office provider and the county of venue is:

(a) _____

| Number and Street | City | State | Zip | County |

(b) c/o: _____

Name of Commercial Registered Office Provider · County

For a corporation represented by a commercial registered office provider, the county in (b) shall be deemed the county in which the corporation is located for venue and official publication purposes.

3. The corporation is incorporated under the provisions of the Business Corporation Law of 1988.

4. The aggregate number of shares authorized is: _____ (other provisions, if any, attach 8½ × 11 sheet)

5. The name and address, including street and number, if any, of each **incorporator** is:

Name _____ Address _____

6. The specified effective date, if any, is: _____

month · day · year · hour, if any

7. Any additional provisions of the articles, if any, attach an 8½ × 11 sheet.

8. **Statutory close corporation only**: Neither the corporation nor any shareholder shall make an offering of any of its shares of any class that would constitute a 'public offering' within the meaning of the Securities Act of 1933 (15 U.S.C. §77a et seq.).

9. **Cooperative corporations only**: (Complete and strike out inapplicable term) The common bond of membership among the members/shareholders is: _____

IN TESTIMONY WHEREOF, the incorporator(s) has (have) signed these Articles of Incorporation this _____ day of _____, 20__.

_____ _____

(Signature) (Signature)

334

Form 06-03
Docketing Statement
Departments of State and Revenue

Check proper box

__Pa. Business-stock __Pa. Business-nonstock Pa. Business-Management __Pa. Professional
__Pa. Business-statutory close __Pa. Business-cooperative Pa. Nonprofit-stock   __Pa. Nonprofit-nonstock
__Foreign-business   __Foreign-nonprofit   __Motor Vehicle for Hire
__Foreign-Certificate of Authority to D/B/A _____

Corporation registering as a result of (check one):

__Incorporation (Pa.)   __Domestication __Consolidation
__Authorization of a foreign corporation __Division   __Summary of Record

1. Name of corporation _____

  _____

2. Location of (a) initial registered office in Pa. or (b) the name and county of the commercial registered office provider:

  (a) _____
    Number and Street/RD number and Box City   State   Zip Code   County

  (b) c/o: _____
    Name of commercial registered office provider   County

3. State or Country of Incorporation: _____ 4. Specified effective date, if applicable: _____

5. Federal Identification Number: _____

6. Describe principal Pa. activity to be engaged in, within one year of this application date: _____

  _____

  _____

7. Names, residences and social security number of the chief executive officer, secretary and treasurer:
  Name   Address   Title   Social Security #

  _____

  _____

  _____

  If professional corporation, include officer's professional license numbers with the respective Pennsylvania Professional Board.

8. Location of principal place of business:

_____

Number and Street/RD number and Box   City   State   Zip Code   County

9. Mailing address if different than #8 (Location where correspondence, tax report form, etc. are to be sent):

_____

Number and Street/RD number and Box   City   State   Zip Code   County

10. Act of General Assembly or authority under which you are organized or incorporated (Full citation of statute or other authority; attach a separate sheet if more space is required): _____

_____

11. Date and state of incorporation or organization (foreign corporation only): _____

12. Date business started in Pa. (foreign corporation only): _____

13. Is the corporation authorized to issue capital stock? ___ YES ___ NO

14. Corporation's fiscal year ends: _____

     This statement shall be deemed to have been executed by the individual who executed the accompanying submittal. See 18 Pa. C.S. §4904 (relating to unsworn falsification to authorities).

Instructions for Completion of Form:

A. A separate completed set of copies of this form shall be submitted for each entity or registration resulting from the transaction.

B. The Bureau of Corporation Taxes in the Pa. Department of Revenue should be notified of any address changes. Notification should be sent to the Processing Division, Bureau of Corporation Taxes, Pa. Department of Revenue, Dept. 280705, Harrisburg, PA 17128-0705.

C. All Pa. corporate tax reports, except those for motor vehicle for hire, must be filed with the Commonwealth on the same fiscal basis as filed with the U.S government. Motor vehicle for hire, i.e., gross receipts tax reports, must be filed on a calendar year basis only.

Form 06-04

Application for Registration of Fictitious Name

In compliance with the requirements of 54 Pa. C.S. § 311 (relating to registration), the undersigned entity(ies) desiring to register a fictitious name under 54 Pa. C.S. Ch. 3 (relating to fictitious names), hereby state(s) that:

1. The fictitious name is: _____

2. A brief statement of the character or nature of the business or other activity to be carried on under or through the fictitious name is:

   _____

3. The **address**, including number and street, if any, of the principal place of business of the business or other activity to be carried on under or through the fictitious name is (P.O. Box alone is **not** acceptable):

   _____

Number and Street	City	State	Zip	County

4. The **name** and **address**, including number and street, if any, of each individual interested in the business is:

Name	Number and Street	City	State	Zip

5. Each entity, other than an individual, interested in such business is (are):

Name	Form of Organization	Organizing Jurisdiction	Principal Office Address	Pa. Registered Office, if any

6. The applicant is familiar with the provisions of 54 Pa. C.S. §332 (relating to effect of registration) and understands that filing under the Fictitious Names Act does not create any exclusive or other right in the fictitious name.

7. **(Optional):** The name(s) of the agent(s), if any, any one of whom is authorized to execute amendments to, withdrawals from or cancellation of this registration in behalf of all then existing parties to the registration, is (are):

   _____

   IN TESTIMONY WHEREOF, the undersigned have caused this Application for Registration of Fictitious Name to be executed this _____ day of _____, 20_____.

_____
(Individual Signature)

_____
(Individual Signature)

_____
(Individual Signature)

_____
(Individual Signature)

_____
(Name of Entity)

_____
(Name of Entity)

By: _____

By:_____

TITLE: _____

TITLE: _____

Form 08-01
Lease Agreement

THIS AGREEMENT MADE and entered into this day of
_____, 20_____ BY AND BETWEEN
_____, a Pennsylvania corporation, having its principal
place of business at _____, _____,
_____, _____, _____,
hereinafter referred to as 'Landlord',

A N D

_____, a Pennsylvania corporation, having its principal
office located at _____, _____,
_____, _____, _____,
hereinafter referred to as 'Tenant'.

    1.   <u>THE PREMISES:</u> FOR AND IN CONSIDERATION of the
rents, covenants, and agreements hereinafter reserved, mentioned, and
contained on the part of the Tenant, its successors, and assigns, to be paid,
kept, and performed, Landlord has demised and leased, and by these presents does hereby demise and lease unto Tenant, and Tenant does hereby
take and hire the following described premises, hereinafter sometimes
called 'the premises' or 'the demised premises', namely:

    A.   ALL THAT CERTAIN warehouse and office area containing
        approximately _____ square feet located _____ as
        shown on the exhibits attached hereto and made a part hereof.

The premises is identified as (address).

Together with the right by the Tenant, its successors, customers,
and employees to use in common with other Tenants of the _____,
their invitee, customers, and employees, the parking facilities, sidewalks, if
any, delivery areas and appurtenances thereto.

    2.   <u>TERM:</u> The term of this Lease shall be for a period of
_____ years, commencing upon _____, and terminating on
_____.

    3.   <u>RENT:</u> Tenant covenants and agrees to pay to Landlord at
_____ or at such other address as specified by Landlord during the
term of this Lease, as rent for the demised premises, the sum of
_____.

    ($___.00) DOLLARS, payable in advance, without prior demand
therefore and without deduction or set-off, in monthly rental installments
as follows:

    (a) _____ ($___.00)DOLLARS on the first day of
_____ as monthly rent for said month and a like and equal sum on the
first day of each and every month thereafter during the term of this Lease
to and including _____.

    (b) The premises is leased in its 'as is condition'.

    (c) Provided Tenant has complied with all the terms of this
Lease Agreement and rental payments are current, Tenant is hereby
granted to option to terminate this Lease Agreement at any time by giving
Landlord at least six (6) months written notice in advance.

    4.   <u>ADDITIONAL RENT:</u> Tenant shall pay, within thirty (30) days
of billing by Landlord, as additional rent, Tenant's pro rata share of all
increases of real estate taxes and assessments levied or imposed upon the
building in which the demised premises is located and the land on which it
is situate in excess of the real estate taxes and assessments for the year
and all increases of all fire, extended coverage, and liability insurance premiums for insurance coverage in said building and the land on which it is
situated in excess of all fire, extended coverage, and liability insurance premiums thereon in effect at the time of the commencement of the term of
this Lease. Said base amount for insurance purposes is ___(.___) cents per
square foot per annum. The term 'real estate taxes' shall include any tax
imposed upon or levied against real estate or upon owners of real estate as
such, rather than on persons generally, rents or occupancy, in lieu of, or in
addition to any present real estate taxes or assessments, and shall also
include the reasonable cost (including fees of attorneys, consultants and
appraisers) of any negotiation, contest or appeal pursued by Landlord in
an effort to reduce any such taxes, assessment, or charge. Landlord shall
have the right, at any time, but not the duty, to contest any such taxes and
Tenant may join in said proceedings if Tenant so desires. Tenant's pro rata
shall be a fraction, the numerator of which shall be the gross leasable floor
area in the demised premises and the denominator of which shall be for
purposes of real estate taxes, the gross leasable floor area in the buildings
in the tax lot in which the demised premises is located, and for purposes of
insurance, the gross leasable floor area in the buildings covered by the
insurance policy insuring the demised premises.

    5.   <u>REPAIRS BY LANDLORD:</u> Landlord covenants and agrees to
keep and maintain the roof, sidewalk, and structural portions of the
demises premises in good order, condition, and repair, except for any
repairs or maintenance required by reason of the act, omission or negligence of Tenant, its contractors, business invitee, and persons making
deliveries to the demised premises, and further, in the event Landlord
installs any new equipment in the demised premises for Tenant and the
new equipment is installed incorrectly or improperly Landlord shall make
repairs to said new equipment.

6. **REPAIRS BY TENANT:** Except as specifically enumerated in the preceding paragraph hereof as an obligation of Landlord, Tenant covenants and agrees to make all repairs, and keep and maintain in good order, condition, and repair, the demised premises, and every part thereof. Without limiting the generality of the foregoing, Tenant shall maintain in good order, condition, and repair, the interior of the demised premises, the heating, ventilating, and air conditioning systems, and the plumbing, sewage, and electrical facilities within the demised premises. Additionally, Tenant shall replace any plate glass or other glass that may be broken or cracked with glass of the same size and thickness, and shall indemnify and save Landlord harmless from any loss, cost, liability, or damages resulting from such breakage or replacement. Tenant shall be responsible to keep all sidewalks in front of the demised premises free and clear of snow and ice. If Tenant does not do the repairs and maintenance required pursuant to this Lease, Landlord shall have the right but not the duty, to do said repairs and maintenance on behalf of Tenant and Tenant shall pay to Landlord the cost thereof, plus ten (10%) percent for profit, as additional rent.

7. **ADDITIONAL COVENANTS OF TENANT:** Tenant covenants as a further consideration for the leasing of the said premises, as follows:

a. **USE:** To use the premises primarily for warehouse and office and for no other purposes whatsoever.

b. **INSURANCE COSTS:** Not to use or occupy or suffer or permit said premises or any part thereof to be used or occupied for any purpose contrary to law or the rules or regulations or any public authority and/or determined to be a fire hazard or in any manner so as to increase the cost of fire and extended coverage and/or liability insurance to Landlord over and above the normal cost of such insurance for the type and location of the building of which the demised premises is a part. Tenant will, on demand, reimburse Landlord for the cost of all extra premiums caused by Tenant's use of the demised premises and discontinue any use (including the removal of equipment) that resulted in the increase of the cost of said insurance to Landlord, whether or not Landlord has consented to such use. If Tenant shall install any electrical lines in the demised premises, Tenant shall, at its own expense, make whatever changes are necessary to comply with the requirements of the insurance underwriters and governmental authorities having jurisdiction thereover.

c. **INSURANCE:** To, at its own cost and expense, procure and continue in force, throughout the entire term of this Lease, general liability insurance covering any and all claims for injuries to persons and any and all claims for damage to property in, on, or about the demised premises.

Such insurance, referred to, shall all times be not less than FIVE HUNDRED THOUSAND ($500,000.00) DOLLARS for injury to any one person, not less than ONE MILLION ($1,000,000.00) DOLLARS for injuries to more than one person in one accident, and not less than TWO HUNDRED FIFTY THOUSAND ($250,000.00) DOLLARS for damage to property with a deductible amount thereunder not to exceed TWO THOUSAND FIVE HUNDRED ($2,500.00) DOLLARS.

Such insurance shall be written with a reputable company or companies authorized to engage in the business of general liability insurance in the Commonwealth of Pennsylvania. Policies of insurance issued by said companies shall name the Landlord as an additional insured and shall bear an endorsement holding and saving Landlord free and harmless and indemnified against any and all claims whatsoever arising out of injury to or death of any person or damage to any property resulting from the use and occupancy of the demised premises. Tenant shall furnish Landlord, at least fifteen (15) days prior to the commencement of the term of this Lease, and thereafter at least fifteen (15) days prior to the expiration of any policy, with customary insurance certificates evidencing such insurance, which provide that Landlord shall receive at least fifteen (15) days prior notice in writing of the cancellation of any such insurance policy. In the event Tenant fails to furnish such certificates, Landlord may, but shall not be required to, obtain such insurance and the premiums on such insurance shall be deemed additional rental to be paid by Tenant to Landlord upon demand.

d. **UTILITIES:** To be responsible for and pay for all public utility service rendered or furnished to the demised premises during the term hereof, including, but not limited to, heat, water, sewage charges, gas, electricity, together with any levies, taxes or other charges on said utility service. In the event Landlord provides said services to Tenant, Tenant shall pay Landlord for the cost of said services, within thirty (3) days of billing. In no event shall Landlord be liable for the quality, quantity, failure or interruption of said service to the demised premises. Landlord reserves the right to meter water and sewage if deemed necessary and charge Tenant for their water and sewage usage and for the installation of said meter.

e. **PERSONAL PROPERTY:** That all personal property of every kind or description which may, at any time, be in or on or about the demised premises shall be Tenant's sole risk, or at the risk of others claiming under or through Tenant, and Landlord shall not be liable for any damage to the said property or loss sustained by any person or persons on account of or by virtue of the business or occupation or activities of Tenant, its agents, servants or employees, or invitee, from any cause whatsoever.

f. **DAMAGES:** To at all times protect, save and keep Landlord forever free and harmless and indemnified from any loss, cost, injury, damage or death which may occur or be claimed by or with respect to any person or persons, property or chattels, on or about the demised premises, or to the property itself, resulting from the neglect, omission, or intentional act of Tenant or those holding under tenant or Tenant's agents, servants, employees or invitee, or from the possession of, condition of, or conduct of Tenant's business on said demised premises, or from any failure of Tenant, in any respect to comply with and perform any of the terms, conditions, covenants and provisions in the within Lease to be performed by Tenant.

g. WASTE: To use, maintain and occupy the demised premises in careful, safe, lawful and proper manner, and not to commit waste thereon, and to return the premises to Landlord upon the termination of the term, or any renewal thereof, an as good condition as received, ordinary wear and tear excepted. Tenant will not permit the demised premises to be used in any way which will injure the reputation of the same or of the building of which it is a part or of the complex or permit the same to become a nuisance, annoyance, inconvenience, or to damage the other tenants of the building or of the complex or neighborhood. Tenant shall not display any merchandise outside its demised premises and shall not place garbage, rubbish, trash, merchandise containers or other incidentals to its business outside of the demised premises. Tenant will be permitted to place an approved refuse container at a specific location with Landlord's written consent. In order to ensure proper use and care of the demised premises, Tenant shall not be permitted to keep dogs, birds or any other animals on the demised premises at any time.

h. ALTERATIONS: Not to make any alternations, additions or improvements to the demised premises without the prior written consent of the Landlord. All alterations, additions and improvements to said premises, including, but not limited to, all chattels affixed by Tenant to the demised premises, all carpeting, and all air conditioning, heating, lighting and plumbing equipment and fixtures installed by Tenant at the demised premises, shall be made in accordance with all applicable laws and shall at once when made or installed be deemed to have attached to the freehold and to have become the property of Landlord and remain for the benefit of Landlord at the end of the term or other expiration of this Lease in as good order and condition as were when installed, reasonable wear and tear excepted; provided, however, that Tenant shall remove any additions and improvements, which were placed in the demised premises by Tenant and shall repair any damage occasioned by any such removal if Landlord shall so notify Tenant prior to the termination of this Lease or within thirty (30) days thereafter. If Tenant fails to comply with such notice from Landlord within ten (10) days of receipt of such notice, Landlord may effect said removals and repair such damages, and, upon demand from Landlord, LESSEE shall immediately reimburse Landlord for Landlord's cost to effect said removals and repair such damage.

i. INSPECTION: To permit Landlord or Landlord's authorized representatives to enter the premises at all reasonable times for inspection thereof, and to specifically enter said premises during the last year of the term thereof, or any renewal, for the purpose of showing the same to prospective Tenants. Landlord shall further have the right of access to make such repairs to the building, or any parts thereof, which Landlord may deem desirable or necessary or to make such repairs as Tenant, by the terms hereof, has covenanted to do and failed to do, but this shall not obligate Landlord to make such repairs.

j. RULES AND REGULATIONS: To abide by all reasonable rules and regulations established by Landlord from time to time, with respect to the common areas, sidewalks, parking areas and roadways. Landlord reserves the right to direct or assign parking if necessary. Tenant, its agents, servants, employees and invitee shall use no more than ten (10) parking spaces at any one time. In general, all parking associated with the building in which the demised premises is located is on a common-use basis. Furthermore, absolutely no abandoned, unlicensed or non-functioning vehicles are permitted to be parked for any period in the complex, furthermore, Tenant agrees to be responsible for all costs associated with the removal of said vehicles.

k. WALLCOVERINGS: The building standard for wall finishes in the premises is either taped and painted drywall or pre-finished wood paneling. Any finishes applied to the walls other than the aforementioned, including but not limited to fabric, vinyl and/or cloth wall coverings, must, at Landlords option, be removed upon lease expiration or any renewal or extension thereof. The wall material must then be prepared so as to receive finish pain, and/or to its original condition. Before applying wall finishes, wall surface must be sized or prepared properly.

8. WAIVER OF SUBROGATION: Landlord and Tenant release each other from any liability on account of loss, damage, cost or expense resulting from fire or other insurable casualty and waive any right of subrogation which might otherwise exist in or accrue to any person on account thereof, provided that such release of liability and waiver of the right of subrogation shall not be operative in any case where the effect thereof is to invalidate any insurance coverage.

9. SIGNS: Tenant herein shall not erect any signs on the premises without first obtaining the written consent of the Landlord, and in the event such written consent is obtained, Tenant agrees to install said signs in accordance with any governmental regulations applicable thereto, and to maintain the same in a good state of repair, and to save Landlord harmless from any loss, cost or damage as the result of the erection, maintenance and removal of the same; and Tenant shall repair any damage which may have been caused in connection with such sign, their erection and removal. Tenant hereby agrees to any sign criteria as set by Landlord.

10. TRADE FIXTURES: Tenant may, upon the termination of the Lease or any renewal thereof, remove any and all trade fixtures owned by Tenant which are not attached to the premises or which may be removed without permanent injury to or defacement of the demised premises, providing, however, that all rents have been fully paid and all damages, if any, to said demised premises incident to such removal are promptly repaired.

11. ENJOYMENT: Landlord warrants that it is seized of good and sufficient title to the demised premises, and further warrants that if Tenant shall promptly pay and discharge all covenants herein contained of rent and otherwise, it shall have quiet and peaceful enjoyment and possession of the demised premises during the term hereof or any renewal, without hinderance from Landlord or other persons lawfully claiming by, through or under Landlord.

12. FIRE OR OTHER CASUALTY:

A. If during the term of this Lease the demised premises is damaged by fire or other casualty which can be repaired within four (4) months of the occurrence of such fire or other casualty, Landlord shall cause such repairs to be substantially completed within said four month period; provided, however, that said four month period shall be extended by any period of delay caused by acts of God, force majeure, strikes, lockouts, labor disturbances or any other cause beyond Landlord's control. In the event of fire or other casualty, the terms of this Lease shall continue in full force and effect, except that the rent shall be equitably prorated during the period of such repairs to the extent that Tenant shall be deprived of the use and occupancy of the demised premises resulting exclusively from said fire or other casualty. Landlord shall not be required to cause such repairs of the demised premises to be made in the event any such fire or other casualty occurs during the last twenty-four (24) months of the term of this Lease. In such event, Landlord shall notify Tenant within sixty (60) days of the date of the fire or other casualty of Landlord's intention not to cause the demised premises to be repaired, and thereafter, the Lease shall continue through the end of the term, with the rent equitably prorated as set forth above.

B. In the event, during the term of this Lease, the demised premises is destroyed by fire or other casualty or suffers substantial damages by reason of fire or other casualty which cannot be repaired within four (4) months of the occurrence of such fire or other casualty, Landlord shall not be required to restore or repair the demised premises but shall have the sole choice or option whether or not to do so, and shall notify Tenant of Landlord's choice or option within sixty (60) days of the occurrence of any such fire or other casualty. In the event Landlord elects not to restore or repair the demised premises, all rights and obligations of the Landlord and Tenant hereunder shall cease and terminate as of the date of such fire or other casualty and prepaid or unpaid rent shall be immediately adjusted as of such date. In the event Landlord elects to and does restore or repair the demised premises, then and in such event, Tenant shall resume occupancy of the demised premises immediately upon the substantial restoration or repair thereof, and the within Lease, and all its terms, conditions, covenants and provisions shall continue from the date that the demised premises is substantially restored or repaired for a term equal to the entire unexpired term of this Lease remaining at the time of the occurrence of such fire or other casualty. During the period of any repairs, the rent shall be equitably prorated to the extent that Tenant shall be deprived of the use and occupancy of the demised premises resulting exclusively from said fire or other casualty.

13. EMINENT DOMAIN:

If the whole of the demised premises shall be taken by any government or public authority under the power of eminent domain, or conveyed in lieu thereof, then the term of this Lease shall cease from the day possession of the demised premises shall be taken and the rent shall be paid up to that day. In the event that less than the whole of the demised premises shall be taken, Landlord shall have the option, to be exercised within thirty (30) days of the date that possession of the part of the demised premises is taken, to terminate this Lease, and the rent shall be paid up to the date of termination.

In the event Landlord does not exercise said option, then this Lease shall continue in full force and effect, except that the rent shall be reduced to an amount bearing the same proportion to the rent before such taking or condemnation as the floor area after such taking or condemnation bears to the floor area of the demised premises before such taking or condemnation.

14. WAIVER BY LANDLORD:

The waiver by Landlord of any breach of any term, covenant or condition herein contained shall not be deemed to be a waiver of any subsequent breach of the same or of any other term, covenant or condition herein contained. The subsequent acceptance of rent due hereunder or any or all other monetary obligations of Tenant hereunder, whether or not denoted as rent hereunder, by Landlord shall not be deemed to be a waiver of any breach by Tenant of any term, covenant or condition of this Lease, regardless of Landlord's knowledge of such breach at the time of acceptance of such rent.

15. OBSERVANCE BY TENANT:

Tenant agrees to perform, fully obey and comply with all ordinances, regulations and laws of all public authorities, boards and officers relating to the premises or the improvements thereon, or to the use thereof, and further, not to use or occupy, or suffer or permit any person or body to use or occupy the premises, or any part thereof, for any purpose or use in violation of any law, statute or ordinance, whether federal, state or municipal, during the term of said Lease or any renewal thereof.

In the event any rule, regulation, ordinance or law, local, State or Federal, generally applicable to buildings of the same size, type and location of the building of which the demised premises is a part, and not in existence or not enforced at the time of execution of this Lease, shall require Landlord to make additions to, modifications of or installation of equipment in the premises and Landlord shall install the same, there shall be added to the monthly rental for the balance of the term of any renewal or extension thereof, the cost of such addition, modification or installation amortized over the expected life of such addition, modification or alternation together with interest at the rate of twelve (12%) percent per annum. In the event any such addition, modification or alteration is required by reason of Tenant's particular use of the premises, then Landlord shall have the additional option of terminating this Lease upon sixty (60) days written notice to Tenant.

16. ASSIGNMENTS: Tenant covenants not to assign this Lease nor to sublet the whole or any part of the premises without the written consent of Landlord first obtained and which consent Landlord agrees it will not unreasonably withhold. In the event Tenant requests Landlord consent to an assignment of the Lease or subletting of all of the demised premises, it shall submit to Landlord, in writing, the name of the proposed assignee or subtenant and the nature and character of the business of the proposed assignee or subtenant. Landlord shall have the option (to be exercised within thirty (30) days from the submission of Tenant's request) to cancel the within Lease as of the commencement date stated in the above mentioned sublet or assignment. If Landlord elects to cancel the within Lease as state, then, the term, tenancy and occupancy of the demised premises, under said Lease or otherwise, shall cease, determine, expire and come to an end as if the cancellation date was the original termination date of the within Lease. If Landlord shall not exercise its option within the time set forth above, its consent to any such proposed assignment or subletting shall not be unreasonably withheld, provided that Landlord shall not be deemed to have unreasonably withheld its consent to a sublease or assignment, if the proposed sublessee or assignee is, at the time, a tenant of Landlord or has been a tenant of Landlord within one (1) year prior thereto provided, however, that the enumeration of the foregoing is not intended to be an exclusive list of reasons as to why Landlord may withhold its consent. If Landlord consent to a Sublease establishing that the tenant is bound by all of the terms and conditions of this Lease and which contains confessions of judgment clauses in favor of Landlord substantially similar to the confession of judgment clauses contained in this Lease and the assignee or sublessee must provide the insurance certificates required by this Lease.

The acceptance of rent from any other person shall not be deemed to be a waiver of any of the terms, conditions, covenants and provision of this Lease or to be a consent to the assignment of this Lease or the subletting of the demises premises or any part thereof.

If this Lease is assigned or if the whole or any part of the demised premises be sublet, Tenant shall nevertheless remain fully liable for the performance of all obligations under this Lease to be performed by Tenant and Tenant shall not be released therefrom in any manner. Any rent or additional rent received by Tenant from any subtenant or assignee of Tenant in excess of the rent or additional rent due and payable under this Lease shall belong to Landlord, and Tenant shall pay said sums to Landlord contemporaneously with the other payments due under this Lease. any consent of Landlord to an assignment or subletting shall not be deemed to waive the obligation to obtain Landlord's written consent to any further assignment or subletting. Any options carried in this Lease do not pass through to subtenant or assignee.

17. BUSINESS PRIVILEGE TAX: Tenant shall also pay to Landlord, within thirty (30) days of billing, the amount of any tax (not including any income or estate tax) payable by Landlord, based on the rents paid by Tenant to Landlord under the terms of this Lease, including, but not limited to a Business Privilege Tax, whether or not said tax is in effect on the date of this Lease.

18. HAZARDOUS MATERIALS OR SUBSTANCES: No goods, materials, or substances shall be brought by Tenant into the demised premises or used by Tenant in and around the demised premises if those good, materials or substances are explosive, hazardous, radioactive, toxic, polluting or hazardous substances or, are considered a 'hazardous substance' or 'hazardous waste' or similar designation under the Comprehensive Environmental Response, Compensation and Liability Act, 42 U.S.C. Section 9601 et seq ('CERCLA'). the Resource Conservation and Recovery Act, 42 U.S.C. Section 6901 et seq, the federal Clean Water Act, 33 U.S.C. Section 1251 et seq or any state or local environmental law, regulation or ordinance, or, whether used singly or by interaction with other goods, materials, or substances, are capable of causing a nuisance or hazard to life or limb unless the storage and handling of said goods, materials or substances is strictly in accordance with all federal, state and local laws. Upon surrender of the demised premises, Tenant covenants and agrees that the demised premises will be left free of any such goods, materials or substances and/or the residue thereof. Tenant covenants and agrees to save Landlord harmless from any loss, cost, injury, damage or death which may occur or be claimed by or with respect to any person or persons, property or chattels on or off the demised premises, or to the property itself, resulting from Tenant's breach of the covenants set forth herein.

19. RELOCATION OF TENANT: Landlord shall have the right to relocate the Tenant to another part of the building in which the premises are located or to another building under the control of Landlord in accordance with the following:

a. Landlord shall give TENANT at least thirty (30) days notice of Landlord's intention to relocate the premises.

b. The new premises shall be substantially the same in size, dimensions, configuration, and nature as the premises described in this Lease, or shall be placed in that condition by Landlord at his cost.

c. The physical relocation of the premises shall be accomplished by Landlord at its cost.

d. The physical relocation of the premises shall take place on a weekend and shall be completely accomplished before the Monday following the weekend in which the relocation takes place. If the physical relocation has not been completed in that time, rent shall abate in full from the time the physical relocation commences to the time it is completed.

e. If the relocated premises are smaller than the premises as they existed before the relocation, rent shall be reduced to a sum computed by multiplying the monthly minimum rent specified in this Lease by a fraction, the numerator of which shall be the total number of square feet in the relocated premises, and the denominator of which shall be the total number of square feet in the premises before relocation.

f. The parties shall immediately execute an amendment to this Lease stating the relocation of the premises and the reduction of rent, if any.

20. <u>SUBORDINATION:</u> Tenant agrees that this Lease shall be subordinated to any mortgage now or hereafter placed upon the demised premises, to any and all advances to be made thereunder, and to all renewals, replacements and extensions thereof. Tenant agrees that immediately upon the request of Landlord in writing, it will, without charge therefor, execute an instrument or instruments to confirm the subordination of this Lease and the lien hereof to the lien of any present or future mortgage, and hereby irrevocably appoints Landlord the attorney-in-fact of Tenant to execute and deliver such instrument or instruments for and in the name of Tenant, in the event Tenant shall fail to execute such instrument or instruments within ten (10) days after written notice to do so. In the event of any mortgagee electing to have the Lease be prior in lien to its mortgage, then, upon such mortgagee notifying Tenant to that effect, this Lease shall be deemed prior in lien to the said mortgage, whether this Lease is dated prior to or subsequent to the date of said mortgage. In the event any person or entity shall succeed to all or part of Landlord's interest in the demised premises, whether by purchase or foreclosure, or otherwise and if so requested or required by such successor in interest, Tenant shall attorn to such successor in interest and shall execute such agreement in confirmation of such attornment as such successor in interest shall reasonably request.

21. <u>WAIVER:</u> The Tenant expressly waives to the Landlord the benefit of Act No. 20, approved April 6, 1951, entitled 'The Landlord and Tenant Act of 1951' requiring notice to vacate the premises at the end of the term or any subsequent term for which this Lease may be renewed and covenants and agrees to give up quiet and peaceable possession, without further notice from Landlord.

22. <u>MECHANIC'S LIEN:</u> Any mechanic's lien filed against the demised premises or the building in which the demised premises is a part for work claimed to have been done or for materials claimed to have been furnished to Tenant shall be discharged by Tenant within thirty (30) days after the filing of any mechanic's lien. If Tenant shall fail to cause such lien to be discharged within the period aforesaid, then, in addition to any other right or remedy which Landlord may have, Landlord may, but shall not be obligated to, discharge said lien either by paying the amount claimed to be due or by procuring the discharge of such lien by deposit or bonding procedures, and any amount so paid by Landlord and all costs and expenses incurred by Landlord in connection therewith, plus interest, shall constitute additional rental payable by Tenant under this Lease and shall be paid by Tenant to Landlord on demand. Nothing contained in or contemplated by this Lease shall be deemed or construed in any way as constituting the consent or request of Landlord for the performance of any work or the furnishing of any materials for which any lien could be filed against the demised premises or the building of which it is a part or the land on which it is situate, nor as gibing Tenant any right, power or authority to contract for or permit the performance of any work or the furnishings of any materials for which any lien could be filed against the demised premises, or the building of which it is a part of the land on which it is situate.

23. <u>HOLD OVER:</u> If Tenant occupies the demised premises after the end of the term hereof with the permission of the Landlord, this Lease and all its terms, conditions and provisions shall be in force for another month and so on from month to month unless either party gives notice to the other party at least thirty (30) days prior to the end of any such month not to continue the within Lease beyond the end of any such month, in which event Tenant covenants and agrees to vacate the demised premises on or before the end of such month. If Tenant remains in the demised premises after the end of the term hereof without the permission of the Landlord or after the effective date of a notice to vacate from Landlord as set forth above, Landlord may treat Tenant as a tenant at will and tenant agrees to pay to Landlord monthly rent in an amount equal to twice the highest monthly rent due hereunder until such time as Tenant vacates the demised premises.

24. <u>SECURITY DEPOSIT:</u> Upon the execution of this Lease by Tenant, Tenant shall deposit with Landlord the sum of 0.00 dollars, to guarantee the return of the demised premises to Landlord upon the termination of this Lease in as good condition as when received by Tenant, reasonable wear and tear and damage by fire or other casualty excepted, and to indemnify Landlord against loss or damage caused by Tenant's occupancy of the demised premises and any other indebtedness due from Tenant. In the event Landlord applied the security deposit, in whole or in part, against any obligation due from Tenant to Landlord, Tenant shall, upon demand by Landlord, deposit sufficient funds with Landlord to maintain the security deposit in the initial amount. At the termination of this Lease or any renewal thereof, the Security Deposit will be returned to Tenant, without interest, within thirty (30) days following the vacation of the demised premises, or within thirty (30) days after Tenant provides Landlord with his new address in writing, whichever comes later, after deducting any amount needed to cover damages to the demised premises, replacement of keys, unpaid obligations to Landlord, cleaning and restoring the demised premises and any other amount due Landlord. It is understood that the Security Deposit is not to be considered as payment toward any rental installment due under this Lease and it shall not be so applied without the written approval of Landlord.

25. <u>BREACHED AND REMEDIES:</u> Any one or more of the following shall constitute an 'Event of Default' under this Lease:

    (a) default by Tenant in the payment of any installment of rent, additional rent or of any sum provided for under this Lease for a period of ten (10) days after the same becomes due and payable;

(b) default by Tenant in the payment of any installment of rent, additional rent or of any sum provided for under this Lease more than three (3) times in any twelve (12) month period, or if Tenant shall, more than three (3) times in any twelve (12) month period, default in the keeping, observing, or performing of any other covenants or agreements herein contained to be kept, observed or performed by Tenant (irrespective of whether or not Tenant shall have timely cured any such payment or other default of which notice was given, if notice is required herein);

(c) breach by Tenant of any covenant or condition contained in this Lease, which breach shall continue after twenty (20) days written notice thereof from Landlord to Tenant;

(d) removal, attempt to remove, or the expression or declaration of an intention to remove any of the goods and chattels from the demised premises for any reason other than in the normal and usual operation of Tenant's business within the demised premises;

(e) abandonment of the demised premises or the expression of an intention to do so;

(f) issuance of an execution against Tenant which is not stayed by payment or otherwise within five (5) days from the date of issuance of said execution;

(g) institution of bankruptcy proceedings by Tenant, or institution of bankruptcy proceedings against tenant which are not withdrawn or dismissed within twenty (20) days after the institution of said proceedings;

(h) an assignment by Tenant for the benefit of creditors, or appointment of a received for Tenant by legal proceedings or otherwise.

In the event that Tenant commits an Event of Default, the entire rent for the balance of said term shall, at Landlord's option, become due and payable as if by the terms of this Lease it were all payable in advance. In such event, Landlord may also serve upon Tenant a written notice that the term of this Lease has terminated and, in such event, Tenant shall have no right to avoid the termination by payment of any sum due or by the performance of any condition, term or covenant broken. Upon the date specified in the aforesaid notice of termination, Tenant shall surrender the demised premises to Landlord. Notwithstanding any statute, rule of law, or decision of any court to be contrary, Tenant shall remain liable, even after termination of the Lease, for rent, additional rent and/or accelerated rent due under this Lease, and for all damages caused by Tenant's breach or breaches of the Lease.

26. <u>CONFESSIONS OF JUDGMENT:</u> For value received and in the event an Event of Default occurs hereunder, Tenant does hereby empower any attorney of any court of record within the Commonwealth of Pennsylvania, to appear for Tenant and with or without declaration filed, confess judgment against Tenant and in favor of said Landlord, his heirs, devisee, executors, administrators or assigns, for the sum due by reason of said default in the payment of rent and other sums, including unpaid rent, and additional rental for the balance of the term and/or for the sum due by reason of any breach of covenant or agreement by Tenant herein, with costs of suit and attorney's commission of then (10%) percent for collection, and forthwith issue writ or writs of execution thereon with release of all errors and without stay of execution.

For value received and in the event an Event of Default occurs hereunder, or upon termination of the term of the Lease and the failure of Tenant to deliver possession to Landlord, Tenant further, at the option of Landlord, authorizes and empowers any such attorney, either in addition to or without such judgment for the amount due according to the terms of this Lease, to appear for said tenant and confess judgment forthwith against Tenant and in favor of Landlord in an amicable action of ejectment for the demised premises, with release of all errors and forthwith issue a writ or writs of possession for the demised premises and a writ or writs of execution for the amount of any judgment and cost, without leave of Court, and Landlord may without notice re-enter and expel Tenant from the demised premises, and also any person holding under Tenant, and in each case, this Lease or a true copy thereof shall be a sufficient warrant of any person.

Tenant covenants and agrees that both of these confession of judgment clauses shall remain in effect subsequent to, and shall survive, the termination of this Lease, for any reason.

27. <u>SURRENDER AND REMOVAL:</u> Tenant covenants and agrees to deliver and surrender to Landlord possession of the demised premises upon the expiration of the term of this Lease, broom clean and in as good condition and repair as the same shall be at the commencement of the term of this Lease or any have been put by Landlord or Tenant during the continuance thereof, ordinary wear and tear and damage by fire or the elements excepted.

28. <u>NOTICES:</u> Any notice, request, demand, approval or consent given or required to be given under this Lease shall be in writing and shall be deemed to have been given on the day when the same shall have been mailed by United States registered or certified mail, return receipt requested, with all postal charges prepaid, addressed, if intended to Landlord to _____, Pittsburgh, PA. __, if intended for Tenant, to Tenant at the demised premises. Either party may, at any time, change its address for the above purposes by sending a notice to the other party stating the new address.

29. **WAIVER OF JURY TRIAL:** The Tenant and Landlord both waive a trial by jury of any and all issues arising in any action or proceeding between the parties hereto or their successors, under or in connection with this Lease or any of its provisions.

30. **REMEDIES CUMULATIVE:** Mention in this Lease or institution of any particular remedy by Landlord shall not preclude Landlord from any other remedies under this Lease, or now or hereafter existing at law or in equity or by statute.

31. **NEGATION OF PERSONAL LIABILITY:** Notwithstanding anything to the contrary herein contained, Tenant agrees that Landlord shall have no personal liability with respect to any of the provisions of this Lease and Tenant shall look solely to the estate and property of Landlord in the Building and the land on which it is situate for the satisfaction of Tenant's remedies or claims including without limitation the collection of any judgment requiring the payment of money by Landlord in the event of any default or breach by Landlord with respect to any of the terms and provisions of this Lease to be observed and/or performed by Landlord.

32. **COMPLETE OBLIGATIONS:** This lease contains the entire agreement between the parties hereto, and neither party has made any statement, agreement or representation, either oral or written, in connection therewith, modifying, adding or changing the terms, conditions, covenants and provisions herein set forth. No modification of this Lease shall be binding unless such modification shall be in writing and signed by the parties hereto.

33. **MISCELLANEOUS:** As used in this Lease and when required by the context, each number (singular or plural) included all numbers, each gender includes all genders and the work 'it' includes any appropriate pronoun as the context requires.

34. **PROVISIONS BINDING:** This Lease and all the terms and provisions hereof shall inure to the benefit of and be binding upon the parties hereto, their respective heirs, administrators, executors, successors, and assigns.

THE UNDERSIGNED TENANT ACKNOWLEDGES THAT HE/SHE/IT UNDERSTANDS THE CONFESSIONS OF JUDGMENT AUTHORIZED IN THIS LEASE, THAT THIS TRANSACTION IS COMMERCIAL IN NATURE AND THAT HE/SHE/IT WAIVES ANY RIGHT TO A HEARING OR TRIAL IN COURT WHICH WOULD OTHERWISE BE REQUIRED BY LAW AS A CONDITION PRECEDENT TO LANDLORD'S OBTAINING THE JUDGMENTS AUTHORIZED BY THIS LEASE.

35. Tenant has twenty (20) days to execute and return this document as of _____, 20___. After said date, this offer to lease shall be considered null and void.

WITNESS THE DUE EXECUTION HEREOF THE DAY AND YEAR FIRST ABOVE WRITTEN.

WITNESS: (NAME)

_____   _____

(Corporate Seal)

WITNESS: (NAME)

_____   _____

(Corporate Seal)

Form 12-01
Employment Agreement, Example 1

Table of Contents

THIS AGREEMENT made as of this _____ day of _____, 20__ by and between _____ (the '**Company**'), a Pennsylvania business trust, and _____ ('**Employee**'), an individual with an address at _____.

WITNESSETH:

WHEREAS, the Company desires to employ Employee to serve in an executive capacity in accordance with the terms hereof; and

WHEREAS, Employee desires to be employed by the Company in an executive capacity in accordance with the terms hereof.

NOW, THEREFORE, in consideration of these premises and of the mutual promises hereinafter contained and intending to be legally bound hereby, the parties hereto do covenant and agree as follows:

Section 1. <u>Employment</u>. The Company agrees to employ Employee, and Employee agrees to serve the Company, during the Employment Period (as hereinafter defined), in a management capacity as a full-time employee of the Company. Employee shall be designated as President of the Company, or shall hold such other title as the Board of Directors of the Company may from time to time designate.

Section 2. <u>Employment Period</u>. The term of Employee's Employment hereunder shall be for period (the '**Employment Period**') commencing as of the date hereof and termination on _____, 20_; <u>provided</u>, that unless either party hereto, not less than 60 days prior to _____, 20_ or any subsequent date to which the Employment Period shall have been extended pursuant to this proviso shall have given written notice to the other such party of its or his intention not to extend the Employment Period, the Employment Period shall be automatically extended for successive 12-month periods until one of the parties Shall have given such notice of intent not to extend; <u>provided</u>, <u>further</u>, that the Employment Period shall, in any event, terminate upon the termination of Employee'S Employment with the Company through application of the provisions of Section 6 hereof. As used herein the term '**Employment Year**' shall mean: (a) for the initial Employment Year, the period commencing on the date hereof through _____; and (b) each successive 12-month period commencing on _____ and on each _____ during the Employment Period; <u>provided</u>, <u>further</u>, that this Agreement shall in no event be renewed for any Employment Period which would extend beyond _____.

Section 3. <u>Salary</u>. For services performed during the Employment Period, the Company shall pay Employee compensation in the amount of $ biweekly (before taxes and deductions). Salary shall be payable to Employee biweekly on or before the fifteenth and final days of each month during the Employment Period.

Section 4. <u>Obligations During Employment Period</u>.

(a) Employee's management, marketing and operating abilities, practices and experience are valuable to the Company. It is the purpose of this contract to employ Employee in an executive and upper management capacity wherein his abilities will be fully recognized and his business judgments be given full consideration.

(b) Employee agrees that during the Employment Period:

(i)   he will faithfully and in conformity with the directions of the Board of Directors of the Company perform the duties of his Employment hereunder, which duties shall be of substantially the same character as those ordinarily performed by persons in similar positionS; provided, that no assignments will be given Employee without his consent which would require his relocating his permanent residence.

(ii)   he will devote his best efforts and attention on a full-time basis to the performance of said duties at all times and will not spend any substantial amount of time on any other business enterprises or investments.

Section 5. Non-Competition; Related Business Interests; Nondisclosure.

(a)   In further consideration of the execution by the Company of this Agreement, Employee hereby represents, warrants, covenants and agrees to and with the Company as follows:

(i)   that presently he has no Related Business Interests (as hereinafter defined) or is currently in the process of terminating his involvement with any such Related Business Interests;

(ii)   that, during the Employment Period, without the prior written consent of the Company, he will not acquire any Related Business Interests;

(iii)   that, during the Employment Period and for a period of one (1) year thereafter he will not, in the Territory (as hereinafter defined), become engaged, directly or indirectly, in any business competing with the Company; and

(iv)   that he will not, at any time, reveal to any person, firm or entity any trade or business secrets or confidential, secret or privileged information about the business of the Company or its clients.

(b)   For purposes of this Section 5:

(i)   **'Related Business Interest'** shall mean any interest whatsoever, direct, indirect, absolute or beneficial, in any entity, business or enterprise, which interest gives rise to a conflict relative to Employee'S position as an executive employee of the Company, specifically including without limitation, any such interest in any customer, competitor or agent of the Company or in any venture in which any such person or any principal or owner of any such person also has an interest;

(ii)   Employee shall be considered engaged in a business competing with the Company if any time as proprietor, partner, shareholder, trustee, employee, representative, director as a consultant or adviser for gain he is engaged in, participates in or furnishes assistance in connection with the operation or management of any business activity which is adverse to or competitive with the business of the Company, or if at any time he is engaged in or participates in any effort to solicit, divert, take away or attempt to take away any customer of the Company or the business or patronage of any such customer;

(iii)   The business of the Company shall include: (A) the retail sale of coffee and tea drinks; (B) the operation of cafes; and (C) any other lawful business in which the Company may later choose to engage.

(iv)   **'Territory'** shall be deemed to be: (A) any geographical area within a radius of fifty (50) miles of _____; or (B) any other geographical area in which the Company then is (or with respect to the two-year period following the Employment Period as referred to in Section 5(a)(iv) hereof, in which the Company, during the last year of the

Employment Period, was) selling or providing services; provided, however, that if at any time Employee diverts or takes away any customer of the Company or the business or patronage of any such customer in violation of this Agreement, **'Territory'** also shall be deemed to include the geographical area in which such customer is or was located during the last year of sales by the Company to such customer.

(c)   Notwithstanding the foregoing provisions, nothing contained in this Section 5 shall prohibit Employee from acquiring or owning not more than five percent (5%) of the securities of any entity whose securities are traded on a national securities market. Further nothing contained in this Agreement shall be construed to prohibit Employee from acquiring or owning any percentage of interest in any entity or business so long as: (1) such entity or business does not constitute a Related Business Interest or a business competing with the Company (as defined in this Section 5); and (ii) Employee remains in compliance with his obligations under Section 4(b)(ii) hereof not to spend any substantial amount of time on any such other business enterprises or investments.

(d)   The parties hereto agree that the rights and privileges of the Company arising under this Section 5 are special and unique, so that the Company shall be entitled to injunctive and other equitable relief including, but not limited to specific performance. In the event it should become necessary for the Company to institute suit to enforce the provisions of this Section 5, the period of noncompetition by Employee shall be extended by a period of time equal to the duration of such litigation.

(e)   The provisions of this Section 5 shall survive the termination of this Agreement.

Section 6. Termination. Notwithstanding any other provisions of this Agreement:

(a)   Upon the death of Employee, the Employment Period shall terminate as of the last day of the month in which such death occurs.

(b)   The Employment of Employee may be terminated by the Company upon receipt by it of a certification by a physician that, by reason of a disability, either physical or mental, of Employee, it may reasonably be anticipate that he will be unable, for a period of at least three (3) months, effectively to perform the obligation, duties and responsibility of this Employment with the Company; provided, that notwithstanding termination of Employee'S Employment pursuant to this Section 6(b), Employee will be entitled to continue to receive salary hereunder for a period of three (3) months from the date of the occurrence of the event or incident resulting such disability or, in the case of any illness resulting in such disability, from the date when symptoms of such illness impairing the ability of Employee to perform the duties of his Employment hereunder were first manifested.

(c)   The Employment of Employee may be terminated by the Company upon the occurrence of any of the following, which for purposes of this Agreement shall be events of cause:

(i)   The violation, breach or default by Employee in the performance or observance of any material term, covenant or condition to be performed or observed by Employee hereunder; or

(ii)   the habitual neglect by Employee of the duties of his Employment hereunder.

(d)   The Employment of Employee may be terminated by the Company upon the occurrence of general business circumstances that make it impossible or impractical for the business of the Company to be continued, <u>provided</u>, that if Employee'S Employment is terminated pursuant to this Section 6(d), Employee'S covenant pursuant to Section 5(a)(iv) hereof shall not be applicable.

(e) This Agreement may terminated at any time by mutual written consent of the parties.

Section 7. <u>Vacation</u>. During the Employment Period, Employee shall be entitled to ___ (_) weeks vacation with full pay during any Employment Year. With respect to the final Employment Year under this Agreement (if same consists of less than 12 months), the amount of vacation to which Employee shall be entitled shall be determined on a proportional basis in relation to the number of months Employee is actually employed by the Company during such Employment Year. Employee shall schedule his vacations so that such vacations are not taken back-to-back, <u>i.e.</u>, linking vacation periods by taking all of one year's vacation in the last months of one year and all of the next year's vacation in the first months of such succeeding year. Vacation time not taken in any particular year shall not accumulate.

Section 8. <u>Special Bonus</u>.
In further consideration of Employee's entering into this Agreement, the Company agrees to pay Employee a Bonus equal to: (a) _% of the net amount of the Company's revenues (after taxes and other expenses) in excess of $___.00 but less than $___.00 in any Employment Period; (b) __% of the net amount of the Company's revenues (after taxes and other expenses) in excess of $___.00 but less than $____.00 in any Employment Period; (c) _% of the net amount of the Company's revenues (after taxes and other expenses) in excess of $____.00 but less than $ .00 in any Employment Period; and (d) _% of the net amount of the Company's revenues (after taxes and other expenses) in excess of $____.00 but less than $____.00. If Employee's employment shall be terminated for any reason other than those set forth in Section 6(c) hereof at any time after the tenth month of any Employment Period, Employee shall remain entitled to receive the Bonus as provided for herein. If Employee's employment shall be terminated for any reason prior to the ninth month of any Employment Period, he shall not be entitled to any Bonus hereunder.

Section 9. <u>Fringe Benefits</u>. Employee shall receive a fringe benefit package during the Employment Period:
- Group Health and Life Insurance Package (as approved by the Board of Directors).
- Ten (10) paid holidays per year.
- Ten (10) paid sick days per year.
- Continuing professional education and development.

Section 10. <u>Non-Alienation of Benefits</u>. Employee shall not assign his interest, rights or obligations under this Agreement without the prior written consent of the Company, nor shall Employee have the right to sell, anticipate, assign, pledge, encumber of alienate his rights to any payment under this Agreement, and no payment to be made to Employee under this Agreement shall become the property of Employee until actually received by Employee. No such payment shall be liable to be taken or levied upon by attachment, execution or any manner in law or in equity for any debt, judgment or liability of Employee.

Section 11. <u>Notices</u>. All notices, approvals, consents, requests or demands required or permitted to be given under this Agreement shall be in writing and shall be deemed sufficiently given when deposited in the mail, registered or certified, postage prepaid, and addressed to the party entitled to receive such notice at the following address or to such other address as that party shall subsequently designate by notice given in accordance with this Section 11:

the Company:

Employee:

If notice is given by any other method, it shall be deemed effective when the written notice is actually received.

Section 12. <u>Non-Waiver</u>. No party shall be deemed to have waived any right, power or privilege under this Agreement or any provision hereof unless such waiver shall have been duly executed in writing and acknowledge by the party to be charged with such waiver. The failure of any party to enforce at any time any of the provisions of this Agreement shall in no way be construed to be a waiver of such provisions, nor in any way to affect the validity of this Agreement or any part hereof, or the right of any party to thereafter enforce each and every such provision. No waiver of any breach of this Agreement shall be held to be a waiver of any other or subsequent breach. All remedies afforded in this Agreement shall be taken and construed as cumulative, that is, in addition to every other remedy provided herein by law.

Section 13. <u>Benefits</u>. This Agreement shall be binding upon and inure to the benefit of Employee, his heirs, executors and personal representatives and to the Company, its successors and assigns.

Section 14. <u>Integration</u>. This Agreement sets forth the entire Agreement and understanding between the parties as to the subject matter of this Agreement and merges and supersedes all prior agreements, commitments, representations, writings and discussions between them; and neither of the parties shall be bound by any obligations, conditions, warranties or representations with respect to the subject matter of this Agreement, other than as expressly provided in this Agreement or as duly set forth on or subsequent to the date hereof in writing and signed by the proper and duly authorized representative of the party to be bound hereby.

By:_____

Its:_____

_____

Form 12-02
Employment Agreement, Example 2

THIS AGREEMENT, is made this __ day of __, 20_ , and shall be effective as of the __ day of __, 20_, (the 'Effective Date'), by and between _____, a Pennsylvania corporation with an office at _____, _____, Pennsylvania _____ (hereinafter referred to as '_____'), and _____, (hereinafter referred to as 'Employee').

WHEREAS, Employee is a salaried employee of _____ employed as a _____ in _____ office located at _____, _____, Pennsylvania _____ (the 'Office'); and

WHEREAS, in the course of Employee's employment with _____, _____ has incurred substantial expenditures of time and money in providing Employee with specialized instruction and training, and has imparted to Employee certain proprietary knowledge and techniques developed by _____; and

WHEREAS, _____ desires to take reasonable action to protect its legitimate business interests by securing certain restrictive employment covenants on the part of Employee; and

WHEREAS, in consideration of said restrictive employment covenants, _____ is willing to enhance Employee's compensation.

NOW, THEREFORE, in consideration of the mutual covenants contained herein, and intending to be legally bound, _____ and Employee agree as follows:

1. <u>Increase in Compensation</u>. _____ and Employee acknowledge that Employee's current compensation is: _____ hereby agrees to increase such compensation as follows effective as of the effective date hereof:_____

2. <u>Noncompetition</u>. Employee agrees and covenants with _____ that at all times during Employees's employment or affiliation with _____ and for a period of two (2) years thereafter Employee shall not, whether as a proprietor, employee, principal, agent, consultant, broker, partner, shareholder, officer, or director or in any other capacity, engage, participate, or have a substantial financial interest in or be connected with, in any manner, a Competitive Business. As used in this Agreement, 'Competitive Business' shall mean an organization engaged in _____located within a _____ (_____) mile radius of the Office.

3. <u>Noninterference</u>. Employee further agrees and covenants with _____ that at all times during Employee's employment or affiliation with _____ and for a period of two (2) years thereafter, Employee shall not directly or indirectly, solicit, contact or recruit any employee, agent, broker, or affiliate of _____ for the purpose of becoming an employee, agent, broker or affiliate of Employee or of any Competitive Business.

4. <u>Nondisclosure</u>. Employee understands and acknowledges that in the course of Employee's employment with _____, Employee has received and/or had access to, and will receive and/or have access to, certain proprietary and confidential information concerning _____ and its business, including without limitation, research and development information, trade secrets, sales and market information, business plans, financial data, commission data, customer and agent lists, and other confidential customer data, and any other information or knowledge concerning _____ and it business, whether or not in tangible form, that are of a proprietary or confidential nature, or have been heretofore or are hereafter treated as secret by _____ or any of it affiliates (collectively, the 'Confidential Information'). Accordingly, Employee hereby agrees and covenants with _____ that Employee shall not disclose, divulge, furnish, or make accessible to any third party, or use for Employee's own purposes other than to perform services for _____, any of the Confidential Information.

5. <u>Reformation</u>. Employee expressly agrees that the foregoing agreements and covenants are reasonably required by _____ to protect the legitimate business interests of _____ and that should a court of competent jurisdiction determine that the foregoing agreements and covenants are unenforceable, in whole or in part, then such court is authorized to modify such agreements and covenants in such respects as such court determines to be required in order that they shall, as so modified, be enforceable.

6. Equitable Remedies. Employee expressly acknowledges and agrees that (i) Employee's covenants herein are of a unique and special nature, (ii) any breach or violation of Employee's covenants herein will result in irreparable harm to _____ for which there is no adequate remedy at law, (iii) in addition to all other remedies, _____ shall be entitled as a matter of right to injunctive relief in any court of competent jurisdiction, and (iv) Employees shall not assert as a defense to any petition or request for injunctive or other equitable relief the claim that _____ has an adequate remedy at law.

7. No Waiver. The failure of either _____ or Employee to object to any conduct or violation of any of the agreements or covenants made by the other under this Agreement will not be deemed a waiver of any rights or remedies. No waiver of any right or remedy arising under this Agreement will be valid unless set forth in an appropriate writing signed by the party to be changed.

8. No Employment Contract. Employee and _____ expressly acknowledge and agree that the purpose of this Agreement is to protect the legitimate business interests of _____ and that this Agreement shall not be construed or enforced as an employment contract or give Employee any right or guarantee to be employed for any specific time or limit _____'s right to terminate Employee's employment at any time, with or without cause.

9. Severability. If any provision of this Agreement is declared void or unenforceable by any judicial or administrative authority, the remaining provisions of this Agreement will not be nullified but will remain in full force and effect.

10. Miscellaneous. This Agreement (i) contains the entire understanding and agreement of the parties and may not be modified or amended except by a subsequent written agreement executed by the parties hereto, (ii) shall be binding upon Employee and Employee's heirs, executors and personal representatives, and upon _____ and its successors and assigns, and (iii) shall be governed by Pennsylvania law and enforceable only in the state and federal courts of Pennsylvania in Pittsburgh, Pennsylvania.

11. Acknowledgment. Employee expressly acknowledges that Employee has been given the opportunity prior to entering into the is Agreement to consult with Employee's own counsel regarding Employee's rights and obligations with respect to this Agreement.

IN WITNESS WHEREOF, the parties hereto have executed this Agreement on the day and year first above written.

ATTEST:

_____   By: _____
                                    Name: _____
                                    Title: _____

WITNESS:

_____   _____

Form 19-01
Profitability Analysis—Gross Margin

Profit and Loss Statement—ABC Manufacturing

Sales Income	**1,500,000**	(1)
Direct costs		
Labor	595,000	
Material	300,000	
Cost of goods sold	895,000	
Gross operating profit	**605,000**	(2)
General and administrative expense		
Rent	25,000	
Office salaries	60,000	
Office expense	25,000	
Sales expense	50,000	
Advertising	35,000	
Travel and entertainment	40,000	
Utilities	20,000	
Depreciation	80,000	
Telephone	15,000	
Officers salaries	104,000	
Interest expense	78,000	
Miscellaneous	15,000	
Total costs	547,000	
net before taxes	58,000	

(2)   605,000   Gross profit divided by the
(1)   1,500,000   sales

$$\frac{605,000}{1,500,000} = .40 \text{ or } 40\%$$

      What is normal is dependent on your type of business and can range from just a few % (high volume grocery store) to high %. Compare from year to year as well as with industry norms.

Form 19-02
Profitability Analysis—Net Profit Margin

Profit and Loss Statement—ABC Manufacturing

Sales Income	**1,500,000**	(1)
Direct costs		
Labor	595,000	
Material	300,000	
Cost of goods sold	895,000	
Gross operating profit	605,000	
General and administrative expense		
Rent	25,000	
Office salaries	60,000	
Office expense	25,000	
Sales expense	50,000	
Advertising	35,000	
Travel and entertainment	40,000	
Utilities	20,000	
Depreciation	80,000	
Telephone	15,000	
Officers salaries	104,000	
Interest expense	78,000	
Miscellaneous	15,000	
Total costs	547,000	
net before taxes	**58,000**	(2)

(2)   58,000   Net profit divided by the
(1)   1,500,000   sales

$$\frac{58,000}{1,500,000} = .04 \text{ or } 4\%$$

      The important concerns here are the trends from year to year and for any individual company. Is this sufficient to meet debt service? Useful to compare with industry norms.

Form 19-04
Accounts Receivable Turnover Ratio

Balance Sheet—ABC Manufacturing

Cash in bank		12,000	
Accounts receivable		**400,000**	(1)
Inventory		500,000	
Prepaid expense		38,000	
Total current assets		950,000	
Fixed assets			
Building	750,000		
less dep.	525,000	225,000	
Machinery & equip	800,000		
less dep.	200,000	600,000	
		825,000	
total fixed assets		1,775,000	
Liabilities			
Accounts payable		450,000	
Current portion–note payable		250,000	
Total current liabilities		700,000	
Long-term balance on note		500,000	
total liabilities		1,200,000	
net worth		575,000	

Profit and Loss Statement—ABC Manufacturing

Sales Income	**1,500,000**	(2)
Direct costs		
Labor	595,000	
Material	300,000	
Cost of goods sold	895,000	
Gross operating profit	605,000	
General and administrative expense		
Rent	25,000	
Office salaries	60,000	
Office expense	25,000	
Sales expense	50,000	
Advertising	35,000	
Travel and entertainment	40,000	
Utilities	20,000	
Depreciation	80,000	
Telephone	15,000	
Officers salaries	104,000	
Interest expense	78,000	
Miscellaneous	15,000	
Total costs	547,000	
net before taxes	58,000	

(2)	1,500,000	Total Sales
(1)	400,000	Accounts receivable

$$\frac{1,500,000}{400,000} = 3.7 \text{ or almost four times per year.}$$

This means that your receivables are turning every 90 or so days so that an invoice sent on January 5 is not likely to be paid until April 5, 90 days later. This can create cash flow problems and should be improved by aggressive collection policies. Monitor this number to see positive progress.

Form 19-05
Accounts Payable Turnover Ratio

Balance Sheet–ABC Manufacturing

Cash in bank		12,000
Accounts receivable		400,000
Inventory		500,000
Prepaid expense		38,000
Total current assets		950,000
Fixed assets		
Building	750,000	
less dep.	525,000	225,000
Machinery & equip	800,000	
less dep.	200,000	600,000
		825,000
total fixed assets		1,775,000
Liabilities		
Accounts payable		**450,000** (1)
Current portion–note payable		250,000
Total current liabilities		700,000
Long-term balance on note		500,000
total liabilities		1,200,000
net worth		575,000

Profit & Loss Statement–ABC Manufacturing

Sales Income	1,500,000	
Direct costs		
Labor	595,000	
Material	300,000	(2)
Cost of goods sold	895,000	
Gross operating profit	605,000	
General and administrative expense		
Rent	25,000	
Office salaries	60,000	
Office expense	25,000	(2)
Sales expense	50,000	
Advertising	35,000	(2)
Travel and entertainment	40,000	
Utilities	20,000	
Depreciation	80,000	
Telephone	15,000	(2)
Officers salaries	104,000	
Interest expense	78,000	
Miscellaneous	*15,000*	(2)
Total costs	547,000	
net before taxes	58,000	

(2)	390,000	Total purchase
(1)	450,000	Accounts payable

$$\frac{390,000}{450,000} = .86$$

Meaning that there are outstanding debts of this company that are over a year old as payables are turning less than one time a year. The possibility of legal action in a company in this circumstance is great and the future is very insecure.

There is no doubt that the company described here is in dire circumstance. However, all of the tools for correcting the problems can be found in the ratios. The ongoing operation is solid as seen by profitability ratio. Debt is serious but not critical and return on equity is low but could improve.

The problem is centered in the inventory, which must be liquidated quickly and not allowed to grow to this proportion. Losses will be taken as it is written off.

Receivables must be collected more quickly, cash flow is inadequate, and payables are dangerously high. With the money received from sale of old inventory and quicker payments for current work, deals could be struck with vendors to prevent any legal action and repair business relationships. This company must be under collection pressure, which takes time and effort away from building a successful future.

Analyze your company this way and see what you will find.

Form 19-06
Inventory Turnover Ratio—Balance Sheet and Profit & Loss

Balance Sheet—ABC Manufacturing

Cash in bank		12,000
Accounts receivable		400,000
Inventory		**500,000** (1)
Prepaid expense		38,000
Total current assets		950,000
Fixed assets		
Building	750,000	
less dep.	525,000	225,000
Machinery & equip	800,000	
less dep.	200,000	600,000
		825,000
total fixed assets		1,775,000
Liabilities		
Accounts payable		450,000
Current portion–note payable		250,000
Total current liabilities		700,000
Long-term balance on note		500,000
total liabilities		1,200,000
net worth		575,000

Profit & Loss Statement—ABC Manufacturing

Sales Income	1,500,000
Direct costs	
Labor	595,000
Material	**300,000** (2)
Cost of goods sold	895,000
Gross operating profit	605,000
General and administrative expense	
Rent	25,000
Office salaries	60,000
Office expense	25,000
Sales expense	50,000
Advertising	35,000
Travel and entertainment	40,000
Utilities	20,000
Depreciation	80,000
Telephone	15,000
Officers salaries	104,000
Interest expense	78,000
Miscellaneous	15,000
Total costs	547,000
net before taxes	58,000

(2)	300,000	Annual inventory cost
(1)	500,000	Current level of inventory

$$\frac{300,000}{500,000} = .60$$

Meaning the inventory has sold less than once in the entire year. This happens when old and obsolete inventory remains on the book year after year and is never turned over. This could represent a warehouse full of unusable goods, which may be liquidated to raise capital and lower debt.

Form 19-07
Debt Ratio

Balance Sheet—ABC Manufacturing

Cash in bank		12,000	
Accounts receivable		400,000	
Inventory		500,000	
Prepaid expense		38,000	
Total current assets		950,000	
Fixed assets			
Building	750,000		
less dep.	525,000	225,000	
Machinery & equip	800,000		
less dep.	200,000	600,000	
		725,000	
total fixed assets		**1,775,000**	(1)
Liabilities			
Accounts payable		450,000	
Current portion—note payable		250,000	
Total current liabilities		700,000	
Long-term balance on note		500,000	
total liabilities		**1,200,000**	(2)
net worth		575,000	

(2)	1,200,000	Total liabilities
(1)	1,775,000	Total assets

$$\frac{1,200,000}{1,775,000} = 68\%$$

This means that 70 percent of the company is financed by debt. A number this high makes it very difficult to acquire any new debt for growth or improvement. Focus should be on cutting costs and paying off existing debt.

Form 19-08
Return on Investment

Requires Profit & Loss and Balance Sheet

Profit & Loss Statement–ABC Manufacturing

Sales Income	1,500,000
Direct costs	
Labor	595,000
Material	300,000
Cost of goods sold	895,000
Gross operating profit	605,000
General and administrative expense	
Rent	25,000
Office salaries	60,000
Office expense	25,000
Sales expense	50,000
Advertising	35,000
Travel and entertainment	40,000
Utilities	20,000
Depreciation	80,000
Telephone	15,000
Officers salaries	104,000
Interest expense	78,000
Miscellaneous	15,000
Total costs	547,000
net before taxes	**58,000** (1)

Balance Sheet–ABC Manufacturing

Cash in bank		12,000
Accounts receivable		400,000
Inventory 500,000		
Prepaid expense		38,000
Total current assets		950,000
Fixed assets		
Building	750,000	
less dep.	525,000	225,000
Machinery & equip	800,000	
less dep.	200,000	600,000
		725,000
total fixed assets		**1,775,000** (2)
Liabilities		
Accounts payable		450,000
Current portion–note payable		250,000
Total current liabilities		700,000
Long-term balance on note		500,000
total liabilities		1,200,000
net worth		575,000

(1) 58,000 Net profit
(2) 1,775,000 Total assets

$$\frac{58,000}{1,775,000} = .033 \text{ or } 3.3\%$$

This means that the money invested in these business assets are returning 3.3%, which is very low for the risk. The rate of return is higher on government-guaranteed bank instruments. Is this a good use of the owner's capital?

Form 26-01

Form 941
Payment Voucher

Purpose of Form

Complete Form 941-V if you are making a payment with **Form 941,** Employer's Quarterly Federal Tax Return. We will use the completed voucher to credit your payment more promptly and accurately, and to improve our service to you.

If you have your return prepared by a third party and make a payment with that return, please provide this payment voucher to the return preparer.

Making Payments With Form 941

Make payments with Form 941 only if:

1. Your net taxes for the quarter (line 13 on Form 941) are less than $2,500 or

2. You are a monthly schedule depositor making a payment in accordance with the **accuracy of deposits** rule. (See section 11 of **Circular E,** Employer's Tax Guide, for details.) This amount may be $2,500 or more.

Otherwise, you must deposit the amount at an authorized financial institution or by electronic funds transfer. (See section 11 of Circular E for deposit instructions.) Do not use the Form 941-V payment voucher to make Federal tax deposits.

Caution: *If you pay amounts with Form 941 that should have been deposited, you may be subject to a penalty. See Circular E.*

Specific Instructions

Box 1. Enter the first four characters of your name as follows:

● **Individuals (sole proprietors, estates).** Use the first four letters of your last name (as shown in box 5).

● **Corporations.** Use the first four characters (letters or numbers) of your business name (as shown in box 5). Omit "The" if followed by more than one word.

● **Partnerships.** Use the first four characters of your trade name. If no trade name, enter the first four letters of the last name of the first listed partner.

Box 2—Employer identification number (EIN). If you do not have an EIN, apply for one on **Form SS-4,** Application for Employer Identification Number, and write "Applied for" and the date you applied in this entry space.

Box 3—Amount paid. Enter the amount paid with Form 941.

Box 4—Tax period. Darken the capsule identifying the quarter for which the payment is made. Darken only one capsule.

Box 5—Name and address. Enter your name and address as shown on Form 941.

● Make your check or money order payable to the United States Treasury. Be sure to enter your EIN, "Form 941," and the tax period on your check or money order. Do not send cash. Please do not staple this voucher or your payment to the return or to each other.

● Detach the completed voucher and send it with your payment and Form 941 to the address provided on the back of Form 941.

▼   **Detach Here and Mail With Your Payment**   ▼   Form **941-V** (2001)

Form **941-V**	**Payment Voucher**	OMB No. 1545-0074
Department of the Treasury Internal Revenue Service (99)	▶ **Do not staple or attach this voucher to your payment.**	**2001**

1 Enter the first four letters of your last name (business name if corporation or partnership)	2 Enter your employer identification number	3 Enter the amount of the payment
		$.

4 Tax period		5 Enter your business name (individual name if sole proprietor)
0 1st Quarter	*0* 3rd Quarter	Enter your address
0 2nd Quarter	*0* 4th Quarter	Enter your city, state, and ZIP code

Privacy Act and Paperwork Reduction Act Notice.
We ask for the information on this form to carry out the Internal Revenue laws of the United States. We need it to figure and collect the right amount of tax. Subtitle C, Employment Taxes, of the Internal Revenue Code imposes employment taxes on wages, including income tax withholding. This form is used to determine the amount of the taxes that you owe. Section 6011 requires you to provide the requested information if the tax is applicable to you. Section 6109 requires you to provide your employer identification number (EIN). Routine uses of this information include giving it to the Department of Justice for civil and criminal litigation, and to cities, states, and the District of Columbia for use in administering their tax laws. If you fail to provide this information in a timely manner, you may be subject to penalties and interest.

You are not required to provide the information requested on a form that is subject to the Paperwork Reduction Act unless the form displays a valid OMB control number. Books and records relating to a form or instructions must be retained as long as their contents may become material in the administration of any Internal Revenue law. Generally, tax returns and return information are confidential, as required by section 6103.

The time needed to complete and file this form will vary depending on individual circumstances. The estimated average time is:

For Form 941:

Recordkeeping	11 hr., 44 min.
Learning about the law or the form .	40 min.
Preparing the form	1 hr., 49 min.
Copying, assembling, and sending the form to the IRS	16 min.

For Form 941TeleFile:

Recordkeeping	5 hr., 1 min.
Learning about the law or the Tax Record	6 min.
Preparing the Tax Record	11 min.
TeleFile phone call	11 min.

If you have comments concerning the accuracy of these time estimates or suggestions for making this form simpler, we would be happy to hear from you. You can write to the Tax Forms Committee, Western Area Distribution Center, Rancho Cordova, CA 95743-0001. **Do not** send the tax form to this address.

Instructions for Form 941

(Revised October 2000)

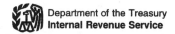

Department of the Treasury
Internal Revenue Service

Employer's Quarterly Federal Tax Return

Section references are to the Internal Revenue Code unless otherwise noted.

Change To Note

Social security wage base for 2000. Stop withholding social security tax after an employee reaches **$76,200** in taxable wages.

General Instructions

Purpose of Form

Use Form 941 to report:
- Income tax you withheld from wages, including tips, supplemental unemployment compensation benefits, and third-party payments of sick pay.
- Social security and Medicare taxes.

Who Must File

Employers who withhold income tax on wages, or who must pay social security or Medicare tax, must file Form 941 each calendar quarter. After you file the first Form 941, you must file a return for each quarter, even if you have no taxes to report (but see the *seasonal employer* and *final return* information below). If you filed Form 941 on magnetic tape or by electronic or TeleFile methods, do not also file a paper Form 941.

Seasonal employers are not required to file for quarters when they regularly have no tax liability because they have paid no wages. To alert the IRS that you will not have to file a return for one or more quarters during the year, check the **Seasonal employer** box above line 1 on Form 941. The IRS will mail two Forms 941 to you once a year after March 1. The preprinted name and address information will not include the date the quarter ended. You must enter the date the quarter ended when you file the return. The IRS generally will not inquire about unfiled returns if at least one return showing tax due is filed each year. However, you must check the **Seasonal employer** box on each quarterly return you file. Otherwise, the IRS will expect a return to be filed for each quarter.

Exception. Employers of the following categories of workers do not usually file Form 941.

Household employees. See **Pub. 926,** Household Employer's Tax Guide, and **Schedule H (Form 1040),** Household Employment Taxes.

Farm employees. See **Form 943,** Employer's Annual Tax Return for Agricultural Employees, and **Circular A,** Agricultural Employer's Tax Guide (Pub. 51).

Business reorganization or termination. If you sell or transfer your business, you and the new owner must each file a return for the quarter in which the transfer occurred. Each should report only the wages it paid. A change from one form of business to another, such as from sole proprietorship to partnership or corporation, is considered a transfer and requires a new employer identification number (EIN). See section 1 of Circular E. If a change occurs, please attach a statement to your return that shows: new owner's name (or new name of the business); whether the business is now a sole proprietorship, partnership, or corporation; kind of change (sale or transfer); and date of change.

When a business is merged or consolidated with another, the continuing firm must file the return for the quarter in which the change took place. The return should show all wages paid for that quarter. The other firm should file a final return.

Final return. If you go out of business or stop paying wages, file a **final return.** Be sure to check the final return box and enter the date final wages were paid above line 1. See the **Instructions for Forms W-2 and W-3** for information on the earlier dates for the expedited furnishing and filing of Form W-2 when a final Form 941 is filed.

Preparing the Form

The following will allow the IRS to process Form 941 faster and more accurately:
- Make dollar entries without the dollar sign and comma (0000.00).
- Enter negative amounts in parentheses.
- File the Form 941 that has your preprinted name and address.

When To File

File starting with the first quarter in which you are required to withhold income tax or pay wages subject to social security and Medicare taxes.

Quarter	Ending	Due Date
Jan.-Feb.-Mar.	March 31	April 30
Apr.-May-June	June 30	July 31
July-Aug.-Sept.	Sept. 30	Oct. 31
Oct.-Nov.-Dec.	Dec. 31	Jan. 31

If you made deposits on time in full payment of the taxes for a quarter, you have 10 more days after the above due date to file. Your return will be considered timely filed if it is properly addressed and mailed First-Class or sent by an IRS designated delivery service on or before the due date. See Circular E for more information on IRS designated delivery services. If the due date for filing a return falls on a Saturday, Sunday, or legal holiday, you may file the return on the next business day.

Where To File

See the back of Form 941 for the mailing address for your return.

Depositing Taxes

If your net taxes (line 13) are $1,000 or more for the quarter, you must deposit your tax liabilities at an authorized financial institution with **Form 8109,** Federal Tax Deposit Coupon, or by using the **Electronic Federal Tax Payment System (EFTPS).** See section 11 of

Cat. No. 14625L

Circular E for information and rules concerning Federal tax deposits.

Reconciliation of Forms 941 and W-3

Certain amounts reported on the four quarterly Forms 941 for 2000 should agree with the **Form W-2,** Wage and Tax Statement, totals reported on **Form W-3,** Transmittal of Wage and Tax Statements, or equivalent magnetic media reports filed with the Social Security Administration (SSA) (Form 6559). The amounts that should agree are income tax withholding, social security wages, social security tips, Medicare wages and tips, and the advance earned income credit. If the totals do not agree, the IRS may require you to explain any differences and correct any errors. For more information, see section 12 of Circular E.

Penalties and Interest

There are penalties for filing a return late and paying or depositing taxes late, unless there is reasonable cause. If you are late, please attach an explanation to your return. There are also penalties for failure to (1) furnish Forms W-2 to employees and file copies with the SSA or (2) deposit taxes when required. In addition, there are penalties for willful failure to file returns and pay taxes when due and for filing false returns or submitting bad checks. Interest is charged on taxes paid late at the rate set by law. See Circular E for additional information.

Caution: *A **trust fund recovery penalty** may apply if income, social security, and Medicare taxes that must be withheld are not withheld or are not paid. The penalty is the full amount of the unpaid trust fund tax. This penalty may apply when these unpaid taxes cannot be immediately collected from the employer or business. The trust fund recovery penalty may be imposed on all persons who are determined by the IRS to be responsible for collecting, accounting for, and paying over these taxes, and who acted willfully in not doing so. See Circular E for more information.*

Ordering Forms and Publications

IRS forms and publications are available by calling 1-800-829-3676 or by accessing the IRS's Internet Web Site at **www.irs.gov.** See Circular E for additional methods of obtaining forms and publications.

Forms W-4

Each quarter, send with Form 941 copies of any **Forms W-4,** Employee's Withholding Allowance Certificate, received during the quarter from employees claiming (1) more than 10 withholding allowances or (2) exemption from income tax withholding if their wages will normally be more than $200 a week. For details, see section 9 of Circular E.

Forms W-5

Each eligible employee wishing to receive any advance earned income credit (EIC) payments must give you a completed **Form W-5,** Earned Income Credit Advance Payment Certificate. The employer's requirement to notify certain employees about the EIC can be met by giving each eligible employee **Notice 797,** Possible Federal Tax Refund Due to the Earned Income Credit (EIC). See Circular E and **Pub. 596,** Earned Income Credit, for more information.

Employer Identification Number

If you do not have an EIN, apply for one on **Form SS-4,** Application for Employer Identification Number. Get this form from the IRS or the SSA. If you do not have an EIN by the time a return is due, write "Applied for" and the date you applied in the space shown for the number. Form SS-4 has information on how to apply for an EIN by mail or by telephone.

Note: *Always be sure the EIN on the form you file matches the EIN assigned to your business by the IRS. Do not show your personal social security number on forms calling for an EIN. Filing a Form 941 with an incorrect EIN or using another business' EIN may result in penalties and delays in processing your return.*

Preprinted Name and Address Information

If any of the preprinted name, EIN, or address information on Form 941 is not correct, cross it out and type or print the correct information.

Generally, preprinted address information on Form 941 is from IRS records. However, if you filed a change of address card with the United States Postal Service (USPS), that address information may be preprinted on your Form 941 and 941Telefile Tax Record. If the preprinted address is from the USPS, your IRS address of record will be changed when your return is filed and properly processed.

Specific Instructions

State Code

If you made your deposits by FTD coupon or by using EFTPS in a state other than that shown in your address on Form 941, enter the state code for the state where you made deposits in the box provided in the upper left corner of the form. Use the Postal Service two-letter state abbreviation as the state code. Enter the code "MU" in the state code box if you deposit in more than one state. If you deposit in the same state as shown in your address, do not make an entry in this box.

Line 1—Number of employees

Enter the number of employees on your payroll during the pay period including March 12 (on the January-March calendar quarter return only). Do not include household employees, persons who received no pay during the pay period, pensioners, or members of the Armed Forces. An entry of 250 or more on line 1 indicates a need to file Forms W-2 on magnetic media. Call the SSA at 1-800-772-1213 for more information on magnetic media filing requirements.

Line 2—Total wages and tips, plus other compensation

Enter the total of all wages paid, tips reported, taxable fringe benefits provided, and other compensation paid to your employees, **even if you do not have to withhold income or social security and Medicare taxes on it.** Do not include supplemental unemployment compensation benefits, even if you withheld income tax on them. Do not include contributions to employee plans that are excluded from the employee's wages (e.g., section 401(k) and 125 plans).

If you get timely notice from your insurance carrier concerning the amount of third-party sick pay it paid your employees, include the sick pay on line 2. If you are an insurance company, do not include sick pay you paid policyholders' employees here if you gave the policyholders timely notice of the payments. See **Pub. 15-A,** Employer's Supplemental Tax Guide, for details.

Line 3—Total income tax withheld

Enter the income tax you withheld on wages, tips, taxable fringe benefits, and supplemental unemployment compensation benefits. An insurance company should enter the income tax it withheld on third-party sick pay here.

Line 4—Adjustment of withheld income tax

Use line 4 to correct errors in income tax withheld from wages paid in earlier quarters of the *same calendar year.* You may not adjust or claim a refund or credit for any overpayment of income tax that you withheld or deducted from an employee in a prior year. This is because the employee uses the amount shown on Form W-2 as a credit when filing his or her income tax return. Because any amount shown on line 4 increases or decreases your tax liability, the adjustment must be taken into account on line 17, Monthly Summary of Federal Tax Liability, or on **Schedule B (Form 941),** Employer's Record of Federal Tax Liability. For details on how to report adjustments on the record of Federal tax liability, see the instructions for line 17 (on page 4) or the instructions for Schedule B (Form 941). Explain any adjustments on **Form 941c,** Supporting Statement To Correct Information, or an equivalent statement. See section 13 of Circular E.

Note: *Do not adjust income tax withholding for quarters in earlier years unless it is to correct an administrative error. An administrative error occurs if the amount you entered on Form 941 is not the amount you actually withheld. For example, if the total income tax actually withheld was incorrectly reported on Form 941 due to a mathematical or transposition error, this would be an administrative error. The administrative error adjustment corrects the amount reported on Form 941 to agree with the amount actually withheld from the employees.*

Line 5—Adjusted total of income tax withheld

Add line 4 to line 3 if you are reporting additional income tax withheld for an earlier quarter. Subtract line 4 from line 3 if you are reducing the amount of income tax withheld. If there is no entry on line 4, line 5 will be the same as line 3.

Line 6a—Taxable social security wages

Enter the total wages subject to social security taxes that you paid your employees during the quarter. Also include any sick pay and taxable fringe benefits subject to social security taxes. See section 5 of Circular E for information on types of wages subject to social security taxes. Enter the amount before deductions. Do not include tips on this line. Stop reporting an employee's wages (including tips) when they reach $76,200 for 2000. However, continue to withhold income tax for the whole year on wages and tips even when the social security wage base of $76,200 is reached. See the line 7a instructions for Medicare tax. **If none of the payments are subject to social security tax, check the box in line 8.**

Line 6c—Taxable social security tips

Enter all tips your employees reported during the quarter until tips and wages for an employee reach $76,200 in 2000. Do this even if you were not able to withhold the employee tax (6.2%). However, see the line 9 instructions.

An employee must report to you cash tips, including tips you paid the employee for charge customers, totaling $20 or more in a month by the 10th of the next month. The employee may use **Form 4070,** Employee's Report of Tips to Employer, or a written statement.

Do not include allocated tips on this line. Instead, report them on **Form 8027,** Employer's Annual Information Return of Tip Income and Allocated Tips. Allocated tips are not reportable on Form 941 and are not subject to withholding of income, social security, or Medicare taxes.

Line 7a—Taxable Medicare wages and tips

Report all wages and tips subject to Medicare tax. Also include any sick pay and taxable fringe benefits subject to Medicare tax. See section 5 of Circular E for information on types of wages subject to Medicare tax. There is no limit on the amount of wages subject to Medicare tax. **If none of the payments are subject to Medicare tax, check the box in line 8.**

Include all tips your employees reported during the quarter, even if you were not able to withhold the employee tax (1.45%). However, see the line 9 instructions below.

Line 9—Adjustment of social security and Medicare taxes

Current period adjustments. In certain cases, amounts reported as social security and Medicare taxes on lines 6b, 6d, and 7b must be adjusted to arrive at your correct tax liability. See section 13 of Circular E for information on the following:

• Adjustment for the uncollected employee share of social security and Medicare taxes on tips.

• Adjustment for the employee share of social security and Medicare taxes on group-term life insurance premiums paid for former employees.

• Adjustment for the employee share of social security and Medicare taxes withheld by a third-party sick pay payer.

• Fractions of cents adjustment.

Enter the adjustments for sick pay and fractions of cents in the appropriate line 9 entry spaces. Enter the amount of all other adjustments in the "Other" entry space, and enter the total of the three types of adjustments, including prior period adjustments (discussed below), in the line 9 entry space to the right. Provide a supporting statement explaining any adjustments reported in the "Other" entry space.

Prior period adjustments. Use line 9 to correct errors in social security and Medicare taxes reported on an earlier return. If you report both an underpayment and an overpayment, show only the net difference.

Because any prior period adjustments shown on line 9 increase or decrease your tax liability, the adjustments must be taken into account on line 17, Monthly Summary of Federal Tax Liability, or on Schedule B (Form 941). For details on how to report adjustments on the record of Federal tax liability, see the instructions for line 17, later, or the instructions for Schedule B (Form 941).

Page 3

Explain any prior period adjustments on Form 941c. **Do not** file Form 941c separately from Form 941. Form 941c is not an amended return but is a statement providing necessary information and certifications supporting the adjustments on lines 4 and/or 9 on Form 941. If you do not have a Form 941c, you may file an equivalent supporting statement with the return providing the required information about the adjustment(s). See section 13 of Circular E.

If you are adjusting an employee's social security or Medicare wages or tips for a prior year, you must file **Form W-2c,** Corrected Wage and Tax Statement, with **Form W-3c,** Transmittal of Corrected Wage and Tax Statements.

Line 10—Adjusted total of social security and Medicare taxes

Add line 9 to line 8 if line 9 is positive (e.g., the net adjustment increases your tax liability). Subtract line 9 from line 8 if line 9 is negative.

Line 12—Advance earned income credit (EIC) payments made to employees

Enter advance EIC payments made to employees. Your eligible employees may elect to receive part of the EIC as an advance payment. Eligible employees who have a qualifying child must give you a completed Form W-5 stating that they qualify for the EIC. Once the employee gives you a signed and completed Form W-5, you must make the advance EIC payments. Advance EIC payments are generally made from withheld income tax and employee and employer social security and Medicare taxes. See section 10 of Circular E and Pub. 596.

If the amount of your advance EIC payments exceeds your total taxes (line 11) for the quarter, you may claim a refund of the overpayment or elect to have the credit applied to your return for the next quarter. Provide a statement with your return identifying the amount of excess payment(s) and the pay period(s) in which it was paid. See section 10 of Circular E.

Line 15—Balance due

You do not have to pay if line 15 is under $1. Generally, you should have a balance due only if your net tax liability for the quarter (line 13) is less than $1,000. (However, see section 11 of Circular E regarding payments made under the *accuracy of deposits rule*). If line 13 is $1,000 or more and you have deposited all taxes when due, the amount shown on line 15 (balance due) should be zero.

Caution: *If you fail to make deposits as required and instead pay the taxes with Form 941, you may be subject to a penalty.*

Line 16—Overpayment

If you deposited more than the correct amount for a quarter, you can have the overpayment refunded or applied to your next return by checking the appropriate box. If you do not check either box, your overpayment will be applied to your next return. The IRS may apply your overpayment to any past due tax account under your EIN. If line 16 is under $1, we will send a refund or apply it to your next return only on written request.

Line 17—Monthly Summary of Federal Tax Liability

Note: *This is a summary of your monthly tax liability, **not** a summary of deposits made. If line 13 is less than $1,000, do not complete line 17 or Schedule B (Form 941).*

Complete line 17 only if you were a monthly schedule depositor for the entire quarter (see section 11 of Circular E for details on the deposit rules). You are a monthly schedule depositor for the calendar year if the amount of your Form 941 taxes reported for the lookback period is not more than $50,000. The lookback period is the four consecutive quarters ending on June 30 of the prior year. For 2000, the lookback period begins July 1, 1998, and ends June 30, 1999.

Caution: *If you were a semiweekly schedule depositor during any part of the quarter, **do not** complete columns (a) through (d) of line 17. Instead, complete Schedule B (Form 941).*

Reporting adjustments on line 17. If the net adjustment during a month is negative (e.g., correcting an overreported liability in a prior period) and it exceeds the total liability for the month, do not enter a negative amount for the month. Instead, enter -0- for the month and carry over the unused portion of the adjustment to the next month. For example, Pine Co. discovered on February 6, 2000, that it overreported social security tax on a prior quarter return by $2,500. Its Form 941 taxes for the 1st quarter of 2000 were: January $2,000, February $2,000, March $2,000. Pine Co. should enter $2,000 in column (a), -0- in column (b), $1,500 in column (c), and the total, $3,500, in column (d). The prior period adjustment ($2,500) offsets the $2,000 liability for February and the excess $500 must be used to offset March liabilities. Since the error was not discovered until February, it does not affect January liabilities reported in column (a).

If excess negative adjustments are carried forward to the next quarter, do not show these excess adjustments on lines 4 or 9. Line 17, column (d), must equal line 13.

Who Must Sign

● **Sole proprietorship.** The individual owning the business.

● **Corporation.** The president, vice president, or other principal officer.

● **Partnership or unincorporated organization.** A responsible and duly authorized member or officer having knowledge of its affairs.

● **Trust or estate.** The fiduciary.

The return may also be signed by a duly authorized agent of the taxpayer if a valid power of attorney has been filed.

Page 4

Form 26-02

Form **940**

Department of the Treasury
Internal Revenue Service (99)

Employer's Annual Federal Unemployment (FUTA) Tax Return

► **See separate Instructions for Form 940 for information on completing this form.**

OMB No. 1545-0028

2000

T
FF	
FD	
FP	
I	
T	

Name (as distinguished from trade name)   Calendar year

Trade name, if any

Address and ZIP code   Employer identification number

A   Are you required to pay unemployment contributions to only one state? (If "No," skip questions B and C.)   ☐ Yes   ☐ No

B   Did you pay all state unemployment contributions by January 31, 2001? ((1) If you deposited your total FUTA tax when due, check "Yes" if you paid all state unemployment contributions by February 12, 2001. (2) If a 0% experience rate is granted, check "Yes." (3) If "No," skip question C.) . . . .   ☐ Yes   ☐ No

C   Were all wages that were taxable for FUTA tax also taxable for your state's unemployment tax? . . . .   ☐ Yes   ☐ No

If you answered "No" to any of these questions, you must file Form 940. If you answered "Yes" to all the questions, you may file Form 940-EZ, which is a simplified version of Form 940. (Successor employers see **Special credit for successor employers** on page 3 of the instructions.) You can get Form 940-EZ by calling 1-800-TAX-FORM (1-800-829-3676) or from the IRS Web Site at **www.irs.gov**.

If you will not have to file returns in the future, check here (see **Who Must File** in separate instructions), **and complete and sign the return** . . . . ► ☐

If this is an Amended Return, check here. . . . . ► ☐

Part I   Computation of Taxable Wages

1   Total payments (including payments shown on lines 2 and 3) during the calendar year for services of employees **1**

2   Exempt payments. (Explain all exempt payments, attaching additional sheets if necessary.) ► **2**

3   Payments of more than $7,000 for services. Enter only amounts over the first $7,000 paid to each employee. (See separate instructions.) Do not include any exempt payments from line 2. The $7,000 amount is the Federal wage base. Your state wage base may be different. **Do not use your state wage limitation.**   **3**

4   Total exempt payments (add lines 2 and 3) **4**

5   **Total taxable wages** (subtract line 4 from line 1) . . . . ►   **5**

Be sure to complete both sides of this form, and sign in the space provided on the back.
For Privacy Act and Paperwork Reduction Act Notice, see separate instructions.   Cat. No. 11234O   Form **940** (2000)

--------------------------------- **DETACH HERE** ---------------------------------

Form **940-V**

Department of the Treasury
Internal Revenue Service

Form 940 Payment Voucher

Use this voucher only when making a payment with your return.

OMB No. 1545-0028

2000

Complete boxes 1, 2, 3, and 4. Do not send cash, and do not staple your payment to this voucher. Make your check or money order payable to the **"United States Treasury".** Be sure to enter your employer identification number, "Form 940", and "2000" on your payment.

1   Enter the first four letters of your last name (business name if partnership or corporation).

2   Enter your employer identification number.

3   Enter the amount of your payment.
$

Instructions for Box 1

—Individuals (sole proprietors, trusts, and estates)— Enter the first four letters of your last name.

—Corporations and partnerships—Enter the first four characters of your business name (omit "The" if followed by more than one word).

4   Enter your business name (individual name for sole proprietors)

Enter your address

Enter your city, state, and ZIP code

Part II   **Tax Due or Refund**

1	Gross FUTA tax. Multiply the wages from Part I, line 5, by .062	**1**
2	Maximum credit. Multiply the wages from Part I, line 5, by .054 . . . | **2**	
3	Computation of tentative credit (**Note:** *All taxpayers must complete the applicable columns.*)	

(a) Name of state	(b) State reporting number(s) as shown on employer's state contribution returns	(c) Taxable payroll (as defined in state act)	(d) State experience rate period		(e) State experience rate	(f) Contributions if rate had been 5.4% (col. (c) x .054)	(g) Contributions payable at experience rate (col. (c) x col. (e))	(h) Additional credit (col. (f) minus col.(g)). If 0 or less, enter -0-.	(i) Contributions paid to state by 940 due date
			From	To					

3a	Totals . . . ▶	
3b	**Total tentative credit** (add line 3a, columns (h) and (i) only—for late payments also see the instructions for Part II, line 6 . . . . ▶	**3b**
4		
5		
6	**Credit:** Enter the smaller of the amount from Part II, line 2 or line 3b; or the amount from the worksheet in the Part II, line 6 instructions	**6**
7	**Total FUTA tax** (subtract line 6 from line 1). If the result is over $100, also complete Part III . .	**7**
8	Total FUTA tax deposited for the year, including any overpayment applied from a prior year . .	**8**
9	**Balance due** (subtract line 8 from line 7). Pay to the "United States Treasury". If you owe more than $100, see **Depositing FUTA Tax** on page 3 of the separate instructions . . . . . ▶	**9**
10	**Overpayment** (subtract line 7 from line 8). Check if it is to be: ☐ **Applied to next return** or ☐ **Refunded** . . . . ▶	**10**

Part III   **Record of Quarterly Federal Unemployment Tax Liability** (Do not include state liability.) **Complete only if line 7 is over $100.** See page 6 of the separate instructions.

Quarter	First (Jan. 1–Mar. 31)	Second (Apr. 1–June 30)	Third (July 1–Sept. 30)	Fourth (Oct. 1–Dec. 31)	Total for year
Liability for quarter					

Under penalties of perjury, I declare that I have examined this return, including accompanying schedules and statements, and, to the best of my knowledge and belief, it is true, correct, and complete, and that no part of any payment made to a state unemployment fund claimed as a credit was, or is to be, deducted from the payments to employees.

Signature ▶   Title (Owner, etc.) ▶   Date ▶

✴   Form **940** (2000)

See the CD-ROM for the IRS Instructions for Form 940.

Form 31-01
Confidentiality Agreement

This **CONFIDENTIALITY AGREEMENT** is made _____
_____, 20___,

between

_____, whose registered office is at

and

_____, whose registered office is at

WHEREAS:

1. _____ and _____ wish to collaborate in the development of _____.

2. During such collaboration each party will have access to technical and commercial information in the other party's possession existing at the above date and during the period of this Agreement relating to _____ (hereinafter referred to as 'Confidential Information') as is reasonably necessary to evaluate such developments.

NOW THEREFORE in consideration of the mutual promises contained herein the parties hereto agree as follows:

1. Each party will reveal to the other party the Confidential Information for the limited purpose of discussion and evaluation only.

2. Each party warrants that it:

   (a)   will use such Confidential Information of the other party only for the purpose of this Agreement and for no other purpose and each party specifically will not use such Confidential Information for any commercial purpose other than pursuant to a further agreement with the other party;

   (b)   will hold in confidence and will not divulge to any third parties all Confidential Information; and

   (c)   will restrict disclosure of all Confidential Information to those of its employees to whom disclosure is necessary in furtherance of the purpose of this Agreement and will ensure that any employees to whom disclosure of the Confidential Information is made will hold the same confidential in accordance with the confidentiality provisions of this Agreement.

3. Notwithstanding anything to the contrary herein neither party shall have any obligation to preserve the confidentiality or be restricted in the use of any information:

   (a)   which at the time of disclosure is the public domain; or

   (b)   which after disclosure becomes part of the public domain or otherwise except as a consequence of disclosure or by a person referred to under Article 2(c) above; or

   (c)   which either party can show by written substantial evidence which existed prior to the time of disclosure by the other party was in its possession and can demonstrate that they recognized prior to such disclosure the significance of that information in the technical area of development.

4. This agreement shall commence on the date hereof and continue in force until terminated by either party giving to the other three months notice in writing. The obligations contained in clause 2 of the Agreement shall survive termination.

5. Upon request each party will:

   (a)   return to the other party promptly on termination of this Agreement all documents and materials (and all copies thereof) containing any Confidential Information; and

   (b)   certify in writing to the other party that it has complied.

6. The Agreement constitutes the entire understanding between the parties with respect to its subject matter and cannot be changed except by written agreement between the parties.

7. This Agreement shall be construed as a U.S. contract and according to the laws of the Commonwealth of Pennsylvania.

   IN WITNESS WHEREOF the parties hereto have caused this Agreement to be signed as of the day and year first above written.

_____   _____
President/Authorized Signature   President/Authorized Signature

Form 32-15

~TRADEMARK/SERVICE MARK APPLICATION (15 U.S.C. §§ 1051, 1126(d)&(e))~

> **NOTE:** The following form complies with the provisions of the Trademark Law Treaty Implementation Act (TLTIA) and the fee increase effective January 10, 2000.

BASIC INSTRUCTIONS

The following form is written in a "scannable" format that will enable the U.S. Patent and Trademark Office (USPTO) to scan paper filings and capture application data automatically using optical character recognition (OCR) technology. Information is to be entered next to identifying data tags, such as <DATE OF FIRST USE IN COMMERCE>. OCR software can be programmed to identify these tags, capture the corresponding data, and transmit this data to the appropriate data fields in the Trademark databases, largely bypassing manual data entry processes.

Please enter the requested information in the blank space that appears to the right of each tagged (< >) element. However, do not enter any information immediately after the section headers (the bolded wording appearing in all capital letters). If you need additional space, first, in the space provided on the form, enter "See attached." Then, please use a separate piece of paper on which you first list the data tag (e.g., <LISTING OF GOODS AND/OR SERVICES>), followed by the relevant information. Some of the information requested *must* be provided. Other information is either required only in certain circumstances, or provided only at your discretion. **Please consult the "Help" section following the form for detailed explanations as to what information should be entered in each blank space.**

To increase the effectiveness of the USPTO scanners, it is recommended that you use a typewriter to complete the form.

For additional information, please see the *Basic Facts about Trademarks* booklet, available at http://www.uspto.gov/web/offices/tac/doc/basic/, or by calling the Trademark Assistance Center, at 703-308-9000. You may also wish to file electronically, from http://www.uspto.gov/teas/index.html.

MAILING INFORMATION

Send the completed form, appropriate fee(s) (made payable to "The Commissioner of Patent and Trademarks"), and any other required materials to:

> Box New App
> Fee
> Assistant Commissioner for Trademarks
> 2900 Crystal Drive
> Arlington, VA 22202-3513

The filing fee for this application is $325.00 *per class* of goods and/or services. You must include at least $325.00 with this application; otherwise the papers and money will be returned to you. Once your application meets the minimum filing date requirements, this processing fee becomes **non-refundable**. This is true even if the USPTO does not issue a registration certificate for this mark.

You may also wish to include a self-addressed stamped postcard with your submission, on which you identify the mark and list each item being submitted (e.g., application, fee, specimen, etc.). We will return this postcard to you, stamped with your assigned serial number, to confirm receipt of your submission.

~TRADEMARK/SERVICE MARK APPLICATION (15 U.S.C. §§ 1051, 1126(d)&(e))~

~To the Assistant Commissioner for Trademarks~

\<APPLICANT INFORMATION>

\<Name>

\<Street>

\<City>

\<State>

\<Country>

\<Zip/Postal Code>

\<Telephone Number>

\<Fax Number>

\<e-mail Address>

\<APPLICANT ENTITY INFORMATION>~*Select only ONE*~

\<Individual: Country of Citizenship>

\<Corporation: State/Country of Incorporation>

\<Partnership: State/Country under which Organized>

 \<Name(s) of General Partner(s) & Citizenship/Incorporation>

\<Other Entity Type: Specific Nature of Entity>

\<State/Country under which Organized>

\<TRADEMARK/SERVICE MARK INFORMATION>

\<Mark>

\<Typed Form>~*Enter YES, if appropriate*~

~*DISPLAY THE MARK that you want to register on a separate piece of paper (even if simply a word(s)). Please see additional HELP instructions.*~

\<BASIS FOR FILING AND GOODS/SERVICES INFORMATION>

\<Use in Commerce: Section 1(a)>~*Applicant is using or is using through a related company the mark in commerce on or in connection with the below-identified goods and/or services (15 U.S.C § 1051(a)).*~

\<International Class Number(s)>

\<Listing of Goods and/or Services>~*List in ascending numerical class order. Please see sample in HELP instructions.*~

\<Date of First Use Anywhere>

\<Date of First Use in Commerce>

~*Submit one (1) SPECIMEN for each international class showing the mark as used in commerce.*~

PTO Form 1478 (REV 12/99)
OMB Control No. 0651-0009 (Exp. 8/31/2001)

U. S. DEPARTMENT OF COMMERCE/Patent and Trademark Office
There is no requirement to respond to this collection of information
unless a currently valid OMB number is displayed.

<Intent to Use: Section 1(b)>~*Applicant has a bona fide intention to use or use through a related company the mark in commerce on or in connection with the below-identified goods and/or services (15 U.S.C. § 1051(b)).*~
<International Class Number(s)>
<Listing of Goods and/or Services>~*List in ascending numerical class order. Please see sample in HELP instructions.*~

<Foreign Priority: Section 44(d)>~*Applicant has a bona fide intention to use the mark in commerce on or in connection with the below-identified goods and/or services, and asserts a claim of priority based upon a foreign application in accordance with 15 U.S.C. § 1126(d).*~
<International Class Number(s)>

<Listing of Goods and/or Services>~*List in ascending numerical class order. Please see sample in HELP instructions.*~

<Country of Foreign Filing>
<Foreign Application Number>
<Date of Foreign Filing>

<Foreign Registration: Section 44(e)>~*Applicant has a bona fide intention to use the mark in commerce on or in connection with the below-identified goods and/or services based on registration of the mark in applicant's country of origin.*~
<International Class Number(s)>

<Listing of Goods and/or Services>~*List in ascending numerical class order. Please see sample in HELP instructions.*~

<Country of Foreign Registration>
<Foreign Registration Number>
<Foreign Registration Date>
<Foreign Registration Renewal Date>
<Foreign Registration Expiration Date>
~*Submit foreign registration certificate or a certified copy of the foreign registration, in accordance with 15 U.S.C. §1126(e).*~

<FEE INFORMATION>

$325.00 x <Number of Classes>	= <Total Filing Fee Paid>

< SIGNATURE INFORMATION>

~Applicant requests registration of the above-identified mark in the United States Patent and Trademark Office on the Principal Register established by Act of July 5, 1946 (15 U.S.C. § 1051 et seq.) for the above-identified goods and/or services.

The undersigned, being hereby warned that willful false statements and the like so made are punishable by fine or imprisonment, or both, under 18 U.S.C. § 1001, and that such willful false statements may jeopardize the validity of the application or any resulting registration, declares that he/she is properly authorized to execute this application on behalf of the applicant; he/she believes the applicant to be the owner of the trademark/service mark sought to be registered, or, if the application is being filed under 15 U.S.C. § 1051(b), he/she believes applicant to be entitled to use such mark in commerce; to the best of his/her knowledge and belief no other person, firm, corporation, or association has the right to use the mark in commerce, either in the identical form thereof or in such near resemblance thereto as to be likely, when used on or in connection with the goods/services of such other person, to cause confusion, or to cause mistake, or to deceive; and that all statements made of his/her own knowledge are true; and that all statements made on information and belief are believed to be true.~

~Signature~_____

<Date>

<Name>

<Title>

<CONTACT INFORMATION>

<Name>

<Company/Firm Name>

<Street>

<City>

<State>

<Country>

<Zip/Postal Code>

<Telephone Number>

<Fax Number>

<e-Mail Address>

The information collected on this form allows the PTO to determine whether a mark may be registered on the Principal or Supplemental Register, and provides notice of an applicant's claim of ownership of the mark or bona fide intent to use the mark in commerce. Responses to the request for information are required to obtain the benefit of a registration on the Principal or Supplemental Register. 15 U.S.C. §§1051 et seq. and 37 C.F.R. Part 2. All information collected will be made public. Gathering and providing the information will require an estimated seventeen to twenty-three minutes. Please direct comments on the time needed to complete this form, and/or suggestions for reducing this burden to the Chief Information Officer, U.S. Patent and Trademark Office, U.S. Department of Commerce, Washington D.C. 20231. Please note that the PTO may not conduct or sponsor a collection of information using a form that does not display a valid OMB control number. (See bottom left side of this form).

LINE-BY-LINE HELP INSTRUCTIONS

APPLICANT INFORMATION

Name: Enter the full name of the applicant, i.e., the name of the individual, corporation, partnership, or other entity that is seeking registration. If a joint venture organized under a particular business name, enter that name. If joint or multiple applicants, enter the name of each. If a trust, enter the name of the trustee(s). If an estate, enter the name of the executor(s).

Street: Enter the street address or rural delivery route where the applicant is located.

City: Enter the city and/or foreign area designation where the applicant's address is located.

State: Enter the U.S. state or foreign province in which the applicant's address is located.

Country: Enter the country of the applicant's address. If the address is outside the United States, the applicant must appoint a "Domestic Representative" on whom notices or process in proceedings affecting the mark may be served.

Zip/Postal Code: Enter the applicant's U.S. Zip code or foreign country postal identification code.

Telephone Number: Enter the applicant's telephone number.

Fax Number: Enter the applicant's fax number.

e-Mail Address: Enter the applicant's e-mail address.

APPLICANT ENTITY INFORMATION

Indicate the applicant's entity type by entering the appropriate information in the space to the right of the correct entity type. Please note that only one entity type may be selected.

Individual: Enter the applicant's country of citizenship.

Corporation: Enter the applicant's state of incorporation (or the applicant's country of incorporation if the applicant is a foreign corporation).

Partnership: Enter the state under whose laws the partnership is organized (or the country under whose laws the partnership is organized if the partnership is a foreign partnership).

Name(s) of General Partner(s) & Citizenship/incorporation: Enter the names and citizenship of any general partners who are individuals, and/or the names and state or (foreign) country of incorporation of any general partners that are corporations, and/or the names and states or (foreign) countries of organization of any general partners that are themselves partnerships. If the applicant is a limited partnership, then only provide the names and citizenship or state or country of organization or incorporation of the general partners.

Other Entity Type: Enter a brief description of the applicant's entity type (e.g., joint or multiple applicants, joint venture, limited liability company, association, Indian Nation, state or local agency, trust, estate). The following sets forth the information required with respect to the most common types of "other" entities:

For *joint or multiple applicants*, enter the name and entity type of each joint applicant. Also, enter the citizenship of those joint applicants who are individuals, and/or the state or (foreign) country of incorporation of those joint applicants that are corporations, and/or the state or (foreign) country of organization- and the names and citizenship of the partners- of those joint applicants that are partnerships. The information regarding each applicant should be preceded by a separate heading tag (<APPLICANT INFORMATION>).

For *sole proprietorship,* enter the name and citizenship of the sole proprietor, and indicate the state where the sole proprietorship is organized.

For *joint venture*, enter the name and entity type of each entity participating in the joint venture. Also, enter the citizenship of those joint venture participants who are individuals, and/or the state or (foreign) country of incorporation of those joint venture participants that are corporations, and/or the state or (foreign) country of organization (and the names and citizenship of the partners) of those joint venture participants that are partnerships. The information regarding each entity should be preceded by a separate heading tag (<APPLICANT INFORMATION>).

For *limited liability company or association*, enter the state or (foreign) country under whose laws the entity is established.

For *state or local agency*, enter the name of the agency and the state and/or locale of the agency (e.g., Maryland State Lottery Agency, an agency of the State of Maryland).

For *trusts*, identify the trustees and the trust itself, using the following format: The Trustees of the XYZ Trust, a California trust, the trustees comprising John Doe, a U.S. citizen, and the ABC Corp., a Delaware corporation. (Please note that the trustees, and not the trust itself, must be identified as the applicant in the portion of the application designated for naming the applicant).

For *estates*, identify the executors and the estate itself using the following format: The Executors of the John Smith estate, a New York estate, the executors comprising Mary Smith and John Smith, U.S. citizens. (Please note that the executors, and not the estate itself, must be identified as the applicant in the portion of the application designated for naming the applicant).

State/Country under Which Organized: Enter the state or country under whose laws the entity is organized.

TRADEMARK/SERVICE MARK INFORMATION

Mark: A mark may consist of words alone; a design or logo; or a combination of words and a design or logo. However, an application may consist of only *one* mark; separate marks must be filed in separate applications. In this space, enter the word mark in typed form (e.g., THE CAT'S MEOW); or, in the case of a non-word mark or a combination mark, a brief description of the mark (e.g., Design of a fanciful cat or Design of a fanciful cat and the words THE CAT'S MEOW). Do NOT include quotation marks around the mark itself, unless the mark actually features these quotation marks. Also, do NOT include any information related to a "pseudo mark" in this field, because only the USPTO controls this field. If the USPTO determines that a pseudo mark is necessary for your particular mark, it will enter this information in the search system.

Typed Form: Enter YES if the mark applied for is in a "typed" format (i.e., if the mark consists of *only* typed words, letters or numbers, and does *not* include any special stylization or design element(s)). Please note that a registration for a mark based on a typed drawing affords protection not only for the typed version of the mark, but for all other renderings of the mark as long as those renderings do not contain any design elements.

Display the Mark: Regardless of whether the mark consists of words alone; a design or logo; or a combination of words and a design or logo, submit on a separate piece of paper a display (drawing) of what the mark is.

At the top of the page, include a heading consisting of (1) the applicant's name and address; (2) a listing of the goods and/or services on which or in connection with which the mark is used; and (3) a listing of the basis for filing (and any relevant information related thereto). Then, in the middle of the page, show the mark:

If the mark is to be in a "typed" form, simply type the mark in the middle of the page *in all capital letters*. For a mark in stylized form or design, in the middle of the page display an image of the mark in black and white, in an area no greater than 4x4 inches.

BASIS FOR FILING AND GOODS/SERVICES INFORMATION

Use in Commerce: Section 1(a): Use this section only if you have actually used the mark in commerce or on in connection with *all* of the goods and/or services listed.

International Class Number(s): Enter the International Class number(s) of the goods and/or services associated with the mark; e.g., 14; 24; 25. If unknown, leave blank and the USPTO will assign the number(s).

Listing of Goods and/or Services: Enter the *specific* goods and/or services associated with the mark. Do NOT enter the broad class number here, such as 9 or 42 (this information belongs in the field above, namely International Class Number(s)). If the goods and/or services are classified in more than one class, the goods and/or services should be listed in ascending numerical class order, with both the class number and the specific goods and/or services. For example, 14: jewelry

                24: towels

                25: pants, shirts, jackets, shoes

For more information about acceptable wording for the goods/services, see the USPTO's on-line *Acceptable Identification of Goods and Services Manual*, at http://www.uspto.gov/web/offices/tac/doc/gsmanual/.

Date of First Use Anywhere: Enter the date on which the goods were first sold or transported or the services first rendered under the mark if such use was in the ordinary course of trade. For every applicant (foreign or domestic), the date of first use is the date of the first such use *anywhere*, in the United States or elsewhere. Please note this date may be earlier than, or the same as, the date of the first use of the mark in commerce.

Date of First Use in Commerce: Enter the date on which the applicant first used the mark in commerce, i.e., in interstate commerce, territorial commerce, or commerce between the United States and a foreign country.
Specimen: You must submit one (1) specimen showing the mark as used in commerce on or in connection with any item listed in the description of goods and/or services; e.g., tags or labels for goods, and/or advertisements for services. If the goods and/or services are classified in more than one international class, a specimen must be provided showing the mark used on or in connection with at least one item from each of these classes. The specimen must be flat and no larger than 8½ inches (21.6 cm.) wide by 11.69 inches (29.7 cm.) long.

Intent to Use: Section 1(b): Use this section if the applicant only has a bona fide intention to use the mark in commerce in the future as to all or some of the goods and/or services, rather than having actually already made use of the mark in commerce as to *all* of the goods and/or services.
International Class Number(s): Enter the International Class number(s) of the goods and/or services associated with the mark; e.g., 14; 24; 25. If unknown, leave blank and the USPTO will assign the number(s).
Listing of Goods and/or Services: Enter the *specific* goods and/or services associated with the mark. Do NOT enter the broad class number here, such as 9 or 42 (this information belongs in the field above, namely International Class Number(s)). If the goods and/or services are classified in more than one class, the goods and/or services should be listed in ascending numerical class order, with both the class number and the specific goods and/or services. For example, 14: jewelry
              24: towels
              25: pants, shirts, jackets, shoes
For more information about acceptable wording for the goods/services, see the USPTO's on-line *Acceptable Identification of Goods and Services Manual*, at http://www.uspto.gov/web/offices/tac/doc/gsmanual/.

Foreign Priority: Section 44(d): Use this section if you are filing the application within six (6) months of filing the first foreign application to register the mark in a defined treaty country.
International Class Number(s): Enter the International Class number(s) of the goods and/or services associated with the mark; e.g., 14; 24; 25. If unknown, leave blank and the USPTO will assign the number(s).
Listing of Goods and/or Services: Enter the *specific* goods and/or services associated with the mark. Do NOT enter the broad class number here, such as 9 or 42 (this information belongs in the field above, namely International Class Number(s)). If the goods and/or services are classified in more than one class, the goods and/or services should be listed in ascending numerical class order, with both the class number and the specific goods and/or services. For example, 14: jewelry
              24: towels
              25: pants, shirts, jackets, shoes
For more information about acceptable wording for the goods/services, see the USPTO's on-line *Acceptable Identification of Goods and Services Manual*, at http://www.uspto.gov/web/offices/tac/doc/gsmanual/.
Country of Foreign Filing: Enter the country where the foreign application upon which the applicant is asserting a claim of priority has been filed.
Foreign Application Number: Enter the foreign application serial number, if available.
Filing Date of Foreign Application: Enter the date (two digits each for both the month and day, and four digits for the year) on which the foreign application was filed. To receive a priority filing date, you must file the U.S. application within six (6) months of filing the first foreign application in a defined treaty country.

Foreign Registration: Use this section if applicant is relying on a foreign registration certificate or a certified copy of a foreign registration currently in force. You must submit this foreign registration certificate or a certified copy of the foreign registration.
International Class Number(s): Enter the International Class number(s) of the goods and/or services associated with the mark; e.g., 14; 24; 25. If unknown, leave blank and the USPTO will assign the number(s).
Listing of Goods and/or Services: Enter the *specific* goods and/or services associated with the mark. Do NOT enter the broad class number here, such as 9 or 42 (this information belongs in the field above, namely

International Class Number(s)). If the goods and/or services are classified in more than one class, the goods and/or services should be listed in ascending numerical class order, with both the class number and the specific goods and/or services. For example, 14: jewelry

24: towels
25: pants, shirts, jackets, shoes

For more information about acceptable wording for the goods/services, see the USPTO's on-line *Acceptable Identification of Goods and Services Manual*, at http://www.uspto.gov/web/offices/tac/doc/gsmanual/.

Country of Foreign Registration: Enter the country of the foreign registration.

Foreign Registration Number: Enter the number of the foreign registration.

Foreign Registration Date: Enter the date (two digits each for both the month and day, and four digits for the year) of the foreign registration.

Foreign Registration Renewal Date: Enter the date (two digits each for both the month and day, and four digits for the year) of the foreign registration renewal.

Foreign Registration Expiration Date: Enter the expiration date (two digits each for both the month and day, and four digits for the year) of the foreign registration.

FEE INFORMATION

The filing fee for this application is $325.00 *per class* of goods and/or services. You must include at least $325.00 with this application; otherwise the papers and money will be returned to you. Once your application meets the minimum filing date requirements, this processing fee becomes **non-refundable**. This is true even if the USPTO does not issue a registration certificate for this mark.

Number of Classes: Enter the total number of classes (*not* the international class number(s)) for which the applicant is seeking registration. For example, if the application covers Classes 1, 5 and 25, then enter the number "3."

Total Filing Fee Paid: Enter the fee amount that is enclosed (either in the form of a check or money order in U.S. currency, made payable to "Commissioner of Patents and Trademarks"), or to be charged to an already-existing USPTO deposit account.

SIGNATURE INFORMATION

Signature: The appropriate person must sign the form. A person who is properly authorized to sign on behalf of the applicant is: (1) a person with legal authority to bind the applicant; or (2) a person with firsthand knowledge of the facts and actual or implied authority to act on behalf of the applicant; or (3) an attorney who has an actual or implied written or verbal power of attorney from the applicant.

Date Signed: Enter the date the form is signed.

Name: Enter the name of the person signing the form.

Title: Enter the signatory's title, if applicable, e.g., Vice-President, General Partner, etc.

CONTACT INFORMATION

Although this may be the same as provided elsewhere in the document, please enter the following required information for where the USPTO should mail correspondence. (Please note that correspondence will *only* be mailed to an address in the U.S. or Canada).

Name: Enter the full name of the contact person.

Company/Firm Name: Enter the name of the contact person's company or firm.

Street: Enter the street address or rural delivery route where the contact person is located.

City: Enter the city and/or foreign area designation where the contact person's address is located.

State: Enter the U.S. state or Canadian province in which the contact person's address is located.

Country: Enter the country of the contact person's address.

Zip Code: Enter the U.S. Zip code or Canadian postal code.

Telephone Number: Enter the appropriate telephone number.

Fax Number: Enter the appropriate fax number, if available.

e-mail Address: Enter the appropriate e-mail address, if available.

Form 33-01

PLAN OF MERGER

OF

(a Pennsylvania corporation)

INTO

(a Pennsylvania corporation)

PLAN OF MERGER approved by the respective boards of directors and shareholders of _____, a Pennsylvania business corporation ('_____'), and _____, a Pennsylvania business corporation ('_____'), with _____ and _____ being sometimes hereinafter referred to collectively as the 'Constituent Corporation.'

1. At the Effective Time (as such term is defined in paragraph 2 hereof) and in accordance with the provisions of this Plan of Merger, the Pennsylvania Business Corporation Law of 1988 (the 'BCL'), the Constituent Corporations shall cause to be consummated a merger (the 'Merger') pursuant to which _____ shall be merged with and into . The separate corporate existence of _____ shall cease and _____ shall be the surviving corporation (hereinafter sometimes referred to as the 'Surviving Corporation') of the Merger. The Surviving Corporation shall continue its corporate existence under the BCL and shall possess all the rights and assets of, and shall be subject to all the liabilities and obligations of, _____ and _____ in accordance with the provisions of the BCL. The name of the Surviving Corporation shall be '_____' until changed in accordance with the requirements of the BCL and the Surviving Corporation shall be a domestic Pennsylvania business corporation.

2. The Merger shall become effective at ___:00 a.m. on _____, 20__, as specified in the 'Articles of Merger' and the 'Certificate of Merger' or if later, upon the later to occur of (i) the filing of 'Articles of Merger,' together with this Plan of Merger, with the Department of State of the Commonwealth of Pennsylvania. The date and time when the Merger shall become effective are herein referred to as the 'Effective Time.'

3. The Articles of Incorporation and By-Laws of _____ in effect immediately prior to the Effective Time shall be the Articles of Incorporation and By-Laws of the Surviving Corporation and said Articles of Incorporation and By-Laws shall continue in full force and effect until thereafter amended or repealed in accordance with the BCL.

4. The directors of _____ immediately prior to the Effective Time shall be the initial directors of the Surviving Corporation until their respective successors are duly elected and qualified. Subject to the authority of the Board of Directors, as provided by the BCL and the By-Laws of the Surviving Corporation, the officers of _____ immediately prior to the Effective Time shall be the initial officers of the Surviving Corporation until their respective successors are duly elected and qualified.

5. The Merger shall be effected and the shares of the Constituent Corporations shall be converted in the following manner:

A. At the Closing, upon surrender to _____ of the certificates representing the issued and outstanding shares of capital stock of _____ (the 'Shares'), the shareholders of _____ shall be entitled to receive, in good funds, by certified or cashier's checks or by bank wire transfer of immediately available United States Federal Reserve funds, a cash payment of $___ (the 'Cash Payment'), and a promissory note in the principal amount of $___ (the 'Note').

B. Each share of common stock of ___, which shall be issued and outstanding at the Effective Time, shall, by virtue of the Merger, remain issued and outstanding from and after the Effective Time. Each of the Shares of ___, which shall be issued and outstanding at the Effective Time and which is represented by the certificates surrendered as set forth above, by virtue of the Merger and without any further action, shall be canceled and retired in exchange for the Merger Consideration as set forth above.

C. At the Effective Time, the Surviving Corporation shall succeed to, as a result of the Merger and without other transfer, and shall possess and enjoy, all the rights, privileges, immunities, powers, and franchises both of a public and a private nature, and be subject to all the restrictions, disabilities, and duties of each of the Constituent Corporations and all property, real, personal, and mixed, and all debts due to any of the Constituent Corporations on whatever account, shall be vested in the Surviving Corporation; and all property, rights, privileges, immunities, powers, and franchises, and all and every other interest shall be thereafter as effectively the property of the Surviving Corporation as they were of the respective Constituent Corporations, and the title to any real estate vested by deed or otherwise in any of the Constituent Corporations shall not revert or be in any way impaired by reason of the merger, except as encumbered by the Mortgage; provided, however, that all rights of creditors, including, but not limited to, past and present shareholders of the Constituent Corporations who were creditors immediately prior to the Effective Time, and all liens upon any property of any of the Constituent Corporations shall be preserved unimpaired, limited in lien to the property affected by such liens at the Effective Time; provided further, however, that none of such rights or liens shall attach to any property owned by NMC.

6. The Merger has been fully approved by the respective boards of directors and shareholders of _____ and _____, all in accordance with the provisions of the BCL.

7. The merger of the Constituent Corporations with and into the Surviving Corporation shall be unauthorized and carried out in the manner prescribed by the BCL.

8. The Constituent Corporations agree that they will cause to be executed and filed and recorded any document or documents prescribed by the laws of the Commonwealth of Pennsylvania and that they will cause to be performed all necessary acts within the Commonwealth of Pennsylvania and elsewhere to effectuate the Merger.

9. Except as otherwise provided in this Plan, nothing herein expressed or implied is intended, nor shall be construed, to confer upon or give any person, firm, or corporation, other than the Constituent Corporations and their respective security holders, any rights or remedies under or by reason of this Plan.

Form 33-02

Microfilm Number _____   Filed with the Department of State on _____

Entity Number_____

_____

Secretary of the Commonwealth

Articles of Merger—Domestic Business Corporation

In compliance with the requirements of 15 Pa.C.S. §1926 (relating to articles of merger or consolidation), the undersigned business corporations, desiring to effect a merger, hereby state that:

1. The **name** of the corporation surviving the merger is: _____

2. **(Check and complete one of the following):**

   The surviving corporation is a domestic business corporation and the address of its current (a) registered office in this Commonwealth or (b) commercial registered office provider and the county of venue is (the Department is hereby authorized to correct the following address to conform to the records of the Department):

   (a) _____

       Number and Street   City   State   Zip   County

   (b) _____

       Name of Commercial Registered Office Provider   County

   For a corporation represented by a commercial registered office provider, the county in (b) shall be deemed the county in which the corporation is located for venue and office publication purposes.

   The surviving corporation is a qualified foreign business corporation incorporated under the laws of and the address of its current (a) registered office in this Commonwealth or (b) commercial registered office provider and the county of venue is (the Department is hereby authorized to correct the following address to conform to the records of the Department):

   (a) _____

       Number and Street   City   State   Zip   County

   (b) _____

       Name of Commercial Registered Office Provider   County

   For a corporation represented by a commercial registered office provider, the county in (b) shall be deemed the county in which the corporation is located for venue and official publication purposes.

   The surviving corporation is a nonqualified foreign business corporation incorporated under the laws of and the address of its principal office under the laws of such domiciliary jurisdiction is:

   _____

       Number and Street   City   State   Zip

3. The **name** and the **address** of the registered office of each other domestic business corporation and qualified foreign business corporation which is a party to the plan or merger are as follows:

4. **(Check, and if appropriate complete, one of the following):**

   ____ The plan of merger shall be effective upon filing these Articles of Merger in the Department of State.

   ____ The plan of merger shall be effective on _____.

375

5. The manner in which the plan of merger was adopted by each domestic corporation is as follows:

Name of corporation   **Manner of adoption**

6. **(Strike out this paragraph if no foreign corporation is a party to the merger).** The plan was authorized, adopted or approved, as the case may be, by the foreign business corporation (or each of the foreign business corporations) party to the plan in accordance with the law of the jurisdiction in which it is incorporated.

7. **(Check, and if appropriate complete, one of the following):**

___ The plan of merger is set forth in full in Exhibit A attached hereto and made a part hereof.

___ Pursuant to 15 Pa.C.S. §1901 (relating to omission of certain provisions from filed plans) the provisions of the plan of merger that amend or constitute the operative Articles of Incorporation of the surviving corporation as in effect subsequent to the effective date of the plan are set forth in full in Exhibit A, attached hereto and made a part hereof. The full text of the plan of merger is on file at the principal place of business of the surviving corporation, the address of which is:

_____

Number and Street   City   State   Zip

    IN TESTIMONY WHEREOF, each undersigned corporation has caused these Articles of Merger to be signed by a duly authorized officer thereof this _____ day of _____, 1993.

_____
(Name of Corporation)

BY: _____
(Signature)

TITLE: _____

_____
(Name of Corporation)

BY: _____
(Signature)

TITLE: _____

Accounts Payable The list of debts that are unpaid to vendors. Normally kept by alphabetical order and listed by date due.

Accounts Receivable The list of customers who have open balances on invoices for goods or services. This is an indication of future cash flow.

Accrual Basis Accounting A system that recognizes income when it is earned, whether collected or not, and expense when it is incurred, whether paid or not.

Assets The value of any tangible property (often the cost less depreciation) owned by the company.

Balance Sheet A summary listing of all assets and liabilities of a company as well as its net worth. Assets and liabilities are listed as current as well as long term and fixed.

Book Value The value of assets shown on balance sheet–the items are listed by cost and then reduced by accumulated depreciation.

By-Laws These are the agreed-upon rules governing the management of the corporation. The by-laws typically identify the roles and duties of the officers, establish the manner in which meetings shall be held and the frequency of those meetings, as well as define the powers of the Board of Directors and officers.

Cash Flow The difference between the cash at the beginning of a period and the cash at the end of the same period. May be increased by loan proceeds or sales of assets or decreased by large purchase or principal debt service.

Contract An agreement between parties that contains specific elements, namely a meeting of the minds and consideration. May be either written or oral.

Confession of Judgment A Confession of Judgment is a document that, when signed by a promisor, entitles the promisee to enter a judgment for a monetary sum at a time agreed to by the parties. No lawsuit, as such, is required and the judgment will act like any other judgment, unless and until such time as it is effectively challenged by the promisor. The Confession of Judgment is not available in all jurisdictions because of its allowance for the entry of a judgment without a hearing.

Corporation A legal entity created under the authority of statute. A corporation is owned by its shareholders, who control the affairs of the corporation through the Board of Directors and officers, although in some jurisdictions, management may be vested in the shareholders, themselves. The most important feature of the corporation is that the shareholders are not liable for corporate financial obligations and all that a shareholder stands to lose is his original investment.

Covenant A covenant is an agreement or promise between two or more people. It is a contract, in its simplest form.

Depreciation The expense of writing down a portion of the usable life of an asset to reflect its devaluation from use.

Direct Costs Also referred to as variable costs, these are expenses directly related to a sale such as raw material and labor. These costs increase and decrease as sales increase or decrease.

FLSA (The Fair Labor Standards Act) A federal statute that governs such matters as minimum wage, length of work week, payment dates, overtime requirements, computation of fixed and piece rate wages, child labor, and a myriad of other issues affecting businesses and employees.

Guaranty The agreement to pay all or part of a financial obligation. This is a document granted by a third party that represents additional security for a lender.

Limited Liability Company A Limited Liability Company is a form of business organization where the owners, like shareholders, are at risk only for the amount of their investment. A Limited Liability Company provides a great range of flexibility in the management structure of the business with much more flexibility and fewer legal requirements that are typically imposed upon a corporation.

Line of Credit An instrument of credit issued by a bank or other lender for a short-term loan (one year). Most lines are revolving meaning they can be drawn down, paid off, and drawn again.

OSHA (Occupational Safety and Health Administration) The federal agency that oversees the workplace environment and regulates safety laws.

Prime Rate This rate is based on the current federal rate for funds that goes up and down on the decisions of the Federal Reserve Board. Most loans are pegged to this rate.

Pro Forma This document reflects future profit and loss from operations as well as changes in the balance sheet. The numbers are based on historical results as well as future anticipated changes.

Shareholder Ownership of a corporation is in the hands of its shareholders. The shareholders invest money in the corporation and receive a return upon their investment in the way of dividends. Shareholders control corporate affairs through an elected Board of Directors and appointed officers, although in some jurisdictions shareholders may, themselves, manage the affairs of the corporation. Shareholders do not own the assets of the corporation because those are owned by the corporate entity. Shareholders own the corporate entity itself.

Tort A wrong or injury committed against another where the harm occurs as a result of a violation of a duty imposed by law upon the person committing the tort. An individual commits a tort upon another when he accidentally injures him, through his carelessness, when there is a duty to refrain from being careless. Personal injury lawsuits are good examples of torts.

UCC Uniform Commercial Code governs the filing of security interests in assets that are used as collateral for financing. These statements are signed by the borrower and filed with the secretary of state where the company operates.

INDEX

FIND MORE ON THIS TOPIC BY VISITING
BusinessTown.com
The Web's big site for growing businesses!

☑ **Separate channels on all aspects of starting and running a business**

☑ **Lots of info on how to do business online**

☑ **1,000+ pages of savvy business advice**

☑ **Complete web guide to thousands of useful business sites**

☑ **Free e-mail newsletter**

☑ **Question and answer forums, and more!**

Accounting
Basic, Credit & Collections, Projections, Purchasing/Cost Control

Advertising
Magazine, Newspaper, Radio, Television, Yellow Pages

Business Opportunities
Ideas for New Businesses, Business for Sale, Franchises

Business Plans
Creating Plans & Business Strategies

Finance
Getting Money, Money Problem Solutions

Letters & Forms
Looking Professional, Sample Letters & Forms

Getting Started
Incorporating, Choosing a Legal Structure

Hiring & Firing
Finding the Right People, Legal Issues

Home Business
Home Business Ideas, Getting Started

Internet
Getting Online, Put Your Catalog on the Web

Legal Issues
Contracts, Copyrights, Patents, Trademarks

Managing a Small Business
Growth, Boosting Profits, Mistakes to Avoid, Competing with the Giants

Managing People
Communications, Compensation, Motivation, Reviews, Problem Employees

Marketing
Direct Mail, Marketing Plans, Strategies, Publicity, Trade Shows

Office Setup
Leasing, Equipment, Supplies

Presentations
Know Your Audience, Good Impression

Sales
Face to Face, Independent Reps, Telemarketing

Selling a Business
Finding Buyers, Setting a Price, Legal Issues

Taxes
Employee, Income, Sales, Property, Use

Time Management
Can You Really Manage Time?

Travel & Maps
Making Business Travel Fun

About the Authors

Suzanne Caplan

Suzanne Caplan has spent almost three decades in a small business environment. After growing up in a family business, she was CEO of a small manufacturing company for over 20 years. She has been a full-time author, speaker, and consultant since 1993. *Streetwise® Small Business Success Kit* is her eighth book; the others have included *Streetwise® Finance and Accounting* and *The Small Business Insider's Guide to Bankers.*

Alan E. Cech

Alan E. Cech has been practicing law in Pittsburgh for 20 years. He received his law degree in 1980 from the University of Pittsburgh School of Law and has served as a bankruptcy trustee and as the Chief of Financial Litigation for the United States Attorney's Office in Western Pennsylvania. Currently in private practice, he focuses on business organizations, workouts, bankruptcy, and commercial litigation.

Streetwise® Small Business Success Kit
CD-Rom Table of Contents

CD-Rom Table of Contents (continued)